# TEXT AND TRADITION

## in Performance and Writing

# Biblical Performance Criticism Series

David Rhoads, Series Editor

The ancient societies of the Bible were overwhelmingly oral. People originally experienced the traditions now in the Bible as oral performances. Focusing on the ancient performance of biblical traditions enables us to shift academic work on the Bible from the mentality of a modern print culture to that of an oral/scribal culture. Conceived broadly, biblical performance criticism embraces many methods as means to reframe the biblical materials in the context of traditional oral cultures, construct scenarios of ancient performances, learn from contemporary performances of these materials, and reinterpret biblical writings accordingly. The result is a foundational paradigm shift that reconfigures traditional disciplines and employs fresh biblical methodologies such as theater studies, speech-act theory, and performance studies. The emerging research of many scholars in this field of study, the development of working groups in scholarly societies, and the appearance of conferences on orality and literacy make it timely to inaugurate this series. For further information on biblical performance criticism, go to www.biblicalperformancecriticism.org.

## Books in the Series

Holly Hearon and Philip Ruge-Jones, editors
*The Bible in Ancient and Modern Media*

James A. Maxey
*From Orality to Orality:*
*A New Paradigm for Contextual Translation of the Bible*

Antoinette Clark Wire
*The Case for Mark Composed in Performance*

Robert D. Miller II, SFO
*Oral Tradition in Ancient Israel*

Pieter J. J. Botha
*Orality and Literacy in Early Christianity*

James A. Maxey and Ernst R. Wendland, editors
*Translating Scripture for Sound and Performance*

J. A. (Bobby) Loubser
*Oral and Manuscript Culture in the Bible*

Joanna Dewey
*The Oral Ethos of the Early Church*

# TEXT AND TRADITION
## in Performance and Writing

RICHARD A. HORSLEY

CASCADE *Books* · Eugene, Oregon

TEXT AND TRADITION IN PERFORMANCE AND WRITING

Biblical Performance Criticism Series 9

Cascade Books
An Imprint of Wipf and Stock Publishers
199 W. 8th Ave., Suite 3
Eugene, OR 97401

www.wipfandstock.com

ISBN 13: 978–1-4982-1680-7

*Cataloguing-in-Publication data:*

Horsley, Richard A.

Text and tradition in performance and writing / Richard A. Horsley.

Biblical Performance Criticism Series 9

xxiv + 340 p. ; 23 cm—Includes bibliographical references and indexes.


1. Bible. N.T.—Criticism, interpretation, etc. 2. Bible. N.T.—Performance criticism. 3. Oral tradition. I. Title. II. Series.

BS2555.5 H66 2013

Manufactured in the USA

# CONTENTS

# INTRODUCTION

THE RESULTS OF SEVERAL LINES OF RECENT RESEARCH ARE now challenging some of the significant assumptions of biblical studies. Because these lines of research have proceeded largely independent of one another it is only slowly becoming evident that their combined effect is to challenge the most fundamental assumptions and constructs of the field. Given the splintering of biblical studies into diverse specialized "criticisms," however, it is difficult to appreciate the extent to which the standard assumptions and procedures of the field have been undermined, on the one hand, and the exciting new possibilities for biblical texts to "come alive" again, on the other.

The standard agenda of New Testament studies, embodied in introductory courses and textbooks, was to identify the "author" ("writer") of each book, the "church" in and for which it was "written," and date of the writing, so that (passages in) the biblical books could be interpreted in their original historical context. It was simply assumed that after they were "written," "biblical books" were circulated and readily available for people to "read" and "interpret." Similarly, it was standard to think of the books of "the Law (Torah) and the Prophets" and at least some of "the Writings" as "biblical," already widely available in writing for most Jews to "read" in "early Judaism" in the second-temple period. "Judaism" was understood as a "religion of the book" in which the Scripture was regularly read and interpreted. It was simply assumed that the "writers" of New Testament texts had copies of the books of the Hebrew Bible ("Old Testament") in front of them, from which they took "quotations." Following in the path of "(early) Judaism" in which it had originated, and pioneering use of the more easily useable codex instead of parchment scrolls, "(early) Christianity" also quickly became a "religion of the book."

This standard agenda of biblical studies indicates that the field is the product of, and deeply embedded in, modern western print culture. In print culture, essays, letters, even stories and poems are composed *in writing*, edited, and then published by printing in multiple identical copies of widely distributed and easily accessible books, pamphlets, or other "hard copy" (and now electronically). Individual "authors" do the "writing," new "editions" are "revised" and "edited," and "printings" are dated. With the increasing availability of texts and information in print, it was unnecessary to hold them in memory since they were readily available for consultation on bookshelves (and now "on-line"). Insofar as the pages and lines were identical in all printed copies (of the same edition), precise quotation was easy and important. The division of biblical books into chapter and verse facilitated quotation and reference even across various editions. Indeed, divided into chapter and verse, biblical books were printed collections of already separated statements easily extracted as "prooftexts" for theological treatises, doctrinal disputes, sermons, and personal devotion. Printed more recently of paragraphs (with topical headings/subtitles), biblical books facilitate identification and accessibility to scriptural lessons for particular dates on the liturgical calendar.

The mission of biblical studies was to serve and facilitate all of these uses of the Scripture(s). Biblical scholars, shaped by and embedded in the fundamental assumptions of the print culture in which their fields originated, understandably projected these fundamental assumptions and concepts onto biblical "books" and their "authors" and "editors." Assuming that there must have been an original (or at least early) Hebrew or Greek text of a book, it was presumed possible to "establish" it by text criticism of later manuscripts (including manuscripts of Latin and other translations) which, except for occasional lapses of attention, had been copied by otherwise faithful copyists. Even though the reconstructed "text" of books was established by text critics on the basis of manuscripts dating from centuries later, biblical scholars standardly interpreted them as "biblical" texts in the context of the "biblical" world in which they originated. "Authors/writers" were assumed to have worked from written copies of earlier sources. Books that included stories and laws that were also in books of "the Bible" were classified as "rewritten Bible." In Gospel interpretation it was assumed that Matthew and Luke, for example, had written copies of the Gospel of Mark and the "Source" (*Quelle*) of Jesus' teaching of Jesus that they shared but was not found in Mark, along with their own special sources, and that they "edited" or "redacted" as they copied their written sources.

In biblical studies as in print culture generally, it was simply assumed that oral tradition was inherently unstable and that only when something was written did it become stable. This was the way of explaining the often verbatim agreement of the Synoptic Gospels (hence the "Two-Source" hypothesis). Such deeply ingrained assumptions persisted through the recent work of the International Q Project in reconstructing the wording of the "Sayings Source." The new wave of European intellectuals' fascination with and study of folklore in the nineteenth century raised biblical scholars' awareness that a period of unstable "oral tradition" of songs, legends, prophecies, and Jesus-sayings had preceded their supposed stabilization in written texts. Form critics, however, embedded as they were in print culture, used (their analysis of) the way that one written text, such as Matthew, had adapted another, Mark, as their model for the oral tradition of the sayings of Jesus. Although they drew analogies from folklore, the fathers of form criticism (in New Testament studies, at least) never devoted much attention to the oral folklore that was still very much alive in the village communities not far from their university towns.

## Challenges Posed by Recent Lines of Research

Just in the last two or three decades, however, several interrelated but largely independent lines of pioneering research are challenging various aspects of the assumptions and agenda of standard biblical studies. Insofar as the results of these lines of research are interrelated and mutually reinforcing, they are beginning to show that the basic agenda of biblical studies and fundamental print-cultural assumptions in which it is embedded have little or no historical basis in ancient cultures. A summary outline should suffice to appreciate the challenges they pose, anticipating fuller summary in chapter 1 and further exploration in the chapters that follow.

The first breakthrough was the recognition by a few biblical scholars and classics scholars that *literacy was severely limited* in the ancient world, indeed in Palestine limited to the scribal (and later rabbinic) elite (2 or 3% of the society). This has become thoroughly researched and documented in sustained studies and is assumed by at least some of the other lines of research. Not always discerned, however, is that the severely limited literacy means that *communication* in antiquity *was largely oral*, almost entirely oral among ordinary people. Writing, moreover, was used mainly by the wealthy and powerful, including the imperial rulers, to enhance their wealth and power.

Closely related but often missed by other lines of research, is that there were different kinds and functions of writing in antiquity, some of which were not designed to be read or consulted. In societies where writing was rare, some writings were numinous, invested with an aura of authority as sacred icons to be worshipped rather than read.

Stimulated by previous research in other fields, such as classics, and having already recognized that the Gospels are whole stories about Jesus' mission, including his speeches on key issues (and not mere collections of sayings and stories), a few New Testament scholars began exploring the oral features of the Gospel narratives, particularly of the Gospel of Mark. This led to fuller discernment that the Gospel must have been performed orally before groups of people rather than read from manuscripts (by individual readers). Ordinary people would certainly have been unable to read the stories. Whether or not the Gospel existed in writing seemed to be a relatively unimportant question for its reception; in a predominantly oral communications environment it would have been orally performed even if it did exist in writing.

A separate line of recent research into Judean scribal practice and later rabbinic culture shows that even the tiny literate Judean elite, while making additional copies of texts on scrolls, learned their texts by repeated oral recitation, so that the texts became "written on the tablet of the heart," that is, inscribed in their memory.

Meanwhile pioneering classics scholars, finding indications in the texts left by elite Greek and Roman intellectuals, recognized that even the highly literate did not compose in writing, but (for example) while lying down or taking a walk, subsequently dictating their texts to a scribe or "secretary," but "publishing" their compositions by oral performance to a group of listeners.

Perhaps the most fundamental challenge to standard assumptions comes from recent text-critical analysis, both of books later included in the Hebrew Bible and of the Gospels. Close study of the manuscripts found at Qumran of the books of the Pentateuch and prophetic books found that in late second-temple scribal circles two or three different versions of these books coexisted and all were still developing. Recent text-critical analysis of early (fragmentary) manuscripts of the Gospels indicated that their Greek texts were highly varied, and that no standardized texts existed until the fourth century and after. The conclusion in both cases is that it is not possible to construct a single early text of these books, but that they were multiform.

What these and other separate lines of research are showing, in their combined results, is that the assumptions and concepts of modern print culture are not applicable to the ancient texts included in the Hebrew Bible and New Testament. These and related studies in other fields are showing that "biblical" texts were embedded in a wider and deeper world of communications that was very different from modern print culture. The difference are striking and highly significant in many respects:

- Whereas in print culture most important communication is done in writing, in pre- or non-print cultures, including among the literate elite, nearly all communication was oral.

- Whereas in print culture nearly all important texts and messages are composed in writing, in pre-print cultures nearly all texts were composed orally (in the mind or in performance).

- Whereas in print culture printed texts are stable, reproducible, and easily referenced (by page and line, etc.), in pre- or non-print cultures hand-written texts change (in detail) in reproduction, like the orally-performed texts with which they are closely interrelated.

- Whereas in print culture information is stored in print, in pre-print cultures all kinds of information, including poetry, stories, and other texts, are stored in memory.

- Whereas in print culture, although writing (in print) is still a means of social control, reading and writing also become means of more democratic empowerment, in pre-print culture writing is primarily a means of wielding power.

- Whereas in print culture the wide availability of information and even propaganda in print reduces the difference and gap between elite culture and popular culture/tradition, in pre-print culture the cultural-political elite's possession of writing compounds the difference and conflict between the "great tradition" and the "little tradition(s)."

## A Fundamental Reorientation of Biblical Studies

It should thus be clear that if biblical interpreters want to understand "biblical" texts in the context of their origins, if they want to deal seriously with the pre-print culture in which these texts were embedded, it will involve relinquishing the fundamental assumptions of print culture in which the field of biblical studies is embedded. The combined results of the lines of recent research indicate a number of interrelated and overlapping ways in which biblical studies would have to abandon its standard concepts and procedures as well as assumptions in coming to grips with the realities they have hidden or obscured.

- Versus the assumption that texts were read (and quoted from written texts), literacy was severely limited to a tiny educated elite while the vast majority of people engaged in oral communication, with no need for writing.

- Versus the assumption that written texts were widely available, manuscripts were expensive, cumbersome, limited to literate circles, largely unintelligible even to the literate who were not already familiar with the text, and extremely difficult to consult.

- Versus the assumption that the books of "the Law and the Prophets" were already the standardized Scripture(s) of Judaism, in the small scribal circles that cultivated written texts these books existed in still-developing multiple versions and their authority was relative to that of other texts (e.g., of torah), both written and oral.

- Versus the assumption that Israelite/Jewish culture or (early Christian) culture consisted only or mainly of written texts, which had various "intertextual" links, the written texts were like the tips of icebergs floating in a sea of Israelite culture or cultural tradition with various identifiable currents.

- Versus the assumption of a relatively monolithic Israelite–Judean tradition available mainly through the Scriptures or "common Judaism," the sources give significant indications of a divide between an official Jerusalem-based cultural tradition and a locally varied popular Israelite tradition cultivated by the vast majority of the people.

- Versus the assumption that texts were quoted from written copies (scrolls/manuscripts), texts were learned by recitation and held in and quoted from memory, by the literate elite as well as by ordinary people.

- Versus the assumption that learned scribes such as Ben Sira (and the texts they produced) read, quoted, and interpreted earlier "scriptural" (written) texts, they rather called for obedience to torah and covenant in general. Insofar as writing had a special sacred aura in societies where it was rare, both late second-temple scribal texts and popular texts appealed to the *authority* of particular laws and prophecies that stood "written."

- Versus the assumption that it is possible to "establish" an original or early text (wording) of written (NT) texts, the extreme variation in early (fragments of) manuscripts suggest that there were multiple versions of written texts that were later included in the New Testament.

- Versus the assumption that (NT) texts were read from written copies, the Gospels, for example, were evidently orally performed for many generations, successive lectors learning the texts from hearing them.

- Versus the assumption that writing a text stabilized it, early (fragmentary) manuscript evidence suggests adjustment of the wording of

Gospel episodes and Jesus-teachings to context and interaction with continuing performance.

- Versus the assumption that the Gospels were "written" by "authors" and/or "editors," the Gospel stories and speeches were evidently composed/developed in repeated performance in community contexts.

As all of these challenges to standard assumptions bear on future interpretation of "biblical" texts, the key shift is from the assumptions of print culture to the recognition of a predominantly oral communications environment in which texts (whether they existed in writing of not) were learned by recitation, held in memory, and performed orally in communities. As recent text-critical research has shown, we cannot establish, for example, the stable early wording of text-fragments such as mini-stories and Jesus-sayings as a basis for exegesis rooted in print-cultural assumptions. Studies of orally performed texts in other cultures and fields, however, can help us appreciate the larger Gospel stories in performance in communities. And this will require fuller understanding of the social-political context in which performed texts resonated with the audience and the cultural tradition in which they were embedded.

A few decades ago we might have interpreted these challenges to the fundamental assumptions of an academic field as the beginnings of a shift in paradigm. I remember thinking, while in graduate school in the late 1960s, after reading Thomas S. Kuhn, *The Structure of Scientific Revolutions* (1962), that the operative assumptions, concepts, and procedures of New Testament studies were problematic with regard to the texts we were interpreting. It was puzzling that prominent New Testament scholars wanted not only to dismantle, but then also to reassemble "the categories" of the field. As Kuhn's analysis began to impact biblical studies some decades later, there was discussion of more profound "paradigm change," sometimes in the perhaps naïve hope that one of the newly emerging "criticisms" could lead the way. A few decades after Kuhn's exciting analysis, however, natural scientists in different fields were no longer talking so much of paradigm shifts.

It is difficult in the extreme for single new paradigms to emerge in highly complex fields. In biblical studies, the various new criticisms have simply become subfields. They challenged certain concepts and procedures and explored new alternatives. Feminist criticism, for example, has effected a significant broadening of discourse in biblical studies and a heightened awareness of gendering in biblical texts and has insisted upon rhetorical analysis of texts that are arguments advocating certain social arrangements and viewpoints. Social-scientific criticism has raised critical awareness of the tendency to project modern western assumptions onto other societies.

But some of the basic synthetic constructs of biblical studies, such as "Judaism" and "Christianity" often remain intact. Postmodernist criticism exposed many ways in which biblical studies was embedded in the conceptual apparatus of modernism. But it is so focused on the modern western Bible as an assemblage of authoritarian, patriarchal, colonial texts that it has little energy left over to investigate whether these texts may have functioned differently in earlier times and places. While adjusting its basic discourse, these new criticisms did not challenge the most fundamental assumptions of the field, which continued in its standard constructs and procedures.

Besides various new "criticisms," there have been more profound challenges to the fundamental orientation, assumptions, and discourse of biblical studies in recent decades. Most basic perhaps are: (1) the challenge to the individualistic orientation of biblical interpretation in striking contrast with the collective/community/social orientation of most texts included in the Bible; and, closely related, (2) the challenge to the reductionist focus on religion in biblical studies that obscures the inseparability of religion from political-economic life in "biblical" texts. Equally basic and closely related to both is (3) the challenge to the synthetic essentializing orientation to "Judaism" and "Christianity" that obscures the division and often outright conflict between rulers and people evident in most texts included in the Bible. These challenges, however, can make little impact on a field that is so deeply embedded in and works in service of individualistic modern western culture that has separated religion from political-economic life and avoided focusing the determinative importance of political-economic divisions.

There is, however, at least a potential convergence of the results of the recent lines of research into ancient communications and the results of recent investigation of the collective orientation, the inseparably political-economic-religious concern, and the political-religious conflict evident in "biblical" texts. There is a potential convergence and mutual reinforcement of the challenges that they pose to the fundamental individualistic and narrowly religious orientation and the print-cultural assumptions of established biblical studies. Recognition that a Gospel, for example, would have been performed orally to a community leads into further investigation of the circumstances of community life. Recognition that literacy was limited basically to the scribal elite, combined with recognition that learned scribes served as advisers and cultural specialists in the Jerusalem temple-state, leads to the recognition that most of the texts later included in the Hebrew Bible would have been produced by circles of learned scribes. That recognition reinforces the impression from various texts of a cultural divide that corresponded to the political-economic divide between rulers and the vast majority of the people evident in many texts. Recent research showing that even the literate scribes learned texts by repeated recitation so that they were inscribed on the tablet of the heart, that is, their memory, calls for recognition of the importance of memory in ancient society, which reinforces the impression that distinctively Israelite popular movements must have been informed by Israelite tradition, by popular social memory. Many more illustrations could be offered. The point is that bringing together results of the various lines of recent research into ancient communications in general, and exploration of texts-in-performance in particular, can be integral to a more comprehensive challenge and alternative to standard biblical studies.

## Terms and Concepts

As the implications of recent research into the ancient communications world become clear, it will only be appropriate to avoid many of the basic concepts of biblical studies that belong to print culture or are otherwise problematic. In anticipation of the many terms and concepts that will emerge in connection with particular texts in the chapters below, some more general cases call for brief discussion at the outset.

First, since it is far from clear that even scribal reciters (much less nonliterate performers) were ("literally") reading from markings on a surface (such as a scroll), it would be problematic to think (and write) in terms of *writings*. I am purposely using the term *text* in its original broader meaning of a texture in reference to a story/epic/speech/prophecy/prayer that could have been oral and/or written. This inclusive term then enables us to become more specific as to whether a given text was oral and/or written, and more specific about when we are referring to its oral or its written mode by the simple addition of adjectives, "oral" or "written." Written texts were like the visible tip of icebergs with their far larger bases invisible, floating in a vast sea of oral culture. They have a certain definite form, but grow from and rest upon (and flow back into) the more amorphous sea of oral tradition.

Similarly problematic is the seeming oxymoron "oral literature" that became used in reference to the epics and sagas of various cultures that by default (of the modern division of academic labor) were taught in departments of literature. It makes more sense to refer to "oral-derived" texts, which better conveys both the relation of modern interpreters who work from written (printed!) versions to the orally-performed versions and the oral cultural processes by which such texts acquired their distinctive forms. In order not to continue projecting the assumptions of print culture onto texts that were later included in the Hebrew Bible or the New Testament, we should not imagine that they were all "written" to be performed. Some may have been, in particular senses and contexts. Some texts of (Mosaic covenantal) torah were written onto scrolls so that they would be numinous sacred objects of worship, and also lend a sacred aura to their performance in public assembly at the Temple (see the suddenly "discovered" writing of torah, in 2 Kings 22–23, and the later written book of torah presented and performed by Ezra, in Nehemiah 8). Paul apparently dictated his letters to particular assemblies of Christ-loyalists so that the performers of the letters had written scrolls of the letters when they "delivered" them. Other texts originated in oral performance and were only subsequently written onto scrolls. Many instructional speeches that the learned Jerusalem scribe Jesus Ben Sira delivered orally to his scribal protégés were written down and included in the collection of his wisdom in the book of Sirach. At the more popular (largely non-literate) level, the stories-with-speeches that we know as the Gospels may well have been performed without consultation of a written version. It is conceivable that the writing of the Gospels on scrolls and codices may have been done because the stories became revered and giving them written form enhanced their authority.

Nearly all historical sources to which we have access because they were written were produced by scribes or other literate elite. Non-literate ordinary people did not leave written texts. Insofar as scribally-produced texts such as the Deuteronomistic history (adapted and) incorporated oral traditions (such as the archaic Song of Deborah), some texts that became written and were later included in the Hebrew Bible originated with ordinary people. The Gospels are not only stories about ordinary people but developed from oral traditions of ordinary people. Thus while most texts were produced (and recited) in circles of scribes, it is important for appreciation and interpretation of texts to discern those that evidently originated in communities of ordinary people.

Performance of texts is a form of communication that involves social relations and dynamic interaction. Since performance is relational, it is only appropriate to think about performance in relational terms. Thus, in contrast to the tendency in biblical studies, as in other academic fields, to move analysis, reflection, and interpretation into static abstract terms (such as those, derived from Latin, ending in "-ity"), it seems more appropriate to refer to the particular relations and dynamics involved insofar as the written texts to which we have access offer indications or clues.

As suggested by the previous two points, the (historical) social relations and political dynamics of texts(-in-performance) and written texts are obscured when boxed into abstract synthetic (and often essentialist) constructs, such as "(early) Judaism/Jewish" or "(early) Christianity/Christian" or "Hellenistic" or "apocalyptic." The texts (recited and written on scrolls) usually located and dated in second-temple Judea (Jerusalem) were all apparently produced in scribal circles either supportive of the temple-state or critical of the incumbent high priestly rulers. It is not clear the extent to which they provide evidence for what Judean villagers thought and practiced. Application of the concept "Judaism" only obscures the origin and function of these texts. The Gospels later included in the New Testament evidently originated in and were performed in communities of Jesus-loyalists. The Gospels of Mark, Matthew, and John, however, are all addressed to communities or movements that had not yet established an identity separate from the people of Israelite cultural heritage and present Jesus as a fulfilment of Israelite tradition. To label them "Christian" only obscures the role of the Gospel stories in the early development of communities in expanding movements that only after several generations established distinctive "Christian" identities and eventually were included institutionally in the established religion of Christianity, with its canon of authoritative written texts.

In contrast to the flat, one-dimensional printed texts that are the passive objects of scholarly study (word-by-word, phrase-by-phrase analysis), texts-in-performance involved live dynamic multidimensional communication and interaction. Not only did the performers interact with the audience, but they did so in particular communities and in broader contexts of life-circumstances. In contrast with study of written/printed texts that usually attempts to establish the meaning of the texts taken in themselves, often without consideration of the historical-social context, appreciation of texts-in-performance requires investigation of the social-historical context as well in order to understand the interaction of text, performer, and audience in context and how the performed texts affect the hearers. To understand the latter, moreover, (as will be discussed below) it is also necessary to gain as much knowledge as possible about the cultural tradition out of which the hearers resonate with the performed text.

## Performance Criticism

Only recently have studies of performance emerged, with a broad range of foci and emphases.[1] Some studies focus more narrowly, on the actor in the theater, the musician in concert, or the artist in the open studio or museum. Others are broad in the extreme, as when anthropologists describe a culture (its rituals and traditions) in terms of performance.

---

1. Bial, *Performance Studies Reader*; Schechner, *Performance Studies*.

Whatever their focus and concern, those who study performance agree that it is action in and upon an audience/community/society in which the cultural-religious dimension is not separate from the political. In relation to certain kinds of modern theater, reflection has often emphasized how performance challenges, moves, or changes the audience. Reflection on ritual (political as well as religious), on the other hand, often emphasizes how performance molds and nourishes people, confirms and reestablishes group identity, and reinforces established power-relations. This can be true even of celebrations that ostensibly subvert or reverse the order of things, such as Carnival or Mardi Gras, which have sometimes been characterized as a "safety-valve" for "letting off steam" before reversion to the established order. Less attention has been paid to how ritual or other performances that reinforce, nurture, and fortify subjugated people also challenge the dominant order to which they are subordinated. While some modern theater challenges the audience and may aim to subvert the political order, performance of ancient Greek drama and other "civil-religious" ceremonies supported the established order while "acting out" its internal tensions.[2]

While reflection on the theater has strongly influenced studies of performance in other fields, parallel criticism and theory has developed in fields such as anthropology and folklore and the interpretation of epic poetry in various times and cultures. At the very least such studies help appreciate the entertainment happening in story-telling or the performance of folktales or traditional epics. But much of this criticism also delves into how such performance carries, renews, and reestablishes the cultural tradition and identities of communities and peoples.

We moderns, whose experience of the relation between text and performance is so deeply rooted in print culture, may have to work at appreciating that most performance in most cultures of the world did not involve, much less depend on, written texts. We experience actors performing from scripts in theaters and on screen and choruses and instrumental ensembles performing from printed scores and we sing hymns from hymnbooks. In the new appreciation of oral-derived texts, we hear Beowulf or the Iliad or the Gospel of Mark performed by someone who has memorized from a printed text (in translation). We may even read "fairytales" from a printed (and illustrated) story-book. But the collection of Germanic folklore by the Brothers Grimm did not put an end to the oral performance of those tales that had been happening for centuries in many local variations. In Appalachia many different tunes-with-poetic wordings of the twenty-third Psalm, for example, have been sung for generations (I would use two or three of

---

2. Schechner and Appel, *By Means of Performance*.

these in classes of urban students most of whom were unable to read music to illustrate traditional psalm-singing when we came to interpret the "book" of Psalms). Most blues-singing and rock-music did not involve written music. And those early ancient performers of the Iliad or more recent Serbian or other bards did not perform from written texts. Even after the invention of writing and popular awareness of the existence of authoritative written texts, performers worked from oral tradition (memory). On the cover of his book *How to Read an Oral Poem*, John Miles Foley has a picture he took of a Tibetan singer performing while holding a piece of paper in front of him—paper which was blank. Performance of many kinds of texts, such as stories and story-cycles, songs, ballads, epics, were done from oral tradition, often in effect re-composed in the performance.

Our continuing experience of theater and musical performances, however, can help us recognize how flat a written text is compared with a live performance of a text. Even with a musical score full of markers of tempo and other dynamics, it is virtually impossible to imagine how alive the text becomes when experienced as a performance, with gestures, movement, facial expressions, tone of voice, and interaction with the audience. And hearing different performances of the same text can help us appreciate how the text comes alive differently and affects us in different ways.

## Performance Criticism in the Reorientation of Biblical Studies

Performance criticism has developed only recently in biblical studies. Studies of performance of texts from the Hebrew Bible have taken cues from performance studies in theater.[3] Performance criticism in New Testament studies has arisen principally from one or the other of two concerns.

On the one hand, pioneering biblical scholars, principally Werner Kelber, taking cues from ground-breaking research in other fields and recognizing that oral communications were dominant in ancient culture, began to explore the relations of oral tradition and oral performance with written texts.[4] These pioneers have been concerned primarily with the origins of biblical texts and their performance in historical context. Some of them have worked in close interaction with the developing performance theory of (the late) John Miles Foley, who drew widely on the ethnography

---

3. Doan and Giles, *Prophets, Performance, and Power.*

4. See esp. Kelber, *Oral and Written Gospel.*

of performance, oral-traditional theory, and oral performance in a wide range of cultures.[5]

On the other hand, pioneering scholars and clergy and others have engaged in performance of biblical texts. Beginning with the Gospel of Mark, David Rhoads has regularly performed several New Testament texts. Videotapes of his performances have been widely used in academic courses and ecclesial contexts, making these texts come alive in new ways. An increasing number of "biblical story-tellers" perform various texts before gatherings of people and gather themselves for mutual reinforcement and reflection. Again led by David Rhoads, they have begun to reflect critically on their performance practices, drawing from wider performance theory, and are appropriating the results of the lines of recent research outlined above.[6] The Biblical Performance Criticism Series (edited by Rhoads) includes explorations that stem from both sides of this spectrum.

Lacking the courage and imagination to engage in performance myself, I have been attempting to appreciate the origins and performance of texts (some of which were later included in the Bible) in historical context. My mentor in sociology, Robert Bellah, insisted that I read Eric Havelock's highly suggestive exploration of the shift from oral communication to writing in classical Greece (*Preface to Plato*) in the mid-1960s.[7] The issues he raised simply festered in my thinking for thirty years. Having been deeply absorbed in research on the political-economic context of the historical Jesus, it was not until I began critically rethinking the Gospel sources for the historical Jesus that I began to "catch on" to some of the more recent research on oral tradition and oral performance. I was puzzled that specialists on the teaching of Jesus parallel in Matthew and Luke were attempting to reconstruct a "critical text" of the sayings in "Q," while some were showing that the "sayings" were formed into "clusters" or speeches. It seemed evident even in the closely parallel Greek versions of Matthew and Luke that the speeches in "Q" had the form of parallel poetic lines, easily memorable, and probably orally performed. In the next several years I began to learn from some of the pioneers in the exploration of orality and oral performance in the Gospel of Mark and other texts (such as Werner Kelber, Pieter Botha, Joanna Dewey),[8] in a series of conferences spearheaded initially by Jona-

5. See especially Foley, *Immanent Art*; *Singer of Tales in Performance*; *How to Read an Oral Poem*; and, more condensed, "Plenitude and Diversity."

6. See especially the programmatic reflections in the two-part article of David Rhoads, "Performance Criticism."

7. Havelock, *Preface to Plato*.

8. See especially Kelber, *Oral and Written Gospel*; and the essays collected in *Imprints, Voiceprints*; the essays of Botha now collected in *Orality and Literacy*; and the

than Draper in South Africa and then especially by Werner Kelber in the United States. Five of the chapters below began as presentations at those conferences.

As will be explained in some of the chapters below, I have been adapting the interdisciplinary and comparative performance theory of John Miles Foley, who gave generously of his wide knowledge and critical reflection at those exploratory conferences and in many sessions at the Society of Biblical Literature.[9] In appreciating the various aspects of performance, Foley focuses particularly on the *text* that is performed, the *context* of the performance, and the performed texts' *metonymic referencing of* the cultural *tradition* shared by performer/text and hearers. The goal of analysis and appreciation is not so much the meaning of the text as the way it affects the (listening) community. Several of the chapters in this volume will include a fuller sketch of Foley's theory. The following outline only illustrates how the key facets of (his theory of) oral performance may fit some of the different texts in the Hebrew Bible and New Testament.

Foley's concept of "oral-derived" *text* is particularly appropriate and helpful for "biblical" texts in historical context once we become aware of the implications of the lines of research outlined above. Ancient Judean texts, some of which were later included in the Hebrew Bible and some not, are really anthologies of separable texts and/or collections of texts that developed and "grew" over many generations before reaching the form and length in which we know them. The book of Psalms is a collection of songs that were sung; the book of Proverbs includes hundreds of proverbs that were used and adapted in oral discourse; the prophetic books are collections of (fragments of) prophecies orally delivered and remembered before being "anthologized." The book of Sirach consists of a few hymns and an epic hymn of praise as well as mostly of instructional speeches of a learned scribe addressed to his students. All of these (collections of) texts have been shaped by professional scribes. But once we recognize that scribes themselves learned and cultivated texts by reciting them, we cannot continue to imagine, for example, that when the scribes began to collect and shape prophetic oracles, the oral tradition ended as the written shaping and transmission began. The Gospels later included in the New Testament bear the features of orally performed stories that include shorter or longer speeches in the larger narrative. It has long been recognized that the Gospel stories developed orally and particularly that the speeches closely parallel in Matthew and Luke (but

---

essays by Dewey now collected in *Oral Ethos of the Early Church* in the Biblical Performance Criticism Series.

9. See note 5 above.

not in Mark) must have developed or been cultivated orally before being included in those larger Gospel stories. It is now being recognized that the Gospels continued to be performed well after they existed in written form.

As for the context in which the texts were performed, the texts themselves often offer indications or clues, or we can deduce the context from matching the text with historical situations as we know them from other sources. The texts of many psalms suggest that they were performed by priests in the Temple, in some cases as part of state ceremonies such as coronation of a king. The (ostensible) historical accounts of texts of Mosaic torah both displayed as numinous sacred writing to be worshiped and formally performed in state ceremonies authorizing centralization of political-economic-religious power in the monarchy or the temple-state (2 Kings 22–23; Nehemiah 8) suggest that such was the performance context (and function) of other texts of torah. The climax of the long hymn of praise in Sirach 44–50 indicates that it was part of a ceremony celebrating and legitimating the Oniad high priesthood in the early second century BCE. The instructional speeches in Sirach were particular components of the oral curriculum in which fledgling scribes were trained (in Ben Sira's "house of instruction"). The performance context of Paul's letters were gatherings of the assemblies of Christ-loyalists that he and his coworkers had catalyzed in Corinth, Thessalonica, and Philippi. We can deduce from a combination of information (for example, their inclusion of performative speeches of Mosaic covenant renewal such as Mark 10 and Matthew 5–7//Luke 6:20–49) that the Gospel stories-and-speeches were performed in communities of movements of Jesus-loyalists.

The *tradition* that both Judean texts later included (or not) in the Hebrew Bible and the Gospels, the book of Revelation, and Paul's letters referenced was, generally speaking, Israelite culture. Given the variety of kinds of text, however, it is possible to be more precise. Most fundamental was the cultural divide between the ruling elite and the circles of learned scribes who served the rulers, on the one hand, and the ordinary people, on the other. This divide between what anthropologists call the "great tradition" and the "little tradition" is so important for understanding ("biblical") texts-in-performance that a chapter (chap 5) is devoted to it. Insofar as a succession of prophets pronounced oracles and circles of scribes continued to collect them, an Israelite prophetic tradition developed. Similarly, insofar as scribes cultivated various kinds of wisdom and trained subsequent generations of scribes, a tradition of scribal instruction and scribal lore developed. As will be examined in some of the chapters below, the Gospels reference mainly the Israelite popular tradition. But they also know of and reference, both positively and negatively, the Judean "great" or official tradition in what have often been taken as "quotations" from "biblical" books.

The explorations in these chapters, primarily of the instructional speeches of Ben Sira, of Q speeches, and of the Gospel of Mark, by adapting the interdisciplinary theory of Foley, aim basically at appreciation of these texts-in-performance in their historical context. It is conceivable, however, that the results might well lead into one or both of two further steps. The one would be how texts-in-performance might be used as sources for historical (re-)construction of (the historical) Jesus-in-movement (that is, understood relationally). The resulting understanding of texts-in-performance in their historical context might also further inform the burgeoning movement of contemporary performance of biblical texts, even though the latter would hardly be confined to "historically-informed" performance. The one step would bring historical investigation onto a more solid footing in appreciation of the oral-performative character of the sources. The other step could provide a solid historical foundation for the texts to come alive again beyond the confining limits of print culture as texts-in-performance in today's context of multiple media of communication and community.

# ACKNOWLEDGMENTS

The author and publisher gratefully acknowledge the permission of the following publishers and journal to include essays that appeared in earlier form:

Chapter 1 originally appeared as: "Oral Communication, Oral Performance, and New Testament Interpretation." In *Method and Meaning: Essays on New Testament Interpretation in Honor of Harold W. Attridge*, edited by Andrew B. McGowan and Kent Harold Richards, Resources for Biblical Study 67 (Atlanta: Society of Biblical Literature, 2011) 125–56.

Chapter 9 originally appeared as: "The Languages of the Kingdom: From Aramaic to Greek, Galilee to Syria." In *A Wandering Galilean: Essays in Honour of Sean Freyne*, edited by Zuleika Rodgers et al., JSJSup 132 (Leiden: Brill, 2009) 401–25.

Chapter 10 originally appeared as: "Oral Performance and Mark: Some Implications of *The Oral and the Written Gospel*, Twenty-Five Years Later." In *Jesus, the Voice, and the Text: Beyond "The Oral and the Written Gospel,"* edited by Tom Thatcher (Waco, TX: Baylor University Press, 2008) 45–70, and is included with the permission of Baylor University Press.

Chapter 12 originally appeared as: "Oral and Written Aspects of the Emergence of the Gospel of Mark as Scripture." *Oral Tradition* 25 (2010) 93–114.

# ABBREVIATIONS

BPCS      Biblical Performance Criticism Series
*CBQ*       *Catholic Biblical Quarterly*
DSS       Dead Sea Scrolls
*JBL*        *Journal of Biblical Literature*
JSOTSup   Journal for the Study of the Old Testament Supplements
*HTR*       *Harvard Theological Review*
JSJSup     Journal for the Study of Judaism Supplements
LAI        Library of Ancient Israel
LXX        Septuagint
MT         Masoretic text
SBLSymS    Society of Biblical Literature Symposium Series
SNTSMS     Society for New Testament Studies Monograph Series
SP         Samaritan Pentateuch
WUNT       Wissenschaftliche Untersuchungen zum Neuen Testament

# 1

# ORAL COMMUNICATION, ORAL PERFORMANCE, AND NEW TESTAMENT INTERPRETATION

MODERN WESTERN PRINT CULTURE GAVE BIRTH TO BIBLICAL studies—and now threatens to hold it captive.[1] Like classicists, New Testament scholars who write mass-produced books and articles for individual silent readers have simply assumed that biblical "books" were widely distributed, readily available, and easily read at least by the time of Jesus and Paul. They assume, for example, that "authors" "wrote" the Gospels, which were fairly quickly "in circulation" to be "read" by early Christians.

Parallel but often separate lines of research in recent decades have shown that literacy was extremely limited in antiquity and that oral communication dominated, even among the literate elite. There was no "Great Divide" between an oral and a literate culture. Written texts in ancient Judea and the Roman empire were embedded in the wider oral communication. In their interface, written texts reflected oral communication and writing influenced oral communication. Many texts that were inscribed on scrolls continued to be cultivated orally. By repeated recitation they had become "inscribed" on the tablets of people's hearts as well as on scrolls.

Ironically our only access to oral communication is through extant written texts. Hence it is important not to impose modern typographical assumptions and concepts in which our scholarship is embedded onto the oral communication that might be discernible in or underneath the written texts that are the only remains visible of the biosphere of communication

---

1. On print culture, see especially Eisenstein, *The Printing Press*.

from which they grew.[2] It is important, therefore, to recognize that histori-cally there have been different oral communications and literacies, and to investigate the specific social practices of reading and writing and oral com-munications. Practices of writing and reading are culturally embedded and ideological. Thus, while estimated percentages of "literacy" may be telling indicators for particular cultural situations, it is more important to discern the different uses of writing and their relationship with various forms of oral communications.[3]

Some significant implications for New Testament interpretation are al-ready clear from the various lines of recent research.[4] Insofar as the medium of communication in antiquity was predominantly oral, and even written texts were recited orally to communities of people, it will be necessary for New Testament interpretation to shift and expand its focus from written texts in themselves, to (oral) *communication as interactive* and the *context(s)* in which it happened. Moreover, just as writing was embedded in wider oral communication, so particular texts, orally performed and/or written, were embedded in wider cultural *tradition(s)* and collective social *memory*, which thus become all the more important for our interpretation. Further-more, insofar as oral and/or written texts (like the "oral traditions" behind them) were used, in repeated recitation and application in communities and their contexts, interpretation would be appropriately focused on their *culti-vation* and not their mere transmission.

## Oral Communication, Literacy, and the Uses of Writing in the Roman Empire

Literacy was limited to a tiny percentage (10%) of the population in the Roman empire. More important than the rate of literacy, however, were the uses and functions of writing. Writing was used mainly by the political and cultural elite, often as an instrument of power. While they knew that it was used by the elite, the vast majority of the people had no use for writing.[5]

The largely localized ancient economy did not require widespread literacy. A tiny minority of urban artisans used brief written forms. By the

2. See especially the call for the field to recognize and critically rethink its own birth and basis in print-culture by the pioneer in the study of orality, Werner Kelber in "Jesus and Tradition," and in many articles since.

3. Street, *Literacy*, 2–3; Foley, *How to Read an Oral Poem*, 66–69.

4. See the reviews of research by Hearon, "The Implications of Orality"; and Iver-son, "Orality and the Gospels."

5. The standard work is Harris, *Ancient Literacy*, on which the following sketch depends.

first century BCE, Roman aristocratic families had written contracts drawn up for large-scale loans and other major transactions. Administration and control of the empire required considerable use of writing, such as the imperial correspondence carried out by slaves in the "family of Caesar." The calculations of how much tribute could be taken from a given territory and its population were kept in writing (the "census" or "enrollment" of Luke 2:1). The Romans built massive monuments inscribed with names, slogans, and lengthy accounts of the great acts of the emperor in bringing Salvation and Security to the cities of the Empire. The operations of the Roman military also required extensive, if less public, writing. Writing in various forms was thus used mainly to maintain or expand military, economic and/ or social power.

Writing also came to play a role in elite "literary" culture. Like every other aspect of life in the ancient world, however, this culture also was largely oral. Poetry of various forms was performed at festivals and in great households. Plays were performed in theaters. Orators displayed their rhetorical prowess at city festivals and before emperors. Sometimes orators used writing in the preparation of their orations. At least some literary culture was requisite for the urban and provincial elite of the Roman empire, although they depended on suitably trained slaves to handle correspondence and read aloud to them. Yet most of their life, including "literary" entertainment and the ceremonial conduct of "political" affairs, proceeded by means of oral communication.

Among the ordinary people in the Roman empire, urban artisans and rural peasants, transactions of all kinds took place in oral communication, usually face to face. Even "legal" agreements such as loans were conducted orally, perhaps confirmed by witnesses, the transfer of symbolic objects, and/or personal oaths. Such interaction was governed by age-old custom and ritual. Personal witnesses and testimony were far more trustworthy than written documents that could be altered by those who might use them for their own advantage. Indeed the people were often suspicious of writing as an instrument of their landlords or rulers.

It is curious that scholars of early Christianity who are aware of this limited literacy in the Roman empire continue to trust older generalizations about general literacy among Judeans and diaspora Jews. "According to Josephus, in first-century Judaism it was . . . a religious commandment that . . . children be taught to read . . . [R]abbinic sources suggest . . . that by the first century CE . . . even small communities had elementary schools."[6] The key passages from Josephus, however, indicate not that children were taught to

6. Gamble, *Books and Readers*, 7.

read but that the teaching and learning of the laws were done through public oral recitation (at Sabbath assemblies). This suggests both that Jews, like others in the Roman empire, were generally not literate and that communications even of the most important matters was oral. Through recitation and hearing the laws would become "engraved on [the people's] souls . . . and guarded in their memory" (*Ant.* 4.210; 16:43; *c. Apion.* 2.175, 178, 204; cf. Philo, *ad Gaium* 115, 210). Earlier studies failed to consider key aspects of the historical context, particularly the social location and power relations of written texts, in the wider context of the dominant oral communications. The rabbinic texts cited for the ubiquity of schools refer rather to rabbinic circles themselves, a tiny segment of the population. And rabbinic sources cited as evidence of the people *reading* (e.g., *m. Ber.* 4:3; *Bik.* 3:7; *Sukk.* 3:10) refer rather to *recitation* of certain psalms and prayers from memory.

More extensive studies of the evidence of literacy and the particular uses of writing have now shown that the rate of literacy in Roman Palestine was much smaller than in the Roman empire generally, as low as three percent.[7] The ability to read and write (Hebrew, Aramaic, or Greek) was limited basically to scribal circles in Judea, the administrations of Rome's client rulers, and nascent rabbinic circles. The DSS provide an unprecedented "horde" of written texts that were kept in scribal-priestly circles, copies of (some of) which were also presumably laid up in the temple. Rabbinic circles evidently continued to teach and learn reading and writing. But it is sobering to realize that they may not have committed the tractates of the Mishnah and Tosefta to writing for several generations and the further elaboration of rabbinic debates and rulings in the Talmuds for many more generations after that. The rabbis, many of whom became wealthy, also used writing for economic transactions and social-religious-economic matters such as marriage contracts, after the second century CE. The Babatha letters found in the Judean wilderness (in Greek) evidently attest the materialist concerns of the local Judean aristocracy.

As elsewhere in the Roman empire, ordinary Judeans and Galileans communicated orally, with no need for writing. Villagers' transactions concerning land, loans, and marriage were evidently conducted by oral agreement and/or ritual action of oaths and witnesses, judging from rabbinic references. People placed their trust in the personal presence of living witnesses. Since writing was often used as an instrument of power over them, as in records of loans drawn up by wealthy creditors, artisans and peasants were sometimes hostile to written documents. One of the first actions in the

---

7. The extensive research in Hezser, *Jewish Literacy*, confirms and much more fully documents what several of us sketched earlier.

popular insurrection in 66 CE was "to destroy the money-lenders' bonds and prevent the recovery of debts" (Josephus, *War* 2.426–27).

## Kinds and Functions of Writing in the Second-Temple Oral Communications Context

In modern print culture it is assumed that writing is for reading. Accordingly in biblical studies it is usually assumed that "biblical" texts were read and interpreted. In the culture of Roman Palestine, however, as in most cultures where writing was unusual, it may have appeared strange and mysterious, especially to the non-literate. It is important to discern the different kinds of writing and their function, lest we project the assumption that writing is for reading.[8] (Note that the Hebrew term *sepher*, "writing," was used for all kinds of writing.)

Certain simple short "writings" were not intended to be read or consulted later. Pertinent to Jesus' dispute with the Pharisees about divorce (Mark 10:2–9) was the provision in Deuteronomy (24:1–4) that a husband could place a simple "writing" of divorce into his wife's hand and send her out of the household. Performative speech, such as a curse, carried the power of effecting what was pronounced. A husband's simple, written (hence permanent) renunciation was even more powerful, a decisively effective action.

A more substantial, extensive kind of writing served to authorize or "constitute" ruling institutions and/or claims to power and control of land and people. The "books" of Chronicles, Ezra, Nehemiah, and possibly the "book" of Deuteronomy, earlier versions of the "books" of the Pentateuch, and many of the "writings" included in them (genealogies, lists of lineages and their claims to land and office, annals of kings, etc.) appear to have been constitutional writings produced to authorize the temple-state and its ruling priesthood. Like many writings placed in temples in Egypt and Mesopotamia, these writings were laid up in the Jerusalem temple, further enhancing their authority, and were not (meant to be) consulted or read, although learned scribes may have known their contents orally-memorially.

"Numinous" writing is very important in authoritative second-temple Judean "books," many of which were later included in the Hebrew Bible. In a society dominated by oral communication, virtually any writing had a certain mysterious authority. The ultimate in numinous writing was that of God, especially his finger engraving his commandments on stone in the

---

8. Important distinctions, which some have not taken into account, by Niditch, *Oral World and Written Word*; on second-temple texts, see Horsley, *Scribes, Visionaries*, chap. 5–6, on which the following depends.

theophany at Sinai (Exod 24:12; 31:18; 32:16; Deut 4:13; 5:22; 9:10). The placement of the stone tablets in the ark of the covenant then made it electric with divine power. "The words" of God were *communicated* by Moses' oral recitation "in the ears of" the people. But the numinous aura of the divine writing gave them awesome authority and power.

Prominent in the cities of the Roman empire was "monumental" writing, which was highly important in the legitimation of imperial and urban institutions and power relations. Monumental writing thus also carried constitutional functions. In the Greek city-states laws were inscribed on stones to display their force and permanence to the public. But knowledge of particular laws was obtained not by reading the inscription on the stones, but by consulting "rememberers." Some "monumental" writings with "constitutional" functions were inscribed on large scrolls or codices rather than on stone arches or "public" buildings. The Domesday Book of medieval England was not a record book to be consulted or read, but an awesome symbolic document of the majestic and unalterable Norman Conquest by William the Conqueror. Its earliest copies were sacred documents, with elaborate multicolored embellishments.[9]

"The writing of the torah/covenant/laws of Moses" was a corresponding "monumental" writing in second-temple Judea that was evidently not primarily for reading or consultation. A whole series of representations in Judean texts that were later included in the Hebrew Bible offer a sense of how "the writing of the torah" was understood, at least in the scribal circles. In addition to the original numinous writing of the covenant "words" on stone and Moses' subsequent writing of the (presumably more extensive) words in a numinous writing placed in the ark of the covenant (Deut 31:24–26; cf. 28:58–61), Joshua "wrote the teaching of Moses on the stones [of the altar he had built]," making the numinous constitutional writing even more monumental (Josh 8:30–35; cf. 24:25–27). Communication of the words to the people was by oral performance, in Moses' and Joshua's recitation. The monumental writing of the covenantal teaching rather externalized and eternalized the covenant between Yahweh and Israel, guaranteeing its continuing force. Even its oral recitation to the people was not (primarily) to help them learn the particular laws but to ritualize the people's commitment to God and his words in a sacred ceremony.

The most telling representations of the torah of Moses as a monumental (and numinous and constitutional) writing were the ceremonial public presentations (followed by recitation) of the "writing of the covenant/teaching" by King Josiah and the learned scribe Ezra. In the latter case (Neh

---

9. Clanchy, *Memory to Written Record*, 18.

8:4–8), Ezra, flanked by other high ranking figures on a raised wooden platform, "opened the writing (large scroll?) in the sight of all the people." The people then acclaimed "'Amen, Amen,' lifting up their hands," and "bowed their heads and worshipped Yahweh with their faces to the ground." This "writing of the teaching of Moses" was clearly a sacred object of great power. The people were bowing before a numinous monumental writing—whose constitutional function was to legitimate the Jerusalem temple-state now in the control of the previously deported Jerusalem aristocracy recently sent back from Babylon by the Persians. Even Ezra's recitation was full of mystery, since it was presumably in Hebrew, unintelligible to the people who probably spoke Aramaic; it had to be "interpreted" (translated).

## The Pluriformity of Authoritative Texts in Late Second-Temple Judean Scribal Circles

The representations of "the writing of the covenant/teaching" as monumental constitutional writing also indicate that the *communication* of the covenant/teaching (torah) was oral, by recitation. The performer, moreover, was the highly literate scribe, Ezra. As recent research into ancient scribal practices is now indicating, the very professional scribes who were trained in reading and writing also learned and cultivated texts orally, by repeated recitation. Ironically perhaps, one of our entries to appreciation of texts in oral performance may be through scribal practice that turns out to have been embedded in oral tradition. First, however, it may help us wriggle out from under the weight of print-cultural assumptions about the cultivation of ancient texts by attending to other recent research, that of text critics on the multiple manuscripts of authoritative texts found in the caves at Qumran.

The written texts of scriptural "books" (in Hebrew) found at Qumran, manuscripts more than a thousand years earlier than any available before, were not standardized and stable. On the basis of over thirty years' examination of these manuscripts, Eugene Ulrich explains how the new evidence they provide challenges older assumptions about these books in two fundamental and interrelated respects.[10] First, evidence from the Qumran manuscripts shows that multiple versions of these texts existed. Second, the multiple textual traditions were all "unstable" and still developing. As they handed on the tradition, creative scribes were enriching it, adding to it, and adapting it. The same process that scholars have concluded was involved in the composition of these (composite) texts evidently continued throughout the second-temple period. One important implication, as Ulrich suggests,

10. Ulrich, *Dead Sea Scrolls*, esp. 11, 14, 40–41, 91–92, 102.

is that if we are trying to achieve a historical perspective on the origins and textual development of these texts, "the first step is not to talk about a Bible," at least until well after the late second-temple period.

Evidence of other texts, not later included in the Hebrew Bible, points to the fluid character of texts and the cultivation of texts.[11] If the numbers of copies of texts found at Qumran is any index of their relative authority, then *Jubilees* (at 15 copies) rivaled Exodus (17) and Leviticus (14). Moreover, alternative texts of torah, the Temple Scroll and the so-called Reworked Pentateuch (5 each) may have been nearly as important as Numbers (8). And those last two texts point to what is striking on the old assumption that the books of *the* Torah were already stable as Scripture that was studied and interpreted. The new exodus and covenant renewal community at Qumran evidently did not look directly to the books of the Pentateuch for the rules and ordinances that guided its life, but produced is own covenantal laws, as evident in the Community Rule and the Damascus Rule. Moreover, rather than "study" and "interpret" the already (relatively) authoritative texts of torah, of which they also made diverse copies, the creative scribes at Qumran also produced new, alternative texts of torah. The recently generated scholarly concepts of "rewritten Bible" and "reworked Pentateuch" are anachronistic misnomers insofar as there was no Bible yet (see further chap. 4). And the Temple Scroll and Reworked Pentateuch, like *Jubilees,* include so much material that was not included (in some version) in the books of the Pentateuch and different versions of some parallel materials. We are thus virtually forced to imagine a wider Israelite/Judean *cultural repertoire* (including torah, prophetic materials, historical narratives, and different kinds of wisdom) in oral tradition that creative scribes drew upon in continuing composition of texts, some of which are extant in written form.

## Scribal Oral-Written Cultivation of Texts

Recent research into scribal practices in ancient Mesopotamia, Egypt, Judah/Judea, and later rabbinic circles is finding that the learned scribe Ezra was not alone in his oral recitation of a complex text. Professional scribes in the service of kings and temples learned and cultivated texts orally, by repeated recitation.[12] To imagine that the "scribal" ("scribality") is a different medium entirely from the "oral" ("orality") may be yet another projection of our print-cultural assumptions, just as the acquisition of knowledge

11. More fully explored in Horsley, *Scribes, Visionaries,* chap. 6.

12. The following depends on van der Toorn, *Scribal Culture*; Horsley, *Scribes, Visionaries,* chaps. 5–6; Carr, *Tablet of the Heart*; and Jaffee, *Torah in the Mouth.*

through the reading and writing of written texts in schools is a modern practice.

The "education" of ancient learned scribes was like a family-based apprenticeship, a "training" or "discipline." In Judea, as in other ancient Near Eastern cultures, the purpose of scribal training was to form a particular type of character suited for service of the temple-state. The skills of reading and writing were fundamental, yet ancillary to the inculcation of culture that would build qualities of personal discipline and obedience to higher authority. In his instructional speeches, the learned scribe Ben Sira admonished his protégés to fear the Lord, lead lives beyond reproach, and defer to their superiors.

Scribal training, while including writing and reading, proceeded mainly in an oral–aural mode. Ben Sira declares that he has "written" understanding "in this writing" (50:27). Yet in his "house of instruction" he teaches not by asking his students to "open a book," but by "opening his mouth" (51:23–25). He presents his own teaching as oral, and his students' reception as aural. "For wisdom becomes known through speech" (4:24). "If you love to listen you will gain knowledge" (6:23). "From the discourse of the sages" the fledgling students would "learn discipline and how to serve princes" (8:8–9). It was only fitting that the goal of scribal training was learning to be "a skillful speaker," insofar as "the assemblies of the rulers," like the society at large, proceeded by oral communication (5:10–11; 5:13—6:1; 11:7–9; 15:5; 21:15–17; 23:7–12; 27:11–15; etc.).

The formation of character, furthermore, was inseparable from and proceeded through the learning of texts and the wider cultural repertoire of which professional scribes were the guardians and cultivators, in service of monarchies and temples-states. Elementary to the curriculum of scribal training were the principal forms of wisdom ("sayings of the famous, . . . parables, . . . proverbs" 39:2–3). But the curriculum also included the other segments of the Israelite/Judean cultural repertoire. The scribe who devoted himself also "held in mind the teaching (torah) of the Most High," and was engaged "with prophecies" (39:1). Like the learning of different kinds of wisdom, the learning of torah and prophecies were also oral–memorial; nothing in Ben Sira's phrases suggests that written texts were involved.

The recent research on the scribal training and scribal practice in Judea and the ancient Near East parallels Ben Sira's observations and practices. Scribes learned a wide range of texts primarily by recitation and repetition. Their instruction in writing and responsibilities for copying and preserving written texts would have influenced and perhaps aided their learning. And scribes' writing and handling of manuscripts may have effected a certain stabilization of texts. It may be significant that scribes understood the internalization of texts in a chirographic metaphor: "written on the tablet of the heart." That metaphor, however, points primarily to the essential role and importance of memory in the cultivation of texts. And memory happened and lived by oral recitation. As is well know, the rabbis taught their students through recitation. They held that once students had heard a teaching or a traditional rabbinic debate about an issue recited three or four times, they should remember it. In medieval European cultivation of important culture texts memorial internalization and recitation were not differentiated.[13] In ancient and medieval elite cultural circles, manuscripts were produced and maintained, but were "almost accidental" or "reference points" to the oral–memorial–aural cycle of repeated recitation by which texts continued their life. Resorting to an analogy from music or drama, plainsong may have been written in the predecessors of our musical scores and manuscripts of medieval mystery plays were written. But the plainsong and the plays had continuing life only in their continuing performance.

As indicated in some of the texts it produced, the scribal Qumran community where written scrolls were kept and (evidently) texts inscribed on new scrolls, embodied the "oral-performative tradition" by which key cultural texts were appropriated and perpetuated, as Jaffee has explained.[14] This is exemplified in a well-known passage from the Qumran Community Rule that has usually been translated by modern scholars as a projection of their own practice of "reading," "studying" and "interpreting" written texts. A more appropriate translation of the passage might be:

> Where the ten are, there shall never lack a man among them who searches the teaching [*dwrs btwrh*] day and night, concerning the right conduct of a man with his companion. And the many shall watch in community for a third of every night of the year, to recite the writing [*lqrw' bspr*] and to search the justice-ruling [*ldwrs mspt*] and to offer communal blessings [*lbrk byhd*] (1QS 6:6–8; my adaptation of the Vermes translation)

All three of the activities mentioned—recitation, "searching," and uttering blessings—were clearly oral. The "writing" is usually assumed to have been a "book" of "the Torah." But even if a scroll of torah were opened in front of the reciter(s), the recitation would have been from memory. The text was inscribed on the memory of the scribes and priests of the community. The function of the recitation of torah at Qumran, like the learning by recitation of texts by scribes-in-training, was not external study and interpretation but the internalization of spiritual-moral discipline, in this case collective

---

13. Carruthers, *Book of Memory*, 156.

14. Jaffee, *Torah in the Mouth*.

as well as individual. The result was also the oral–memorial knowledge of many texts and the wider cultural repertoire in which those texts were embedded.

## Popular Oral Cultivation of Israelite Oral Tradition

If even the literate scribes cultivated texts and the broader cultural tradition orally, then how much more the ordinary people, who were not literate.[15] It is difficult to imagine that the latter had any direct contact with authoritative written Judean texts. And there is no evidence that the people had indirect contact with such texts via "the scribes and Pharisees."

Not only could the vast majority of people in Roman Palestine not read and write, but scrolls were expensive and cumbersome. The picture in Luke 4 of Jesus opening a scroll and reading in a synagogue was a projection perhaps based on what might have happened at a gathering of a well-off Jewish congregation in a Hellenistic city. In Judea scrolls were kept in the Jerusalem temple and scribal circles valued and copied them. Considering that the texts were also "written on the tablets of their hearts," it seems questionable whether even scribes regularly consulted or read from the cumbersome scrolls (which had primarily iconic value). Josephus comments more than once that the Pharisees were recognized (mainly in Jerusalem) as experts on the laws. But he also explains that they focused on promulgating laws that were derived from "the tradition of the elders" and not written in the laws of Moses (*Ant.* 13.288, 296–97). Further, we have no indication outside of the Gospel of Mark (and Matthew and Luke, that depend on Mark) that the Pharisees or other scribes were active in Galilee in the first century CE, when the temple-state in Jerusalem no longer had jurisdiction over that area. There is thus no evidence that they were defending, much less reciting or teaching, the contents of scriptural texts in the villages of Galilee or Judea. Scribal teachers and Pharisees were active mainly in Jerusalem, teaching their protégés. The people who lived under the rule of the Jerusalem temple-state surely knew of the existence of authoritative written scrolls of "the Law and the Prophets." But it is difficult to imagine they had any direct contact with the (still developing) authoritative written texts, or even how they might have acquired indirect knowledge of their contents.

Their lack of contact with authoritative written texts, however, did not mean that Galilean, Samaritan, and Judean villagers were ignorant of Israelite tradition(s). We can no longer use written Judean scriptural texts

15. Fuller discussion in Horsley with Draper, *Whoever Hears You Hears Me*, esp. chaps. 5–6.

as evidence for what "the Jews" or "Judaism" generally knew and practiced. But we do have sources that provide evidence, however indirect, that Galileans and Judeans in late second-temple times knew and acted upon Israelite traditions.

Josephus' accounts of popular movements in the generations before, during, and after Jesus' mission indicate that they took one or another of two distinctively Israelite forms.[16] In the decades immediately after Jesus' mission, the prophet Theudas led a large group out to the Jordan River where he promised to divide the waters for a path into the wilderness, and a prophet (from Egypt) led thousands of followers up to the Mount of Olives opposite Jerusalem where the walls would fall down so they could take the city. These and other popular prophetic movements were clearly informed by memories of Moses leading the exodus and/or of Joshua leading the people against kings in fortified cities such as Jericho. In the popular messianic movements, several in 4 BCE and another during the great revolt in 66–70, again large numbers of villagers acclaimed their leader as "king," attacked Herodian fortresses, took back the goods taken there, and held off the Roman military for months or even years. The form taken by all of these movements was informed by memories of how the Israelites acclaimed ("messiahed") the young David as their king to lead them in their struggle against the Philistines (2 Sam 2:1–4; 5:1–4). The formative traditions of Israel were not only cultivated among the villagers but were so vivid that they provided the patterns for the sizeable movements led by popular prophets and messiahs.

More briefly, Josephus' accounts of several actions by "the Galileans" in attacking Antipas' palace in Tiberias or Herodians indicate that they were acting in defense of Mosaic covenantal commandments.[17] The Gospel of Mark, clearly a popular and not a scribal text, not only presents Jesus as a new Moses and new Elijah, but as defending the covenantal "commandments of God" against the Pharisees' "traditions of the elders" and what "Moses" allowed (Mark 7:1–13; 10:2–9; cf. Deut 24:1–4). These sources provide telling indications that Israelite traditions of the exodus, the land, the Mosaic covenant, the young David and the struggle against the Philistines, and Elijah–Elisha were alive, even formative among the villagers.

Studies of many other agrarian societies find that the people have their own version of their cultural tradition that parallels but differs in emphases and implication from the official or dominant version of the cultural tradition, which may appear (partly) in written texts. Anthropologists have

---

16. See further Horsley with Hanson, *Bandits, Prophets, and Messiahs*, chaps. 3–4.

17. References and analysis in Horsley, *Galilee*, 152–55.

referred to these parallel yet different version of culture as "the little tradition" and "the great tradition."[18] Because the official tradition is usually cultivated by cultural specialists, such as scribes, it is usually more unified and standardized (but not necessarily in stabilized written form). Popular tradition, which is cultivated in oral communication locally in village communities, has regional variations. These studies of other societies that find "little traditions" running along "underneath" the politically-religiously dominant cultural tradition may give us confidence that Israelite popular tradition was cultivated orally in village communities, even though we do not have the direct sources to reconstruct its substance and "behavior" in detail.

The cultural context in which Jesus worked—and in which the Gospel tradition developed from Jesus' interaction with people—was thus Israelite popular tradition that continued to be cultivated orally in village communities. The authoritative "books" later included in the Hebrew Bible and other Judean "writings" produced in scribal circles do not provide direct access to this culture. Israelite popular tradition was not a mere transmission of several texts, but a culture in which the people were embedded. It was the cultural medium in which the people communicated and interacted, like the biosphere in which they lived.[19]

## Implications of Recent
## New Testament Text Criticism

As we struggle to grasp the implications of oral communication in antiquity, the lack of literacy among the vast majority of people, and the relative unavailability and illegibility of written texts, we are perpetually in the ironic situation of relying for our evidence on the surviving manuscripts. Significantly, recent research by text critics that challenges long-standing assumptions is also providing important evidence for the continuing oral cultivation of texts included in the New Testament.

18. Especially helpful is Scott, "Protest and Profanation." For application to Jesus and the Gospels, see the essays in Horsley, ed., *Hidden Transcripts*.

19. Recognition of the dominance of oral communication in Roman Palestine has led to renewed exploration of the oral transmission of Jesus' teachings and traditions about Jesus, most notably by Dunn, *Jesus Remembered*. Moving directly to the oral transmission of Jesus tradition may be premature, however, once we recognize that the Gospels or the Q speeches behind Matthew and Luke are embedded in and permeated by oral communication. (See the works mentioned below on Mark and Q.) In this connection, much more critical analysis remains to be done on how social memory is operative in the Gospel tradition. See the preliminary explorations in many of the essays in Kirk and Thatcher, eds., *Memory, Tradition, and Text*; and Horsley, *Jesus in Context*, chaps. 3–7.

Not until the fourth century do manuscripts show evidence of some standardization of the text the Gospels. This standardization, moreover, was related to the establishment of Christianity in the Roman empire. The newly converted Emperor Constantine sent instructions to the learned bishop Eusebius that he should "order fifty copies of the divine scriptures . . . for the instruction of the church, to be written on well-prepared parchment by copyists most skillful in the art of accurate and beautiful writing" (Eusebius, *Life of Constantine* 4.36).[20] Contrary to the earlier scholarly assumption of (and effort to "establish") a normative early (or "original") written text of the Gospels, early manuscript and fragmentary papyrological evidence indicates considerable variation. As leading text critic David Parker says, "the further back we go, the greater seems to be the degree of variation."[21] If anything, the variation in the written textual witnesses is greater on the most frequently cited statements of Jesus, such as on marriage and divorce. As Parker lays out, the variation in the versions in manuscripts of Mark 10, Matthew 5 and 19, and Luke 16 is as much or more than that between the respective Gospel versions. This suggests that the considerable differences across early manuscripts is not due simply to the way copyists copied already written copies. Rather it seems to have much to do with the importance of the teaching of Jesus to people's lives, particularly on key matters of concern. As Eldon Epp explains, early manuscripts show marks of the social contextualizations of the Gospel texts. On this basis he also argues that textual *authority* was pluriform, in contrast to the previous print-cultural assumptions of text critics who took textual "variants" in early manuscripts as "tampering with the text" or "misquoting Jesus."[22]

One possible explanation would be that producers of Gospel manuscripts, like earlier Judean scribes, were themselves performers of the texts they transcribed. In the wider Greco-Roman world, however, the copyist/scribe was a person different from the composer/performer of a text and not necessarily someone with education for literary composition. Important evidence suggests more of an *ad hoc* production of written texts as an occasional occurrence in the course of the continuing performance of revered texts in Christian communities. Prior to the fourth century there are strikingly few references to copyists engaged in making written copies of Gospels and other Christian texts.[23] A plea from a community in upper

---

20. Gamble, *Books and Readers*, 79, n. 132.

21. Parker, *Living Text*, 188.

22. Epp, "Multivalence of 'Original Text,'" and "Oxyrhynchus New Testament Papyri," 10; in contrast to Ehrman, *Orthodox Corruption*; and *Misquoting Jesus*.

23. Haines-Eitzen, *Guardians of Letters*, 38–39.

Egypt to "make and send me copies of books" suggests four interrelated aspects of the active cultivation of nascent scriptural texts. First, the existence of written copies of texts was known to (leaders of) communities, but they were not readily available. It was desirable (at least to the leaders) to possess written copies of these books. Someone in or hired by (a leader of) another community could make copies. There was probably some interaction between the text already orally-memorially known in the copying and sending community and the making of a new copy—especially if, as was likely, copying was done at dictation by someone who knew and could recite the text. Recent text-critical research is thus indicating that the production of written texts of New Testament books that were so "fluid" and "free" happened in the course of the continuing oral performance of those books in the diverse early Christian communities. Those texts were repeatedly "reactivated" in oral performance.

## Learning and Performance

The implications of recent text-critical research that the considerable variation in early manuscripts of New Testament books is related to their continuing performance is only further confirmation of other evidence that early Christian texts were orally cultivated even if written copies were available. According to the print-cultural assumptions of biblical studies, the teaching of Jesus and other material in the "Synoptic Tradition" was "transmitted" and developed in oral tradition for several decades. Then the "writing" of the Gospels provided a more stable written form of those teachings and stories, some of which were variously "edited" or "redacted" by later Gospel "writers." As Paul Achtemeier laid out clearly twenty years ago, however, the texts that were (also) written were spoken to hearers, the words "sounded."[24] In our professional investment in written texts, we seized upon evidence that Christian communities possessed at least some written copies of at least some of their revered texts already in the second century. But we were "deaf" to other "voices."

The few early Christian references to oral communication and writing indicate that the communities of Christ and their intellectual leadership did not just prefer oral communication, but were suspicious of or reticent about writing. The later bishop Eusebius, who supplied fancy standardized copies of books in response to the emperor, remembered that Papias, bishop of

---

24. Achtemeier, "*Omnes verbum somnat.*" The following discussion relies on the plentiful references and analysis of Shiner, *Proclaiming the Gospel*, with particular citations from 26 and 47.

Hierapolis in the early second century, "did not suppose that things from books (*ek ton biblion*) would benefit [him] so much as things *from a living and abiding voice* (*zoes phones kai menouses*)" (Eusebius, *H.E.* 3.39.3–4). The sophisticated theologian Clement of Alexandria apologized for committing the teaching of the church to writing, which he knew was weak and lifeless in comparison with oral discourse.

As it turns out, early Christian communities continued to cultivate orally not only the teaching of Jesus but the Gospel texts as well for several centuries after they were composed. Recent research into performance in Hellenistic and Roman culture is showing that this was not at all unusual, since texts of all kinds, some of them also written, were orally performed. It is clear in this context that the "readers" of the Gospels in the assemblies of Christ did not need to learn to read from a codex. A person could learn the text from hearing others recite it. According to Justin Martyr, at Sunday assemblies "the memoirs of the apostles or the writings of the prophets" were recited for as long as time permitted. A few generations later, Hippolytus reported that scriptures were recited by a succession of lectors at the beginning of services until all were gathered. The practice of reciting continued through the time of Augustine. He comments that many people learned to recite large portions of the Gospels themselves from hearing them recited in services.

## Composition

In the oral communication environment of the ancient Mediterranean world, composition was not done in writing. Texts with a more traditional content, moreover, were often the result of a longer process of (repeated re-) composition over a period of time.

Even the literate elite in the Roman empire did not compose their letters or histories of other texts in writing. Pliny offers a fascinating account of his own practice (Letters 9:34; 2.10; 3:18; 7:17).[25] Awaking before daylight, he composed in his head while lying in bed. Arising after some hours, he called in a capable secretary to take dictation as he spoke his text. To disseminate his composition he then performed his text to a group of friends or in public. His "public-ation" of his composition was thus assisted or "backed up" by a written text, but the composition was not done in writing.

Composition of letters was similarly done by oral dictation and the text was re-oralized, re-performed before the addressee(s). This is evident

---

25. Discussion of Pliny and others in composition in the ancient media context in Small, *Wax Tablets of the Mind.*

in nearly every account of letters in the Hebrew Bible, where a king dictated to a scribe at one end of the communication and a scribe/official "read" it out aloud to the intended recipient(s). This is evidently how the apostle Paul (and others) proceeded in long-distance communication with the assemblies of Christ. As indicated by his comment at the end of Galatians as he "signed" the letter—"see what large letters I make when I am writing in my own hand"—he was dictating his complex extended arguments (Gal 6:11; cf. Rom 16:22; 1 Cor 16:21). It has been speculated, with sound basis in the epistolary practice of antiquity, that one of his associates (e.g., Timothy) or a member of the assembly he is addressing (e.g., Stephanas, Fortunatus, Achaicus, 1 Cor 16:20) were the bearers of the letter: they heard him speak the text, then carried the written text, and after arriving at the destination "read" aloud (performed) the text to the assembled community.

Many texts in antiquity were "traditional," in the sense that they were repeatedly recited or performed. The best known examples are surely the *Iliad* and the *Odyssey*. We may continue to think of "Homer" as their composer. But at the very least classics scholars are aware that "Homer" is a cipher, that these poetic epics not only were never composed in writing, but their texts developed over centuries of repeated performance. Among texts that later became "biblical," the book of Isaiah is an anthology of prophetic oracles, some of which may have been developed orally from what was delivered orally by the prophet Isaiah in eighth-century Judah. A major section of the "book" (Isaiah 40–55) is a sustained prophetic poetic drama pertaining to anticipated events early in Persian imperial rule. If we trust what text critics are saying, however, the text of that prophetic poem continued to develop for centuries before we can catch sight of its development in scrolls of Isaiah from Qumran. In what sense, then, could we think of the text of "Second Isaiah" as having been composed in writing around 540 BCE?

Once we become aware of the various lines of parallel research into oral communication in antiquity and the contingencies of the writing of texts, it is difficult to imagine that the Gospel of Mark, for example, could have been composed in writing. It is clearly a story about a figure and movement among the ordinary people of Galilee in opposition to the political-religious and (literate) cultural elite and is clearly addressed to ordinary people. But virtually no ordinary people could write. So did "Mark" compose and dictate the text to a scribe? Even if we insist on the highly unlikely (anachronistic) scenario that a literate "author" composed the Gospel in writing, the text would have been recited orally in communities of ordinary people. And even text critics are now suggesting, in effect, that what we have access to are different versions of the Gospel that were integrally related to its repeated performance over many generations.

The Gospel of Mark is the New Testament text that has been most carefully and creatively explored as an oral–aural narrative. Werner Kelber pioneered the appreciation of the healing and exorcism episodes and the parables in Mark in terms based on studies of the behavior of oral narrative, pushing decisively past the previous projection of print-cultural assumptions onto "oral tradition" by form criticism.[26] In a whole series of highly suggestive articles over the last two decades, Joanna Dewey has explored the oral patterns and echoes and the oral–aural "event" detectable in the narrative.[27] David Rhoads and several others have for years performed Mark's story in English to various audiences. In an imaginative study thoroughly informed by research into ancient performance practices of Greek texts in Hellenistic-Roman culture, Whitney Shiner has suggestively explored how Mark could have been performed in its historical context.[28] More recently Antoinette Clark Wire has skillfully crafted a persuasive, step-by-step explanation of why and how Mark was composed in performance.[29]

## Communication in Oral Performance

As written texts, the books of the New Testament have served many functions for different people in various circumstances: an anthology of readings for worship and preaching, compendia of prooftexts for theologies, collections of verses for Bible study and personal devotion, colonial texts of Christian missions during western imperial expansion, ideological texts in the subordination of some people to others or challenges to that subordination, and "culture texts" of "western civilization." Increased recent attention to the dominance of oral communication in antiquity leads to the consideration of New Testament texts as *communication* in the course and context of their composition and cultivation. In biblical studies developed on the basis of print-culture, we have usually objectified text-fragments (verses, sayings,

26. Kelber, *The Oral and the Written Gospel*—the groundbreaking work that opened investigation and discussion of orality and New Testament interpretation.

27. Dewey, "Oral Methods in Mark"; and "Mark as Interwoven Tapestry. See further the collection of Dewey's articles forthcoming in the Biblical Performance Criticism Series. Another ground-breaking article was Botha, "Mark's Story as Oral Traditional Literature. See also Horsley, *Hearing the Whole Story*.

28. Shiner, *Proclaiming the Gospel*.

29. Wire, *Mark Composed in Performance*. See also Shiner, "Memory Technology and Mark"; Horsley, "Oral Performance and Mark"; and Dewey, "Mark and Oral Hermeneutic."

brief stories, pericopes, etc.) as artifacts the meaning of which (in them-selves) we strive to discern. In the context of composition, performance, and further cultivation, however, those fragments were integral components of whole texts. And those texts were the negotiated messages in processes of communication between composers/performers and communities of hear-ers in particular social contexts.

While there has been little investigation into communications theory in New Testament studies, during the last generation or two other fields have seriously investigated how communication happens. The insights of socio-linguistics may be particularly relevant to New Testament texts in historical context, since they were orally performed, as indicated in the researches just summarized.[30] Within the field of New Testament studies, recent rhetorical criticism has helped to reestablish sensitivity to the larger text in the communication process, particularly in Paul's letters, in which his arguments on key issues gives us only one side of the conversation or argument. To appreciate oral communication, however, requires more at-tention to the social and cultural context(s) than rhetorical criticism has usually devoted. Moreover, it will likely be more difficult for us to discern the views and sensitivities of the hearers through rhetorical criticism (or its equivalent) of the Gospels than it has been for Paul's letters.

The texts in the New Testament, however, are not just any kind of communication, such as conversations or the (mere) transmission of infor-mation. They are special forms of communication: the foundational story of the hero-prophet-messiah and his expanding movement performed in communities of committed participants; and arguments on key issues of concern by an envoy of the exalted hero-messiah performed in a commu-nity in whose formation he had played a key role. These special forms of communication may be significant not so much for the meaning of their statements as for the *work* they do, the effect they have when performed in a community (such as narrating the foundational story, healing the individual and collective body, reviving the *esprit de corp*, and/or memorializing an event).

To interpret New Testament texts, therefore, it will be necessary to understand special communications as interactive and contextual, a far more complex undertaking than considering the meaning of written texts as artifacts, as we have been trained to do. Considering the circumstances of the early Jesus movements, our situation may be analogous in many ways to having only a few transcripts of the sermons delivered to the often nightly church services in small towns in the South in the early 1960s as

30. See Halliday, *Language as Social Semiotic.*

some demonstrators were welcomed out of jail and other teams prepared to attempt sit-ins the next day. Adequate appreciation and interpretation would require not just a sense of the rhetorical tone and rhythm of the respective speech, but a sense of the hearers' life circumstances and their historical situation and cultural tradition in which they hear and respond to the speeches.

Our training in biblical studies, like that in fields of modern and ancient literatures, has not prepared us to appreciate, understand, and interpret texts-in-performance. Again, however, we may be able to learn from and adapt the pioneering interpretive practices and theory being developed by leading scholars in other fields. Particularly helpful may be the work of John Miles Foley, perhaps the leading theorist of oral poetry and performance, who has interacted fruitfully with biblical scholars for over twenty years. In continuing theoretical reflection on oral poetry from a wide range of cultures, Foley has drawn on performance theory and ethnopoetics and called special attention to the importance of the referencing of cultural tradition in oral performance.[31] The following discussion is an adaptation of Foley's suggestive synthetic theoretical reflection. Of greatest import for understanding texts in oral performance is giving careful attention to three key interrelated facets of a text-in-performance. In order to hear and interpret New Testament texts, it is necessary to discern the contours of the *text*, to determine the historical *context* of the community of the responsive/ interactive hearers, and to know as much as possible the cultural *tradition* out of which the voiced texts resonate with the hearers.

*Text*

Biblical studies based in print culture has usually focused on text-fragments "cut out" of longer texts. To interpret texts-in-performance it is first necessary to discern the contours of whole texts. The texts-in-performance as communication, moreover, were interactive with groups of hearers in their respective contexts. To take a particular "paragraph" out of the longer argument in 1 Corinthians 1–4, for example, will almost certainly miss how in one "paragraph" (step in the argument) Paul is "setting up" (some of) the hearers for his disagreement or disapproval in a subsequent "paragraph." Sensitivity to the oral performance of the argument can lead to hearing

---

31. I have found most helpful for oral communication/performance and New Testament interpretation recent works by the leading cross-cultural theorist John Miles Foley, esp. *Immanent Art*; *Singer of Tales in Performance*; *How to Read an Oral Poem*; and, more condensed, "Plenitude and Diversity." See also the theoretical reflections specifically for New Testament interpretation by Rhoads, "Performance Criticism."

the "tone of voice" that might be sarcastic in one step and authoritarian in another.

Recent reading of the Gospels as sustained stories has helped move beyond their habitual fragmentation into verses or weekly lessons. Mark's story, for example, develops in a sequence of rapid-fire episodes, the earlier setting up the later. Reading the whole story results in the recognition of the multiple conflicts that are interwoven in the sequence of episodes. *Hearing* the whole story makes those conflicts seem all the more dramatic, particularly that between Jesus and his followers and the Jerusalem rulers and their scribal representatives. The importance of hearing the whole story of Mark and other Gospels is reinforced by the implications of the recent text criticism. Given the diversity of wording in ancient manuscripts, it is not possible to "establish" a standard written text for particular teachings of Jesus, as on marriage and divorce, as noted above. Studies of oral performances of epics and other oral narratives much longer than the Gospels, however, finds that while the particular lines and "stanzas" of oral performances vary, the overall story persists from performance to performance. The implication—ironically for the previously standard study of the Gospels focused on determining and interpreting words, phrases, and verses as precisely as possible—is that the overall story of Mark or Matthew was probably more stable than the wording of particular episodes and sayings.

## Context

In order to understand a special form of oral communication it is necessary to hear it in the appropriate (historical) collective context: wedding, funeral, political rally. The context determines the expectation and the appropriate hearing of the text. Traditional oral performances were always already in the appropriate context. Ancient Greek dramas were performed in a theater in Athens or other city-states. Standing in the ruins of ancient Greek theaters and knowing something of the history and culture of Athens helps our informed historical imagination in appreciating the enacted drama for which we have only the script.

The earliest contexts in which Paul's letters or the Gospels were performed, however, are more difficult to reconstruct in our informed historical imagination. Generally these would presumably have been gatherings of communities of the new and expanding movements of Jesus-loyalists or Christ-believers. At least we have become aware that the contexts addressed by different texts were different in many significant ways—and that essentialist scholarly constructs such as "Christian" simply obscure particular historical contexts about which we are gaining ever more precise historical information. Tradition had it that because "Mark" was Peter's interpreter, the Gospel of Mark was addressed to a community in Rome. The text, however, would seem to have been more appropriately heard in communities in Syrian villages where circumstances were more similar to those of the Galilean villages in which Jesus is portrayed as healing and preaching. Each of the cities and their populations in which "assemblies" emerged in response to the work of Paul and his coworkers was distinctive. The contexts, such as the circumstances of the people and the issues addressed in each letter were different, as can often be discerned through Paul's arguments.

### Tradition

In a performance the text resonates with the audience as they hear it in the group context. This is clearly the case in traditional texts in performance, such as Greek plays, weddings, funerals, or political rallies. In performance, meaning happens in a way very different from a private reading of a modern literary text. A modern novelist individually manipulates inherited or idiosyncratic materials in a new direction or from a particular perspective, thus conferring meaning on her fresh new literary creation that is read silently by an individual reader. Performed traditional texts resonate with the hearers by referencing the cultural tradition and evoking meaning that is inherent. The evocation is often metonymic, as a part evokes a whole cultural pattern or complex memory.

Certain special texts in performance do not simply evoke meaning but do work on or among the group of hearers in the context. Some sermons, speeches on special national or other political events, or some performances of Mozart's "Requiem" or Bach's "St. Matthew Passion" evoke renewed religious-ethical commitment, renewal of group identity, or inspire and give expression to collective mourning and religious devotion. This happens through especially "effective" referencing of traditional memories, patterns, and expressive forms. To illustrate how the text resonates by referencing, in which a part represents or evokes a whole, let me reference what happens to many in the United States in mid-January each year. When those of us who were involved in the civil rights movement in the 1960s hear even a short excerpt from one of Martin Luther King's speeches on the radio ("I have a dream. . ."), it resonates deeply in our memory, evoking a whole period of our lives as well as recommitment to certain concerns.

In New Testament interpretation we are already aware of this referencing of the cultural tradition at least at a surface level. Biblical studies rooted in print culture has looked for this in the form of New Testament texts' quotations of "Old Testament" texts. This widened a bit and shifted into "mixed media" as "echoes" of and allusions to particular lines or phrases in Scripture. Discussion of "intertextuality" recognized this extensive interrelationship of texts. The interrelationship, however, was far deeper and more important than that between texts, as performed texts referenced cultural tradition that was more like a cultural biosphere in which texts, performers, and hearers were embedded. Recent interpreters of the Gospels of Mark and Matthew have recognized that they are addressed to communities that still have a strong sense of Israelite cultural identity and heritage. Exploration of these texts as/ in oral performance can sense all the more how they repeatedly reference Israelite tradition, evoking whole patterns of meaning and social relationship, such as the renewal of the Israelite people and the Mosaic covenant and prophetic pronouncements against rulers. More than evoking meaning, however, the performed Gospel of Mark may have also affected the community of hearers by referencing tradition, in a renewal of community identity and solidarity and collective commitment to the direct rule of God for which Jesus had been martyred.

The arguments in Paul's letters also repeatedly reference Israelite tradition. But Paul is addressing communities comprised largely of people(s) who were not familiar with this cultural tradition except insofar as Paul and his coworkers had taught it during their sojourns. Insofar as they were rooted in other cultures and/or had been listening to rival apostles, the performance of Paul's letters may have involved miscommunication, as the referencing of Israelite tradition failed to resonate with the hearers.

The goal of interpretation to be sought by exploring these three aspects of performance would be to discern, appreciate, and understand not the meaning of the text in itself, but the work done among the community of hearers by the text in performance.

## Interpretation of the Speech in Luke 7:18–35 // Matthew 11:2–19 as Orally Performed

As pioneering New Testament scholars have been explaining for twenty years or so, typical features of oral performance and "oral-derived" texts include poetic form, parallel lines, repetition of sounds, and additive and repetitive style. These were noted particularly in the Gospel of Mark and in the closely parallel speech material in Matthew and Luke, what has long been designated as "Q." In order to have a manageable text in which to illustrate the questions that emerge when we explore the implications of the predominantly oral communication in antiquity for New Testament interpretation, we focus on a speech of Jesus that is almost "verbatim" in Matthew and Luke.[32]

Recognition of the predominance of oral communication in antiquity raises serious questions about the print-cultural basis on which the Synoptic Problem was discussed and solutions proposed. There is little or no basis for assuming that written texts of Mark or Matthew or Luke or Q were sufficiently "circulated" shortly after their "writing" so that the "author" of one could have been "copying" from the written text of another. On the other hand, on the basis of comparative studies of lengthy oral narratives, it is striking that Matthew and Luke are telling the same basic overall story as Mark and that they greatly expand and complicate the story with what are virtually the same speeches of Jesus in much the same sequence. As we learn more about oral–written texts embedded in oral communication and cultivated by oral performance, it will be fascinating to see how discussion of the relations between the Gospels will shift its basis and focus. With regard to the speeches of Jesus closely parallel in Matthew and Luke (with only a few similar short speeches, such as a mission-discourse and Beelzebul debate in Mark) what we are learning about the almost exclusively oral communication among ordinary people makes it difficult to imagine a written "Synoptic Sayings Source."

If, on the other hand, we listen to how the text of the Jesus speeches sounds it is striking what we hear (or even see when it is printed out as poetry). Within and across "sayings" or "verses" are frequent repetition of sounds, verb forms, words, whole phrases and ideas/points. Not only do "sayings" take the form of parallel lines, but parallel lines/statements/ thoughts occur in a sequence of sayings, and words and multiple sounds are repeated in a sequence of "sayings." This is poetry. As poetry in Greek, moreover, it is unusual. The parallel lines consisting usually of three or four basic words, with repetition of sounds, seem like Hebrew or Aramaic poetry, and they include phrases that are not idiomatic in Greek but appear to be translations of Aramaic idioms (and presumably the early cultivation of Jesus' speech was in Aramaic). The "sayings," moreover, are not separate, but come in sequences that focus on an issue and move to a point or conclusion. The teaching of Jesus dubbed Q is thus not a collection of sayings but a series of short "discourses" or "speeches" on particular issues or concerns of the community(ies) addressed (such as mission, prayer, subsistence, exorcisms, or the Pharisees). To illustrate these and other points in exploring

---

32. The following builds on the extensive analysis and interpretation of the speeches of Q in oral performance in Horsley with Draper, *Whoever Hears You Hears Me*.

the implications of the predominantly oral communication in the ancient context, we focus on the speech parallel in Matt 11:2–19 and Luke 7:18–35, concentrating on three of the basic aspects of oral performance.

### Text

It bears repeating that the teaching of Jesus closely parallel in Matthew and Luke is not a mere collection of sayings but a series of short speeches on various issues. Among the clearest is the speech that addresses anxiety about subsistence, concluding with the reassurance "seek first the kingdom of God and all these things will be added" (Luke 12:22–31; included in Matthew's long covenant renewal speech at 6:25–34). Another clear example is the speech addressing persecution, including the sanctioning admonition about bold public confession (Luke 12:2–9; Matt 10:26–33; cf. the similar speech in Mark 8:34–38). The speech parallel in Luke 7:18–28, 31–35 and Matt 11:2–11, 16–19 develops in three more distinct steps: in response to John's question about "the coming one," Jesus points to how the longings of Israel are being fulfilled in his mission; he then points to John as the greatest of the prophets to exclaim how great life in the kingdom of God will be; and he concludes with the reassurance that despite their being attacked, their work will be vindicated. These speeches evidently belonged in a coherent sequence of speeches, hence should be interpreted in relation to each other.

Ironically, given our print-oriented minds, a printed transliteration may help our aural imagination hear the poetic form, the sequence of lines, the repetition of sounds and words, and the "rhetoric" of the speech. Readers should "re-oralize" the text by reading (and thus hearing) it *aloud*. The following printed version of the speech is, however experimentally, laid out for oral performance in a way intended to help discern the repetition of sounds and forms. In the few instances where the words are not verbatim in Matthew and Luke, this version usually follows (the modern text of) "Matthew."

### The text of the speech parallel in Luke 7:18–35 and Matthew 11:2–19

(for reading aloud, with visual display of lines and repetition of sounds, words, verbal forms)

| | | | |
|---|---|---|---|
| *Ioannes* | *pempsas* | *dia ton matheton autou* | *eipen auto* |
| *su ei* | *ho erchomenos* | *e heteron* | *prosdokomen?* |
| *kai apokritheis* | *eipen autois* | | |
| *poreuthentes* | *apaggeilate Ioanne* | *ha akouete* | *kai blepete* |

| | | | |
|---|---|---|---|
| *tufloi* | *anablepousin* | *kai choloi* | *peripatousin* |
| *leproi* | *katharizontai* | *kai kufoi* | *akouousin* |
| *nekroi* | *egeirontai* | *[kai]ptochoi* | *euangelisontai* |
| *kai makariois estin* | *hos ean me skandalisthe* | *en emoi.* | |
| | | | |
| *Erxato* | *legein* | *tois ochlois* | *peri Ioannou* |
| *ti exelthate* | *eis ten epemon* | *theasasthai?* | |
| *kalamon* | *hupo anemou* | *saleuomenon?* | |
| *alla ti* | *exelthate* | *idein?* | |
| *anthropon* | *en malakois* | *emfiesmenon?* | |
| *idou* | *ta malaka* | *en tois oikois* | *ton basileion eisin.* |
| *alla ti* | *exelthate* | *idein?* | *propheten?* |
| *nai,* | *lego humin,* | *kai perissoteron* | *prophetou* |
| *outos estin* | *peri hou* | *gegraptai* | |
| *idou apostello* | *ton aggelon mou* | *pro prosopou sou* | |
| *hos kataskeuasei* | *ten hodon sou* | *emprosthen sou.* | |
| *lego hymin,* | | | |
| *meizon* | *en gennetois gunaikon* | *Ioannou* | |
| *ho mikroteros* | *en te Basileia tou theou* | *meizon* | *autou estin.* |
| | | | |
| *Tini* | *homoioso* | *tes geneas autes* | |
| *homoia estin* | *paidiois* | *kathemenois* | *en tais agorais* |
| *[ha prosfonounta* | *tois heterois* | *legousin]* | |
| *eulesamen hymin* | *kai ouk orchesasthe* | | |
| *ethrenesamen* | *kai ouk ekopsasthe* | | |
| *elthen* | *gar Ioannes* | *mete esthion* | *mete pinon* |
| *kai legousin* | *daimonion* | *echei.* | |
| *elthen* | *ho huios tou anthropou* | *esthion* | *kai pinon* |
| *kai legete* | *idou* | | |
| *anthropos* | *fagos* | *kai oinopotes* | |
| *telonon* | *filos* | *kai hamartolon.* | |
| *kai edikaiothe* | *he sophia* | *apo ton ergon aute!* | |

As most of us have experienced personally, even our modern print-oriented minds retain poetry and songs (especially with the tunes) far more easily than prose. As studies of oral tradition and the performance of (oral-derived) texts have found, a speech such as this, with parallel lines, profuse repetition of sounds, words, verbal forms, and rhetorical questions, is both readily remembered (and repeated/recited by a performer) and easily heard by a communal audience. The repeated sounds and thoughts duplicated or piled up in parallel lines make for effective communication.

## Context

Presumably this speech along with other speeches in the sequence would have been performed in communities of a Jesus movement and, once included in Matthew, in the assemblies to which the Gospel of Matthew was addressed. Because this and other *speeches* parallel in Matthew and Luke sound like they may represent a Greek version of Aramaic speech, they may well have been developed and cultivated in Aramaic-speaking village communities in Galilee (see the villages named in Q/Luke 10:13–15). The Greek version (behind Matthew and Luke) would have resonated most readily with other communities of villagers. Greek-speaking or bilingual village communities in Syria would have been the closest in proximity. The circumstances of people in villages and small towns in Syria who formed communities of the rapidly expanding Jesus movements would have been similar to those of the Galilean villagers among whom Jesus had worked. Most of the ordinary people, who comprised around 90% of a traditional agrarian society, lived at the subsistence level. And the villagers of Syria, like those of virtually any area in the eastern Roman empire had lived under imperial rulers and their local clients (Tyre, Sidon, Damascus, the Decapolis, etc.) for centuries and had experienced some of the same violence of periodic conquest, such as the recent Roman expeditions led by the warlords Pompey, Crassus, and Cassius. A message of deliverance from poverty and illnesses into a new life of wholeness and justice would have resonated with them as well as with Galilean villagers.

## Tradition

While not as continuously as the Gospel of Mark, this and other speeches parallel in Matthew and Luke reference Israelite tradition repeatedly and prominently. The speech as a whole and in its three principal steps presents both John and Jesus as prophets of fulfillment in the long line of Israelite prophets. The first and second steps of the speech make explicit reference to particularly prominent points of Israelite tradition that would have resonated readily with those rooted in or even just familiar with the culture.

On the assumption that the "books" of "the Law and the Prophets" were widely available and familiar to the "writer" of Q, it has been thought that the response to John's question in Luke 7:22//Matt 11:5 is a "quotation" from the book of Isaiah. The problem was always which particular text was being "quoted": Isa 35:5–6 or 42:6–7 or 61:1 (or a combination of phrases from them)? But how long must a phrase be to be credible as a quotation, as opposed to an allusion or an echo or a phrase in memory? Even before the recent recognition of how prominent oral cultivation of texts and cultural tradition was, we might have asked what to make of these parallel lists in Isaiah of what will happen in the future to people in certain conditions.

Now that we are aware of the oral–written scribal cultivation of texts such those included in the Isaiah anthology and the oral scribal cultivation of the wider cultural repertoire, which regularly included material from the popular tradition, at least one possibility suggests itself. Isaiah 35:5–6; 42:6–7; and 61:1 are all combinations of phrases that express the longings of the people living in conditions of imperial conquest and ongoing imperial rule. Two of the three also have allusions to (memories of) the exodus liberation. These different passages in the "book" of Isaiah included some of these phrases of longing for deliverance from the common Israelite cultural repertoire. It seems quite possible, considering the continuing subjection of Judeans, Samaritans, and Galileans to one empire after another, that these phrases would have continued to be cultivated in the Israelite popular tradition. The speech here is not "quoting" from the written text of Isaiah, but referencing the people's longings in what had become standard phrases. Moreover, a few "parts" signal the "whole" of the people's longings for liberation and justice, one prominent image of which, deeply rooted in the collective memory, was the exodus, as also projected onto the role of a future prophet, as in the Isaiah passages. But what scholars focused on written texts saw as quotation can be more easily explained now as the oral cultivation of Israelite tradition referenced at several points in development of the text of Isaiah and then again many generations later in this Jesus-speech.

The next step in the speech identifies John with what appears to be an explicit quotation, introduced by a quotation formula: "it is written." But what text-fragment is being quoted? Is it Mal 3:1a or Exod 23:20a, and from the Septuagint or in a Greek translation of a proto-Masoretic Text? As text critics are now explaining, we do not have the stable textual "data" on the basis of which we can "control" the evidence in our analysis of written texts. "It is written," however, can now be understood not as a cue of a quotation of a written text, but as an appeal to the authority of what stands "written"—in the "written" texts of great tradition laid up in the temple. God's declaration that he would "send a messenger to prepare the way," as attested in Exodus, was evidently an important statement in the foundational Israelite narrative of the exodus and coming into the land. Malachi provides a clear illustration of how it was used (coopted?) in a "writing" in support of the temple-state. Although they were unlikely to have known in which "writing" it was "written," ordinary people such as Jesus and his followers would have known that such a prominent divine promise stood "written," hence all the more authoritative.

It may be significant that this allusion to a future prophet-messenger to prepare the way for deliverance, which alludes to the exodus narrative, is the only reference to what "is written" in the speeches of Q.[33] The many other references (allusions, echoes, etc.) to particular Israelite figures, events, themes, covenantal teachings, etc. evidently arose from (orally cultivated) Israelite popular tradition. And the citation of "the messenger to prepare the way . . ." also derived from Israelite popular tradition, in which the people knew some of the contents of what was "written," but did not have direct contact with or access to written scrolls.

These two explicit references to prominent points in Israelite tradition are what articulate the main point or message of the speech as it resonates with the hearers. Jesus' preaching and manifestation of the kingdom of God are the fulfillment of the longings of Israel for a new exodus-like deliverance and a common life of personal and communal justice and wholeness. John, the greatest in the long line of Israelite prophets, is/was the messenger who would prepare the way of God's deliverance, hence life in the kingdom of God will be even more remarkable. In Israelite tradition, of course, the prophets had opposed and been opposed and attacked by the rulers. In this regard too, the speech presents John and Jesus as opposed to and attacked by the rulers. The final line of the speech, however, offers reassurance that these prophets in whose work the fulfillment of the people's longings for justice and wholeness is happening will be vindicated.

We are only beginning to discern the ways in which increasing recognition of the dominance of oral communication in antiquity, along with the limits and uses of writing, will pose challenges to the standard assumptions and approaches of New Testament interpretation. Given the inertia and conservative bearing of the field, developed on the basis of print-culture and dedicated to the interpretation of the printed sacred Scripture (i.e., written text), it seems likely that the implications of oral communication as the medium in which New Testament texts originated will be resisted. Greatest leverage will likely come from text criticism, which is now explaining

33. That is except for the temptation dialogue, usually judged a late and poorly fitting addition to Q, but another text in which the lines that are cued as "written" cannot be "controlled," that is identified as specific quotations.

that early manuscript evidence indicates not standardized early texts, but pluriformity of authoritative texts that were likely related to continuing oral recitation. Further exploration of texts-in-performance as oral communication, however, would lead into and reinforce further research and understanding in areas that have become important to New Testament interpreters for other reasons. There would be such "overlap" especially with the efforts to attain more precise knowledge of particular social contexts of texts and fuller understanding of the Israelite popular tradition in which Jesus movements were rooted.[34]

It may be significant that recognition of the dominance of oral communication in antiquity is emerging as the new electronic communications media are challenging and replacing print culture. The new electronic media are now showing both their possibilities and their problems for social and political life. In this time of media exploration and innovation, it is possible that rediscovery of how, in oral performance, texts were alive in and had profound effects on communities of hearers will lead to creative modes of re-performing those texts in today's world with its rich mix of communications media.

34. Exploratory efforts to link these investigations can be seen in Horsley with Draper, *Whoever Hears You Hears Me*; Horsley, *Hearing the Whole Story*; Horsely, *Jesus in Context*; and Wire, *The Case for Mark*.

## 2

# THE ORIGINS OF THE HEBREW
# SCRIPTURES UNDER IMPERIAL RULE

## *Numinous Writing and Ceremonial Performance*

A CENTRAL FEATURE OF THE STANDARD PICTURE OF ANCIENT "Judaism" at the time of Hillel and Jesus has been an already well-defined canon of Scripture, the Hebrew Bible, consisting of Torah, Prophets, and (some of the) Writings. This Scripture, moreover, was supposedly being read by a highly literate Jewish people educated in ubiquitous schools who possessed scrolls of the Bible.[1] Even recently, scholars who otherwise acknowledge that literacy was limited in Greco-Roman antiquity still take at face value Luke's portrayal of Jesus in the Nazareth synagogue reading from the scroll of the prophet Isaiah (4:16–20). This view, like much of the rest of the modern understanding of life in ancient Judea and Galilee involves heavy projection of the assumptions of modern print culture into a time when literacy was extremely limited and the Judean scriptures had not yet developed into what later became the Hebrew Bible. Three recent recognitions in particular, all based on extensive new research, require the deconstruction of this standard view.

First, some pioneering scholars pointed out that oral communications were predominant in ancient Judean and other ancient Mediterranean societies.[2] In Judea literacy was limited mainly to the scribal elite. The vast

---

1. Hengel, *Judaism and Hellenism*, 78–83; Safrai, "Education," especially 952, 954; Gamble, *Books and Readers*, 7.

2. Botha, "Greco-Roman Literacy"; Harris, *Ancient Literacy*; and Hezser, *Jewish*

majority of people, peasant villagers and urban poor whose lives did not require literacy, would have been unable to read. Moreover, scrolls were both cumbersome and prohibitively expensive, and until late antiquity Judean and Galilean villages had not begun to construct synagogue buildings in which to house such scrolls.[3]

Second, even though the Pharisees and other learned scribes in second-temple Judea may have had access to scrolls of scriptural texts, they engaged primarily in oral communication. The Pharisees, say both Josephus and the Gospel of Mark, promulgated for the people a whole set of oral rulings (the "traditions of the elders," *Ant.* 13.296–98; Mark 7:1–13) in addition to those in the written torah of Moses. The highly educated rabbis learned and debated thousands of issues of *halakhah* (legal rulings) orally both before and after they were codified in written form in the Mishnah and Tosefta (after 200 CE). The later compilers of earlier rabbinic traditions "were pedagogically and ideologically committed to the *oral* mastery of the traditions . . . Written texts were preserved . . . Yet their use in instruction was discouraged. Rather, the exposition of Sages' teachings took place in a highly ritualized setting designed to recreate and represent an original imparting of oral tradition from Moses to his disciples."[4] The rabbis and their predecessors the Pharisees and other learned scribes, along with the famous renegade Paul, cultivated even authoritative texts that had (also) been "written" (the derivation of "scripture") primarily by oral recitation. "Neither Paul nor the Sages had writings before them as they composed their discourses."[5] They were working from authoritative texts committed to memory, not from scrolls in a scholarly study.

The third will probably be most threatening, but ultimately most convincing for Jewish and Christian Scripture-scholars embedded in the assumptions of print culture. Close study of the actual scrolls of authoritative written texts discovered among the DSS at Qumran is now demonstrating that there was a remarkable textual (in a more precise sense) plurality even among literate circles in late second-temple Judea.[6] The diversity of scrolls discovered in the Judean wilderness indicates that there were different versions of the scriptural books, varying textual traditions, not simply textual variations in a single textual tradition. It is becoming clear, therefore, that

---

*Literacy*, provides extensive documentation for Roman Palestine.

3. Botha, "Greco-Roman Literacy," 201; Horsley, *Galilee*, 222–27.

4. Jaffee, "Writing and Rabbinic Oral Tradition," 143–44; see now Jaffee, *Torah in the Mouth.*

5. Jaffee, "Figuring Early Rabbinic Culture," 70–71.

6. Ulrich, *Dead Sea Scrolls.*

we can no longer speak of a Hebrew Bible as a canon of authoritative books with a standardized textual tradition prior to at least the second century CE. Rather, literate Judean scribal circles such as at Qumran (and presumably others in Jerusalem) had a number of scriptural scrolls (in the sense of revered and/or authoritative writings), many of them in two or three versions.

The number and sequence of books in the Pentateuch was standard, but different versions of particular books such as Exodus and Deuteronomy coexisted. There was a collection of "prophets," but the particular prophetic texts included and their sequence were not standardized and some prophetic "books," especially Jeremiah, existed in very different versions. Most suggestive of all is that different versions (or "editions") of many scriptural "books" coexisted, in some cases resembling the Septuagint versions, in some cases resembling the later Masoretic Text versions, and in others resembling those included in so-called Samaritan Pentateuch, which apparently was based on an earlier textual tradition current in late second-temple Judea. The scrolls of various versions of these "books" thus appear to represent literature that was revered and authoritative, i.e., Scripture. But those scriptural "books" were still pluriform, not yet standardized in Judea. Moreover, the variation among the versions suggests that the same process that characterized the composition of these books from their beginnings, i.e., of additions and revisions as well as "editing," continued all the way through the second-temple period.

This situation—where we find revered authoritative texts in various versions in a society, but the vast majority of people removed from their use as well as composition and further development, and even from their scribal cultivation in memory and oral discourse in scribal circles—invites further investigation into their origin, development, and function. The first step would appear to be to break with the kind of Christian theological essentialism represented in the standard construction of the Scripture or "Hebrew Bible." That is, we must pointedly cease thinking in terms of "Judaism," i.e., a modern construction of a "religion" that did not yet exist. Instead we must begin thinking in terms of a concrete historical world of political-economic-religious power-relations that structured societal life and determined the dynamics of cultural developments in ancient Judea.

## Written Torah and Performed Torah in the Temple under Imperial Rule

The formation of the temple-state in Jerusalem and the compilation(s) or composition of Judean laws were both sponsored by imperial regimes as instruments of imperial rule, starting with the Persian regime. This is coming increasingly to scholarly recognition, in contrast to the earlier construal of Judea as virtually autonomous, politically and religiously.

Prior to the Babylonian conquest in 587/6 BCE the people of Judah had been ruled by the Davidic monarchy, which in turn sponsored the temple in Jerusalem as part of its divine legitimation, according to historical tradition included in authoritative Judean texts. After destroying the city and its temple, the Babylonian imperial regime took the Jerusalem ruling class, the royal family and their ranking retainers, including leading priestly and scribal families, into "exile" in Babylon (2 Kings 24–25). Fifty years later, however, when the Persians took over Babylon and its empire, they reversed the policy of deporting local ruling elites and restored (at least many of) them to their positions of power and privilege, partly to serve as representatives of imperial order. Among the early Persian emperors, Darius in particular pursued the policy of rebuilding temples (i.e., restoring temple-states) throughout the empire as extensions of the imperial administration. He thus gained the goodwill of the various priesthoods in the provinces and posed as a beneficent ruler who restored the cultures of subjected peoples. Conveniently for maintenance of the imperial order, a temple served a variety of functions simultaneously: along with a restoration of a local elite's (and people's) service of their own deity(ies), a temple constituted a local financial administration for the imperial regime's revenues, the point of establishing an empire in the first place.[7] Not only did the Persian imperial regime encourage the exiled Judean elite to return to Jerusalem, but it virtually mandated the rebuilding of the temple, indeed financed the project out of the imperial treasury, as indicated in biblical traditions (Ezra 1).[8]

The restored Judean elite and the rebuilt temple in Jerusalem thus constituted a virtual colony of the Persian regime in Judea, with many of the power-relations associated with colonialism.[9] The Babylonians had deported only the Jerusalem ruling class, while leaving the Judean peasantry on the land, albeit in vastly reduced numbers. During the seventy or so years between the Babylonian destruction of Jerusalem and the Persian-sponsored rebuilding of the temple local leadership would have emerged in Judea, including perhaps ordinary priestly groups and Levites who had not been among the deportees. The deported Jerusalem elite had meanwhile become dependents of empire and now owed their restoration to Persian imperial sponsorship. To complicate matters further, after their return to

---

7. Berquist, *Judaism*, 52–57, 63; Schaper, "Jerusalem Temple."

8. Blenkinsopp, "Temple and Society," 51.

9. See now Horsley, *Scribes, Visionaries,* chap. 1, and recent studies cited there.

Jerusalem, the restored Judean elite began to intermarry with powerful families elsewhere in Palestine such as the priestly aristocracy in Samaria, immediately to the north. Nor did the restored Jerusalem elite's dominance over the people who had remained on the land go unchallenged. Indeed, the multiple conflicts within early second-temple Judea, whether between factions competing for power in the temple-state or between the people and the restored ruling elite, emerged within the first generations of the restoration, as evident in Haggai, Malachi, and Isaiah 56–66. Indeed they became sufficiently severe that the Persian regime was forced to intervene by mid-fifth century.

The successive missions of Nehemiah and Ezra just after mid-fifth century attempted to "reform" the situation that was threatening to dissolve into severe conflict, as evident in the "memoirs" that offer somewhat confusing accounts of the circumstances and events. Almost certainly connected with the struggle for power among the wealthy and powerful, the "nobles and officials" of Judah had been severely exploiting the peasants economically, charging them interest (against Judean covenantal torah), forcing them into debt, debt-slavery, and loss of their ancestral lands (Neh 5:1–6). The Persians of course had a vested interest in a viable provincial peasantry, which served as their own as well as the temple-state elite's "tax-base." The Achaemenid regime thus found it necessary to re-impose order in Judah from above through a military governor. It is significant surely that the three governors mentioned in our sources all had either a Babylonian name (Zerubbabel) or roots in the Persian court (Ezra and Nehemiah).[10] Although all three apparently had ties with the exiled Judahite elite in Babylon, they were all clearly taking orders from the Persian imperial court.

Although Nehemiah is traditionally understood as a Judahite hero of the restoration, it is clear from his "memoirs" (the later book of Nehemiah) that he was sent by the Persian court as governor and escorted by Persian officers and mounted troops—which he needed, given the strong opposition from various wealthy and powerful figures competing for power in Judah (Neh 2:9). Besides his commission to rebuild the walls of Jerusalem, he was clearly also responsible for regularizing the revenues of the imperial regime and the Jerusalem temple alike. Not only did Nehemiah expropriate payments in kind (allotments of grain, wine, and silver) from the populace (Neh 5:14–15) and see that "the king's tax" on cultivated land was collected (Neh 5:4), but he also regularized the contributions of goods and funds to central storage area of the temple for the support of the priestly families (10:26–29,

---

10. Berquist, *Judaism*, 136.

40).[11] In what is surely a mark of the previous irregularities he confronted, he established a regular supervision of collections and disbursements by a panel consisting of one priest, two representatives of the lower clergy, and a certain Zadok, who was apparently his own representative (Neh 13:13; cf. 2 Macc 3:5–6, 10–12; Josephus, *War* 6.282; *Ant.* 14.10–13). It is also clear that Pethahiah the overseer was an imperial appointee.[12]

We can thus discern from the reform of Nehemiah that the Jerusalem temple-state was supposed to serve simultaneously as a largely self-governing body (under minimal imperial supervision) and a branch of the imperial fiscal administration. Under imperial supervision, the officers of the temple were evidently to operate both the imperial and the local tax systems, that is the collection and payment of the tribute, a poll tax, and a land tax to the emperor (Ezra 4:13, 20; 6:8; 7:24; Neh 5:4), and the collection of the first fruits or *teruma* for the temple revenues (Neh 10:26–29, 40).[13]

The mission of Ezra has proven less susceptible of historical verification. But the account in the book of Ezra portrays it as an implementation of Persian policy and directed by the imperial regime. Even more sharply than Nehemiah's reform, Ezra's aimed to consolidate the position of the previously exiled elite in Yehud. Indeed, virtually by definition in these reforms, the *Yehudim* were identical with the returned (*golah*) community. In repeatedly reinforcing the power of the returned Judahite elite the Persians were backing a ruling class with both roots in traditions of the Davidic dynasty and Solomonic temple and strong cultural ties with and understandable allegiance to their Persian "liberators."[14] But this colonialist policy either excluded the indigenous "people of the land" or subordinated them to the temple-state as second-rate or lesser-status people.[15] To reinforce the severe exclusivity of the returned Yehud community, intermarriage was strictly forbidden. To retain their positions of power, priestly aristocrats were supposedly forced to dissolve their alliances with other, non-Yehudite families of prominence in the region. Thus the very exclusive definition of who belonged to Yehud, while presumably strengthening the dominant group, would have alienated rather than integrated the people of the land in Yehud itself and other powerful families in the region from the dominant faction that controlled the temple-state.

---

11. Gottwald, *Politics*, 110.

12. Blenkinsopp, "Temple and Society," 49.

13. Schaper, "Jerusalem Temple."

14. Berquist, *Judaism*, 136.

15. Blenkinsopp, "Temple and Society," 44–47, drawing somewhat on Weinberg, *Temple Community*; cf. Horsley, "Empire, Temple"; Carter, *Emergence*, 297–306.

Besides restoring temples and their administrations throughout the empire, the Persian regime "promoted the codification and implementation of local traditional law as a closely related instrument of the *pax Persica* throughout the empire."[16] It remains unclear whether the Jerusalem elite restored to power in the late sixth century brought with them some sort of law or law-book. In any case, Ezra, who was a priest and "a scribe skilled in the law of Moses" that the God of Israel had given, became the great symbol of the "restoration" of the Law. According to the (at least extensively edited) "copy" of the official "letter," Ezra was commissioned by the Persian emperor Artaxerxes to enforce obedience to "the law of your God and the law of the king" on "all the people in the province Beyond the River who know the laws of your God." He was to do this by appointing (apparently Persian) judges and magistrates who would enforce "the laws of your God" under threat of confiscation or goods, banishment, imprisonment, or death (Ezra 7:25–26). Obedience to "the law of your God" is also obedience to "the law of the King," which is probably a reference to the transcendent Law/Justice by which the King established Order in the empire.[17] The principal account of the establishment of "the law of God" in Judah thus clearly presents it as authorized, imposed, and enforced by the Persian imperial regime.

Although we can infer certain contents of Ezra's law-book from the text of Ezra and Nehemiah (e.g., Neh 10:20–39), we have insufficient basis for identifying it with any bodies of law now included in the Hebrew Bible. Although some of the allusions to and citations of laws in Ezra and Nehemiah bear some relationship to Deuteronomic laws and others some relationship to the Priestly laws, some of the references (e.g., Ezra 9:11, 12) do not appear in what we know as the Pentateuch.[18] It thus seems unlikely that "the law of God" or "the law of Moses" that Ezra supposedly enforced was an early form of what we know as the Pentateuch. But the law enforced by Ezra clearly reflected the interest of the priestly aristocracy that it legitimated and lent imperial authority and enforcement. Moreover, in sponsoring a written composition of Judean law, the Persian imperial regime also in effect imposed a particular story that "defined what Yehud was, rhetorically limited Yehud's own self-understanding, and kept it within certain ideological confines."[19]

16. Blenkinsopp, "Mission"; "Temple and Society," 24; Berquist, *Judaism*, 24. See the broader discussion in Watts, *Persia and Torah*; and see now Fried, *Priest and King*.

17. Fried, *Priest and King*.

18. Blenkinsopp, "Pentateuch," 57; Gottwald, *Politics*, 102, 109.

19. Berquist, *Judaism*, 138.

What the Persians sponsored as the normative law in Yehud, enforced by the imperial regime, however, would have been only one or two forms of Judah' legal legacy, that derived from the exiled and then restored Jerusalem ruling class, to the subordination or exclusion of rival versions of Judean law. Yehud, like Babylon and Egypt, had its own law, under the umbrella of Persian imperial rule. But it would have been contested among the population of Yehud itself that still operated according to its own, alternative versions of Judean tradition. The defining story, self-understanding, and ideology imposed by the Persian regime would have taken a long time to "filter down" and "sink in," if it ever did too effectively. In sum, we need do no more than read the "memoirs" of the imperial "reformers" Nehemiah and Ezra to discern that, whatever the law-book was that Ezra presented to the *Yehudim* in Jerusalem, it was also in effect something sponsored by the Persian imperial regime as an instrument of imperial policy.

That Ezra's law-book served as a constituting authority of the Jerusalem temple-state (as part of the imperial order) is also evident in the very special kind of writing it was and in its *ceremonial performance* before the people. Ezra's "writing" of covenantal torah/the laws of Moses was both presented and venerated as a *numinous constitutional writing* and *communicated to the people in* a dramatic *oral performance* by Ezra. This can be discerned clearly in his ceremonial performance before a grand assembly of the (returned) Judahites (Nehemiah 8).

According to the accounts in books later included in the Hebrew Bible, Ezra's grand performance of the written torah/law-book stood in (and was modeled after) a long tradition of earlier ceremonial performance of writings of Mosaic torah/law. Contrary to the assumptions of modern print culture, many (and perhaps most) kinds of writing in antiquity were not for reading and/or consultation or interpretation. In societies where writing was unusual and the vast majority of people were not literate, writing had a numinous quality. Writing was mysterious and fraught with power. What was "written" thus had a special, transcendent, even divine authority. The inscription of a text on stone or parchment etherealized it and gave it inviolable permanence.[20] This can be seen frequently in the references to "writings" in the "writings" ("books") that were later included in the Hebrew Bible, especially in the writing by God on the tablets of stone or in the heavenly books of divine records.

---

20. Although evidently unaware of the extensive studies (such as Harris, *Ancient Literacy*; Hezser, *Jewish Literacy*; and Niditch, *Oral World*) in the previous decades that "documented" just how limited literacy and writing were in antiquity, Najman, "Symbolic Significance of Writing," emphasizes the authority of writing.

This mysterious, numinous quality inheres in *monumental* writing, such as the inscription of laws on stones in Athens and the inscription of the *Res Gestae* of the emperor Augustus on imperial monuments in the Roman empire or copies of the Domesday Book in medieval England (discussed in chap. 1). Such monumental writing could also be *constitutional*, that is, constitutive in authorizing the power of the state and its rulers. The law codes that Hammurabi had inscribed on steles, for example, provided authority to the imperial power he exercised over the Babylonian empire. A similar constitutional, monumental, numinous quality is projected onto the writing of the covenantal torah (laws) given by God to Moses that then Joshua, in turn, had inscribed on stone monuments (Deut 31:24–26; cf. 28:58–61; Josh 8:30–35; 24:25–27).

Such numinous monumental and/or constitutional writing, however, was not for the people to read, not a means of communicating information or the contents of the laws. Communication of God's (Moses') torah/laws was by oral performance (see again Deuteronomy 31; Josh 8:30–35). And even this oral performance of God's torah was not so much a communication of information (the contents of the laws) as a *ceremony in which the people submitted* to the demands of God (or the prophet or king) and committed themselves to obedience (for example, Joshua 24).

The prototype for Ezra's awesome presentation of the writing of the torah/laws of Moses and his ceremonial performance before the people was the "discovery" of a "writing of the torah" in the temple and its performance before the people under King Josiah (2 Kings 22–23; that this "writing of the covenant" contained "commandments and laws" indicates that its torah was Mosaic-covenantal, 23:2–3). The story of the "writing of torah" that was "found" in the temple (stated repeatedly, 2 Kgs 22:8, 13; 23:2, 24), such that it both required and then authorized Josiah's "reform" (2 Kings 23), illustrates that a written law-book was unusual, perhaps unprecedented even at the center of power in the Davidic court and Jerusalem temple. This suddenly-discovered scroll was certainly not simply a dusty old copy of "the Law" that had somehow gotten displaced (or suppressed by a previous regime) from "the temple library" where it would previously have been "read" or "studied" by priests, or from the royal "archives" where such law-books would supposedly have been regularly consulted by royal scribes or other officials. Communications in the royal court and in the temple were largely oral (the royal scribe Shaphan recited/proclaimed the contents of the writing ["book"] aloud to Josiah [2 Kgs 22:10], which was the way that the king had "read" it [22:16]).

The "book of the law" discovered during repairs to the temple was more likely composed for the purpose of mandating and authorizing the centralization of political-religious power in Jerusalem, the systematic purge that followed the royal covenantal ceremony (2 Kgs 23:4–25). This is similar to the function of "found book" traditions that legitimated innovation in highly traditional societies. This worked only because writing was not a familiar aspect of life that was simply taken for granted, as in modern print culture. Only because writing in general was utterly unusual in ancient Judah did the discovery of a written law-book "work," evoking the awe of the people. Like the covenant tablets written by God given to Moses on Mount Sinai, this suddenly "found" *sepher* was endowed with aura and mystery. "It validates reform not only because it is written and true, but because it is unusual, mysterious, and divinely sent."[21] In authorizing the centralization of power, the scroll, inscribed with the sacred words of God, whose contents and authority was managed by the royal scribes and priests all the way, was performed "in the hearing" of all the people (23:2).

The story of Ezra's "reading" in Nehemiah 8 similarly portrays "the writing of the torah/law of Moses" as a numinous sacred object.[22] Ezra proclaims (from) the scroll to the assembly of the Judahites returned to Jerusalem from exile in an unprecedented founding ceremony on the first day of *Tishre*. Ezra was "standing above all the people" on a platform made specially for the occasion. "And Ezra opened the scroll in the sight of all the people . . . and when he opened it, all the people stood up. Then Ezra blessed the LORD, the great God, and all the people answered, 'Amen, Amen,' lifting up their hands" (8:4–6). That is, Ezra holds up the scroll of the torah as a virtual sacred icon before which the people bow.[23]

That this formal public performance of the sacred writing had to be "interpreted" or "translated" for the people, who (it is believed) spoke Aramaic, indicates that it was (probably) composed-and-written in Hebrew, to authenticate its hoary antiquity as a/the torah/law of Moses. That the "citations" concerning the Festival of Booths (8:14–15) "found written in the torah/law which the Lord had commanded by Moses" do not appear in the older material contained in the Pentateuch, however, indicates that Ezra's "book of the torah/law of Moses" was written to authorize a new foundation, that of the temple-state under the Persians. Ezra's law-book was written to serve as the numinous sacred law, and then it was orally proclaimed before a founding ceremonial assembly to authorize the (new) temple-state as the political-economic-religious order in Yehud.

21. Niditch, *Oral World*, 104. Na'aman, "'Discovered Book.'"

22. Ibid., 105–6.

23. Van der Toorn, "Iconic Book," suggests an "analogy" between the Babylonian cult of images and the veneration of written torah in second-temple and subsequent texts.

Having been established under Persian imperial sponsorship, the temple-state and its "books" of torah/law continued under the Ptolemaic and Seleucid empires, even if as less purposeful instruments of imperial policy. Although they indeed founded new cities with Greek language and constitution, the respective successors of Alexander the Great's rule over Egypt and the territories from Syria to Bactria continued the Persian practice of working through temple-states as instruments of their control and economic exploitation of indigenous peoples. The complex of intrigue and negotiation between rival factions among the Jerusalem elite and rival Ptolemaic and Seleucid imperial regimes for control of Judea, particularly from mid-third to mid-second century BCE, provides a vivid illustration that the principle concern of the imperial regimes was to secure and maximize their revenue.[24] In the mid-third century when the Tobiad Joseph outbid the incumbent Oniad high priest for the contract to collect taxes from Judea for the Ptolemies, it presumably weakened the position of the high priesthood. When the Oniad high priestly party then changed their loyalty to the Seleucids just as the latter finally succeeded on taking control of Palestine, the power of the high priesthood, its role in tax collection restored, was presumably strengthened. Ironically it became an attractive plum for rival elite factions who miscalculated the strength and importance of Judean/Israelite tradition that presumably continued to be cultivated, by recitational learning and performance, among the indigenous priests and scribes.

We catch a glimpse of the close association of the now written but ceremonially proclaimed sacred torah/law closely linked with the high priesthood at the beginning of Ptolemaic rule over Judea. A fragment from Hecataeus of Abdera, writing at the beginning of the Ptolemaic period, i.e., late fourth or early third century BCE, observes that

> The Judeans believe that the high priest acts as a messenger to them of god's commandments. It is he who in their assemblies and other gatherings announces (orally) what is ordained, and the Judeans are so docile in such matters that straightway they fall to the ground and do reverence to the high priest when he expounds the commandments to them. (Diodorus Siculus 40.3.5–6).

It is difficult to tell, however, whether this refers to the high priest's proclamation of divine torah/law from a sacred scroll kept in the temple or to his pronouncement of rulings simply on his own authority.

What is striking, in contrast with modern print culture in which written texts are read silently by individual readers, is that in the Judean

---

24. Horsley, *Scribes, Visionaries*, chap. 2.

temple-state written texts of the torah of God/Moses were "monumental" writings housed in the temple that were not read or consulted. After all, literacy was severely limited, confined to the scribal elite that comprised a tiny minority of the population. Rather the written texts were presented to the people as authoritative numinous symbols of divine authority. Communication of the contents of the texts then happened by means of public oral proclamation by scribes or priests.

By the third century BCE, collections of prophetic oracles had presumably also been written on scrolls. The story of Jeremiah's dictation—twice—of his prophetic oracles to the scribe Baruch, full of political intrigue, provides one example of the how the writing of the orally delivered pronouncements of prophets may have begun (Jeremiah 36). But we have no sources that describe the development or use of the prophetic books other than the later written copies of the books themselves found among the DSS. It is thus difficult to do more than speculate about how the prophetic books developed prior to the second century BCE. It is generally agreed that the third set of books later included in the Hebrew Bible, the "Writings," originated in late second-temple times, although some included earlier materials.

## The Continuing Scribal Oral Cultivation of Authoritative Written Texts

In fact, there is a gaping hiatus between the very limited sources we have for early second-temple times (e.g., the memoirs of Ezra and Nehemiah) and texts from late second-temple Judea. This makes all the more important the later sources that were produced by the scribes of the second and first centuries BCE, some loyal to incumbent high priestly regimes and most sharply dissident. These sources do not give us access to some generalized second-temple "Judaism." But they do indicate how a tiny literate elite, the scribes/sages, who were professionally devoted to the cultivation of the Judean cultural heritage, cultivated the nascent authoritative texts of torah, prophets, and writings, both in regular oral performance and (some of them) on written scrolls.

In the very structure of the imperial order established in the Jerusalem temple-state, scribes were the mediators of power-relations. In the ancient Near East scribes had traditionally served as intellectual "retainers" in priestly, royal, and imperial regimes.[25] Their possession of reading and writing skills provided the basis for their many functions in service of

25. Horsley and Tiller, "Ben Sira"; Horsley, *Scribes, Visionaries*, chap. 3, including references.

the rulers, such as record-keeping, diplomatic correspondence, astronomy and calendrical construction, divination and dream interpretation, and the political-religious self-presentation of the regime. The books of Chronicles indicate that scribes played important roles in the temple-state in earlier second-temple times (1 Chron 18:16; 24:26; 27:32; 2 Chron 34:8–13). It is significant that Antiochus III's charter for Judea at the beginning of the second century lists "scribes of the temple" (along with the *gerousia*, the priests, and the temple singers) among the principle officers and staff of the temple-state.

The instructional speeches and other "wisdom" of Ben Sira provides a first-hand source for the social location and role(s) of Jerusalem scribes/sages. Ben Sira portrays the learned scribes as engaged in the service of the ruling aristocracy of the temple-state. The majority of the "wisdom" anthologized in the book of Sirach consists of his instructional speeches to his scribal protégés, younger scribes-in-training. The purpose of the highly disciplined scribal learning was to prepare to provide advice and counsel in the councils of ruling Jerusalem aristocracy. In contrast to the artisans and farmers below them on the social scale, who worked with their hands, the scribes/sages had the leisure (*schole* in Greek) to learn a broad Judean cultural repertoire (Sir 38:24—39:11). Their curriculum consisted not just of proverbs and the sayings of famous men, but of the torah of the Most High and prophecies as well. It is understandable how, on the basis of their special responsibility as the carriers and guardians of this wide-ranging Judean cultural repertoire, perhaps the torah of the Most High in particular, learned scribes would have developed a sense of their own authority independent of their service of the temple-state.

In several of his instructional speeches Ben Sira also indicates that learned scribes could be "caught in the middle," caught in a conflict between the ruling aristocrats on whom they were economically dependent and the ordinary people and between their service to the rulers and their loyalty to the cultural tradition. While he encourages the payment of tithes and offerings to the priests, he comments on how the wealthy and powerful rulers exploit the people and encourages his protégés to mitigate the worst effects on the destitute. He also warns the scribes about the dangers of their own vulnerability to their wealthy and powerful patrons.[26]

Ben Sira himself was a strong supporter of the incumbent high priesthood—although he conveniently ignores its recent restoration and sponsorship by the Seleucid imperial regime. The long section at the end of the book of Sirach ( chaps. 44–50) is a sustained paean of praise of the great

---

26. Horsley, *Scribes, Visionaries*, chap. 3.

office-holders of prophets, kings, and priests, an ideology that grounds the Oniad high priesthood in the hoary cultural tradition of Israel's past leaders and rulers. That the praise takes the form of a long hymn indicates clearly that, like the book of Mosaic torah that Ezra recited before the assembled Yehudim, this paean was performed, probably in a ceremony in the temple.

It has often been claimed on the basis of the historical rehearsal of office-holders in this hymn that Ben Sira knew virtually the whole (later) canon of scripture, at least the books of the Torah and the Prophets. While he does seem to know of the principal prophets, including the twelve "minor prophets," however, nothing in his laudatory rehearsal of heroes suggests that he has derived any of his information from (earlier versions of) the books later included in the Hebrew Bible. It is also often claimed that Ben Sira was engaged in interpretation of the Torah. But he rarely mentions torah and does not cite, much less interpret, any particular passage or law from books of the Pentateuch.

Ben Sira does, however, understand the torah of the Most High as the divine authorization of the temple-state—again as in Ezra's grand presentation of the torah and public proclamation—and presents a legitimating ideology of the high priesthood at the head of the temple-state and authority in divine torah. In the well-known self-praise of heavenly Wisdom, one of his several hymns to Wisdom, Ben Sira explicitly identifies the personified transcendent ethereal Wisdom with the torah/law of Moses (Sirach 24). Thus, when he declares that "all this (i.e., Wisdom) is the book of the covenant of the Most High God, the torah/law that Moses commanded us" (24:23), he thereby locates the latter in the temple. As the personified heavenly Wisdom declares, "In the holy tent I ministered before him, and so I was established in Zion . . . In the beloved city he gave me a resting place, and in Jerusalem was my domain" (24:10–11). That is, the torah/law of the Most High (= the entextment of divine Wisdom) is under the custody of, while lending its divine authority to, the high priesthood in the temple. Again it seems evident that this hymn of (self-)praise of Wisdom would have been performed in a ceremony in the temple that legitimated the temple-state and its official torah/law.

In his praise of the great ancestral rulers, moreover, Ben Sira grounds the authority of the current Oniad high priestly regime in a glorious adulation of Aaron and his descendants. They had received from God an "everlasting covenant" to be the (high) priesthood over the people and were also ordained by Moses as teachers of the torah/law. "In his (Moses'? God's?) commandments, he gave him (Aaron) authority and statutes and judgments, to teach Jacob the testimonies, and to enlighten Israel with his torah/law" (Sir 45:17). Especially fascinating is the climax of Ben Sira's hymnic performance of praise legitimating the Oniad high priesthood, the final step in which it describes the high priestly performance of the sacrifices at the temple altar (Sirach 50). The pomp and circumstance in the performed paean of praise are awesome indeed—although it seems likely that the principal attendees would have been only the Jerusalem elite.

Although Ben Sira understood the torah of the Most High, which he identified as the written embodiment of heavenly Wisdom, as the divine authorization of the temple-state, he does not appear to be working with, much less interpreting, a particular written text of torah. His lack of references to specific laws or other passages (in what we know as the books of the Pentateuch/Torah) suggests he does not know torah/law as a set sacred text that he or other scribes/sages or priests were interpreting. Judging from the anthology of his instructional speeches (that comprise most of the book of Sirach), Ben Sira is deeply devoted to the covenant/torah, to which he calls his students to obedience. He also claims that scribes/sages learn the torah/law of the Most High (along with prophecies and wisdom, 38:24—39:4). Like the later rabbis and their students, Ben Sira and his scribal protégés learned the torah of the Most High, as part of their character formation and preparation for service in the temple-state, by repeated recitation—so that they could recall and *publically perform* from it as appropriate to the situations in councils of state. But he does not interpret or apply the laws in the materials included in the book of Sirach.

While Ben Sira ardently supported the incumbent high priest as well as the high priesthood as an institution, other learned scribes attacked the incumbent high priestly rulers and some even seem to have rejected the institution of temple and its high priesthood.[27] The Epistle of Enoch (*1 Enoch* 92–105), a text that may be more or less contemporary with Ben Sira, pronounces God's condemnation of the wealthy and powerful (apparently the incumbent priestly rulers). The Animal Vision of "Enoch" (*1 Enoch* 85–90) declares the whole period of the second-temple period to be "a perverse generation" and the temple itself as corrupted, and envisions the future fulfillment of history beyond imperial oppression in idyllic terms, including the restoration of Israel/Judea as the house of God that conspicuously lacks its "tower" (i.e., temple; *1 Enoch* 90:28–38).

The scribal circles' active opposition to the incumbent high priesthood that developed after 175 BCE is fairly clearly rooted in their sense of their own authority, vis-à-vis that of their aristocratic patrons, that scribes had developed as the professional guardians of the official Judean cultural

---

27. Fuller analysis and discussion of texts in Horsley, *Scribes, Visionaries*, chaps. 8–9.

repertoire, including the nascently authoritative written texts. What touched off the widespread scribal, priestly and even popular resistance to the incumbent high priesthood and its imperial sponsors, however, was a series of successful maneuvers by the dominant aristocratic faction to change the long-standing recognition of the developing torah/law of Moses as the authoritative basis on which the Jerusalem temple-state was constituted as the ruling body in Judea. The Seleucid empire included *poleis* with constitutions (*politeiai*) patterned after Greek city-states, as well as a few indigenous temple-states, such as in Jerusalem. The priestly elite in Jerusalem who had acquired a taste for Hellenistic culture, led first by Menelaus and then by Jason, offered the ever-needy Seleucid imperial regime greater sums of tribute for the privilege and power of the high priesthood and transformed Jerusalem into a *polis* with a Greek-style constitution. That move, however, eliminated the traditional function of the professional scribes, along with their economic support. Thus it should not be surprising that scribal circles might resist their displacement, in whatever ways they could. And it is evident in the visions-and-interpretations in Daniel 10–12; the Animal Vision in *1 Enoch* 85–90; and the *Testament of Moses* that several different scribal circles did resist the high priests' Hellenizing "reform" and its enforcement by the Seleucid emperor, Antiochus IV Epiphanes, to the point that they were martyred.[28]

It may be a significant indication of the still nascent role and authority of the books of torah/law and prophetic books, however, that the scribes who produced the texts of resistance that we classify as "apocalyptic" literature do not appeal to any of them as the basis of their resistance or as the basis of the restoration of the people that they anticipate. In fact, as these texts indicate, their scribal producers were desperately seeking alternative sources of revelation, of clarification of the historical crisis that had come upon them, evidently contrary to what they expected on the basis of the "Mosaic" or "Deuteronomic" torah central to the developing authoritative books of torah. It is clear in the visions-and-interpretations in Daniel 7 and 10–12 that Antiochus Epiphanes and/or his allies in the dominant "reforming" high priestly faction have broken the (Mosaic) covenant in some general way. But the interpretations of the visions make no particular reference to anything recognizable from the nascent scriptures. Conspicuous by the absence in the anticipated restoration of the people in both Daniel 7, 8, 10–12 and Enoch texts are both any books of torah/law and the temple.

Only in Daniel 9 do we find reference to "the books" (9:2). And there the scribal producers of the vision mention more specifically knowledge of

---

28. Fuller discussion in Horsley, *Revolt of the Scribes*.

God's words about the seventy years to the prophet Jeremiah (but no quotation) and "the curse and oath written in the torah/law of Moses (again with no specific reference, although we know such in both Deut 29:15–45 and Lev 26:14–22). Here at least is an indication that scribal visionaries knew of books of both torah and prophecies and could refer to (although they did not quote) particular contents of those books, even if they did not appeal to them as the basis of their resistance and hope for future restoration.

It would be inappropriate as historical method to use the book of 1 Maccabees as a source for Judean resistance to the imperial order on the basis of scriptural torah, despite its theme of "zeal for the Law" that supposedly fires the rebellion against the repressive military forces of Antiochus Epiphanes. First Maccabees is clearly the propaganda of the Hasmonean regime that resulted from the leaders of the revolt maneuvering themselves into power as the new high priests in the same imperial system. Thus the Hasmoneans themselves needed as well as desired legitimation as the defenders of the temple-state's law/torah, with its authority as the glorious and ancient Israelite tradition.

In fact, no sooner had the Hasmoneans set themselves up as the new rulers of the temple-state than significant numbers of scribes and priests reacted strongly. The discovery of the DSS vastly increased the sources available for late second-temple Judean history. Most remarkable both for its own actions and for the light it sheds on affairs in the Judean temple-state more generally is the group of scribes and priests who, in a new exodus, withdrew from Jerusalem into in exile in the wilderness at Qumran where they established the renewed Mosaic covenantal community of Israel. Evident from the texts these people abandoned in nearby caves are a number of significant features of the development of the Judean scriptures and their oral and written cultivation in late second-temple times.

First, the many copies of scriptural books found among the DSS indicate that by the first century BCE at least the books of the Pentateuch and the prophets had taken more or less the contours we recognize as the books of Pentateuch and the books of the prophets. The multiple scrolls of various scriptural books indicate that different versions coexisted and were still developing, however, so that there was no standardized textual tradition for particular books.[29]

Second, other forms of torah/law-codes/law-books were, nevertheless, being composed and cultivated. Moreover, judging from the number of copies found, which sometimes rival those of books later included in the Hebrew Bible, these alternative texts of torah or prophetic books held

29. Ulrich, *Dead Sea Scrolls.*

authority that rivaled and relativized that of the books of the Pentateuch and the prophets. The book of *Jubilees* contains a law-code different from while overlapping those the Pentateuch. And the Temple Scroll now gives us an example of a relatively extensive authoritative book of torah/law, both evidently intended as alternatives to or at least supplemental the torah included in the Pentateuch. These alternative books of torah/law indicate that, while the books of the Pentateuch had become authoritative, perhaps by weight of the length of time they had held official sacred status in the temple, by no means did all Judean scribal circles recognize the books of the Pentateuch as the only authoritative books or traditions of torah.

Third, the *pešarim* ("interpretations") of several particular prophetic books found among the scrolls provide the first examples of explicit interpretation of scriptural texts. Working through particular prophetic books in sequence of statements, the *pešarim* then relate what was prophesied by a prophet to events or persons of their own historical situation. In fact, the *pešarim* on the prophets might be explained as having originated in the very crisis by which the community went out to the wilderness in self-imposed exile.

Fourth, by contrast with the *pešarim* on prophetic books, however, the Qumranites do little or no interpretation of books of torah or of particular statements from them. It is clear from the texts produced by Qumran scribes themselves that they were thoroughly imbued with "scriptural" language and idiom. But rarely do they quote (implicitly or explicitly) from authoritative books of torah in the texts they produced themselves, such as their Community Rule (1QS, very seldom) or the Damascus Rule (CD, more frequently). And in these instances they appeal to the *authority* of a given phrase or clause, with the formula "(as) it is written," yet may or may not identify the book in which it stands "written."

Several such appeals to the authority of a clause or phrase that "is written" occur in the highly fragmentary text 4QMMT, "Some Observances/ Legal Rulings of the Torah." This is a "letter" written to the high priest by some proto-Qumranites evidently prior to the decisive leadership exercised by the Teacher of Righteousness. It delineates the dissidents' Sabbath and festival calendar and twenty-eight or so rulings of a purity code pertaining to sacrifices and offerings that differ from current practices in the temple (leading to their withdrawal from participation).[30] At the end the letter calls upon the high priest to "understand {the book/s of Moses}and the book[s of the pro]phets and David," which appears to be an appeal to the authority of the scriptural books recognized by both the dissident scribes and the

---

30. Schiffman, "*Miqsat Ma'aseh ha-Torah.*"

addressee(s). It should be noted that this fragmentary text required frequent conjectural restorations, as in the preceding translation, meaning that interpretation involves conjecture as well. In connection with four or perhaps five of the "observances/legal rulings," the text appeals for authority to what "is written," in three of which a brief phrase is cited, but only in one case is the phrase followed by an interpretation. In closing, the text cites or alludes to the prophesied blessings and curses toward the end of Deuteronomy (30:1–2; 31:29) as currently being fulfilled—as punishment for the missteps of the established priesthood and the (hoped for) repentance and agreement with the dissidents.

While this can be called application of particular phrases of Scripture, we can hardly call this "interpretation of Scripture" in our sense of focusing on a scriptural text and then figuring out its meaning or significance. It is significant to note in this connection that although the Qumranites' own Community Rule is clearly a renewed Mosaic covenant, complete with covenantal ceremony, their *mišpatim* (justice-rulings) that comprise the rules for community life are not derived from and do not refer to particular laws or *mišpatim* in the books of the Pentateuch, the "books of Mosaic covenant."

It is thus clear that, in contrast with modern scripture scholars, the scribes and priests at Qumran were not engaged in the study and interpretation of books of torah. The scribes and priests at Qumran did not appropriate the torah by reading, study, and interpretation. Rather they appropriated authoritative texts of torah and the texts they produced themselves by *collective recitation* and other performance. This should have been clear in the often mistranslated passage in the Community Rule that lays out the proper procedure when the minimum group of ten is gathered together:

> Where the ten are, there shall never lack a man among them who searches (the) torah [*dwrš btwrh*] day and night, concerning the right conduct of a man with his companion. And the many shall watch in community for a third of every night of the year, to recite the writing [*lqrw' bspr*] and to search the justice-ruling [*ldwrš mšpt*]and to offer communal blessings [*lbrk byhd*]. (1QS 6:6–8; my adaptation of Vermes' translation)

Note that all three of those exercises are oral performances: the recitation of the writing as well as the searching of the justice-ruling and the communal blessings. As was standard practice among scribes in Judea and throughout the ancient Near East, they learned authoritative texts by repeated recitation until they were "written on the tablet of the heart" (in their memory; Prov 3:3), as well as inscribed on scrolls. The special covenantal renewal community at Qumran then extended the recitation of texts of torah and other texts to collective oral recitation. In doing so, their purpose was the collective discipline as well as personal discipline, certainly not some sort of discursive interpretation.

The Qumranites appropriation of scriptural torah by regular collective recitation thus resembled the relation between other celebrations and performances in their community life in relation to the inscription of those performances on scrolls. This can be seen in connection with three of the Qumran texts that have been edited, translated, and studied the longest: the Hymn Scroll (1QH), the Community Rule (1QS), and the War Rule (1QM). The Hymn Scroll contains hymns. But hymns are sung or chanted orally— that is, performed. The texts are held in memory and scrolls do not have to be unrolled and read. The Community Rule includes instructions for ceremonies of covenant renewal and reception of members into the community. On a more elaborate basis than the singing of hymns (although perhaps including collective hymns), covenant renewal ceremonies were enacted, complete with pronouncement of blessings and curses. The War Rule as well appears to be instructions for the rehearsal, in elaborate performance, of ritual warfare, with banners and maneuvers and pronouncements, against the *kittim* (the Romans), the imperial embodiment of the demonic forces (1QM 1–2; 1QpHab 8–12). The special texts produced at Qumran were indeed inscribed on scrolls. But the texts are copies of instructions for the conduct of ritual performances. The regular evening communal recitations of writings (presumably of torah), along with the searching of the community rules and the communal blessings, were merely less dramatic and elaborate performances of authoritative/scriptural texts that had become written on the tablets of their hearts.

In connection with the multiple versions of the books of the Pentateuch (laws of Moses) still developing and the alternative texts of torah, both evident among the DSS, we should also raise the question of another scribal circle: the Pharisees. In contrast with the scribes and priests who withdrew from the temple-state to the community at Qumran, the Pharisees emerged under the early Hasmonean high priesthood as the leading party of scribes in service of the temple-state (Josephus, *Ant.* 13.288–98, 408–15). According to Josephus' accounts, they continued to be considered the most accurate or astute in knowledge of the laws. It has been assumed that they were interpreters of the books of torah (in reference to passages such as *Ant.* 18.12–17; *Life* 191). But Josephus does not say exactly that. According to his earliest account, in contrast to the Sadducees, who accepted as authoritative only the written laws of Moses, the Pharisees promulgated (other) legal rulings not written in the laws of Moses that they had received as ancestral tradition. These "traditions of the elders" were recognized as official state law under John Hyrcanus and again apparently under Alexandra Salome (*Ant.* 13.288–98, 408–10).

The Pharisaic traditions of the ancestors have previously been identified with the "oral torah." But Martin Jaffee has recently explained definitively that the concept of "torah in the mouth" is of much later origin, among the Palestinian Amoraim.[31] Some scholars have also argued that the Pharisees, like the Qumran scribes, derived their rulings, like the later rabbis their *halakhot*, from interpretation of laws or other passages in the Torah.[32] Jaffee, again, has explained that this is not the case, pointing out that the term/concept of *halakhah* does not even occur in the Qumran texts among the DSS. But there is also no textual evidence that the Pharisees, any more than the Qumranites, derived their special rulings from interpretation of laws or passages in books of torah (laws of Moses). As Josephus says explicitly, their rulings derived from ancestral tradition. There is also no evidence that they were written. Yet even if they were, the Pharisees cultivated them orally, reciting them as appropriate to the particular issue or occasion, just as the scribes generally had traditionally learned cultural tradition and texts that were also written by repeated recitation, held them in memory, and recited them as called for by the issue or occasion. The rulings of the Pharisees not written in the laws of Moses, their tradition of the ancestors, thus comprise yet another set of authoritative torah supplementary to or rival to the books of the Pentateuch and the alternative texts of torah, such as the book of *Jubilees* and the Temple Scroll.

## The Origins of Judean Scriptures and their Continuing Oral Performance: A Summary

One of the principal factors, perhaps the principal factor, leading to written scrolls of Israelite/Judahite law and other cultural traditions was the Persian imperial practice of sponsoring the writing of indigenous legal traditions as a device to strengthen and legitimate (the restoration of) native/local elites as the governing infrastructure of the empire. One particular version of Israelite/Judean law and tradition was installed as the official founding history-and-lawbook that provided divine authorization of the temple-state in sacred constitutional writing and its accompanying ceremonial performance. Numinous monumental writing and oral performance went hand in hand in the consolidation of power in the temple-state. Other versions

---

31. Jaffee, *Torah in the Mouth.*
32. Schiffman, *Halakhah.*

and law-codes continued and/or developed, perhaps among subordinated priestly-scribal or other groups, learned and recited orally.

Scribes played a special role in the development and cultivation of Scripture. As the professional literates, scribes serving directly under the regime that sponsored the composition of a law-book as "scripture," were necessarily involved in its composition and perpetuation. It is understandable that the scribes would develop a sense of their own authority rooted in their knowledge of the Judean cultural repertoire, and authority independent of that of their high priestly patrons. And scribes' sense of their own authority based in Judean tradition thus became a factor of structural conflict in the imperial order. When the Jerusalem priestly rulers collaborated with their imperial patrons in ways that violated Israelite cultural tradition, such as the Mosaic covenant, circles of scribes mounted resistance. Yet they did not appeal specifically to authoritative texts of torah as the basis of either their resistance or their expectation of restoration of the people to independence.

The DSS now provide evidence that by the first century BCE the books of the torah and the prophets had taken the basic contours that we know from the much later written manuscripts that previously provided the basis of our knowledge of the books of the Hebrew Bible. But the copies of proto-biblical books found among the Scrolls indicate that the written texts of these books existed in more than one version and were still developing. Moreover, the alternative texts of torah such as the book of *Jubilees* and the Temple Scroll, as well as the Pharisees' legal rulings derived from ancestral traditions, were authoritative texts supplemental or rival to the authority of the books of torah and the prophets that were later included in the Hebrew Bible.

Texts produced by the Qumran community also include the first examples of what could be called interpretation of scripture in the *pešarim* of prophetic books. Yet other Qumran texts cannot be said to display a parallel interpretation of books of torah. Rather, as a key passage in the Community Rule clearly indicates, appropriation of texts of torah was still primarily learning by repeated recitation and collective performance.

# 3

# ORAL–WRITTEN SCRIBAL CULTIVATION OF TORAH—NOT "RE-WRITTEN BIBLE"

THE RESULTS OF RECENT RESEARCH IN SEVERAL AREAS POSE serious challenges to standard assumptions, approaches, and concepts in the fields of biblical studies and Jewish history. Because we are all focused so heavily on our own specialty, however, we may not even be aware of the challenges, much less find time for the reconsideration that might be required. Particularly important for the future of biblical studies and Jewish history are the results of recent research in five areas: (1) the historical political-economic structure and dynamics of second-temple Judean society, particularly the social location and role of scribes/sages; (2) the limits of literacy and the predominantly oral communications environment in antiquity; (3) the close relationship between the oral and written cultivation of texts in scribal circles; (4) the manuscripts of books that were later included in the Hebrew Bible found among the DSS; and (5) previously unknown books among the DSS that have been classified as "rewritten Bible." With the possible exception of ##2 and 3, many scholars working in each of these particular areas have, until recently at least, seemed relatively unaware of the results of research in the other areas. Yet the results of these heretofore separate lines of research can potentially be mutually reinforcing. Serious conversations across these lines of research could produce some important new insights and new possibilities for understanding ancient texts in historical social-cultural context. The problem is how to bring together these potentially mutually reinforcing lines of research. I would like to sketch four steps that would move in that direction.

## The Social Role of Scribes in Judea and the Emergence of Dissident Circles of Scribes

It is possible to discern the political-economic-religious structure of second-temple Judean society, particularly the social location and role(s) of Judean scribes/sages, from information in key texts produced by learned scribes themselves, particularly the book of Jesus ben Sira. This information can be critically assessed with the aid of two sets of comparative material. The first is recent studies of the role of scribes elsewhere in the ancient Near East. The second is comparative historical studies, while being critical of how those studies may have been used in previous historical sociology.[1]

The instructional speeches of Ben Sira attest a society sharply divided between a very wealthy aristocracy that headed the temple-state in Jerusalem and the vast majority of Judeans, economically marginal villagers who supported the temple and priesthood with tithes and offerings. In between, but by no means forming a modern "middle class," were a relatively small number of scribes/sages who served the temple-state as advisers (historical sociologists would call them scribal retainers). Their role was "to serve the magnates/rulers" (*megistasin; sarim*, Sir 8:8; 39:4), generally as advisers of the collective ruling aristocracy (6:34; 7:14 15:5; 21:17; 38:32–33). Learned scribes, for example, might function as advisers in courts and assemblies, as Ben Sira indicates in his comment that "they understood the decisions of courts and could expound judgments" (4:9; 11:7–9; 38:33; 42:2).

As professional servants of the temple-state, without a separate economic base of their own, the wise scribes were economically dependent on, hence vulnerable to, the priestly aristocrats who headed the temple-state. This is the obvious implication of Ben Sira's contrast between the various kinds of artisans and farmers, whose long hours of labor were necessary to support the city of Jerusalem (as well as their families), and the wise scribes who have the "leisure" to acquire the wisdom necessary to serve among the rulers (38:24–34). How did they have such leisure? Evidently because they were supported economically from temple revenues. The sage must therefore bow low to the rulers (4:7). Ben Sira's repeated warnings to his protégés to mind their words and "watch their backs" when dealing with the powerful aristocrats (8:1; 13:8–11, 13; 31:12—32:13, esp. 32:9) indicate how vulnerable they were. It is not by accident that the scribal training exemplified in the instructional speeches that comprise most of the book of Sirach was designed to instill a conservative ethos and disposition of obedience in

---

1. See the fuller treatment in Horsley and Tiller, "Ben Sira and Sociology"; Horsley, *Scribes, Visionaries*, chap. 3.

the scribal trainees aspiring to take their fathers' places in the service of the temple-state. Comparative studies of other ancient Near Eastern societies show that in all these respects, the role of scribes in second-temple Judea resembles that of earlier generations of scribes in Egypt and Mesopotamia.[2]

Ben Sira, who was a prime propagandist for the incumbent Oniad high priesthood, however, conveniently leaves out a determinative dimension of temple-state politics, one that is also obscured by the standard synthetic concept of early "Judaism." Far from being independent and free standing, the Judean temple-state had been set up and maintained as a local ruling institution subject to imperial rule.[3] And just at the time of Ben Sira, with the rivalry between the Ptolemaic and the Seleucid regimes for control of Judea, it had become clear that the priestly aristocracy depended upon an imperial regime for its own power and privilege. It was also clear, after the machinations of the Tobiads with the Ptolemaic regime, that an ambitious faction within the aristocracy could manipulate the imperial regime for its own purposes, which could be threatening to scribes who steadfastly adhered to Judean cultural tradition.

The principal basis of the wise scribes' role as advisers to the aristocracy of the temple-state was their wisdom, their knowledge of the Judean cultural repertoire, of which they were the professional guardians (38:34–39:4, 8–11). Scribes such as ben Sira devoted themselves personally and professionally to learning the wisdom of the ancients, the torah of God, and prophecies (38:34). Knowledge also meant obedience. If Ben Sira is typical of other learned scribes in the service of the temple-state, they put great stock in obedience to the covenant (of Moses) and its commandments. All of their wisdom, however, the scribes understood as coming from God and as having the authority of God (39:5–8; cf. 24:8–12, 23–34; similarly the contemporary scribal circle that produced "Enoch" texts). Learned scribes thus had an authority of their own, their God-given wisdom, independent of the authority they derived from their aristocratic patrons, who were the representatives of God to the people (as well as the representatives of the interests of the empire). From their knowledge of the torah of the Most High, the wisdom of the ancients, and the prophecies, scribes had a clear sense of their own about how the temple-state should be run. This set up the potential for conflict if the priestly aristocracy did not operate the temple-state according to the criteria to which the scribes were committed and/or if their collaboration with the empire conflicted with the torah of the Most High.

2. Carr, *Tablet of the Heart*; Horsley, *Scribes, Visionaries*, 141–43.
3. See the fuller discussion in Horsley, *Scribes, Visionaries*, chaps. 1–3.

As is well known, such a conflict did emerge at least by early in the second century and came to a head in 175 with the Hellenizing reform led by the dominant faction in the aristocracy in collaboration with Antiochus Epiphanes.[4] We know of at least three circles of dissident scribes that opposed the reform and resisted the imperial attempt to enforce it: the "Enoch" scribes who produced the Book of Watchers, the Animal Vision, and the Epistle of Enoch (*1 Enoch* 1–36; 85–90; and 92–105, respectively); the *maskilim* who produced the visions-and-interpretations in Daniel 7, 8, and 10–12; and the *hasidim* who joined in the Maccabean Revolt (1 Macc 2:42; 7:12–16). Then, we think, after the Hasmoneans set themselves up in high priesthood, another circle of dissident scribes and priests went out to form the *yahad* at Qumran in the Judean wilderness.

## Scribes' Cultivation of the Judean Cultural Repertoire

The many texts from Qumran offer us an abundance of previously unavailable evidence that confirms the statement of Ben Sira that wise scribes were the people who cultivated all segments of the Judean cultural repertoire. Because of scholarly specialization, this evidence comes from often separate lines of research. But these can be brought together in order to discern their mutual implications that challenge standard assumptions, approaches, and concepts.

Because biblical scholars focus primarily on texts (especially "biblical" texts), they often allow literary categories to determine soci(ologic)al constructions. It has been commonplace to think that prophetic oracles and books were produced by prophets, wisdom teaching and books by sages/scribes, and law-collections by priests. This is exemplified in the titles of recent books on the patterns of leadership in ancient Israel or "Judaism," with variations on the "Priests, Prophets, and Sages."[5]

We need only take a closer look at Sirach to see that Ben Sira himself not only cultivated several kinds of wisdom but covenantal torah and prophecies as well. Speeches of *instructional wisdom* comprises the bulk of the book of Sirach. But Ben Sira indicates clearly that he knows and produces other kinds of wisdom, samples of which are included in Sirach: *reflective (speculative) wisdom,* mainly in the form of hymns to or about the figure of Wisdom, and *cosmological wisdom*, also usually hymnic in form. In passing

---

4. See the fuller discussion in Horsley, *Revolt of the Scribes.*

5. For example, Blenkinsopp, *Sage, Priest, Prophet*; Grabbe, *Priests, Prophets, Diviners, Sages.*

Ben Sira also indicates that he knows of another kind of wisdom of which he is suspicious and critical: secret, *mantic wisdom* (of which we can see examples in the book of Daniel). So scribes and scribal circles cultivated a range of different kinds of wisdom, as is also evident in Enoch texts.[6]

The range of Ben Sira's learning, however, is far broader than several different kinds of wisdom. Precisely when he is discussing the scribe's service among rulers, he proudly points to the wide range of materials to which the scribe devotes himself. The scribe's learning included the three main divisions of what much later became the Hebrew Bible: the torah of the Most High, the wisdom of all the ancients, and prophecies (38:34—39:3). Whether or not Ben Sira was working with written scrolls of the books that later became biblical, the point here is that scribes cultivated all segments of the Judean cultural repertoire.[7]

The torah, prophecies, and wisdom learned and taught by wise scribes such as Ben Sira surely included already composed texts that existed in written as well as oral form. For example, collections of prophecy-fragments that derived from prophets such as Amos, Micah, or Isaiah were further developed by addition of later materials. And as indicated in the case of Jeremiah and Baruch (Jeremiah 36), scribes probably had a role in the production of such collections of prophecies. The three principal segments of the Judean cultural repertoire, however, also included traditional lore that was not included in those texts and alternative versions of some traditional materials that had been incorporated into particular texts. It has previously been asserted that Ben Sira knew and used the "books" of all or most of the nascent Hebrew Bible. The basis for this claim was mainly his long paean of praise of all the great Israelite-Judean office holders (Sirach 44–49). But neither in that long rehearsal of famous figures nor elsewhere does Ben Sira quote or even clearly allude to any particular passage that could be identified in the any of those books. His (and other scribes') knowledge of Judean tradition/cultural repertoire does not depend upon, and is surely not confined to books, that is written texts, but is far wider and deeper.

Probably one of the reasons why scholars find much influence of "wisdom" in the book of Deuteronomy is that certain scribes who cultivated instructional wisdom cultivated and further developed the book of Deuteronomy. One of the reasons why scholars find "sapiential" and "Deuteronomistic" influences in prophetic books is that scribes who cultivated the former also cultivated and further developed the latter. Ancient Judean scribes probably specialized, just as their modern intellectual counterparts

---

6. Fuller sketch in Horsley, *Scribes, Visionaries,* 126–28.

7. More extensive discussion in Horsley, *Scribes, Visionaries,* chap. 6.

specialize. Ben Sira specialized in instructional wisdom. "Enoch" scribes who produced the Book of Watchers and the Animal Vision drew heavily on and combined prophetic forms and visions and both mantic and cosmological wisdom.[8] The scribes, as the professional intellectuals of the temple-state, were engaged in cultivating all segments of the Judean cultural repertoire and, in the process, shaped and continued to develop all of the books later included in the Hebrew Bible: the Torah and Nebi'im, as well as the Ketubim.

Recent research on the limits of literacy in antiquity strongly reinforces the conclusion that scribes were the people who cultivated and developed all segments of the Judean cultural repertoire—hence were responsible for the shaping and continuing development of what became the books of the Hebrew Bible. Contrary to previous (and continuing) claims of widespread literacy and the availability and reading of books, especially among ancient Jews, ever more fully documented and sophisticated researches are concluding that literacy in antiquity was limited to the cultural elite. In the Hellenistic and Roman empires only about 10–15% of the populace was minimally literate. Thoroughly documented recent studies of Jewish literacy in early rabbinic times conclude that the rate was considerably lower in Jewish Palestine, limited mainly to scribal circles and their successors.[9] The clear implication is that almost "by definition" books in written form on scrolls were the product of scribal circles and that the scribes would have been the principal, perhaps almost the only, people in the society who were thoroughly acquainted with their contents.

Even though literacy was limited mainly to scribal circles in antiquity, the mid-twentieth-century construct of a "great divide" between literate culture and oral culture does not fit. For one thing, writing had various functions, some of which did not depend on widespread literacy, but on its opposite. Since it was rare and awesome, writing was mysterious and authoritative, particularly to those who could not read. As can be seen in the Gospel of Mark, for example, the non-literate knew of the writings possessed by the elite whose authority they recognized (in the formula "it is written"), even if ambivalently. Writing whose main function was monumental or constitutional served mainly as a permanent written record, and was not necessarily consulted.[10]

Most important for our purposes in trying to understand scribal practice at Qumran and elsewhere in second-temple Judean society, what

8. Horsley, *Scribes, Visionaries,* chap. 8.

9. Hezser, *Jewish Literacy.*

10. See further Niditch, *Oral World.*

is emerging clearly in recent research is that in the predominantly oral communication environment writing was embedded in oral communication. There was close interaction between writing and oral communication. Popular culture may have been almost exclusively oral. But for scribal culture we need a hyphenated term and what it points to: scribal practice was "oral–written."

Recent studies of scribal practice in ancient Near Eastern societies and more recent studies of scribal practice in Judah and Judea are concluding that scribal training and practice involved a mixture of writing and oral cultivation.[11] Scribes serving in the administrations of ancient kingdoms and temple-states made additional chirographs of various texts in a given state's cultural repertoire, and they could read what they or others had written on a scroll or clay tablet. But they learned texts as much or more by oral recitation. And the result of their learning texts was that the texts were now "written on the tablet of the heart" (that is, memory) as well as on the scrolls laid up in temples or court storage facilities (which were not the equivalent of modern "archives"). Since we are only beginning to understand scribal oral–written cultivation of texts in a provisional way, the following exploration will be elementary, perhaps even a bit experimental.

Ben Sira gives no indication that he is working with written texts. It is clear from numerous passages that he delivers his own instructional wisdom orally. "For wisdom becomes known through speech, and education through the words of the tongue" (4:24).[12] Interpreters often claim that Ben Sira is interpreting the Torah, as if he had a written scroll in front of him. But he never cites a particular passage that he is supposedly interpreting. If we look more closely, Ben Sira repeatedly refers to obeying the commandments or being faithful to the covenant, but not to studying or interpreting the law(s). All of the activities Ben Sira mentions in the scribe's learning involve oral cultivation: "devoting themselves to the understanding of the torah of the Most High," "seeking out the wisdom of the ancients," "preserving the sayings of the famous," and "concerned with prophecies" (38:34—39:3).

Some of the previously unknown texts discovered at Qumran are particularly informative in this connection. As is commonly recognized, the later rabbis taught and their students learned Torah (and Mishnah and Talmud) by repeated oral recitation. Drawing on the same comparative study of oral performance and cultivations of texts that some of us in biblical studies

---

11. See the treatment of scribes in ancient Judah/Judea (and the summary of studies on scribes in the ancient Near East, by Carr, *Tablet of the Heart*; and Horsley, *Scribes, Visionaries*, chap. 4.

12. See further, Fox, "Wisdom and the Self-Presentation"; and Horsley, *Scribes, Visionaries*, chap. 5, esp. 90–91.

have been exploring, Martin Jaffee has illuminated the "oral-performative" cultivation of torah among the rabbis. Jaffee suggests about the rabbis and their predecessors at Qumran and among the Pharisees what modern scholars of the ancient Near East suggest about scribal practice in earlier Mesopotamia and Egypt.[13] The texts became inscribed on their memory as much or more than on the scrolls. Scribes could then access the texts from memory. That enabled them, for example, to (in turn) teach them by recitation, or apply a passage to a case before a court or an issue before a council of state or a community. To illustrate how learning texts by recitation and devotion to the texts by further recitation could have worked, Jaffee refers us to a key Qumran text, one that is by now very familiar in translations skewed toward our own modern academic practice. The following attempt at retranslation aims at avoiding our modern scholarly assumptions.

> Where the ten are, there shall never lack a man among them who searches the torah [*dwrs btwrh*] day and night, concerning the right conduct of a man with his companion. And the many shall watch in community for a third of every night of the year, to recite the writing [*lqrw' bspr*] and to search the justice-ruling [*ldwrs mspt*] and to offer communal blessings [*lbrk byhd*]. (1QS 6:6–8; my adaptation of Vermes' translation)[14]

These gatherings were not engaged in interpretive scholarly *study* of texts on scrolls unrolled in front of them, but in three successive oral activities, starting with recitation of a book (presumably of torah, accessed from memory). As is more familiar to students of religion from rabbinic learning of Torah and Talmud, from Muslim learning of the Qur'an, and medieval Christian monks' and others' learning of the Bible, those who have learned such texts by repeated recitation can easily access them from memory and can recite, apply, or otherwise use them as called for by particular occasions. Such "scholars" have often mastered vast quantities of texts of considerable complexity (often with sophisticated techniques) and are able to access them memorially. Perhaps most important for our approach to scribal practice in late second-temple times, it is clear that even after texts existed in written form, much if not most of their cultivation or use was oral.

The recently published results in two particular sub-areas of research on the scrolls found at Qumran further complicate our investigation of scribal practice. One is close analysis of the manuscripts of the books that were later included in the Hebrew Bible. The other is study of previously unknown books or previously known books that were not included in the

---

13. Jaffee, *Torah in the Mouth*.

14. Adaptation of translation by Vermes.

Hebrew Bible that parallel or overlap with books that were included. We have known for some time that the canon of the Hebrew Bible was not formally defined until at least after the second-temple period. Yet many of us have been writing as if we assume that the "biblical" books had already been "written" in definitive form and/or have been anachronistically referring to the books of the Pentateuch and the Prophets, etc., as "Bible/biblical."[15]

After close study of manuscripts of books later included in the Hebrew Bible found at Qumran, manuscripts over a millennium earlier than those previously known, Eugene Ulrich has drawn two major interrelated conclusions.[16] (1) At Qumran, and perhaps in Jerusalem as well at the time, there were multiple textual traditions or versions of the books of the Pentateuch, Isaiah, etc. (proto-Masoretic, proto-Samaritan, proto-Septuagintal). (2) Those different textual traditions were still undergoing development similar to what scholar had detected about them earlier in second-temple times. There was no stable standard text or version yet of the books that later became "biblical" and scribes cultivating those books seemingly had no problem with the coexistence of different versions which they also had no problem with further developing as they copied them.

Also found at Qumran were previously unknown written texts of torah such as the Temple Scroll (11QT), Some Observances Concerning the Torah (4QMMT), and Reworked Pentateuch (4QRP). Some of these, like the previously known *Jubilees*, present parallel but different versions of much of the same history and/or legal material presented in books that later became biblical. But not only do these documents show that there were alternative texts of torah coexisting and perhaps competing with the texts of torah (books of the Pentateuch) that later became biblical. Insofar as these alternative texts of torah include material not known from those later canonized texts, they attest an oral stream of traditional torah that had been running parallel to texts of torah that had taken shape earlier and were being cultivated orally as well as written on scrolls.

The authority of the books that were later included in the Hebrew Bible was thus still relative in three ways: relative to the different versions of those books then in use; relative to other texts that presented alternative versions of some of the same cultural materials; and relative to oral tradition of torah that may not (yet) have been included in any oral–written texts.

---

15. Even in articles accepted for publication in the leading critical journals in the field, such as Schmid, "Canon and Cult." See also the many recent books and articles referred to in Zahn, "Genre and Rewritten Scripture."

16. Ulrich, *Dead Sea Scrolls*.

# The Temple Scroll, "Reworked Pentateuch," and *Jubilees* as Case Studies

That scribal cultivation of texts was oral in close interaction with writing may be the basis on which we can understand the composition of texts such as the Temple Scroll (11QT) and the so-called "Rewritten Pentateuch" (4QRP) better as the continuing composition of alternative texts of torah than as "rewritten Bible."

## *Adaptable Torah and Alternative Torah*

Scholars have classified and interpreted a number of documents found in the caves near Qumran as "rewritten Bible" (or "reworked Pentateuch" or "rewritten scripture"). This classification had been designed to cover early Judean texts such as *Jubilees* that supposedly took their literary framework from the "biblical" text and (presumably for clarification) made changes by omission, expansion, and insertion.[17] The Temple Scroll and the fragments of several scrolls (4Q364–367 and 4Q158) recognized as belonging to the same document, labeled "Reworked Pentateuch" by Qumran scholars, have also been placed into this category. The editors and others judged that, despite different degrees of reworking and/or rephrasing, these texts were "based on an accepted form of the Bible," that they provided "a running text of one or more biblical books," and that "the exact wording of the biblical text is usually clearly recognizable."[18]

In recent years scholars of the DSS have carried out an intense debate about how the concept of "Rewritten Bible" (or "Rewritten Scripture" or "Reworked Pentateuch") should be understood (as a genre).[19] This debate, however, has been conducted without taking into account the implications of the important separate lines of research outlined just above, for example: (a) that authoritative texts had not yet been recognized and collected as "the Bible" or formally defined and officially designated as "Scripture"; (b) that, given the scribal *oral*–written learning and oral recitation of texts, new texts

---

17. See Vermes, *Scripture and Tradition*; Harrington, "Adaptations of Biblical Narratives." Alexander, "Retelling the Old Testament," even claims that "rewritten bible" was a genre. On Qumran, see especially Brooke, "Between Authority and Canon."

18. Tov, "Biblical Texts as Reworked," 112–13.

19. From the extensive debate, see for example Brooke, "Rewritten Bible"; Zahn, "Rewritten Scripture"; Machiela, "Rewritten Scripture"; Bernstein, "Rewritten Bible"; and Falk, *Parabiblical Texts*. While he retains the concept for modern scholarly purposes, Petersen, "Rewritten Bible," recognizes that "Rewritten Scripture" would not have been a meaningful category to ancient Judeans (scribes).

were probably not produced by physically writing on a scroll while visually consulting highly cumbersome already-inscribed scrolls; and (c) that new texts were probably composed in and for certain political-religious circumstances. Without having taken the implications of these largely separate lines of research into account, (continuing use of) the concept "Rewritten Bible/Scripture," along with its variants "reworked Bible" and "parabiblical," is problematic as well as anachronistic.[20]

This can be seen in the trouble that scholars have in describing texts such as "Reworked Pentateuch" and the Temple Scroll. Assuming that certain books were already biblical, and were not only ready to hand and eye but also *the* source of knowledge for narratives and laws, they assume that the "writer" doing the "reworking" was following "a running text of one of more biblical books." Yet the omissions of "biblical" materials and the additions of other materials are sometimes lengthy, and materials from several *different* books of the Pentateuch are brought together *topically* in a narrative context parallel to incidents in Genesis.[21] But how can a supposedly derivative "rewritten Bible" text be following a "running text" of the Pentateuch if it frequently changes the sequence and rearranges material? When a sufficient degree of similarity appears in the two texts, scholars of the scrolls find that "the exact wording of the biblical text is usually clearly recognizable," yet this is "sometimes only vaguely."[22] The "organizing principle" in scholarly analysis of such "exegetical texts" is the degree of closeness to "the biblical text." Insofar as there were different textual traditions of the "biblical" books found at Qumran, however, the same "rewritten Bible" document can be seen as following a proto-Masoretic version at some points and a proto-Samaritan or proto-Septuagint version at others—and at still others it

---

20. Brooke, "Between Authority and Canon," 1, recognizes that the concept "puts too much emphasis on the closed demarcation of one set of writings and the entirely secondary or derivative nature of the other" and suggests the broader category of "authoritative scripture." Emanuel Tov, "Biblical Texts as Reworked," 113, 133–34, comments in passing that in terms of genre such texts are mostly *sui generis*, yet concentrates his analysis only on the difference between "rewritten Bible" which "involves exegetical additions, omissions, and reordering," and "rephrased Bible," which also changes the wording itself. But (for example) if 4Q422 is a historical psalm focused on incidents of the exodus, like Psalm 78 and especially Psalm 105 (Tov, "Biblical Texts as Reworked," 121–22, 133), why not call it another historical psalm, not "rewritten Bible"? Najman, *Seconding Sinai*, 7–8, 42–46, raises objections to the concept "rewritten Bible" that are separate from its basis in print-cultural assumptions.

21. Tov, "Biblical Texts as Reworked," 114, 115, 124, 127, 128; Crawford, "Rewritten Pentateuch."

22. Tov, "Biblical Texts as Reworked," 113, 115.

resembles Jubilees.[23] And at yet other points, the relation to "biblical" texts is merely paraphrase or allusion.

Analysis of texts as "rewritten Bible" presupposes that the "author" scribe was working with written texts. But this would have been impossibly awkward: the scribe would have been sitting with large, unwieldy scrolls of two or three different versions of different books of the Pentateuch in front and beside him, plus whatever other written sources he was drawing on, with his eyes—and necessarily his body as well—moving back and forth and all around to select a phrase from one and a clause from another for the narrative that paralleled a story in Genesis, only to stop and insert a law from Numbers and another from Leviticus and another from Deuteronomy, and checking on different versions of each of those law-books.

In addition to requiring ancient "authors" as well as modern Qumran scholars to engage in highly complicated mental gymnastics, however, the "rewritten Bible" concept is based on (standard old) assumptions that are challenged (and rendered anachronistic) by the recent researches directly pertinent to the investigation of Judean scribal practice. Not only is the concept "Bible" anachronistic, but the very existence of texts such as the Temple Scroll and *Jubilees* along with the various versions of the books that were later included in the Bible suggests that the latter had only relative authority and were not the only sources of scribal knowledge of torah. If the number of MSS of particular "books" found at Qumran is any guide, *Jubilees* would appear to have been as authoritative ("scriptural") as Leviticus or Numbers. Scribes, moreover, had texts as well as parallel and additional materials that were not also written on scrolls accessible in memory for composition as well as recitation or application.

It makes sense, therefore, to explore scribal practice in our analysis of such texts as the Temple Scroll and 4QRP on the basis of appropriate new assumptions suggested by the relevant recent researches outlined above. Like scribes elsewhere in the ancient Near East, the Judean scribes who cultivated torah materials, including versions of "books" such as Genesis and Deuteronomy, could have accessed them memorially, without necessarily consulting written scrolls. Given the wide range of authoritative texts of torah and other torah materials in their cultural repertoire and the ongoing cultivation of the books of the Pentateuch in multiple versions, moreover, it seems evident that no particular version was sacrosanct and unalterable in a settled sequence and wording. Scribes apparently felt free to continue to adapt, or compose somewhat creatively on the basis of, already existing

23. Tov, "Biblical Texts as Reworked," 113–14, where he uses a modern composite of Masoretic, Samaritan, and LXX versions as his base-line "Biblical" text; Brooke, "Rewritten Bible," 778.

texts (just as earlier Mesopotamian scribes had done). They might follow a widely known sequence of events not confined to Genesis and Exodus, with some variations. Conscious of current practice in the temple or their particular scribal circle and/or in the interests of systematizing the diverse traditions of Torah, they might understandably combine laws on the same issues of purifications or sacrifices or festivals from different books, such as Leviticus and Numbers and Deuteronomy.

I suggest that the Temple Scroll or 4QRP or *Jubilees* could have been composed in just such a scenario. All I can do here is sketch the broad parameters of how the composers of *Jubilees* and the Temple Scroll may have worked with cultural materials in their memory.

### Alternative Torah—Jubilees *and Temple Scroll*

It is often said that the book of *Jubilees* takes its framework or structure and much of its contents from the narrative in the beginning of Genesis to the covenant-making scene at Sinai in Exodus 19.[24] But that is only a minimal and not a very determinative characterization of the book. While at points it appears to follow the wording of Genesis or Exodus closely (in a proto-Samaritan version), at others it is hardly even a paraphrase or allusion. It not only does not include much contained in Genesis and Exodus, but it includes a great deal not in those books. The book mentions matriarchs and other figures and places not known in Genesis. It includes stories about Abraham, for example, some of which appear also in the *Apocalypse of Abraham*.[25] Such materials suggest that the legendary lore behind Genesis was much broader than what was known from the book that was later included in the Bible. From the materials on Enoch not known from Genesis (4:15–26) it is evident that *Jubilees* was familiar with several of the writings attributed to Enoch, four of the five parts of what we know as *1 Enoch*.[26] It also makes use of *Aramaic Levi* or the Hebrew tradition behind it, and uses isolated passages in Isaiah and the Psalms. It is thus drawing on other authoritative texts (written texts?) in addition to Genesis and Exodus.

Most significant perhaps, with regard to the torah texts that were later included in the Bible, *Jubilees* almost systematically "relocates" legal materials from where they appear in Leviticus, Numbers, and Deuteronomy—that is, organizes legal material in ways different from what we are familiar with—to the points in its narrative of the patriarchs and matriarchs where

---

24. Nickelsburg, *Jewish Literature*, 69; VanderKam, *Jubilees*, 136.

25. VanderKam, *Jubilees*, 138–39.

26. Ibid., 137.

the issues that those legal materials address first appear in the sequence of episodes about the ancestors. The result in *Jubilees* is that the ancestors prior to Moses received revelation of and/or practiced the laws of (Mosaic) torah long before they were declared at Sinai. And those laws sometimes include rulings that do not appear in one of the legislative sections of the Pentateuch.[27] In a book that insists on strict observance of (Mosaic) torah the composers of *Jubilees* were free not just to rearrange legal materials and to add additional legislation, but to have these revealed before the definitive revelation of (the) torah at Sinai.

The Temple Scroll is a utopian charter for the (final) temple that God will construct. It is set in the covenant-making on Sinai in Exodus 24–31 or covenant renewal and construction of the tabernacle in Exodus 34–40. Description of the construction of the sanctuary and altar (cols. 3–13) is followed by a calendar of annual festivals and their sacrifices (13–29). Prescriptions for the construction of the temple display a different version of some of the descriptions of the tabernacle in Exodus 26 and 35, Solomon's temple in 1 Kings 6 and 2 Chronicles 3–4, and the ideal temple in Ezekiel 40–48. Instructions for festivals and their sacrifices are similar to some of those in Numbers 28–29 and Leviticus 23, but include prescriptions for festivals not mentioned in pentateuchal texts, and follow the 364-day calendar known also in *Jubilees* and *1 Enoch* 72–82. The next sections continue construction of the temple into huge courtyards and their buildings (cols 30–45), followed by a collection of purity laws for the temple and the city of Jerusalem (cols. 45–51). The final section (cols. 52–66) is another version of the legal teaching in Deuteronomy 12–23, which follows the order in Deuteronomy, adding pertinent materials at points, and expands significantly on "the law of the king" known in a shorter version in Deut 17:14–17.

The Temple Scroll is clearly a *constitutional* text (a text composed to "establish" or "institutionalize" a particular [ideal-future] political-religious order). Drawing on descriptions of the earlier tabernacle and Solomonic temple along with Ezekiel's ideal temple-design, it presents prescriptions for the utopian (eschatological) temple to be built by God, in which a system of courtyards and purity regulations protect the sanctity of the temple-cult, the priesthood, and the holy people. Festivals and sacrifices are expanded and enhanced beyond what was prescribed in the pentateuchal books that were already authoritative.[28] The elaborate design for the ideal new temple

---

27. See further ibid., 100–109.

28. Levine, "Mo'adim of the Temple Scroll," 62–64.

implies that the existing temple needs to be replaced, and revision of the codes in Deuteronomy implies that this new code is a replacement.[29]

The continuing composition of new texts of torah suggests strongly that the pentateuchal books had no monopoly on authority, either in the Qumran community or more widely in scribal and priestly circles. In fact, both the Temple Scroll and *Jubilees* claim higher authority than the pentateuchal books claim. Whereas the latter refer to God in the third person, the Temple Scroll has God speak in the first person. Its prescriptions for the temple, sacrifices, and purity regulations are all the very words of God, Moses serving merely as God's amanuensis. In fact in the Temple Scroll Moses is only *implicitly* the addressee, being in the same position as the general audience of God's direct address. *Jubilees* even more pointedly presents its historical narrative and legislation in a new setting: that of a revelation disclosed to Moses on Sinai, but revelation that had already been written on heavenly tablets and was dictated to Moses by the angel of the presence.[30] By presenting itself and its contents as having been written on heavenly tablets from the beginning of creation, and then dictated by an angel of the presence, *Jubilees* claims an authority far higher than the other books of Mosaic torah parts of which it drew upon. As represented especially in Ezra's formal ceremonial presentation and recital, the book of Mosaic torah held the authority of sacred writing as well as a constitutional function for the temple-state. Presumably the books of torah continued to carry this authority and function in the Judean temple-state, including scribal circles. The exhortation at the end of "Some Observances of the Torah" (4QMMT) appeals to just this authority as it calls upon its addressees to again acknowledge just this function of (the) Torah. The book of *Jubilees* claims an even higher authority than sacred writing. It claims to be a transcription of the ultimate in numinous writing, divine writing on heavenly tablets (as discussed in the previous chapter), writing that has the power to make history happen.

The effect of this claim to contain the very speech of God or the divine writing of the heavenly tablets is to relativize other books of (Mosaic) torah. The Temple Scroll dictated directly by God trumped books of torah produced by Moses.[31] The contents of the Mosaic books included in *Jubilees* are included in what had been inscribed on the heavenly tablets, so that they too share in the higher authority. But other legal materials were also included

---

29. Wacholder, *The Dawn of Qumran*; and Wise, *Temple Scroll*.

30. VanderKam, *Jubilees*, 11–12; 87–91, 136. See further the discerning discussion in Najman, *Seconding Sinai*, 53–68.

31. This is an important reason to think of these texts as texts of *torah* rather than "Mosaic discourse"; but cf. the arguments for the latter concept in Najman, *Seconding Sinai*, 9–16.

in the contents of the heavenly tablets, and particularly the solar calendar and its festivals, some of which are not mentioned in the pentateuchal books. Moreover, much of the legal contents of the pentateuchal books are revealed to patriarchs from the heavenly tablets, including in writing, long before they were revealed to Moses on Sinai, according to Exodus. Thus they have authority equal to, and in the antiquity of their revelation, prior to the Mosaic legislation. At points *Jubilees* even makes a distinction between itself and "(the book of) the first law/torah" (2:24; 6:22; 30:12).[32] Moses' own authority is in effect downgraded insofar as he appears as only a later one among many, such as Enoch, Abraham, Jacob, and Levi, who had the skill of writing and wrote books of torah that were transcripts of the heavenly tablets well before Moses received his legislation on Sinai.[33]

Whether related to their implicit claim to divine authority, the Temple Scroll and especially the book of *Jubilees* occupied an authoritative status in the Qumran community, judging from the many copies found and its quotation in other documents alongside books that were later recognized as biblical. This also suggests that the pentateuchal books had only relative authority, at least at Qumran and possibly in other circles. They may have been the principle sources of Mosaic torah, but there were other books of torah and all of those texts were grounded in and being further developed from a broader cultural tradition of (Mosaic) torah.

## Continuing Scribal Production and Cultivation of Legal Torah

That the books of the Pentateuch and alternative books of torah were cultivated orally as well as inscribed on scrolls helps us understand the importance of (rival?) scribal circles in ongoing generation of legal torah (teaching/rulings). Again the discoveries at Qumran offer a remarkably rich store of potential information about scribal practices. Three examples from Qumran texts and one mainly from Josephus can illustrate various ways that scribal circles derived, understood, perpetuated, and adapted legal torah.

In approaching these illustrative texts it is important to allow the meaning of particular terms to emerge from literary context, and not be determined by anachronistic scholarly assumptions. There was no Bible yet, so we cannot take certain books as "biblical." We cannot simply assume that the Hebrew word *torah* refers either to the books of the Pentateuch or to a text in written form. Depending on the literary context, *the torah* may refer

---

32. VanderKam, *Jubilees*, 136–37.

33. See further Najman, "Interpretation as Primordial Writing," esp. 388, 391, 399.

to a body of teaching that includes material in the Pentateuch, but may also include more. The term (*ha-*)*sefer* (of Moses) may not refer to the written books of the Pentateuch, but may refer, e.g., to the book of Deuteronomy. "It is written" in Hebrew (or in Greek) may be more of an appeal to the *authority* of the written text, which is being cited from memory. Many legal teachings and rulings and laws that appear in our written texts may have been derived from social practice (local custom), ceremonial practice (e.g., in the temple), and continued in social practice.

We may also want to question the standard impression that scribes were "interpreting" particular texts from a written copy of a pentateuchal book. The Qumranites did indeed practice interpretation of the prophetic books. But the *pešarim* are distinctive to their use of the prophets. We find nothing similar to this in texts such as the Community Rule, Damascus Rule, 4QMMT, or Temple Scroll. In sections of the Damascus Rule are many echoes and references to texts from the Pentateuch, prophets, and even the writings, as proof texts or exhortations to observe a teaching, etc., but not as interpretation of a specific text. So it is inappropriate, probably simply incorrect, to say that scribes/priests at Qumran were deriving their legal rulings (*halakot*) by exegesis from (written) texts of the Torah (Pentateuch).[34]

Several particular texts illustrate how scribes understood and adapted legal torah:

First, in Observations Concerning the Torah (4QMMT) some dissident scribes and priests first present their rulings on more than twenty matters of offerings, sacrifices, and purifications ("concerning X . . . we say Y . . ."). This text has been taken to contain "disputes over the interpretation and practice of the Torah."[35] It appears rather to be an appeal to authorities in the temple to break with their current practices of sacrifices and purifications in favor of the rulings presented. Only a few times does the text clearly have the term "it is written" (4Q395:10; 4Q397 [conflated with 4Q394]:27; 4Q296 1–2 iii [with conflations]:66; 4Q396 1–2 iv [conflated with 4Q397]:76). Other apparent instances in the translation are scholarly surmises about what stood in lacunae in the manuscript-fragments. In two cases no words of potential quotation are identifiable, another cites only one or two words (possibly from Jer 2:3), and in another a longer paraphrase states the issue, not a supposedly scriptural solution. The rulings in 4QMMT are derived not from texts of the Pentateuch, but from a combination of the dissident scribes' tradition of ceremonial practice and their own teachings. Only after laying out their rulings do the dissidents appeal to the authority

---

34. Schiffman, *Halakhah at Qumran*.

35. Nickelsburg, *Jewish Literature*, 147–49.

of "{the book of Moses} and the book[s of the pro]phets and Davi[d and all the events] of every age" (especially the kings)—again note the scholarly surmises—as part of a warning (evidently) to the temple authority(ies) about having violated the Mosaic covenant (4Q397:10–12, as reconstructed from 4Q398:14–17, which quotes Deut 30:1–2, evidently from memory). The "Deuteronomic" context suggests that the surmised "the book of Moses" may refer to Deuteronomy (not The Torah = Pentateuch). If the phrase "some of the observances of the torah" toward the end is a reference to their own rulings laid out earlier in the text, then they also understand their rulings to be in accordance with "the torah." But that would be only in a very general sense, since they do not present their rulings as derived from or interpretations of specific rulings in the Pentateuch.

Second, the Community Rule states that members are to be examined on their understanding and practice of the torah (1QS 5:20–21). The rules that the members are to observe in community life, in 1QS 6:24—9:12, however, are not derived from the Pentateuch. They do echo language of scriptural books, not surprising for those who have been reciting passages of "the book" (1QS 6:6–8). But the rulings are not citations or paraphrases or adaptations or applications of laws or teachings from books of the Pentateuch. Rather, the rulings are given on the authority of the leaders of the community itself as the renewal of Israel. Torah is to be recited regularly so as to inform interaction in the community. But obedience to torah is understood in a general way. This seems implied in the broad general statement of the way they are to walk in "the searching of the torah which God commanded by the hand of Moses that they may do according to all that has been revealed from age to age, and as the prophets have revealed by His Holy Spirit" (1QS 8:15–16; my adaptation of Vermes' translation). Members are to obey the scripture in general, with the *Rule* giving no attention to particulars. Meanwhile the leaders formulate new legal torah on their own authority specifically for the community.

Third, the Temple Scroll, on the other hand, takes over legal torah that derives from, or parallels material in, the books of the Pentateuch and other legal torah that comes from other texts (presumably of oral tradition). As noted above, moreover, it frames its new presentation of legal torah as derived directly from God and heavenly books, the "first" torah. Having a higher authority than the torah of Moses, it thus relativizes—or "trumps"— the books of the Pentateuch and, by implication, Moses himself. Far from appealing to the authority of the books of Moses, it may even have been intended as a replacement for the Pentateuch. The jury is evidently still out on what circle of scribes may have produced the Temple Scroll. It was not necessarily the Qumran community itself. If the books of the Pentateuch were closely linked with the (Hasmonean) temple-state, the Temple Scroll may well have been produced as an alternative by a dissident scribal circle. Whether or not there was overlap, the Qumran community originated as a dissident community of scribes and priests and at least at some point had hopes of replacing what they considered an utterly illegitimate high priesthood in Jerusalem. In that connection, some of the community's cultivation of Mosaic torah may well have been done by scribes anticipating that they would again serve (with) a legitimate priesthood in the temple.

Fourth, contemporary with the scribes and priests at Qumran was another circle of scribes that did serve in the temple-state, the Pharisees, known from the accounts of Josephus. Certain Qumran texts indicate that the Qumran community opposed a rival circle of scribes, the "smooth interpreters," who are usually thought to be the Pharisees. The three documents from Qumran just examined all give examples of scribal production and cultivation of legal torah, whether the preferred ceremonial practices of a dissident scribal circle (4QMMT) or rulings for intra-community relations (1QS 6–8) or a combination of legal torah from Pentateuchal books and legal torah from some other source(s). All of these are cases of oral cultivation of legal torah before and almost certainly continuing after it was written on scrolls. Josephus' accounts of the Pharisees mention their oral cultivation of legal torah that, so far as we know, was not also written on scrolls. And yet it was an integral component of official "state law."

> The Pharisees passed on to the people certain regulations (*nomima*) handed down from ancestors, which were not inscribed in the laws (*nomoi*) of Moses. And on account of this the Sadducees reject these (regulations), saying that it is necessary to adhere to those regulations that are written, but not to keep those from the tradition of the ancestors. (Josephus, *Ant.* 13.297–98, my trans.)[36]

Josephus says that John Hyrcanus "rescinded these [unwritten] regulations" that the Pharisees "established for the people" and excluded the Pharisees from his administration. Later he mentions that Alexandra Salome reinstalled the Pharisees to the administrations and restored their regulations as part of the laws of the temple-state (*Ant.* 13.405–409).

The implications of Josephus' account are that the Pharisees' oral rulings from the tradition of the ancestors were parallel to the written laws of Moses and that both were part of the official laws of the temple-state, although dependent on the pleasure of the high priest or other head of state.

36. An important study of the traditions of the elders is Baumgarten, "Pharisaic *Paradosis.*"

Again the authority of the written laws of Moses are relative and only one component among others of the legal torah operative in Judean society, alongside other legal torah cultivated mainly or only orally. There is no indication in Josephus' reports or in the Qumran texts that the oral legal torah was somehow derived from or interpretation of the written laws of Moses.

In sum, in late second-temple times scribes were cultivating legal torah in several parallel forms. The books of torah that were later included in the Bible had taken their distinctive forms, but continued in multiple textual versions, each of which was still developing. Far from their having enjoyed exclusive authority as scripture, however, scribes were composing alternative books of torah, some of which appear to have been intended to replace or supersede the books of the Pentateuch (hence to rival and replace their authority). That the alternative texts of torah drew on material that came from sources other than the pentateuchal books, some of them oral (not also written), points to the continuing cultivation of (Mosaic) legal torah orally. Some of this may not have been formed into discernible texts. But texts that were (also) inscribed on scrolls were also cultivated orally, taught and learned by oral recitation. Finally, both the Qumranites, as evident in 1QS, and the Pharisees, formulated and cultivated legal torah orally, the former for their own community life and the latter for the temple-state as well as themselves.

# 4

# ORAL COMPOSITION-AND-PERFORMANCE OF THE INSTRUCTIONAL SPEECHES OF BEN SIRA

For wisdom becomes known through speech,
and education through the words of the tongue.
—*SIRACH 4:24*

My tongue is like the pen of a skilled scribe.
—*PSALMS 45:2*

IN THE FIELD OF BIBLICAL STUDIES WE ASSUME THAT THE Wisdom of Jesus son of Sirach, like other "biblical books," was written, i.e., composed in writing, by an author named Yeshua ben Sira. It is assumed that writing was involved not just at the stage of collecting the component materials into a book, but throughout Ben Sira's learning and composition. Scholars assume, for example that influences on his teaching from earlier Judean or Greek or Egyptian culture came from his having read written texts, such as the book of Proverbs, or a written text of Theognis or of the Instruction of Phibis (Papyrus Insinger).[1]

References to reading and written texts are difficult to find, however, when we look at the teachings of the wise that are extant in writing.[2] Ben

---

1. As discussed, for example, by Middendorp, *Stellung Jesu Ben Siras*; Sanders, *Ben Sira*; Collins, *Jewish Wisdom*, 39–41.

2. I first noticed this in 1992 when working through Sirach in preparation for a SBL presentation. Among prominent scholars of wisdom literature that discuss the orality

Sira knows about writing. He mentions that the sacred vestments of the prototypical high priest Aaron included "precious stones engraved . . . to commemorate the twelve tribes of Israel" (45:11). He knows that ancestral figures had "put verses in writing" (44:4).[2] Yet he consistently and repeatedly represents his own teaching as oral and his students' learning as aural. The "children" receiving instruction are to "listen" to their father and mother (3:1–3).

> Listen to me, my child, and acquire knowledge,
> And pay close attention to my words. (16:24–25; cf. 31:22)

> For wisdom becomes known through speech,
> and education through the words of the tongue. (4:24)

The learning of fledgling scribes happens by listening to spoken discourse (6:23, 33–35; 8:8–9; 9:14–15). Ben Sira teaches in his "house of instruction" not by asking his students to open a book, but by "opening his mouth" (51:23–25). In a more public role, the sage instructs others as a skillful speaker (37:16–26). Indeed, according to the teaching of Ben Sira it seems that oral communication was dominant in the social ethos in general (5:10—6:1; 6:5; 14:1; 22:22, 27; 23:7–12; 27:11–15; 33:4; 37:16), as well as in the court and assembly (11:7–9; 15:5; 21:15–17).

The book of Proverbs represents learning similarly as happening by listening and holding the words in the heart (Prov 4:1–5; 5:12–13). In circles of learned scribes wisdom was communicated, not through reading and writing, but by speech (Prov 12:15, 18; 15:2, 31; 16:21, 23; 18:15; 23:12). Even in the section of "the words of the wise" where the teacher had "written" thirty sayings, learning happened by "inclining the ear" and having the words learned "ready on the lips" (22:17–21). The only use of the verb *katab* ("to write") is metaphorical or symbolic, that students should write their instruction on "the tablet of the heart" (Prov 3:3; 7:3).

These repeated references in Sirach and Proverbs to teaching and learning as oral–aural suggest that scribal instruction was oral (or, insofar as scribes were also trained to write and read, oral–written). The book of

---

of Ben Sira's instruction or in Proverbs are Crenshaw, "The Primacy of Listening in Ben Sira's Pedagogy"; *Education in Ancient Israel*, 177–83; and Fox, "Wisdom and the Self-Presentation."

3. The passage in Sir 48:10 that Elijah is to come at the appointed time to calm the wrath of God and restore the tribes of Jacob (48:10) is introduced by what appears to be a quotation formula, "it is written." But Wright, "Eschatology without a Messiah," 320, concludes that the Hebrew behind the Greek meant something more like "it is ordained," in the Wisdom of Ben Sira.

Ben Sira's wisdom, of course, was obviously written in the prototype(s) of the manuscripts from which derive the Hebrew and Greek manuscripts that form the basis of the modern critical text and translations—or we would not have it to read and interpret.[4] Yet it is difficult for us as modern scholars embedded in the assumptions and procedures of print culture to imagine how an ancient intellectual could have composed except in writing.[5]

In a sensitive and nuanced treatment, Michael Fox argues that the persistent references to speech and listening in Proverbs refer to the original instruction and to subsequent oral instruction that relies on written instructional materials. For the relation between the author(s) of Proverbs and the book's readers, however, orality is a rhetorical fiction. "Wisdom literature is self-consciously literate and does not envision oral transmission of memorized sayings."[6] The prologue to the book of Proverbs, he suggests, presents a complex layering of speakers and audiences. The audience of the book is "the callow or untutored child" (1:4). But "since a naïve untutored boy can hardly be expected to educate himself by independently studying the book," the book must be intended for the sage (1:5) who is to use the book to educate the young. So while the sage uses the medium of speech to instruct the "sons," the author of Sirach uses the medium of writing to address other wise teachers.[7]

Awkward for this hypothesis, however, is that in Prov 1:5 the sage is instructed not to read something written, but to hear something oral. As noted just above, the only reference to writing in Proverbs is to inscribing the instruction on the tablet of the heart (3:3; 7:3). The goal of instruction is to internalize the teaching. And as Fox explains, just as the parent/teacher instructs the child/student orally, so the parent/teacher had previously been instructed by his parent/teacher orally–aurally. Instruction obviously took written form in the anthologies of Proverbs and Sirach. But the continuing instruction did not cease to be oral–aural. The same "coexistence" and relationship existed in other texts as well. The Song of Moses was to be written down, but it was also to be taught to the people, "place[d] in their mouths"

---

4. If the cultivation of instructional wisdom was predominantly oral–aural, then perhaps Ben Sira's comment at the very end of his book (Sir 50:27), "Instruction in understanding and knowledge I have *written* in this *book*," refers to the compilation and *writing down* (not the composition) of his wisdom and hymns.

5. See, for example, the concluding reflections in Fox, "Wisdom and the Self-Presentation." For a pointed contrast between the print culture in which modern biblical scholarship is embedded and the oral sensitivities in which ancient scribal practice was embedded, see Kelber, "Jesus and Tradition, 140–41; and Ong, *Presence of the Word.*

6. Fox, "Wisdom and the Self-Presentation," 169–70, 163.

7. Ibid., 159–60.

(Deut 31:19–22).[8] And throughout the books of Exodus, Deuteronomy, and Joshua, Mosaic torah is to be written down, but also taught orally to the people, who were to internalize, recite, and observe it (e.g., Exod 17:14; 24.4–7, Deut 6:6–9; 11:18–21; 31:24–31; Josh 1:8; 8:30–35; 24). Is it possible that the self-presentation of Proverbs and Sirach as oral is more than rhetorical fiction? Is it possible that, while written copies of anthologies such as Proverbs and Sirach existed, the teaching and learning of the contents of such wisdom instruction were primarily oral–aural?

It should be possible to supplement Fox's sensitive discussion of the relation of written book and oral instruction with the suggestive results of the burgeoning recent research into orality and writing in the ancient world.[9] This research is inducing us to question some of the standard assumptions of biblical studies and to rethink our approaches to biblical texts. But it also offers possibilities of a fresh understanding of how the contents of cultural tradition were cultivated in relation to written texts that continued to develop.

First, in the ancient Near East and the Roman empire, literacy was limited mainly to the political and cultural elite.[10] Recent examination of Jewish literacy in Roman Palestine provides extensive documentation that writing and reading were confined mainly to administrative, scribal, and rabbinic circles, and those who used writing to enhance their own power and privilege.[11] Some have argued from archaeological evidence for widespread literacy in the later monarchy.[12] In the earlier ancient Near East, and in the history of Judah/Judea, however, writing was of interest mainly to

---

8. Fox, "Wisdom and the Self-Presentation," 164, citing comparative cases examined by Hurowitz, "Aspects of Oral and Written Transmission," 11–30.

9. Fox, "Wisdom and the Self-Presentation," 164–65, does use to advantage the collapse of the dichotomy between orality and literacy in important studies such as Niditch, *Oral World*.

10. See esp. Niditch, *Oral World*; and Harris, *Ancient Literacy*; and the refinement on different kinds and uses of writing in the essays in Beard, ed., *Literacy in the Roman World*.

11. Hezser, *Jewish Literacy*, with full documentation that underwrites shorter arguments that the extent and uses of literacy were severely limited in Galilean and Judean society, where communication was predominantly oral; e.g., Kelber, *The Oral and the Written Gospel*; Botha, "Greco-Roman Literacy"; Horsley, " Oral Communication Environment."

12. See, for example, Barkay, "Iron Age II–III," 349; Millard, "Evidence for Writing," 301–12; even with a more critical and nuanced sense of ancient writing, Schniedewind, *Bible Became a Book*, 91, 111, is still confident that "the use of writing spread throughout society" by the time of Josiah.

rulers and their administrators, to keep records of tax collection, to carry out official correspondence, and to enhance their culture.[13]

Second, scribes, the specialists in literacy and culture who were employed mainly in royal and temple administrations, produced different kinds of writing, but not necessarily for consultation and reading.[14] Some texts were written as legitimating charters to be laid up in temples. The "book of the teaching/covenant of Moses" that Ezra ceremonially presented to the people (who bowed before it) and then recited to them orally (Nehemiah 8) was a sacred, numinous document that served a constitutional function in authorizing the temple-state.[15] Even after certain texts of great authority in scribal and priestly circles existed in multiple written copies, they were not read but (ritually) recited in group gatherings. An important passage from the Community Rule at Qumran usually taken (and translated) by scholars to refer to the "study" of the Torah refers instead to ritual recitation, apparently of an authoritative text of torah:

> The many shall watch together for a third of every night of the year, to recite the book (*liqro' hasseper*), to search law/justice (*lidrosh mispat*), and to bless together (*lebarek beyahad*). (1QS 6:6–8)

Third, and only just becoming clear from recent studies of ancient Near Eastern and Judean texts and scribal practice, even the scribes, specialists in literacy, continued to cultivate orally texts that were also written, that is they learned and recited them orally. In an important application of emerging theory of the close interrelationship of orality and writing, Martin Jaffee discerned that scribes and priests at Qumran, like the later rabbis, had in effect "inscribed" authoritative texts on their memories as much as on their scrolls.[16] They possessed scrolls and knew how to make new cop-

---

13. See the critical survey of the kinds of evidence for writing in ancient Israel and Judah by Niditch, *Oral World*. In the ancient Mesopotamia of cuneiform writing and the Egypt of hieroglyphics literacy was even more narrowly confined, perhaps to one percent of the population, mainly those trained as scribes. See Larsen, "What They Wrote on Clay," 134; Baines and Eyre, "Four Notes on Literacy"; writing linked to the structure of Egyptian society in Baines, "Literacy and Ancient Egyptian Society"; and "Literacy, Social Organization."

14. The analysis of different kinds and functions of writing in Niditch, *Oral World*, is an important basis for a more nuanced further discussion of orality and writing in ancient Judea.

15. Discussed in Niditch, *Oral World*, 55, 103–6; and Horsley, "Origins of the Hebrew Scriptures," 112–14; cf. the discussion of the Domesday Book in medieval England in Clanchy, *From Memory to Written Record*, 18, 125.

16. Jaffee, *Torah in the Mouth*, chap. 2.

ies of texts, but they did not necessarily need to consult them in order to recite texts. Recent studies of ancient Mesopotamian and Egyptian texts are drawing similar conclusions about scribal practice. Scribal training and practice involved familiarity and copying of written texts. But emphasis lay on the memorization and oral recitation of texts, often in a wide-ranging cultural repertoire.[17] David Carr recently presented a sustained case that scribal practice in ancient Judea was more or less the same.[18] In the training and professional practice of scribes and sages, "written copies [of texts] were a subsidiary part of a much broader literate matrix, where the focus was as much or more on the transmission of texts from mind to mind as on transmission of texts in written form."[19]

It is just at this point, however, that we may reach an impasse. We biblical scholars so deeply rooted in the assumptions of print culture find it difficult to imagine, let alone understand, just how texts of wisdom may have been transmitted "from mind to mind." Studies of oral performance and of "oral-derived" texts in other academic fields such as ethnopoetics and ethnography of performance, however, may be suggestive. A foremost theorist of verbal art, John Miles Foley, whose work has already proven useful to the work of Niditch, Jaffee, and others, has synthesized creative work in several fields. Central to his theory is analysis of communication in the field of socio-linguistics, particularly the work of M. A. K. Halliday.[20] Fox has, in effect, explained that texts such as Proverbs 1–9 are oral-derived, i.e., originated in the oral teaching of the "author" to be again recited orally after being written down. And insofar as the material is wisdom instruction from parent/teacher to child/student, it is clearly communication (not just dead artifacts to be memorized by rote). Taking a few tips from Foley and the works he drawn upon, perhaps close attention to key aspects of communication in wisdom instruction can help us understand how this material was learned and transmitted orally. Accordingly we focus on the unit/form of communication, the message or the *text*, the typical *context* in which communication took place, and how the message is stated in a *register* of

17. For Mesopotamia see Veldhuis, *Education in Nippur*; Gesche, *Schulunterricht in Babylonien*. For Egypt, see Morenz, *Schriftlichkeitskulture*.

18. Carr, *Tablet of the Heart*, has summarized the results of studies by specialists on Mesopotamian, Egyptian, and other scribal cultures and drawn out their implications for scribal practice in Judah/Judea.

19. Carr, *Wax Tablet*, 5.

20. Most pertinent probably are Foley, *Imminent Art*; Foley, *Tales in Performance*; Foley, *How To Read an Oral Poem*; and Halliday, *Language as Social Semiotic*. For application of Foley's theory to biblical studies, see Culley, "Orality . . . Prophetic Texts"; and Horsley, "Recent Studies of Oral-Derived Literature."

language appropriate to the typical context (or topic) of communication, which would have been traditional in that (or any) society.

## The Form and Context of Ben Sira's Instructional Speeches

Wisdom has been understood in biblical studies primarily as proverbial wisdom. A deeply ingrained habit of focusing on individual verses, moreover, has reinforced a tendency among interpreters to identify the "literary genre" of Ben Sira's teaching narrowly as the *mashal* (proverb, aphorism, maxim, or saying).[21] Much of the prototypical wisdom book, Proverbs (10–22; 25–29), does indeed take the form of individual proverbs and maxims, with no obvious topical grouping involved and no discernible principles of organization. And it is often claimed that Sirach was modeled on the book of Proverbs.[22]

There is an inherent contradiction involved, however, in identifying the fundamental form and unit of Ben Sira's wisdom teaching as the individual proverb or maxim. The latter are not forms of interpersonal communication, which is virtually by definition involved in teaching. To function in communication, a proverb or maxim must be applied in some social and rhetorical context.[23] Interpreters' "mixed messages" with regard to the form of Ben Sira's wisdom, however, indicate that his teaching is more complex than individual sayings. Most interpreters still proceed verse by verse, saying by saying, focusing heavily on the theological and ethical. Yet some interpreters have noticed that proverbs are organized around themes,[24] or that Sirach includes "several short treatises."[25] Others organize their commentaries according to clusters of sayings grouped into stanzas, and even

21. DiLella, in Skehan and DiLella, *Ben Sira*, 21–27; cf. McKane, *Proverbs*, 3, that the fundamental form-critical unit of the instruction is the imperative or admonition; Crenshaw, *Old Testament Wisdom*, 17–19, similarly focuses on "proverbial sentences," having the older material in Proverbs 10–22 primarily in mind.

22. For example, Collins, *Jewish Wisdom*, 44. Indicative of the orientation of scholarly interpreters to individual saying is that they often discern certain "blocks of material" in Sirach or that the book is more "organized" than Proverbs 10–22 (e.g., Coggins, *Sirach*, 27), but do not analyze those "blocks" for rhetorical patterns.

23. Fontaine, *Traditional Sayings*, insisted that the field recognize the proverb comes alive only in the context in which it is applied, in its "performance meaning." This is true not only of proverbs in narrative, but in instructional speeches as well, as recognized by Fox, "Wisdom and the Self-Presentation," at least for proverbs in literary context in Proverbs 1–9. But the principle of contextual meaning should be even more obvious for oral performance, as in Ben Sira's speeches of instructional wisdom.

24. Middendorp, *Stellung Jesu Ben Siras*, 28; Sanders, *Ben Sira*, 54, 92–93.

25. Collins, *Jewish Wisdom*, 44.

draw attention to the fact that many clusters of such maxims or admonitions consist of twenty-two lines or bi-cola (the number of letters in the Hebrew alphabet).[26] Those are all pointers to the fact that virtually all of the instruction presented in the book of Sirach takes the form of *short speeches focused on particular topics*.[27] And in this regard the form of instructional wisdom in Sirach resembles that in certain sections of Proverbs (1–9; 22:17—24:34; and 31:10–31), which takes the form of speeches.

The instructional speeches in Sirach, moreover, (like those in Proverbs 1–9; 22:17—24:34; 31:10–31) assume variable patterns.[28] In each an argument, with various rhetorical devices, is easily discernible, although the particular structure of the argument may be different in nearly every speech. Yet the speeches have certain common typical features that can be readily detected and thus enable us to appreciate how their respective arguments proceed. The most basic form is an admonition followed by a motive clause, as in Prov 24:21–23. The admonition and/or the motive clause may be multiplied, and another, similar admonition may form an inclusio at the end of the speech. Often a proverb or maxim serves as an admonition or a sanctioning motive clause, as in Prov 24:3–6, where the final proverb provides the motive for the preceding ones. Maxims or proverbs and illustrative examples may reinforce the basic point made in the admonition(s). Often at the end of the speech a proverb or other saying can provide a sanctioning promise of reward or threat of punishment. This shifting back and forth from admonitions to proverbs and illustrative examples also involves a shifting from second person/imperative address to third person (which thus should not be taken as shifts to new units of communication). Similar patterns of speeches can be found in a wide range of instructional literature from the ancient Near East, particularly in Egyptian texts.[29]

The book of Proverbs includes a section of short, simple speeches (22:17—24:34) as well as the opening section of more complex speeches (1–9). Many of the latter are introduced by a call to the child/son (student) "to listen to/obey" the teaching of the father (teacher). In these speeches the series of admonitions with lengthy motive clauses that forms the main body

---

26. Some significant illustrations in DiLella, *The Wisdom of Ben Sira*.

27. Harrington, "Sirach and Qumran Sapiential Work A," more clearly than previous studies of Sirach, discerns that Ben Sira's wisdom instruction takes "the form of short packets or paragraphs on various topics." I use the term "speeches" to indicate that the teaching was oral, including that they are "oral-derived" in their current appearance in the anthology collected in Sirach.

28. This paragraph leans heavily on the critical discussion in Kirk, *Composition*, 93–151, with references to earlier treatments.

29. See further Kirk, *Composition*, 93–104, 130–51.

of instruction is followed by maxims or proverbs that state the consequences of wise or foolish behavior. The speech in Prov 5:1–23, for example, begins with the call to listen and motive clauses that announce the topic (5:1–2, 3–5). Then, following a brief renewed call (5:7), come two programmatic admonitions with extensive motive clauses (5:8–14; 5:15,16–19), followed by a rhetorical question and proverb (5:20, 21). The speech concludes with a double parable about the fate of the wicked (5:20–23).[30]

Ben Sira's speeches display similar patterns of argument. This suggests that he stands in a tradition of learned scribes who delivered their instruction in speeches comprised of various configurations of admonitions, motive clauses, and maxims. The contours of particular speeches of varying length are discernible in most of the book of Sirach. The coherence as well as the variation in pattern can be illustrated from speeches on various issues.[31]

The speech on honoring one's parents in 3:1–16 opens with an appeal to "listen" to the father/teacher coupled with an appeal to the children's self-interest (3:1), followed by a maxim as a motive clause (3:2). Three parallel bicola of maxims in the form "those who honor/respect their father/mother" (3:3–7) then set up the principal admonition to "honor your father" in the center. with motive statement (3:8–9), followed by another admonition with motive clause (3:10) and a maxim that functions as a further motive statement (3:11). The speech concludes with a call that includes a detailed admonition to "help your father in his old age . . ." (3:12–13), followed by a similarly complex motive statement (3:14–15) and a double "whoever . . ." maxim as a divine sanction (3:16).

The speech on seeking wisdom in 6:18–37, one of several with twenty-two bicola, develops in three steps, each with the opening address to "my child" (6:18–22, 23–31, 32–37). The first step moves from opening admonitions and motive clause (6:18–19) to maxims that provide counter-instances (6:20–22). The second stacks up admonitions (6:24–27), followed by motive clauses (28–31). The third, starting with parallel conditional admonitions (6:32–33), offers two examples of how to become wise (6:34–37a), the latter of which leads to the concluding reward of wisdom (6:37b). Insofar as the multiple motive statements in 6:28–31 form a fitting climax or "pay-off" to the discipline called for in 6:18 that entails "fetters" and bonds" in 6:24–25, it is conceivable that the first two steps originally comprised a complete speech. The third step could have formed a complete speech on its own exploring the discipline that leads to wisdom. Yet the statement in 6:37 forms

---

30. See ibid., 101–3.

31. Helpful analysis of the speeches in Sir 15:11–20; 27:30—28:7; and 39:13–35, in Kirk, *Composition*, 143–48.

a suitable conclusion to 6:18-37 as a whole, with "wisdom" as an *inclusio* corresponding to the goal of the "discipline" in 6:18.

The speech about scribes' association with the wealthy and powerful in 13.1–13 begins with a warning proverb that sets up the general admonition not to associate with one more powerful. Another proverb illustrates the danger (13:1-2), and an additional proverb and several other sayings illustrate the exploitative behavior of the rich (13:3-7). After several more illustrative admonitions, followed by a motive clause (13:8-11), come another maxim and a concluding general admonition sanctioned by a warning motive-clause (13:12-13).

A speech on properly disciplining a child in 30:1-13 begins with three statements in the form of "He who whips/disciplines his son" with beneficial results (30:1-3), followed by three more statements of the results (30:4-6). Then the teacher gives a statement of and proverbs illustrating the counter-instance of "spoiling his son" (30:7, 8, 9) and moves into admonitions with motive clauses about the results (30:10-13).

Some speeches consist almost completely of one proverb after another, some of which serve as motivation (showing the good and bad result of certain behavior), followed perhaps at the end by admonitions that apply them to the student's own behavior. Such are the speech on taking care what one says (curbing one's tongue, watching one's mouth, 28:13-26), the speech(es) on the good (and bad) wife (26:1-9, 13-18), and the warning against selling and buying (26:29—27:3).

Discerning these variable but clear patterns in Ben Sira's speeches should enable us better to appreciate that they were delivered orally.[32] There are clear signs, of course, that such poetic speeches, a fundamental expression of scribal culture, were influenced by the literacy in which learned scribes specialized. Principle among these is the fact that some of the speeches in Sirach (such as the speech on seeking discipline sketch above, Sir 6:18-37; cf. 1:11-30), like many in Proverbs 1-9, were composed in 22 lines or bi-cola (two parallel lines, usually synonymous). The closing, autobiographical poem, like the speech on the "good wife" at the end of Proverbs, is a well-crafted alphabetic acrostic of 23 bicola (with *pe* duplicated).[33] Other

---

32. The speeches in the book of Sirach would be examples of texts described as "oral derived texts" or "voices from the past." See the analysis and discussion in Foley, *Tales in Performance*; and *How to Read an Oral Poem*, esp. 22-53.

33. Directly pertinent and illuminating of such poems/speeches is Hanson, "Alphabetic Acrostics," esp. 47; he discusses the proposals made by Skehan ("Song of Moses," 160n13) and Murphy (*Wisdom Literature*, 173) that the final *pe* makes the first, middle, and final letters spell *aleph*—the first letter of the alphabet and the word meaning "to teach, learn."

features, however, mark Ben Sira's speeches clearly as oral communication. Among these are the frequent assonance, alliteration, and rhyme evident in the Hebrew, and often discernible even in the Greek text and in English translations (examples evident in the speeches outlined just above would be words and sounds in 6:19; 13:1, 2.). Chiastic patterns are occasionally evident (e.g., in 6:22, 37). And the repetition of a key term or an idea in both the opening and closing lines often constitutes an *inclusio* that ties the whole speech together as a coherent unit of communication.[34]

That instructional wisdom in the book of Sirach takes the form of short speeches on particular topics means that it is inappropriate to take sayings or "verses" in isolation, separated from the speeches of which they are integral components. To discern how Ben Sira's speeches were designed to persuade it is necessary for interpreters to appreciate their rhetoric. A proverb used in a speech has a rhetorical function in the speech as a whole, which will go undetected if it is interpreted it as if it had a meaning in itself.

Ben Sira's speeches cannot be appreciated as oral instruction, however, in purely formal terms. A particular message or text in any communication is addressed to a context, but this is all the more important in oral communication. Narrowly speaking the context may be "literary" or rhetorical and often a stereotyped and typical one. But the context of teaching is also always social, even political. Ben Sira's speeches offer numerous indications that the social-political context of his teaching was the training of scribes to serve among the rulers of Judean society.[35] In the most informative speech (38:24—39:11) he boasts that the standing of learned scribes with leisure to learn wisdom is respectably above those who support a city economically with their manual labor, but below and indeed in service to the rulers of the society. Passing references in many other speeches indicate that the learned scribes function as advisers and administrators for the collective aristocracy (38:32–33; 6:34; 7:14; 15:5; 21:17). Yet they have at least some ability and responsibility to defend the poor against the worst effects of exploitation by the powerful (4:1–10; 7:32; 13:18–23; 29:1–20; 34:24–27). That Ben Sira makes exhortations about dutiful payment of tithes and offerings (7:29–31; 35:1–12; 45:20–21), on the one hand, yet cautions his listeners about their vulnerability to the rulers, on the other (4:7; 13:8–11; 31:12–24; 32:9), suggests that they were economically dependent on the ruling aristocracy.

34. See further DiLella, *The Wisdom of Ben Sira*, 64–74.

35. See the more extensive analysis and discussion of evidence derived from Ben Sira, critically evaluated in comparison with studies of other agrarian societies some of which seem similar in political-economic structure (along with a critique of historical sociological models) in Horsley and Tiller, "Ben Sira and Sociology."

The topics of the speeches, moreover, cohere around the relationships and special interests of scribes and sages.[36] The prominent topics of seeking wisdom/discipline, fear of the Lord as the beginning of wisdom, and vigilance about speech (tongue, mouth, gossip, slander) are all distinctive to scribes and scribal training. As Ben Sira says with scribal pride, those who labor with their hands, such as artisans, do not have the leisure for the pursuit of wisdom (38:24), and it is the wise scribes whose role it was both to speak in councils and to take care lest they offend their superiors. It might seem that topics such as disciplining children, honoring parents, good and bad wives, and friendship would pertain to the general populace. A closer look at the specific contents of Ben Sira's speeches on these topics, however, suggests that these familial and social relations are particular to those in the scribal role. And speeches focused on the topic of domestic servants or slaves would hardly have been pertinent to peasants and artisans who themselves worked close to the level of subsistence. Finally, speeches on topics such as association (dining and drinking) with the wealthy and powerful, warning against selling and buying, economic relations between the very rich and the poor, and exhortations to look out for the poor are all specially pertinent to the mediating role that scribes played in the Judean political-economic-religious structure.[37]

Confirmation that the social context of Ben Sira's speeches was scribal training comes from recent studies of scribal practices evident in Mesopotamian and Egyptian texts. Even in those more complex large-scale societies the education of scribes took place not in separate "schools" with professional "teachers," but in an apprenticeship-like atmosphere in homes of scribal masters; and, as Carr argues, scribal training in Judah/Judea must have been similar.[38] The teacher was the "father" (and sometimes "mother"), literally or figuratively, and the student was a "child/son" in what was probably a mainly hereditary profession in service of a monarchy or temple. And scribal training was as much or more an enculturation into the distinctive ethos of scribal service. Nearly all of the speeches on the topics covered in Ben Sira's instruction fit in what must have been just such a process of "socialization" and "character-formation" of apprentice scribes in second-temple Judea.

36. Rather than categorizing Ben Sira's teaching according to standard theological categories, such as "ethics," "the problem of evil," etc., as practiced in interpretation of the scriptures for modern appropriation (e.g., in Collins, *Jewish Wisdom*), I am attempting to discern the function and context of his speeches on particular topics in second-temple Judean society.

37. See further Kovacs, "Is There a Class-Ethic in Proverbs?"

38. Carr, *Tablet of the Heart*, 12–13, 21, 31–34, 67, 113.

## Traditional Registers of Speech Dedicated to Standard Topics of Instruction

Closely related to the form and context of Ben Sira's wisdom as short speeches in the "house of (scribal) instruction" is the appearance of multiple speeches on key topics in which he repeats many of the same images, motifs, and phrases and even similar lines. Where Proverbs has speeches and/or individual sayings on the same topics as Sirach, moreover, they also contain many of the same images and motifs and even variant versions of the same proverbs, maxims, or admonitions. There was evidently a particular standard set of language for each topic of instruction.

This, of course, is similar to what socio-linguistics has observed about communication in general.[39] Spoken or written language is keyed to particular typical contexts of communication. The one major variable, determined by social location or class, is usually called *dialect*. The speech of upper class people differs from that of urban workers or rural peasants. There are also local and regional dialects, although these can disappear in some modern societies under the influence of mass media. The other major variable is the style of speech determined by the typical situation or activity or set of relations to which speech is addressed. For this socio-linguists use the term *register*.

The concept can be illustrated more easily than explained. In modern American society a distinctive language is dedicated to the stock market report, another to theatre criticism. Within the general register of sports broadcasts, further, particular sets of language are devoted to particular sports, such as football or tennis. Similarly there is a distinctive set of language appropriate for worship in churches and synagogues, and more particular registers for particular contexts, such as funerals or weddings or, within the general register of the mass, the particular sets of language for adoration or penitential prayer or offering.[40]

In the Judean tradition of wisdom teaching, similarly, there was a general register of speech appropriate to the instructional context, and within that were distinctive sets of language appropriate to particular topics such as friendship or honoring parents. Each of these particular "registers" of

39. Socio-linguistic theory of communication in general, such as Halliday, *Language as Social Semiotic*, has been adapted for the appreciation of oral performance by ethnographers and others. Foley has integrated some of these efforts in a theory of verbal art in *Imminent Art*; *Tales in Performance*; and *How to Read an Oral Poem*.

40. Helpful broad general discussion of register in relation to context and tradition in Foley, *Immanent Art*, 2–60; adapted to biblical studies in Culley, "Orality and Writtenness," 50–51, 56–64; Horsley, "Studies of Oral Derived Literature," 168–70.

speech, moreover, was rooted in its own deep tradition. Particular registers included proverbs and standard admonitions that focused on particular concerns of scribal culture, such as acquiring wisdom, speaking, or relations with powerful patrons, or on typical familial and social relations, such as husbands-wives, parents-children, rich-poor. The idiom and imagery of each register thus depended on the particular relationship in focus. Over many generations scribal teachers had generated a store of illustrative examples of the consequences of certain behavior in those basic relationships, often formulated in proverbs and maxims. Given the larger context of relations with the divine, nature, and social custom, particular speech-registers had developed typical sanctions or motive-clauses that fit particular topics.

Classical rhetorical culture offers somewhat of an analogy to Ben Sira's instructional speeches on typical topics and their distinctive language registers. Walter Ong attempted sometime ago to remind scholars in biblical studies and the humanities generally that from classical times until the demise of rhetoric in western education, much of western culture was comprised by "commonplaces," *loci communes*.[41] As we know not only from a Cicero or a Quintilian but also from Renaissance humanists such as Erasmus who codified them, Greek and Latin orators cultivated a stock of material on a wide variety of topics such as honesty, loyalty, treachery, and "things-are-going-to-hell" upon which they drew in composing-and-performing orations. Such traditional materials were grouped, for easy memory and recall, around typical social relations and interaction and evolved in a plethora of formulaic phrases and sayings and examples. The cultural memory at the disposal of orators was thus organized according to standard topics and the discourse (terms, motifs, phrases, proverbs, exempla) dedicated to each. Individual orators such as Cicero formed set pieces out of the general cultural store of these topical registers on a whole range of topics in advance and stored them in their minds (and sometimes in writing) for use in public orations or court cases. In their concern for fluency in their own rhetoric (*copia*), Renaissance humanists made books of snippets of classical rhetoric on a myriad of topics, hence the term "copybook."

Instead of formulating set pieces on various topics to combine into longer orations, Ben Sira used the standard registers devoted to standard topics to formulate short speeches aimed to inculcate scribal character and to socialize the fledgling scribe into the scribal ethos of service to the temple-state. The book of Sirach can thus be understood as a collection of "commonplaces" of Judean scribal instruction, a collection of short speeches

---

41. Ong, *Presence of the Word*, 56–57, 79–87.

formulated out of the traditional topical registers stored in the memory for easy access in the composition and performance of instructional wisdom.

Our ability to discern and appreciate the many distinctive registers of language dedicated to particular topics from which Ben Sira composed his instructional speeches is hampered by the limited amount of extant instructional wisdom. For ancient Judea, the latter is confined largely to the books of Proverbs and Sirach.[42] Our procedure here is thus limited to (while made possible by) an examination of the parallel speeches on several topics that appear in Sirach itself and/or parallel speeches or proverbial wisdom on the same topics in Proverbs and occasionally comparative Egyptian instructional texts. After gaining an appreciation of the particular sets of language devoted to several different topics for which we have multiple speeches and/or other sapiential materials we can then begin to sense how speeches on other topics are similarly rooted in certain distinctive sets of language. By this procedure we can perhaps begin to appreciate that Ben Sira commanded a general repertoire of instructional wisdom constituted by a range of different registers of speech, and how he would have composed and delivered speeches on particular topics by drawing on these registers at his command.

It is awkward and difficult to represent the sounds and extra-textual features of oral teaching in the print medium. We can take some cues from ethnographers such as Dennis Tedlock and Dell Hymes, who focused on oral performance of epic poetry or simple storytelling.[43] For a more complete appreciation of Ben Sira's speeches we should be dealing with the patterns of words and sounds in parallel lines in the original Hebrew, or in the Greek translation where the Hebrew is not available. To appreciate the basic reality of the dedicated sets of language (images, motifs, proverbs, etc.) in which speeches on given topics were couched, however, we can work with English translation accessible to readers who lack familiarity with Hebrew or Greek. It is possible here only to summarize the analysis discursively with selected illustrations.

---

42. In a more extensive and longer-range study it might be possible to find further evidence in Job, Ecclesiastes, and a few later Judean texts, and to find supporting evidence in the richer supply of instructional wisdom from Egypt and Mesopotamia. Earlier studies on related subjects, such as Sanders, *Ben Sira;* and Humbert, *Sources egyptiennes*, provide a good start. Archaic Greek culture probably had parallel registers for parallel topics of instruction, an exploration that could begin from the study of Middendorp, *Stellung Jesu Ben Siras.*

43. Tedlock, *Spoken Word;* Hymes, "Ways of Speaking."

*Friendship*

The five speeches on friendship in Sirach offer one of the most obvious cases of a distinctive register of language. Without taking the space to print out all of these speeches, we can take note of several lines in each that include some of the key images, motifs, and phrases devoted to this topic (printed in bold for easier identification, underlined where repeated in parallel lines). To appreciate the traditional character of this language, we first take note of some older proverbs on friendship that would presumably have been familiar to Ben Sira as he formulated these speeches.

One who **forgives an affront** fosters friendship,

> but one who dwells on disputes will alienate a friend. (Prov 17:9)

A **friend loves at all times, and kinsfolk are born to share adversity**. (17:17)

Some **friends play at friendship**

> but a **true friend sticks closer than one's nearest kin.** (18:24)

**The poor are disliked even by their neighbors,**

> but **the rich have many friends**. (14:20)

**Wealth brings many friends,**

> **but the poor are left friendless.** (19:4)

If **the poor are hated even by their kin,**

> how much more are they shunned by their friends. (19:7; cf. Job 19:19–21)

This same set of terms is easily detectable in the longest speech on friends in Sirach, in 6:5–17:

> . . . gain **friends** through testing,
>
> > and **do not trust** them hastily. (v. 7)
>
> . . . **friends** when it suits them,
>
> > but they will <u>**not stand by you in time of trouble**</u>. (v. 8)
>
> . . . **friends who change into enemies,**
>
> > and tell of the quarrel to your disgrace. (v. 9)
>
> . . . sit at your table,
>
> > but will <u>**not stand by you in time of trouble**</u>. (v. 10)
>
> **When you are prosperous** they become your second self . . .
>
> > but if you are **brought low,** they turn against you . . . (vv. 11–12)
>
> Keep away from your **enemies,**
>
> > and **be on guard with your friends.** (v. 13; cf. not trusting in v. 7)
>
> <u>**Faithful friends**</u> are . . . (repeated three times in vv. 14–16)

Some of the same key motifs and images are evident again in the speech in 12:8–18:

> **A friend is not known in prosperity,**
>
>> nor **an enemy hidden in adversity.**
>
> One's **enemies are friendly when one prospers,**
>
>> but in **adversity** even one's friend disappears.
>
> **Never trust your enemy** . . .
>
>> take care to **be on your guard** . . .
>
> An **enemy** speaks sweetly . . .
>
>> but in his heart he plans . . . evil. . . (12:8–12,16–17)

The speech in 22:19–26 focuses on alienation and reconciliation, while sharing with the other speeches the motifs of trust and adversity/poverty. Along with common elements, the speech in 27:16–21 includes the theme of betraying secrets. The fifth speech, in 37:1–6, focuses on the common theme of being a friend in name only, but not in time of trouble. These speeches attest a common traditional set of images, motifs, and even phrases devoted to the topic of friendship that Ben Sira drew upon as he composed them.[44]

### Seeking Wisdom

The book of Sirach also includes several speeches on seeking and finding wisdom. Each of the speeches has distinctive features. Yet they all draw on the same motifs, images, and phrases and combine them in similar ways. This suggests that there was a standard traditional discourse dedicated to the topic of seeking and finding wisdom. In attempting to appreciate this particular register and how it informs all of these speeches we can take two interrelated steps.[45]

First, we chart key motifs and images that occur prominently, in somewhat different sequence, in the speeches devoted to this theme, with parallels in traditional proverbs. There may be some risk in relying on a chart of textual parallels, since such charts have previously been used to indicate words written in scrolls or books. Perhaps, however ironically, it will be possible for us modern readers, from this visual medium, to appreciate

---

44. The register of Judean instruction on friendship (and other topics) was surely influenced in indirect ways, requiring reexamination of possible influence by explicit reading of manuscripts, by earlier Egyptian instruction on friendship. Critical reexamination could begin from the pointers in earlier studies such as Sanders, *Ben Sira*, 64.

45. Pertinent here is Johnson, *Seeking the Imperishable Treasure.*

how composition in the oral medium would have worked from a register of language deeply embedded in the cultural memory of Ben Sira.

### Key Images in 'seeking wisdom' register.

| | Sir 4:11–19; | 6:18–37; | 14:20–15:10; | cf. Proverbs |
|---|---|---|---|---|
| Wisdom as teacher (mother), | | | | |
|   wise as students/children | 4:11a; | 6:32; | 15:2 | Prov 3:11 |
| ways/paths of wisdom | (4:17, 19) | 6:26b | 14:21, 22 | Prov 4:11–14, 18–19, 26–27 |
| Wisdom as house/tent | | | | Prov 7:6ff; 9:1 |
|   gates/doors, windows | | | 14:22–24 | |
| wisdom as tree (24:13–17) | | | 14:26–27 | |
|   (3:18, tree of life) | | | | |
| Wisdom as mother, bride, wife | | 6:32 | 15:2 | cf. Prov 1:20–33; 7:4 |
|   giving bread and drink (1:16) | | | 15:3 | Prov 9:2–6 |
| wise as children | 4:11 | 6:18, 23, 32 | (15:2–4) | |
| wise as seekers | 4:11b, 12 | 6:27a | (14:22ff) | |
| wise love wisdom | 4:12ff | | | Prov 3:16, 18; 8:17, 35 |
| secrets | 4:18b | | 14:21 | |
| discipline, toil | | 6:18–19, 32 | | Prov 5:12 |
|   yoke/fetters | | 6:24–25, 29–30 | | |
|   trial, torture, torment: | 4:17; | 6:20a,21a | | Prov 3:11–12 |
| wise exalted/crown/glory/name | 4:13a; | 6:29–31; | 14:5,6; | Prov 4:8–9 |
|   (1:18, 19; 39:9–11) | | | | |
| inherit/obtain wisdom, etc. | 4:16; | 6:18b, 33, 37; 15:1, (7) | | |
|   fruits | | 6:19bd | | |
| eloquence in assembly | | | 15:5 | |
|   (1:30) | | | | |
| contrast with fools, sinners, etc. | 4:19a | 6:20–21 | 15:7–9 | |
|   ruin/destruction/Hades | 4:19b | | | |
| relate to Wisdom, relate to God | 4:14 | | | Prov 8:35 |

Second, we supplement the chart of key images and motifs of the "seeking wisdom" register with other indications of how Ben Sira was drawing on traditional language and even standard phrases in composing his speeches on this topic. In the speech in 4:11–19, in which virtually all the images and phrases are directly from the standard register, the introductory lines (in an artful a-b-c-b'-a' pattern) provide an especially good example of how Ben Sira could compose in a traditional idiom.

> Those who love her love life;
>> those who seek her out win the Lord's favor.
> Those who hold her fast inherit glory;
>> wherever they dwell, the Lord bestows his blessing.
> Those who serve her serve the Holy One;
>> those who love her, the Lord loves. (Sir 4:12–14, DiLella)

Several lines from the earlier instructional speeches on seeking wisdom in Proverbs 1–9 illustrate the rich resource of standard phrases and images that Ben Sira was drawing on.

> Long life is in her (wisdom's) right hand,
>> in her left hand are riches and honor. (Prov 3:16)

> She is a tree of life to those who lay hold of her,
>> and those who hold her fast are called happy. (3:18)

> I (Wisdom) love those who love me,
>> and those who seek me diligently find me. (8:17)

> Whoever finds me finds life
>> and obtains favor from the LORD. (8:35)

In the speech in 6:18–37, the opening address of each of the three sections ("my child/listen my child") immediately signals the register of 'seeking wisdom,' just as it had in the earlier speeches in Proverbs 1–9. Virtually all of the ensuing images and motifs are derived from the distinctive language devoted to this topic. In 6:33, for example, "My child, . . . If you love to listen you will gain knowledge, and if you pay attention you will become wise" sounds like Ben Sira's more elaborate version of what must have long been a standard admonition, as in Prov 8:32–33 ("And now, my children, listen to me . . . Hear instruction and be wise"). In contrast with 4:11–19, the speech in 6:18–37 is striking for the creative special emphases and twists Ben Sira gives to the traditional register. For example, he downplays the toil and harshness of the discipline that the wise choose, displacing them to the fools, who are the standard foils in such discourse (6:20–21). The next step of the speech, again adapting standard images, acknowledges the typical difficulties of wisdom's discipline, but insists that the search will result in rest and peace, the fetters become a defense and the collar a glorious robe, indeed a royal cord and crown (6:23–31). In the final step, Ben Sira supplies his own special understanding of what the discipline of wisdom consists, i.e. meditating on the commandments of the Lord as well as gaining knowledge from the discourse of the wise (6:32–37).

In the longest speech, 14:20—15:10, the opening in 14:20 illustrates how traditionally formulaic this language register was ("Happy the person(s) who meditate on/find wisdom," cf. Prov 3:13).[46] A few lines later (14:23–24), Ben Sira uses the standard images of "peering through her windows/listening at her doors/tenting near her house" that are widely attested in discourse on seeking wisdom (e.g., Prov 7:6–7; 8:34; 9:1; Job 8:22; 22:23; 29:4; Cant 9:2). The complex metaphor of wisdom as the mother and/or bride who feeds with the bread of learning and water/wine of wisdom (15:2–3) was similarly a standard component of the register ready for Ben Sira to utilize (Prov 5:18; 7:1–6; 9:5; Cant 4:9, 12; 5:1–2).

The alphabetical acrostic speech about seeking wisdom placed at the conclusion of the book of Sirach and found also in a Psalms scroll at Qumran (11QPs^a) also utilizes most of the images and motifs in this register. In the "autobiographical" first person, the sage speaks of avidly seeking wisdom and walking on her path (51:13–15, 19–21). The speech characterizes wisdom herself less elaborately than the others, picking up only the images of wisdom (or God) as teacher and as supplying food and drink (51:17, 24). As in 6:18–37, so here the toil under her yoke is not burdensome (51:18, 26–27), while the results of obtaining wisdom and eloquence in instruction (51:21–25) and the rewards of serenity and wealth (51:27–28, 30) are great. The possibility that this speech is not from Ben Sira himself only enhances the point that these speeches are all composed in the standard traditional idiom of the register of "seeking (and finding) wisdom."

### Fear of the Lord as the Beginning of Wisdom

Ben Sira's multiple speeches on the fear of the Lord as the beginning of wisdom enable us to hear not only the distinctive register in which he was speaking, but the way he (or the line of teachers in which he stood) worked creatively with it. That this identification was already a standard theme in instructional wisdom is evident from its frequent appearance and crucial placement in the speeches in Proverbs 1–9 (esp 1:7 and 9:10; cf. 1:29, 2:5,

---

46. Hanson ("'How Honorable!' 'How Shameful'") suggests "honorable" as a more appropriate translation.

etc.) and at the conclusion of the wisdom speculation in Job 28 (cf. Ps 110:10). In one of his speeches on the traditional topic (34:14–20) Ben Sira stays with the evidently standard language of health, life, blessing, and other rewards that flows from fear of the Lord as wisdom.

In three other speeches (1:11–30; 19:20-24; and 32:14—33:3), however, he combines fear of the Lord as wisdom with fear of the Lord as keeping the commandments/torah. In Deuteronomy, on the other hand, "fear of the Lord" had become synonymous with hearing God's words, walking in his ways, and keeping the commandments (e.g., 4:9–10; 8:5–6; 10:12, where there is no mention of wisdom, even though in other passages in Deuteronomy keeping the commandments is identified with wisdom). Ben Sira simply assumes the three-way identification, which is central to instructional wisdom, as can be seen in several variant formulations (15:1; 19:20; 21:11; cf. 23:27; 25:10–11). The short speech in 19:20-24 is almost barebones in its tight focus on the identification of wisdom with fear of the Lord and keeping the law.

The embellishment of the three-way identification as a creative adaptation of the traditional register of fear of the Lord as wisdom (as in 34:14–20) can be heard in the two longer speeches in 1:11–30 and 32:14—33:3. The speech in 32:14—33:3, which, after an opening reference to wisdom, emphasizes the keeping of the torah, then focuses on the same benefits of health, blessing, a secure basis of life, and divine favor and deliverance integral to the language dedicated to fear of the Lord as wisdom in 34:14–20. In the longest and most programmatic speech (placed as a preface to the book of Sirach in 1:11–30), the identification of the fear of the Lord with (the beginning of) wisdom is stated in 1:14 and again 27, with variations (fullness/crown/root of wisdom) in 1:16, 18, 20. Again the language dedicated to this topic features the many blessings of happiness, health, abundance, fame and glory (especially 1:11–20). This speech also includes some language from the register devoted to the topic of seeking wisdom, perhaps not surprising when the topic here is the wider identification of and dedication to wisdom. In addition to the basic three-way identification in the other speeches, Ben Sira's creativity here includes also includes reference to the professional reputation of aspiring scribal addressees in his concluding admonitions (1:28–30).

These speeches on fear of the Lord and keeping the law as the equivalent of wisdom are not as similar to one another as the speeches exhorting students to seek wisdom. Yet they all do develop the same theme, with varying emphases, by using the same basic motifs and phrases. We can sense how the scribal teacher, Ben Sira, makes creative innovations even as he composes these speeches from the standard traditional register of language dedicated to the topic of fear of the Lord as wisdom.

### Guarding the Tongue and Subtopics

Sirach includes a number of speeches on discretion in the use of one's "mouth," "lips" or "tongue" in various connections (for example, 5:9–12; 19:5–17; 23:7–15; 28:13–26). Previous generations of scribes had left a rich store of proverbs dealing with speech in its different aspects (e.g., Proverbs 10:11, 19, 20, 31, 32; 12:6, 13, 18, 19; 16:21, 23, etc.). This is understandable, since communication was predominantly oral in antiquity, and learned scribes depended on speaking, along with writing, for their economic livelihood: "The lips of the righteous feed many, but fools die for lack of sense" (Prov 11:21). Indiscretion in speech could be costly: "Those . . . who open wide their lips come to ruin" (Prov 13:3). In his speeches on speech, Ben Sira thus built on a register rich with proverbs as well as certain images distinctive to the use of the mouth. The latter are evident in Ben Sira's petition to "the Father and Master of my life" to "set a guard over my mouth. . .so that my tongue may not destroy me" (22:27—23:3). In prayer as well as instructional speech about speech, Ben Sira composed with the typical images and phrases of the register devoted to the topic.

   Speech about speech appears to have become divided into sub-topics, and its register into sub-registers in the tradition on which Ben Sira draws in his composition. The introduction to the speech in 23:7–15, beginning with the signature instructional "lead-in," signals the general topic of 'speech': "Listen, my children, to instruction concerning the mouth. . .." The substance of the speech is then devoted to the sub-topics of 'oaths' and 'foul language' (23:9–11, 12–15). The speech in 19:5–17 focuses on the sub-topic of gossip; that in 28:13–26 on yet another sub-topic, slander. These speeches use a number of comparisons that look like they were specific to the dangers of oaths, foul language, gossip, and slander, respectively. The dangers of loose lips are dramatized in ominous images, what seem to us like rhetorical overkill, suggesting that Ben Sira and the instructional line in which he stood were sharply aware of the difficult social relations in which they and their students operated.

### Economic Relations: Aiding the Poor and Wealth and Poverty

Judean instructional wisdom also included a set of topics concerning wealth and poverty. On the topic of aiding the poor Sirach contains two parallel speeches in 3:30—4:10 and 29:8-13. While they have different links (for example the more proactive "rescuing of the oppressed from the oppressor" in 4:9, 10–11; cf. Prov 31:8–9), the parallel motifs in the speeches suggest that this was yet another topic on which Ben Sira was drawing on a traditional speech-register in his composition. Again the book of Proverbs provides a window onto the tradition of proverbial wisdom devoted to this topic. "Whoever is kind to the poor lends to the LORD, and will be repaid in full" (Prov 19:17; cf. Prov 14:21, 31; 17:5; 21:13; 28:27). In both speeches in Sirach the core consists of a series of parallel admonitions.

| Sir 3:30—4:10 (4:1–4) | Sir 29:8–13 (8–9) |
|---|---|
| Do not keep needy eyes waiting. | Do not keep the humble waiting for alms |
| ... Or delay giving to the needy, | |
| Do not reject the suppliant in distress ... | Do not send [the poor] away empty handed. |
| Give a hearing to the poor. | Help the poor for the commandment's sake |

The speeches also have highly similar motive clauses, the one at the start ("almsgiving atones for sin," 3:30), the other at the conclusion ("Store up almsgiving in your treasury, and it will rescue you from every disaster," 29:12–13). And in another parallel, the one speech alludes to covenantal principles or laws and the other links helping the poor directly to the covenantal commandments (4:6; 29:9, 11).

A related topic was wealthy and poverty. Sirach has no other speech on this topic with which we can compare the speech in 13:15–24. It is nevertheless evident that this speech is composed from a traditional register, including several proverbs. Scribes who served wealthy and powerful rulers in agrarian societies where the vast majority of peasants hovered on the edge of subsistence could not help but observe the relative position of the rich and poor. "The wealth of the rich is their fortress; the poverty of the poor is their ruin" (Prov 10:15; cf. 14:20; 18:23). Just such traditional proverbs provide the content of the speech on the rich and the poor in Sir 13:15–24. This can be seen clearly in Sir 13:21, which is another version (or adaptive performance) of the proverb that the rich have many friends while the poor are disliked even by their neighbors, known from Prov 14:20. The proverbs included in 13:15–24 also make clear the direct relationship between wealth and poverty. "Wild asses in the wilderness are the prey of lions; likewise the poor are feeding grounds for the rich" (13:19; cf 13:17, 18, 21–22). The point to which this speech is driving is articulated finally in the concluding maxim: "Riches are good if they are free from sin . . ." (13:24)—an ideal but unlikely possibility, from what the scribes knew in the real world of economic relations.[47]

### Scribes' Relations with Rulers

Along with many passing comments on this subject (e.g., 4:7, 27; 7:4–7; 8:1–2; 9:13; 20:27–31), Sirach includes a speech on the general topic of association with the great (13:1–13) and one on the more particular sub-topic of behavior at banquets (dining and drinking) hosted by the wealthy and powerful (31:12—32:13). Ben Sira's passing comments on these issues in other contexts and the many proverbs and even short speeches on them in Proverbs indicate that these two speeches are both rooted in traditional registers of language. Considering the learned scribes' vulnerability to the rulers whom they served, of course, it is not surprising that their relations with "the great ones" was an important topic of instruction.

Ben Sira's speech on association with rulers,[48] which configures proverbs, admonitions, analogies, and (proverbial) illustrations, displays not just standard terms and motifs but adaptation of earlier proverbs and brief speeches. Proverbs includes both several proverbs and simple speeches on the topic (14:35; 19:12 = 20:11; 22:11; 24:21–22; 25:6–7). The formulations in Sirach 13:8–10 are addressed to the same situation and its perils as indicated in Prov 25:6–7, and give virtually the same advice.

> When a ruler invites you, be reserved,
>     and he will invite you all the more insistently.
> Do not be forward, or you may be rebuffed;
>     do not stand aloof, or you will be forgotten. (13:9–10)

And the concluding admonition (picking up the illustrations of Sir 13:3–4, 7) repeats the same ominous concern as Prov 20:2 (cf. Sir 9:13; Prov 24:21–22).

> Be on your guard and very careful,
>     for you are walking about with your own downfall. (13:13)

In his more elaborate speech on the topic of behavior at banquets sponsored by patrons among the aristocracy, in 31:12—32:13, Ben Sira is again clearly building on and adapting traditional proverbs as well as terms

---

47. Sirach also has two parallel speeches on not being drawn into the pursuit of wealth, in 5:1–8 and 40:18–27, in which 40:26 is an adaptation of the proverb in Prov 15:16 (cf. an alternate version in Prov 16:8; and cf. Prov 22:7, 8, 16).

48. On who the wealthy/powerful/rulers are, to the *nadib* of 13:9, cf. Job 21:28; 34:18; Prov 8:16; etc. An earlier Egyptian form of instruction on the same topic is in Phibis x 12—xi 23, as discussed by Sanders, *Ben Sira*, 92–93.

and motifs. Well before the time of Ben Sira, proverbs and speeches warning about drinking had become standard in instructional wisdom ("Hear my child, and be wise, do not be among the winebibbers and gluttons," Prov 20:1; 21:17; etc.; 23:19–22). Longer speeches combining rhetorical questions, proverbs, and illustrations were built around admonitions such as "look not upon the wine when it is red. . . and goes down smoothly" (Prov 23:29–35). Building on such wisdom, speeches about the scribes' own vulnerability focused on how to conduct themselves when "sitting down to eat with a ruler" (Prov 23:1–3). Such speeches had deeper roots in the instructional wisdom of Egypt, where banqueting with rulers was a standard topic, as evident in several extant collections.[49]

Ben Sira' speech stands directly in this standard instructional discourse on the topic of banqueting. Indeed 31:12–24 is an elaboration, mainly in admonitions, of shorter speeches such as Prov 23:1–3, warning hungry sages against appearing greedy at the table of the great. Ben Sira adds the very practical suggestion that, should one overeat, "get up to vomit" (31:21). In 31:25–31 he simply builds on the standard traditional Judean and ancient Near Eastern proverbial wisdom on the importance of moderation in wine-drinking. And in 32:3–12 he draws on the traditional idiom of Judean instruction on moderation in speech (32:3–12), always central to scribal service of the rulers.

## Conclusion

The above exploration of the components of communication in Ben Sira's oral instruction may enable us to better appreciate how the composition of speeches on particular topics occurred in (immediate connection with) performance. As a learned scribe who had himself undergone intensive scribal training, he would have been thoroughly familiar with the various patterning of instructional speeches as well as the various registers of speech dedicated to the standard topics of scribal instruction. The ideal for the wise scribe, which presumably he attempted to pursue, moreover, was life-long learning of the cultural heritage that included the torah of the Most High and prophecies but most importantly "the wisdom of all the ancients, [including] . . . sayings, . . . parables, . . . and proverbs" (38:34—39:3). On the basis of these traditional forms and sets of dedicated language that he had internalized, he could formulate speeches, as appropriate to the instructional context, on a wide range of standard topics. To his students as well

49. E.g., the Instruction of Ptah-hotep, the Instruction of Kagemi, and the Instruction of Amenemope, as discussed by Sanders, *Ben Sira*, 67.

as himself, each of those speeches would have been readily memorable (but not in the sense of verbatim memorization that we "print-culture" people rely on). "Those who are skilled in words become wise themselves, and pour forth apt proverbs" (18.29).

In its creation out of thoroughly familiar formal patterns and dedicated sets of language, Ben Sira's composition-in-performance might be compared roughly with improvisational jazz performance or traditional blues singing, or perhaps the prayers that experienced pastors and priests perform as appropriate to the context of celebration, memorial, or bereavement.

We may thus be able to begin to appreciate how Ben Sira worked in oral composition. The next question then becomes how his oral speeches became written and anthologized (beginning the process by which we have access to them). The answer to that question, if we follow the indications in other ancient Judean texts, may lie in "dictation" (re-performance)—as by Jeremiah to Baruch (Jeremiah 36) or by Yahweh to Moses (Exod 24:3–4), followed by continuing development, by editing and copying, which were other skills and responsibilities of learned scribes such as Ben Sira and his protégés—ones that we modern-day successors may be more familiar with. We can certainly surmise that Ben Sira himself and/or his students did the dictating, writing, and anthologizing, as his "grandson" suggests in the prologue to Sirach. As suggested by Fox and by the discovery of wisdom teaching such as *Sapiential A* at Qumran, however, Ben Sira's students and other scribal teachers would have continued to draw on the registers or discourses devoted to the various topics of wisdom instruction in formulating speeches to their students.

# 5

# CONTESTING AUTHORITY

## Popular vs. Scribal Tradition in Continuing Performance

I HAVE VIVID MEMORIES FROM THE EARLY 1960s AT HARVARD Divinity School of beginning to question the then standard assumption in biblical studies that "the Jews" at the time of Jesus were expecting the imminent eschatological coming of *the Messiah*. The book assigned as the climax of the two-semester "Introduction to the Old Testament," Sigmund Mowinckel's *He That Cometh,* offered an extensive synthetic survey of "Old Testament" and "late-Jewish" expectation of *the Messiah.* Closer examination of Judean texts produced just prior to the time of Jesus, however, indicated that, aside from "the anointed son of David" in *Psalms of Solomon* 17 and a few passing references to "the anointed ones of Aaron and Israel" in certain of the DSS, late second-temple Judean texts do not refer much to a messiah. A few years later, having read a recent article on the subject,[1] Krister Stendahl led a graduate seminar that confirmed my suspicions.

In his histories, however, the Judean historian Flavius Josephus gives considerable attention to movements in the countryside led by popularly acclaimed kings that managed to assert their independence of Roman and/ or Herodian rule for months and years before they could be suppressed by Roman reconquest. Three such movements, independent of one another, occurred in 4 BCE, in Galilee and in the transJordan as well as in Judea after Herod's death in 4 BCE. What became the largest fighting force in the great revolt against Rome in 66–70 CE took the same social-political form, with

---

1. Our suspicions were confirmed by de Jonge, "The Word 'Anointed.'"

Judeans over a fairly extensive area acclaiming Simon bar Giora as their king (*War* 2.56–69, 652–53; 4.503–13, 529–34, 574–78; *Ant.* 17.271–85).

This discrepancy between the lack of interest in an anointed figure in texts produced by the intellectual elite and the emergence of concrete movements headed by a popularly acclaimed king led me to suspect that there was a difference between elite culture and interests and popular culture and interests. I began to suspect that what my "Old Testament" teacher Frank Cross had analyzed as "northern" and "southern" Israelite ideas of kingship[2] could be more appropriately understood as the Israelite popular tradition of kingship (detectable, e.g., in 2 Sam 2:1–4; 5:1–4; 1 Kings 12; 2 Kings 9), on the one hand, and the official ideology of the Davidic monarchy in Jerusalem (Pss 2; 89; 110; 2 Samuel 7), on the other. The Israelite tradition of popular acclamation of kings that began with the people's "anointing" of the young David as chieftan to lead the people against the Philistines can be traced for at least two hundred years through texts later included in the Hebrew Bible. It emerged again in the anointing of Jeroboam to lead the Israelite revolt against Solomon's son Rehoboam and yet again in Elijah/Elisha's anointing of Jehu to lead the revolt against the successor of Ahab and Jezebel. That this tradition continued "underground" in collective social memory of the people would help greatly to explain why and how the several widespread popular revolts in 4 BCE, again in 67–70 CE, and again in 132–35 CE all took the same discernible social form of "messianic" movements led by popularly acclaimed kings.[3]

Anthropologists and others had developed a standard distinction between the "great tradition" and the "little tradition." This distinction is evident particularly in traditional agrarian societies in which urban-based elites rule over and expropriate the produce of peasants who live in semi-self-governing village communities. James C. Scott's comparative analysis is particularly suggestive for ancient Judean and Galilean society.[4] He finds clear differences between the distinctive patterns of belief and behavior valued by the peasantry and the corresponding patterns among a society's elite, sometimes embodied in written documents. While parallel and in regular interaction, the respective traditions display significant differences in emphasis and interests, the "little tradition" often expressing a set of values and concerns counter to those of the "great tradition." In recent books and articles, some of us have applied this distinction between "great" and "little" traditions (and Scott's article in particular) to what are clearly contested Is-

---

2. Cross, *Canaanite Myth.*

3. Horsley, "Popular Messianic Movements."

4. Scott, "Protest and Profanation."

raelite traditions in the speeches of Jesus parallel in Matthew and Luke ("Q") and Jesus' disputes with the Pharisees in the Gospel of Mark, as well as to the popular messianic and prophetic movements mentioned by Josephus.[5]

Recent lines of research on the limits of literacy and the dominance of oral communication in antiquity, on scribal cultivation of texts, and in text-criticism of the manuscripts found among the DSS, are now further destabilizing and problematizing standard assumptions and constructs in biblical studies. The results of this research suggest that the distinction between the official tradition and the popular tradition may be more widely relevant for understanding the considerable diversity among ancient Judean and Galilean groups and movements, the tension between scribal groups and their patrons among the ruling aristocracy, and the conflict between popular movements and their rulers. The results of this recent research, however, also suggests the importance of having an adequately complexified understanding of the "great" and "little" traditions, their historical relations, and their diversity in second-temple Judean (and Galilean) society.

More particularly, it is clear that the "great" tradition should not be understood only or even mainly as embodied in written texts (scriptures), even though the latter did play a distinctive role. Scribal tradition and texts, moreover, were not necessarily identical with the expressions of the rulers' interests and practices, for there was considerable diversity among scribal circles in the cultivation of the Judean great tradition. At the level of the "little," or as I would prefer, the *popular* tradition, it is increasingly clear that our knowledge of it is elusive. We cannot use "biblical" texts that we know from later manuscripts as anything like direct sources. We can use such extant texts, that are almost always produced by the intellectual elite, only with critical caution. Moreover, there would have been regional and even local variations in the popular Israelite tradition. All of these particulars will be clear if we begin with a clearer sense of the relations and differences between the official/scribal tradition(s) and the popular tradition(s).

## Traces of the Historical Interaction of Scribal and Popular Israelite Traditions

The assumption by modern biblical scholars that "the Jews" (generally) were reading the books of the Torah and the Prophets (the "Old Testament") has generated a great deal of false knowledge. It has also blocked discernment of

5. Horsley, *Jesus and the Spiral*, chap. 5; *Hearing the Whole Story*; Horsley with Draper, *Whoever Hears You Hears Me*; Herzog, *Jesus, Justice*; Crossan, *Historical Jesus*; and the articles by Herzog and Horsley in Horsley, ed., *Hidden Transcripts*.

the power relations and dynamics between the vast majority of the Judean and Galilean people and their imperial and Jerusalem rulers. The vast majority of people in any ancient agrarian society were peasants living in villages. And because Judean peasants were non-literate, they could not have read the scriptures.[6] Considering how large, costly, and unwieldy scrolls were, it seems doubtful that villagers even had direct contact with or access to them.

That the peasants were non-literate, however, does not mean that they had no knowledge of their cultural tradition(s) or that they acquiesced in the arrangement of Judean cultural traditions by the priestly and scribal elite. Recent research has demonstrated that even the literate elite, learned scribes such as Jesus ben Sira, cultivated texts and traditions orally, learning them by repeated recitation and performance as appropriate to various situations.[7] But ordinary people as well would have cultivated Israelite tradition orally, in their households and village communities. Literacy was hardly necessary to recite well-known psalms or to tell well-known stories about figures such as Moses and Miriam or Deborah and Elijah.

Studies of the great and little traditions in other agrarian societies have shown that, while noticeably different, they are often parallel and develop and function in at least some interaction.[8] Such overlap and interaction may be minimal in cases where one people or its rulers have come to rule over another, subjected people. In such cases a dominant (official) and a subordinated culture may continue parallel but in tension if not conflict, as happened to many peoples under the Hellenistic empires after Alexander the Great's conquests. Insofar as the monarchy in Judah and the later Jerusalem temple-state attempted to legitimate their rule on the basis of Israelite-Judean tradition, however, the official-scribal tradition and the popular Israelite tradition were overlapping and interactive for centuries.

Their difference and interaction can be seen in key aspects of Israelite tradition as we know them in the field of critical biblical studies. The basic story of the exodus of Israelites from bondage in Egypt, for example, developed initially among early Israelites who valued their independence of oppressive rulers, as can be seen in the very early "Song of the Sea," whose language is an early northern Israelite dialect.[9] The story of the exodus, including the "Song of the Sea," however, were taken up into and overwritten by the so-called Yahwist's and subsequent histories composed for the Judean

6. Botha, "Greco-Roman Literacy"; Hezser, *Jewish Literacy*.

7. Jaffe, *Torah in the Mouth*, chap. 1; Carr, *Tablet of the Heart*; Horsley, *Scribes, Visionaries*, chaps. 4–5.

8. Scott, "Protest and Profanation."

9. Rendsberg, "Galilean Background."

monarchy and/or temple-state aristocracy. In these histories, ironically, the liberation from foreign monarchy became a major early event in the longer sequence of events that led to the fulfillment of the promise to the ancestors that Israel would become a great nation and have land, under the monarchy of David and Solomon. The Jerusalem regime's centralization of the Passover celebration of the exodus in the Jerusalem temple attempted to attach the basic story of liberation to Jerusalem rule.

The absorption of the exodus story into the official or scribal tradition in Jerusalem, however, did not end its cultivation and continuing role in resistance and renewal among villagers. After chafing under the forced labor imposed by Solomon, the Israelites remembered that their ancestors had escaped similar "forced labor" under Pharaoh in Egypt (1 Kings 12). Nearly a millennium later, in the decades just after the mission of Jesus, popular prophets such as a Samaritan, a Judean returning from Egypt, and a Judean named Theudas led large numbers of villagers onto a sacred mountain, up to the Mount Olives, or out into the wilderness of the Jordan where they were to experience new acts of deliverance patterned after the divine acts of deliverance led by Moses and/or Joshua (Josephus, *Ant.* 18.85–87; 20.97–98, 169–71; *War* 2.261–63).[10]

The Jerusalem elite drew upon the exodus and the way through the wilderness to their land in a very different way when they were themselves subjected and exiled in Babylon. They themselves now looked for a new exodus, only now to restore them to their positions of power and privilege in Zion (Isaiah 40–55, 55–66; and in particular, Isa 42:6–9; 61:1–7; 35:1–10, which belonged with Isa 40–66). In yet a different way, the dissident scribalpriestly movement that withdrew to the wilderness at Qumran carried out a new exodus, escaping the incumbent Jerusalem high priestly rulers they found oppressive (1QS).

The conflicting uses of the exodus story in the Jerusalem temple and in the Judean (and Galilean) popular tradition is vividly dramatized in the celebration of Passover right around the time of Jesus. The high priestly aristocracy maintained in power by the Romans continued the centralized celebration of the exodus in the Passover in the temple, which provided a considerable percentage of their revenues and the livelihood of the city of Jerusalem. Not surprisingly under Roman rule, however, Passover became a time of intense yearning among the people to again gain their freedom from oppressive alien rule. The Passover festival became not just a potential but an actual time of public agitation against Roman and high-priestly rule. Accordingly the Roman governors posted Roman soldiers on the temple

---

10. Horsley, Two Types of Popular Prophets"; Popular Prophetic Movements."

porticoes, exacerbating the already high tensions by embodying their subjugation in a show of force. But that only exacerbated the tension, so that
a provocation by a Roman soldier might easily touch off an agitation by
the crowd of pilgrims celebrating their liberation of old (Josephus, *Ant.*
20.105–12).

Just as official or scribal tradition and texts took up the exodus story
from early Israelite popular tradition, so the law-codes that now appear in
the books of the Pentateuch/Torah took over and adapted principles and
mechanisms of the Mosaic covenant. It is clear that key covenantal principles such as not coveting and stealing one another's goods, the land as
the inalienable possession of lineages given them by YHWH, not demand-
ing interest on loans, sabbatical cancellation of debts, and release of debt-
slaves, provided protection of peasant villagers' economic livelihood.[11]
They were taken up into the covenant code in Exodus 21–23, the book of
Deuteronomy, and the "Holiness Code" now in Leviticus (17–26), adapted
to serve the interests of centralization of power in the late monarchy and/or
the temple-state in Jerusalem. Nevertheless, the people and/or their prophets still appealed to these principles in stories and prophetic speeches that
protested violation of these principles (covenant commandments) by kings,
their officers, and priestly aristocracy (e.g., 1 Kings 21; Amos 2:6–8; Mic
2:1–5; Neh 5:1–10).

Another illustration of the interaction, yet continuing opposition,
between the popular and the elite tradition can be seen in the way Elijah –Elisha narratives were used. The style of the Elijah–Elisha stories in
1 Kings 17–21 and 2 Kings 1–9 is very different from the accounts of the
reigns of the kings of Judah and Israel that comprise the rest of the books of
Kings. They were evidently overwritten to serve the purposes of the Judean
composers of the books of Kings. Perhaps partly because of the legends
surrounding his disappearance, Elijah was adopted as a figure who would
return to restore Israel (Mal 4:5–6; Sir 48:1–12). But he must have continued
to be remembered as a great hero in popular circles as well. At least in the
Gospel tradition, both John the Baptist and Jesus were understood as Elijah-
like figures in their program of renewal of Israel, by the covenant renewal
ritual of baptism and by the manifestations of renewal in healings.

While traditions that originated and continued among the people
were taken up into the great tradition in the case of the exodus and Elijah
stories, materials or traditions promulgated by scribal circles and/or the
temple regime in turn influenced the popular tradition. Clearly the centralization of the Passover festival influenced the way villagers celebrated

---

11. References and discussion in Horsley, *Covenant Economics*, chaps. 2–3.

the exodus, including their yielding up precious family resources to the priestly and other officers who presided over the festival in the Jerusalem temple. In such a context, psalms that originated in circles that staffed the temple would have become known by pilgrims from the villages as well. And presumably the body of laws in the books of Moses that pertained to the support and operation of the temple cult would have become known to, if perhaps also resisted by, the villagers whose tithes and offerings were required by the temple and priestly officers and staff. On a more general level, even the terms, images, phrases, narratives, and psalmic formulae in which originally popular materials that had been reworked by the scribal-priestly elite would inevitably have influenced the popular continuation of those materials, most likely through contacts at festival times.

A significant factor in the interaction of ordinary people and their Israelite popular tradition, on the one hand, and the Jerusalem rulers and their scribal representatives and the Jerusalemite "great" tradition, on the other, would have been the authority of the scriptures, the texts that stood *written* on scrolls. Contrary to common scholarly assumption and claims, later second-temple Judean texts refer to or "quote" particular laws or narratives of the books of the Pentateuch fairly rarely. Nevertheless the sacred texts of the temple-state commanded a certain authority. This was partly because in a largely non-literate society, almost any writing was mysterious and certain writings had an aura about them that was almost numinous. The written texts of the temple-state held authority partly because they stood *written* on the scrolls that were all the more mysterious since they functioned as sacred objects (as in the worship of the sacred writing of Mosaic torah by the assembly of Judeans when it was held aloft by the scribe Ezra, in Nehemiah 8).

## Differences between Official/Scribal Tradition and Popular Tradition

While overlapping in much of their "contents" and interactive in certain ways, the scribal tradition and the Israelite popular tradition were significantly different. Scott explains that the great and little traditions are usually not simply variations on the same cultural tradition, certainly that popular culture is not merely a watered-down version of what filtered down from the elite.[12] They are rather distinct patterns of belief and practice. And these are closely related to the political-economic-religious structure of traditional agrarian societies. Traditional societies such as ancient Judea and Galilee lacked integrating factors such as the mass media. As historical so-

---

12. Scott, "Protest and Profanation," 7–9.

ciologists and others point out, an aristocracy and its retainers such as lived in Jerusalem can be almost a semi-separate society from the village communities scattered through the countryside. The most dramatic illustration, perhaps, is that the *Yehudim* that the Persians had supported in establishing the temple-state in Jerusalem were immigrants who had previously been deported to and lived for several generations in Babylon. In their "return" from exile they came to rule over the people who had remained on the land after the Babylonian conquest. And as stated explicitly in the book of Ezra, they insisted that as the true *Yehudim* they had in effect a divine right to control the land as well as the apparatus of the temple-state (Ezra 2; 8).

Second-temple Judean society was thus structured in concentric circles, with the high priesthood at the apex and center, with its wealth and privileges and special purity codes, surrounded by the circle of ordinary priests and the Levites, who had declined in status and function by late second temple society (Sirach 50). (In Judea as in other traditional agrarian societies, there was nothing corresponding to the "middle class" of modern industrial societies; the "scribes and Pharisees" were not a middle class, but the "retainers," the assistants and representatives of the ruling priestly aristocracy.) Although some priestly families lived in villages, most village communities were comprised of ordinary Israelites not expected to keep purity codes. So far as we know, from indications in later rabbinic literature, village communities operated according to the fundamental Mosaic covenantal principles and local customs. It must have seemed a blatant violation of those principles, therefore, that the Jerusalem rulers lived in mansions and enjoyed the finest cuts of meat and fine bread and wine, while the villagers languished in debts and hunger and perhaps loss of their ancestral lands because of their obligations for tithes, offerings, and interest payment on loans (Neh 5:1–4; 10:32–39; 13:5; Sir 13:17–22).

The official and/or scribal Jerusalem tradition and the popular tradition of village communities were also separated by language differences. Judean and Galilean villagers apparently spoke different dialects of Aramaic. The various versions of proto-scriptural Judean texts cultivated in Jerusalem, however, were in ("biblical") Hebrew, an archaic literary language that was no longer spoken among ordinary people (Neh 8:8). The elite/popular divide was also maintained by education. Scribes and presumably priests as well were trained, indeed apparently drilled, in the learning of texts, including (some of) the proto-scriptural texts (Sir 38:34—39:3; 1QS 6:6–8). Peasants, on the other hand, of necessity having to produce crops for the elite as well as themselves, had no time or use for formal education (Sir 38:24–33), although they learned Israelite traditions in the course of family and community interaction and communication. There would thus have been a considerable gap and difference between the elite Israelite tradition in Jerusalem and popular Israelite tradition(s) in the village communities.

## Scribal Traditions, Diverse and Contested

"The Torah" has been assumed to have been a stable reference point even in much recent discussion of early "Judaism" and emerging "Christianity." Other, parallel written texts such as *Jubilees* and the *Biblical Antiquities* of Pseudo-Philo have been labeled and thereby interpreted as "rewritten Bible," that is derived directly from "the Bible" and of secondary importance.[13] The "Oral Torah" is set confidently over against the "Written Torah" (and often identified with the Pharisees' "traditions of the elders") and *halakah* is understood to be derived by "interpretation of the Torah." All of these standard scholarly beliefs are based on assumptions that there was such a thing as a stable Torah in late second-temple times, that we know what the Torah was (the written books of the Pentateuch), and that we have access to it (or have it) in the standard scholarly editions of the Hebrew Bible. Recent research and rethinking, however, are challenging such concepts and assumptions as unwarranted and anachronistic.

As discussed briefly in chap. 1, the text of the books of the Pentateuch was not yet stabilized. Among the DSS were a great number of manuscripts of these books that were later included in the Hebrew Bible. After close examination of these manuscripts, more than a millennium older than previously known manuscripts of the books of the Pentateuch, Eugene Ulrich has reached two decisive and far-reaching conclusions.[14] (1) Coexisting at Qumran and presumably in other scribal circles were two or three different textual traditions (proto-masoretic; proto-Samaritan, and a Hebrew text corresponding to the LXX). (2) Those textual traditions were still fluid, still undergoing development, through the end of the second-temple period. Although the component books of the Pentateuch and their order and, to a degree, even the sequence of episodes in the narratives and law-codes, appear to have been relatively constant across these still fluid textual traditions, there is some variation in the inclusion of episodes and their sequence. This evidence of several still-developing textual traditions of the books of the Pentateuch fits the recent late critical dating of their composition in something like the version with which we are familiar through those textual traditions.

13. Vermes, *Scripture and Tradition.*
14. Ulrich, *Dead Sea Scrolls.*

Forty years ago my generation's mentors such as Krister Stendahl hammered away at their students that it was utterly unacceptable to continue to project a "normative Judaism" derived from rabbinic texts of the third century CE and later back to the Pharisees in the time of Hillel and Jesus. Now the evidence for different and still-developing textual families of the books of the Pentateuch are about to force us to quit projecting the concept of a stable text of "the Torah" as standard scripture back into late second-temple times. No wonder that in documents such as the Qumran Community Rule as it is often quite unclear what the term 'torah' is referring to. How would we determine in a given case, such as the histories of Josephus, what the terms "law(s) of Moses" or "books of Moses" or "laws of the Judeans" were referring to?

Complicating and diversifying the scribal tradition, other written narratives and written law-books coexisted and competed with the books of the Pentateuch in their various developing textual traditions. We already knew about the book of *Jubilees* and the *Biblical Antiquities* of Pseudo-Philo. These and the more recently discovered Temple Scroll from Qumran, however, evidently are not derived directly from, but are parallel to and perhaps alternatives to, the historical legends and law-codes in Exodus, Leviticus, and Deuteronomy (as discussed in chap. 3). Further, the combination of the existence of such alternative law-books and the variety and fluidity of the text of the Pentateuch in late second-temple times calls the concept of "rewritten Bible" seriously into question. Daniel Harrington laid out nearly twenty years ago why "re-written Bible," midrash, and targum and related concepts were problematic when applied to several late second-temple Judean texts.[15]

A more appropriate hypothesis would be that texts such as *Jubilees*, *Biblical Antiquities*, and the Temple Scroll represent parallel, alternative versions of Judean-Israelite historical and legal traditions (as discussed in chap. 3), rather than re-writings of already standardized texts of "the Bible" or "the Torah/Pentateuch." This fits with the striking lack of explicit citation of supposedly scriptural books (Law and Prophets) in late second-temple (non-Qumranic) Judean texts such as Sirach and the sections of *1 Enoch*. Similarly in legal texts produced by the Qumran community (such as the sections of regulations in the Community Rule and the Damascus Rule), explicit citation of other texts that were supposedly recognized as scripture are largely absent or strikingly rare. For the scribal circles that produced them, moreover, these alternative versions of Israelite historical and legal

---

15. Harrington, "Palestinian Adaptations of Biblical Narratives"; Brooke, "Between Authority and Canon."

traditions would have possessed authority that rivaled that of the already well-defined texts of torah. The discovery of the Temple Scroll at Qumran reinforces the previous impression from the book of *Jubilees* and the *Antiquities* of Pseudo-Philo that scribal circles produced and cultivated alternative books of torah.

Schiffman, Qimron, and others argued that *halakhah* like that of later rabbinic circles is found in Qumran documents and that such *halakhah* is derived by interpretation of the Bible/Torah.[16]

> The legal materials of the sect are to a great extent derived from biblical interpretation, an activity that took place at regular study sessions as part of sectarian life, most probably in the main center at Qumran. The decisions reached at such sessions were recorded in lists of sectarian laws called *serahkim* (e.g. component parts of 1QS and CD) . . . for the most part [the sectarian laws] were made up of snatches of biblical phraseology woven together. Only rarely do we find explicit quotation. By examining these paraphrases, we can discover the[ir] biblical basis.

He even pictures the "halakhah" at Qumran as having originated in "decisions" similar to those imagined for the post–70 CE "council at Yavneh."[17]

Schiffman, however, drew this conclusion before much of the recent research on scribal practices was carried out that now challenges standard assumptions in biblical studies. The results of this research give us a very different sense of scribal culture, whether in Jerusalem or in the Qumran community. Not only were multiple textual versions of the books of the Pentateuch current, but they were still undergoing development. Not only was literacy in ancient Judea limited to scribal circles, but even in scribal circles its uses were embedded in the dominant oral communication environment.[18] Not all kinds of writing, moreover, were written to be read and studied. Written scrolls, which were extremely costly and cumbersome, were treated as holy objects to be venerated.[19] Written texts (scrolls) were not necessarily read or consulted and they were not studied and interpreted in anything like the way canonical texts are today. In rabbinic circles learning consisted of disciples repeating aloud and memorizing their masters' orally-

16. Schiffman, *Reclaiming the Dead Sea Scrolls*, 247.

17. Saldarini, "Johanan ben Zakkai's Escape"; L. I. Levine, "Jewish Patriarch," and others, however, have argued that the rabbinic passages claimed as evidence for the supposed academy or council at Yavneh are legendary at best, and not reliable historical accounts.

18. Hezser, *Jewish Literacy*; Jaffee, *Torah in the Mouth*.

19. Niditch, *Oral World and Written Word*; Horsley, *Scribes, Visionaries*, chap. 6.

presented torah, teachings, and legal opinions.[20] Studies of Judean scribal practice have concluded that learned scribes cultivated and appropriated "texts" by repeated recitation, in teaching, memory, and performance.[21] As indicated in compositions of the Qumran community, they emphasized keeping torah and covenantal rulings, not (reading and) interpreting. As for the "oral torah," Jaffee has shown that the concept of "torah in the mouth" gradually emerged among the Amoraic rabbis well after the formulation of the Mishnah and Tosefta, was not operative in late second-temple times, and should not be identified with the Pharisees' traditions of the elders or the chain of tradition in the Mishnah tractate *Aboth*.[22]

The results of recent research thus put in a very different light the "study sessions" that Schiffman imagined, evidently on the basis of the key passage in the Community Rule that gives instructions for procedures in the communal life. In the sequence of the three ceremonial procedures mentioned, the eating in common, the blessing in common, and the rule for (deliberations in) the assembly, Schiffman finds "study" of the Bible from which *halakhah* was derived in the nightly sessions of communal blessing. We start with an alternative translation that does not project modern scholarly practices of study and interpretation onto this key passage.

> And where the ten are, there shall never lack a man among them who search torah (*dwrs btwrh*) day and night, concerning the right conduct of a man with his companion. And the many shall watch in community for a third of every night of the year, to recite the writing (*lqrw' bspr*) and to search justice-ruling (*ldrws mspt*) and to offer communal blessings (*lbrk byhd*). (1QS 6:4–8; my translation, adapted from Vermes' translation)

Cutting through the problematic old assumptions, with reference to this key passage and others, Fraade and others insist that we not project later rabbinic developments back into Qumran texts and point out that the legal rulings in the Community Rule and other Qumran texts are not derived by means of scriptural interpretation.[23] Having earlier emphasized "study," "(scriptural) interpretation," and "interpretive study of Torah," after close examination of Observations Concerning the Torah" (4QMMT), Fraade recognizes that such a rendering of *drš/mdrš* is problematic, that its root sense

20. Hezser, *Jewish Literacy*, for example, 82, 98, 460, 463, 480.

21. Ibid., 451; Jaffee, *Torah in the Mouth*; Carr, *Writing on the Tablet of the Heart*; Horsley, *Scribes, Visionaries*, chap. 5.

22. Jaffe, *Torah in the Mouth*.

23. Fraade, "Interpretive Authority," 51n15; Meier "Is There *Halaka*?"

is not "study" or "interpretation" of scripture, but "searching."[24] Indeed, if we attend to the repeated emphasis in the Community Rule, the "searching" of torah or of *mišpat(im)* was done with the purpose of the interrelational communal observance of torah and "justice-ruling." There is nothing in 1QS 6:6–8 or related texts to indicate that *drš* or related terms refer to "*exegetical* activity that *derives* the communal laws from the Torah."[25] In contrast with the *pešarim* on several prophetic texts from Qumran, "nowhere [in the Community Rule and other such texts] is it suggested that the laws themselves were uncovered through the methods of scriptural exegesis."[26] The Community Rule states that the community's "justice-rulings" it lists were *revealed*, progressively, as it were, "from age to age," and more recently to the priestly leaders and members of the community (e.g., 1QS 8:12–16).[27] As Schiffman's own observation that "sectarian laws" display "snatches of biblical phraseology woven together" suggests, the justice-rulings in the Community Rule were not paraphrases of an already stable "scripture" but continuing development of a diverse and still-developing scribal tradition of torah and/or regulations composed by scribes thoroughly familiar with the idiom and phrasing of authoritative torah.

As both Fraade and Jaffee point out, the three communal activities mentioned in 1QS 6:6–8 (reciting *sefer*, searching *mišpat*, and offering blessings) all comprise a sustained communal *ritual performance*. The point or purpose of the ritual performance, moreover, is a communal social-economic performance, in the interaction among the members of the covenantal *yahad*: doing torah and justice-rulings. Although the Qumran community possessed written texts of books of torah and produced written copies of their own compositions, both torah and *mišpat(im)* were *recited or performed orally* in the gatherings of the community.

While the *communal* performance or recitation of torah may have been unusual for scribal circles in their cultivation of tradition, their continuing development of justice-rulings that were not included in the (written) laws of Moses—and not derived from interpretation of those laws—was paralleled by the rival scribal circle whom they accused of being "smooth interpreters," the Pharisees. Josephus declares firmly that under the Hasmonean high priests the Pharisees were promulgating regulations (*nomima*) for the society that had been handed down from the succession of fathers and were not written in the laws of Moses (*en tois Mouseos nomois*)" (*Ant.* 13.297).

24. Fraade, "Looking for Legal Midrash."
25. Ibid., 67.
26. Ibid., 76.
27. Ibid., 77.

But nothing in his account suggests that these regulations were somehow derived by interpretation of "the laws of Moses." And, as Jaffee has now decisively clarified, these Pharisaic "traditions of the ancestors" cannot be understood as "oral torah," which concept had not yet emerged.[28]

As manifest in both the development of justice-rulings in the Qumran community and the promulgation of regulations derived from the tradition of the ancestors by the Pharisees the developing scribal tradition in late second-temple Judea included ongoing production and oral learning and recitation of torah that might also be written down (in 1QS?) or not (the Pharisees *nomima*). The diversity of the scribal tradition thus included these new products of oral composition and performance in addition to the still-developing texts of the Pentateuch (both written and in continuing oral recitation) and other, alternative torah such as the Temple Scroll (both written and in continuing oral recitation).

In yet a further refinement of how the Judean scribal tradition was developing in late second-temple Judea, the Pharisees' regulations/traditions of the ancestors and the new justice-regulations at Qumran, as well as the alternative texts of torah illustrate how the scribal tradition was not necessarily the official tradition of the Jerusalem temple-state. *Jubilees,* the Temple Scroll, and Observations Concerning the Torah" (4QMMT) were evidently produced as alternatives to what was the official policy and practice at the time. The *nomina* established by the Pharisees illustrate how what was included in official tradition depended on the incumbent rulers. According to Josephus, John Hyrcanus had authorized but later rescinded these regulations as part of the official "state law" of the regime (*Ant.* 13.288–298). His successor Alexander Jannai fought with and evidently crucified hundreds of opponents (probably including Pharisees) who had the audacity to oppose him (*Ant.* 13.379–83). But his wife and successor Alexandra Salome reauthorized the Pharisees regulations as part of official Hasmonean state law (*Ant.* 13.405–8). These passages and Josephus' other references to "the laws of the Judeans" in various connections, moreover, suggest that it is difficult to judge what may have constituted officially operative tradition (law, etc.). There appear to be no particular indications in extant Judean texts that the books of the Pentateuch (often referred to as "the Torah") were the primary, much less the only texts of torah/law according to which the high priestly rulers operated the temple-state. In the summer of 66 CE, when the priests officiating in the temple services led by the temple-captain Eleazar refused to accept any sacrifices in honor of Rome and Caesar, the high priests put

---

28. Jaffee, *Torah in the Mouth,* chap. 1.

forward priestly experts on the ancestral traditions; but Josephus does not mention any consultation of sacred texts in his account (*War* 2.409–17).

The picture that is now emerging for the scribal circles, in contrast to the old one of a stable scriptural text of "the Torah" and variant interpretations of it, is that of a diverse "great tradition" in which written scrolls played what might be called a supporting role. Far from a stable single text of commonly revered "scripture," alternative versions of Judean/Mosaic law competed with different versions of the Pentateuch. Parallel and perhaps virtually equal in authority, whether for a scribal community such as Qumran or for Hasmonean state law, were collections of legal rulings, traditions of ongoing revelations to the leaders and community (at Qumran) or traditions of legal promulgations by the Pharisees (and their ancestors). Even though scribal circles were literate and presumably had access to written scrolls, both the various versions of (also written) torah/laws of Moses or alternative (written) law-codes, such as the Temple Scroll and 4QMMT, and the (partly written) collections of on-going *mišpatim*, such as 1QS 6–9, were cultivated by memory and oral recitation, indeed at Qumran partly or primarily by collective oral performance. This is not a stable (written) scripture and variant interpretations (partly written) but a richly varied and still developing scribal (but not necessarily official) tradition cultivated primarily in oral communication and performance by various (rival) scribal circles.

## Popular Tradition

As we begin to appreciate the diversity and diffuse authority in the Judean scribal tradition concentrated in Jerusalem (and evident in the texts from Qumran) we can also begin to imagine the considerable social space in which the Israelite popular tradition could flourish in the village communities of Judea and Galilee. No one version of the great tradition had been able to achieve a dominating authority across the various factions of the priestly rulers and different scribal circles. Even less would one version of Israelite tradition have been able to become standard across the semi-self-governing village communities in the various areas of Israelite heritage. While there was some interaction between the scribal and popular traditions, it was not necessarily direct. Given the results of recent research, it is now unclear that villagers would have had direct contact with the scribal tradition, whether in written texts or oral teaching. Scrolls were expensive, cumbersome, and impossible for the non-literate people to read. And while the Pharisees had promulgated rulings for the society, there is no evidence that they or any other scribes serving the temple-state taught torah in the villages. As what sociologists would call "retainers" in the service of the temple-state, they lived and taught in Jerusalem. Thus even in the villages of Judea, which had been ruled by the temple-state for centuries, it is unclear what contact the people may have had with the written texts or even the orally-cultivated regulations of scribal tradition.

The different histories of Galilee and Judea, of course, only served to compound the differences between Jerusalem tradition and popular tradition in the north. During the centuries that Galileans had been independent of Jerusalem rule the Jerusalem scribal/official tradition would have developed with little or no impact on Galilee. Upon taking control of Galilee in 104 BCE, according to Josephus' account, the Hasmonean High Priesthood required the inhabitants (presumably mainly of Israelite heritage as descendants of the most northerly Israelites) "to live according to the laws of the Judeans" (*Ant.* 13.318–19). The latter phrase presumably referred to some significant components of the official tradition developed in Jerusalem and serving as state law.[29] It is historically utterly unrealistic to imagine the Hasmonean regime could somehow have displaced the local customs of Galilean village communities and replaced them with the laws of the Pentateuch and/or the Pharisaic "traditions of the fathers/elders." Presumably "the laws of the Judeans" that the Hasmoneans imposed on the Galileans pertained to the political-economic-religious relations between the temple-state and the villagers, i.e., those pertaining to tithes and offerings, and other "interests" of the temple-state.

It is doubtful that scribes and/or Pharisees would have taught in the villages of Galilee any more than those of Judea. The only sources that ostensibly place them in Galilee prior to the great revolt in 66–67 CE are the Gospel of Mark and the Gospels of Matthew and Luke, which are presumably dependent on Mark. That Pharisees just happen to appear now and then in a village here and there must be explained as stage-setting for their disputes with Jesus. As Mark twice states explicitly, the scribes and Pharisees "came down from Jerusalem," where they were active in service of the temple-state (Mark 3:22; 7:1–2). But Jesus and other Galileans can have known what the scribes and Pharisees stood for without having direct contact with them from the hundred years they lived under the rule of the temple-state prior to the lifetime of Jesus. In Galilean villages there was thus even more "social space" than in Judean villages for Israelite popular tradition to flourish. Rulers were primarily interested in receiving their revenues, and so long as they were forthcoming, did not intervene much in village communities, which had charge of their own local affairs.

29. Analysis and discussion in Horsley, *Galilee*, 39–52.

The most acute problem in attempting to gain a sense of Israelite popular tradition in the villages of Galilee and Judea (and Samaria) is the paucity of sources, particularly direct sources from the people themselves. Because there was interaction between the scribal tradition and the popular tradition in ancient Israel–Judea, however, we do have indirect sources for the latter in the former. As noted above some early Israelite popular traditions were taken up into the Jerusalemite great tradition. The archaic victory songs of Miriam and Deborah and what are clearly popular legends of Moses' and Joshua's leadership and of Elijah and Elisha as prophetic leaders of popular resistance were inserted in Judean scribal epic narratives, as noted above.[30] Yet they would have continued to be cultivated in popular circles, perhaps particularly in Galilee (as evident in the prominence of Elijah in the synoptic gospel tradition). Taken up into the Exodus narrative were the "decalogue" and the "Covenant Code" (in Exodus 20, 21–23), both derived from or reflecting Israelite popular tradition. And at several points in the Deuteronomic history of the rise of the young David to the kingship and the revolts of northern Israelites against kings we find windows onto the Israelite tradition of the popular acclamation ("messiahing") of kings.

While we cannot project the continuing operation of these popular traditions simply on the basis of what we know in the books of the Hebrew Bible, other sources happen to give indications that such popular traditions were indeed still operative in late second-temple times. Elite sources rarely focus on the lives of ordinary people. When the people become unruly and make trouble for their rulers, however, elite sources sometimes give accounts, usually hostile. So while we cannot put much credence in the attribution of motives to popular protests, movements, or revolts by elite sources, they do provide windows onto the actions of the people and at points even indicate the cultural roots of their actions. Josephus provides these in two important connections.

As noted briefly at the outset, Josephus' accounts of the popular prophetic movements and popular messianic movements enable us to discern that they were rooted in memories of the acts of deliverance led by Moses and Joshua and memories of the people having "anointed" the young David as their king to lead them against foreign rulers.

Josephus also provides a window onto the continuing operation of the Mosaic covenantal commandments among the Galilean villagers, whose uprising against Roman and Herodian rule in 66–67 CE he was attempting to control. In several incidents of which he had direct knowledge Galileans attacked Herodians or their officers. In the interrelated fields of New

30. Coote, *Elijah and Elisha.*

Testament studies and ancient Jewish history these accounts were previously used as evidence for the presence of the Law of Moses in Galilee, even for Galileans' faithfulness to "the Law."[31] Closer examination of Josephus' accounts of these actions by groups of Galilean peasants, however, indicates that in every case they were acting in defense of one or another of the basic Mosaic covenantal commandments, which they saw their rulers as violating. Josephus' accounts provide no evidence of Galilean loyalty to (the books of) the Pentateuch/ Torah, but they do indicate that the Mosaic covenant commandment continued to function in the village communities, indeed that at least many Galilean villagers were more committed to observance than were either their Herodian rulers or Josephus and his fellow envoys sent by the Jerusalem high priestly junta to control the situation in 66–67.[32]

With regard to Israelite popular tradition in late second-temple times we are in the unusual position of having sources that derive from movements that originated among Galilean villagers, the Gospels. While the Gospel of Matthew is often deemed to have certain scribal traits and the Gospel of Luke is thought to exhibit a bit of literary sophistication, the Gospel of Mark and the "source" ("Q") of the speeches that are closely parallel in Matthew and Luke clearly derive from circles of ordinary people. In the Gospel tradition generally, Jesus and his disciples are portrayed as working in villages or among villagers in Galilee and nearby areas. Leaving the speeches of Jesus for the next chapter, we can focus here on passages where Mark portrays Jesus as challenging the oppressive practices of the scribes and Pharisees as based in and authorized by their scribal tradition, which was partly written and partly oral. "Jesus," moreover, does this on the basis of Israelite popular tradition. This can be seen in several episodes often called "controversy stories" or "pronouncement stories," usually set up by the Pharisees' challenging Jesus on a particular issue of law.[33] In a prominent previous reading of these stories, based in the assumptions of modern print-culture, Jesus was understood to be challenging "the Law" of "the Jews/Judaism." They can now be read with the fresh perspective provided by the recent research summarized above. We focus on two in particular, one in which Jesus appeals to the popular tradition in opposition to the Pharisees' "traditions of the elders" (Mark 7:1–13) and the other in which he appeals to popular tradition in opposition to the Pharisees' claim of Deuteronomic torah as their authority (Mark 10:2–9).

---

31. Freyne, *Galilee*.

32. Horsley, *Galilee*, 147–57.

33. Horsley, *Hearing the Whole Story*, 161–76.

*Mark 7:1–13*

"The Pharisees and some of the scribes *who had come down from Jerusa-lem*" at the opening of this episode positions this controversy in the broader religious-political-economic conflict between Jerusalem rulers and Galilean villagers. That they challenge the practices of Jesus' Galilean disciples sets Jesus up as spokesperson for Galilean customs and interests in opposition to the representatives of Jerusalem. The representatives of the Jerusalem temple-state use the disciples' failure to wash their hands to illustrate their general failure to conduct their life according to "the tradition of the elders." These were presumably the same as the Pharisees' "tradition of the ances-tors" that Josephus explained as regulations that, at times, had carried the authority of temple-state law.

The parenthetical explanation about the Pharisaic/scribal purity rules focuses on the regional as well as class/caste differences in practices: up there in Jerusalem the Pharisees and all those Judeans . . . ! To Israelite in-siders, including Josephus in both of his histories, the term *Ioudaioi*, often mistranslated as "the Jews," referred to people in/from Judea proper, as dis-tinguished from their Israelite cousins, "the Samaritans" and "the Galileans" to the north. It is relevant to remind ourselves that during the lifetime of Jesus and the first decades of the Jesus movements, Galilee was not under the official jurisdiction of Jerusalem, but that of Herod Antipas and his suc-cessors. Nothing in the episode suggests a conflict between an old legalistic religion (Judaism) and a nascent ethical-universalistic religion (Christian-ity). The maintenance of purity by washings of hands, food, and vessels was a matter of concern for the priests who handled holy objects in the temple. Only occasionally and temporarily when visiting the temple would ordinary Judeans and more distant Israelites have been concerned about matters of purity.[34] The Pharisees, who evidently included purity in their regulations were viewed by the scribes and priests at Qumran as lax ("smooth") in their rulings. But Mark here caricatures them as being particularly concerned about purity in their "tradition of the elders."

In reply, Jesus first attacks the Pharisees' and scribes' obsession with their oral "traditions of the elders" with a reference to a prophetic fragment in their own written scriptures, what we recognize as a version of Isa 29:13. With that entry, he quickly drives a wedge between their "traditions of the elders" and the basic "commandment of God," which all Israelites would have known and supposedly observed. He also decisively changes the sub-ject from purity codes to the deployment of the limited economic resources

34. Neusner, *Judaic Law.*

available to peasant families. He pointedly chooses as an example of the commandment of God, by which he clearly means the decalogue of the Mosaic Covenant, "honor your father and mother." He thus focuses attention on an issue that would form the most sacred and fundamental of duties in any agrarian society, people's care for their aging parents. The scribes and Pharisees, says Jesus, prevent the people from honoring their parents, effectively rejecting or making void the basic (Mosaic covenantal) commandment of God, the very basis of Israel's common life. This they do by urging peasants to devote (*qorban*) a portion of their crops or the produce of part of their land to (the support of) the temple. But that means that those resources could then not be used in support of parents who had become non-productive in their older years.

The political-economic circumstances of Jesus' defense of Israelite popular tradition in Galilee in opposition to the Pharisees may not be far to seek. Under the last Hasmoneans and Herod as client rulers of the Romans, the temple continued to have jurisdiction over Galilee and could presumably expect various revenues from Galileans. After Herod died in 4 BCE, however, the Romans had placed Galilee under the rule of Antipas, who must have taxed the Galileans fairly rigorously in order to support his construction of two cities within the first twenty years of his reign. Encouraging Galileans to "devote" some of the produce of their land to the temple would presumably have been a device to recoup some of the revenues it had lost after 4 BCE.

In any case, the point here is that in defending the covenantal commandment of God against the traditions of the elders Jesus takes his stand on what was most basic to the Israelite popular tradition in attacking the Pharisees' use of part of their scribal tradition to garner more economic support of the temple. One suspects throughout, particularly from the focus of attention first on "the basic commandment of God" before introducing the key issue of honoring parents, that the latter is a focal instance in a general charge against the representatives of the temple-state that in their economic exploitation of the people they are making it impossible for them to live according to the traditional Mosaic Covenant, the core of the Israelite popular tradition. Jesus claims the basic covenant commandment of God as a higher authority in insisting that those resources are needed for local economic support of families.

*Mark 10:2-9*

Earlier in Mark's story John the Baptist is arrested and then executed for prounouncing that "it was not lawful" for Herod Antipas "to have his broth-er's wife," evidently on the view that divorce and remarriage constituted adultery. In the episode of Mark 10:2–9 the Pharisees now "test" Jesus on whether "it is lawful" for a man to divorce his wife. Why was divorce such a "loaded issue" for Herodian rulers and their popular prophetic opposition? Divorce was presumably not very frequent among village families since it would have broken up the fundamental household unit of production, which was barely viable under normal circumstances. Among elite families, on the other hand, marriage, divorce, and remarriage were instruments of rearranging and consolidating political-economic power. Antipas' remar-riage to the last remaining member of the Hasmonean family would have had considerable implications for further consolidation of Herodian rule and power in Roman Palestine. Permissive divorce laws enabled ruling fam-ilies and their ambitious underlings to maneuver for position and power via remarriage. This had ominous implications for the peasantry in at least two principal respects. Peasants indebted to Herodian officers could be caught in the middle of such manipulations.

Jesus' argument with the Pharisees over divorce revolved completely around references to key pieces of Israelite tradition, starting with Jesus counter-question to the Pharisees: "What *to you* did Moses *command*?" The form of the question is the opposite of trying to establish common ground ("What did Moses command {us}?"). When the Pharisees respond that "Moses *allowed* a man to divorce" and Jesus refers again to what Moses said to them as a *command*, it is clear that Jesus is making far more of what Moses said to them then they are. It is standardly recognized that what they say Moses allowed alludes to the teaching on divorce and remarriage in the Deuteronomic code (which we know in Deut 24:1–4). That the text of Deut 24:1, whether in Hebrew or Greek, does not lend itself to description as a command suggests that the formulation in Mark makes this allusion on the basis of limited popular knowledge, not by tinkering with the text of scripture.

Why is Mark's Jesus separating himself from "them" with regard to a legal formulation in Deuteronomy? As noted above, it seems highly unlikely that Galilean villagers would have had knowledge of the Deuteronomic law-code. It had developed in Jerusalem scribal circles, and Jerusalem did not come to control Galilee until a hundred years before Jesus' birth. On into later centuries, as later rabbinic sources inform us, many of the cus-toms and practices of the Galileans were more conservative than those of

Jerusalemites as known from earlier text (now including the objections to their laxity known in Qumran texts). Once the rabbis moved north into Galilee, they found that the Galileans apparently had no need for liberal regulations addressing the kind of contingencies of marriage, divorce and remarriage that had appeared in Judea (*m. Ketub.* 1:4, 5; 4:12; *Yeb.* 4:10). The provisions in Deut 24:1–4 would have appeared to Galileans as liberal laxity of the permissive urban elite.

Jesus sharpens the attack still further. His retort to the Pharisees' recitation of "Moses'" permissiveness both mocks their attribution of authority to their torah of Moses and, in effect, attacks their written law as the virtual opposite of the will of God. "To incite your hardness of heart [Moses] wrote you this command!" suggests that such permissiveness to the wealthy and powerful in fact exacerbates the Pharisees' hardness of heart that has deleterious effects on the people. Apparently Mark's Jesus is alluding to the disintegrating effects on popular life, in its families and village communities, of their advocating permissive laws that enable the wealthy and powerful to control more and more economic resources (for example, by manipulating property arrangements, as implied in Jesus' dispute with the Sadducees about Levirate marriage, in Mark 12:18–27).

In the controversies in both Mark 7:1–13 and 10:2–9 as in other debates with the Pharisees in Mark, Jesus rejects or attacks particular strands of the great tradition, along with the representatives of the Jerusalem temple-state who cultivate and espouse them. Mark 7:1–13 shows Jesus condemning the Jerusalem based Pharisees' traditions of the elders, as exploitative of the people. Mark 10:2–9 shows Jesus rejecting the supposedly scriptural Law of Moses, as a threat to the people's fundamental social forms (family and village community). In both episodes he insisted upon the most fundamental commandments of God (in the Mosaic Covenant) as *the* authoritative basis of Israel's societal life. The commandments of God constituted the core of the Israelite popular tradition in which he and his movement that produced and heard the Gospel of Mark were deeply rooted.

## Continuing Oral Performance

In the process of (re-)"discovery" of the dominance of oral communication in antiquity, the distinction (or even contrast) was drawn between "scribal" culture, in which (presumably) reading and writing of chirographs was dominant, and the "oral" culture of ordinary people. Recent investigation of scribal culture in Judea and the ancient Near East is now also discovering that scribal culture was also oral, or rather "oral–written," insofar as the scribes who were trained to inscribe texts on scrolls learned texts by oral recitation so that they became "written on the tablet of the heart," that is, inscribed in their memory (as discussed in chap. 1). As the early second-century BCE scribe Ben Sira makes clear, a learned scribe trained his "sons" in his "house of instruction" not by having them open a scroll, but by "opening his mouth (Sir 51:23–25), again as discussed in earlier chapters. Like the later rabbis, earlier sages drilled their students in recitation both of already defined texts, some of which were also inscribed on scrolls, and of yet unwritten oral tradition.

This explains how the scribes and priests at Qumran could "recite the writing" and "search the justice-ruling" as well as offer communal blessings in their nightly communal gatherings (1QS 6:6–8). It also explains what modern scholars embedded in the modern print-cultural assumptions of established biblical studies often take as "quotations" of scripture or the "rewriting" of the Bible. In closer examination what are identified as "quotations" are only a phrase or a few words and it is difficult to discern just what "biblical text" they are supposedly "quoting." Rather, the scribes who composed the texts at Qumran such as the Community Rule or the Damascus Rule were so thoroughly imbued with traditional language and idiom that they thought and composed in language that is closely similar to that familiar to biblical scholars from their study of texts that were later included in the Hebrew Bible. The broader streams of oral tradition of torah and various kinds of wisdom were articulated in the same language idiom. Thus when the scribes and priests at Qumran defined regulations (mišpatim) for their community or the Pharisees promulgated regulations not included in the written torah of Moses they appear to scholars embedded in the assumptions of modern print-culture as derived through exegesis of texts of (already "biblical") Torah. The Qumran community was surely unusual in having communal recitations at nightly gatherings. But it is becoming clearer from recent investigation of ancient scribal practice that in scribal training and in scribal circles text and tradition were both cultivated (learned and applied) by oral recitation.

If text and tradition were cultivated by oral(–written) recitation even in scribal circles, it should be clear that Israelite popular tradition was cultivated in oral performance in families and village communities. As in other traditional peasant societies, stories of heroes and heroines would have been told and retold. Stories and pronouncements of the prophets' opposition to oppressive kings would have bolstered the collective resolve of villagers to endure their often difficult circumstances and even engage in what James C. Scott calls "hidden forms of resistance," such as sequestering crops from the probing eyes of tax-collectors. The time-honored customs and covenantal laws and teachings according to which local social-economic relations were managed would have been learned from parents and village elders, for example as particular cases came up for their application. Key passages in the scribal book of Deuteronomy offer a few indications of what may have become local customs and practices, perhaps at scribal urging. These passages indicate that the people knew of the existence of writing, and that it had an authoritative numinous aura. Yet communication was clearly oral and had its effect by the internalization of law and custom by repeated recitation. The Deuteronomic scribes insisted upon the writing of covenantal commandments "on the doorposts" of houses (Deut 11:18–21). But those are symbolic of the permanence of the commandments as the people recite them repeatedly, thus internalizing them in their personal and communal discipline. Similarly, that "Moses" and his scribal successors are to speak laws and songs "into the ears" of the people indicate that oral performance was the way in which the people learned their traditions and then continued to perform them in local praise and practice. While already defined texts stood "written" on scrolls, both the scribal texts and tradition and the popular tradition came to life and *worked* in a process of continuing oral performance.

# 6

# ISRAELITE TRADITION AND THE
# SPEECHES OF JESUS IN Q

WHILE MARK IS COMMONLY AGREED TO BE THE EARLIEST
Gospel story of Jesus, the teaching of Jesus closely parallel in Matthew and
Luke (but not in Mark) is probably the earliest definable text in the synoptic gospel tradition. Identified as the source "Q" (short for *Quelle*, German term for "source"), this is thought to have been formulated within twenty or thirty years Jesus' mission.

Influenced by the habitual reading of the Gospels verse by verse, saying by saying, Q was understood as a mere collection of originally separate sayings of Jesus, the "Sayings Source." Recent "composition criticism" by scholars in North America, however, has led to increasing recognition that Q was a series of Jesus' speeches on various issues important to communities of a Jesus movement.[1] Clearly discernible in the parallel speeches in Matthew and Luke are a covenant renewal speech (behind Luke 6:20–49 and Matthew's "Sermon on the Mount"); a speech that commissions envoys to expand Jesus' own mission into more village communities (Q/Luke 10:2–16); Jesus' response to the charge of casting out demons by Beelzebul (Q/Luke 11:14–20/26); a series of prophetic woes against the scribes and Pharisees (Q/Luke 11:39–52); Jesus' exhortation to bold confession in court (Q/Luke 12:2–12); a speech on anxiety about subsistence living (Q/Luke 12:22–31); and others that may be less obvious.

As the earliest discernible source in the synoptic gospel tradition, closest to the time and context of Jesus' mission in Galilee, the speeches of Q would presumably reflect the Israelite cultural tradition in which Jesus and

---

1. Kloppenborg, *Formation of Q*; Horsley, "Q and Jesus"; Horsley with Draper, *Whoever Hears You Hears Me*, chap. 4.

his first followers would have been rooted. In recent decades, after Q was no longer taken as early Christian catechism supplementary to the Christian Gospel (in Mark, etc.), scholars have included Israelite tradition as a significant factor in their interpretation. "Deuteronomistic theology" has been suggested as the key to the formation and "argument" of Q materials.[2] Some who hypothesize a formative "sapiential" stratum and a secondary "apocalyptic" layer find the teachings in the former to be "unconventional" or "countercultural."[3] Ironically that claim is paired with the hypothesis that after the "itinerant radicals'" mission to "Israel" failed, they tapped into Israelite culture for judgmental sayings in the secondary layer of sayings with which they condemned "all Israel" for rejecting their countercultural message.[4]

All such interpretation of the relation of Q to Israelite tradition, particularly scripture, is based on two interrelated sets of assumptions and concepts, those of the modern print-culture in which biblical studies is deeply rooted, and those left over from the Christian theological origins of biblical studies, such as the synthetic essentialist constructs "Judaism" and "the Law." Recent research in several interrelated areas, however, has undermined and moved well beyond both of these problematic sets of assumptions and concepts, inviting fresh analysis of the relation of the Q speeches to Israelite tradition on assumptions more warranted by evidence for ancient realities.

## The Implications of Recent Research

Results of several lines of recent research, largely separate, but overlapping and mutually reinforcing, are undermining some of the most basic assumptions and concepts previously standard in biblical studies and setting up fresh perspective and new possibilities for understanding texts in historical context. Extensive historical analysis has led to a far more extensive and precise understanding of social life and politics in first-century Roman Palestine. And several separate lines of research into the communications media of antiquity are leading to significant shifts in our understanding of cultural life in ancient Judea and Galilee.

2. Steck, *Geschick der Propheten*; Jacobson, *First Gospel*.

3. Mack, "Kingdom that Didn't Come."

4. Criticism of hypotheses of sapiential and apocalyptic "strata" in Q in Horsley and Tiller, *After Apocalyptic*, chaps. 8–9.

## *The Fundamental Division in Roman Judea and Galilee*

The fundamental division in Roman Galilee and Judea was between the wealthy and powerful Herodian and priestly aristocracies placed in power by the Romans, on the one hand, and the vast majority of people living in hundreds of villages around the countryside, on the other. This is both presupposed and portrayed by our principal sources, such as Josephus' histories and the Gospels. As in other traditional agrarian societies, the power and privilege of the rulers was derived from their expropriation of resources in the form of taxes, tithes, and offerings from the villagers. More than in most traditional agrarian societies, the Judean and Galilean villagers and even the ordinary people in Jerusalem mounted repeated protests, movements of resistance and renewal, and even periodic widespread revolts against their rulers in late second temple/early Roman times.[5]

The Pharisees and other circles of scribes belonged on the elite side of this divide. One need only read Ben Sira's comments the role and activities of scribes/sages in relation to others in society (e.g., Sir 38:24—39:11) indicate clearly that learned scribes served as advisers to the aristocratic priestly rulers of the temple-state. While they may well have attempted to mitigate some of the worst exploitation of the peasants by their aristocratic patrons, they were themselves apparently economically dependent on their patrons in the priestly aristocracy. There is no evidence that points to scribal leadership of popular protests or to peasants or Jerusalemites following scribal figures. The Gospels and Josephus portray the scribes and Pharisees in collaboration with the ruling elite and popular resentment of scribal functions.[6]

A cultural divide corresponded to the political-economic division between the rulers and their scribal retainers, on the one hand, and the Judean and Galilean villagers, on the other. The respective cultures of the Jerusalem temple-state and the villagers corresponds to what anthropologists have discussed in terms of the "great tradition" and the "little tradition," as explored in the previous chap. 5. In short, the priestly aristocracy conducted and controlled the sacrifices and other ceremonies in the temple, as legitimated in authoritative books laid up in the sacred precincts and cultivated by the scribes/sages. But Israelite tradition was also cultivated and operative among the villagers as well. According to Josephus' accounts, most of their protests, movements, and revolts were informed by and patterned after Israelite memories and prophecies. The messianic movements

---

5. Among the many studies are Goodman, *Ruling Class*; Hanson and Oakman, *Palestine*; and Horsley, *Jesus and the Spiral*, chaps. 1–4; *Sociology*; and *Galilee*.

6. Horsley and Tiller, "Ben Sira and Sociology"; Horsley, *Scribes, Visionaries*, chap. 3–4; *Jesus and the Politics*, chap. 6.

headed by a peasant leaders acclaimed by their followers as "kings" were clearly informed by stories of the young David "messiahed" by the Israelites as their king. The movements led by prophets such as Theudas and the "Egyptian" who led their followers out into the wilderness to see the waters of the Jordan divided or up to the Mount of Olives to see the walls of Jerusalem collapse were clearly patterned after stories of Moses and Joshua leading the exodus or entry into the land.[7]

### Limited Literacy amid the Dominant Oral Communication

Ever more extensive research in the last several decades has demonstrated that literacy was very limited in the ancient Roman world and used mainly by the wealthy to enhance their power, as discussed in chap. 1 above.[8] In Roman Palestine literacy was limited mainly to scribal circles.[9] Given the limited literacy, it is clear that oral communication dominated in Judean, Samarian, and Galilean society. The learned scribes were thus the only people in the society who could have produced the authoritative texts (scriptures) that were inscribed on scrolls and laid up in the temple. Furthermore, it is not clear that Hebrew, the language in which authoritative texts (scriptures) were written, was still spoken or understood by anyone outside of scribal circles. It is thus quite unclear how, in the predominantly oral communications environment, villagers might have had direct contact with, or knowledge of the contents of, written scrolls of the books of Moses and the books of the Prophets. Yet they were very familiar with many aspects of Israelite tradition, such as the stories of Moses and Joshua and the young David, as indicated by the popular movements patterned after them.

### Regional Differences between Galilee and Jerusalem

Compounding the differences between rulers and ruled, scribal circles and peasants, scriptures and the stories of Israelite popular tradition, were the differences in historical experience between Galileans and Judeans. After having been independent of Jerusalem rule for centuries, Galilee was taken over by the Hasmonean high priesthood a hundred years before Jesus was born. Galileans were then subjected to Jerusalem rule and "the laws of the

---

7. Fuller analysis and discussion key texts in Horsley, "Popular Messianic Movements"; and "Two Types of Popular Prophets."

8. See especially Harris, *Ancient Literacy*.

9. Hezser, *Jewish Literacy*.

Judeans" for a hundred years before being placed under the separate juris-diction of Herod Antipas during the lifetime of Jesus.

Since these regional differences have not often been recognized, the implications have not been much explored.[10] It seems unwarranted to iden-tify "the laws of the Judeans" as the books of the Pentateuch. Were some of the laws in them included in Josephus term? Since "the laws of" a given people (or rather their rulers) was a term for their polity in Hellenistic texts, Josephus' account may mean that the Hasmoneans were forcing the Galile-ans to live subject to the Judean (temple-)state. It seems historically unlikely that the Pharisees or other scribal retainers would have brought knowledge of the Judean scriptures to the Galileans. As retainers of the temple-state, they were based in Jerusalem and did their teaching there, not in villages. The Gospel of Mark (on which Matthew and Luke depend) is the only source that portrays the Pharisees as active in Galilee, and Mark's picture of their having Jesus under active surveillance is one of the least credible aspects of the Gospel story historically. There is also no good evidence of Judeans, oth-er than Herodian officers and troops, moving north into Galilee. Galileans who, like Judeans, cultivated Israelite popular tradition would presumably have become aware that authoritative books existed, at least in Jerusalem. But it is quite unclear how they, including the people who produced and cultivated the Jesus speeches in Q, could have become acquainted with the scriptures produced and cultivated by Judean scribes/sages.

### *Different Kinds of Writing and their Functions:*

Closely related to the limited literacy and the dominant oral communica-tion in ancient and medieval societies were the different kinds of writing and their functions.[11] In societies where writing is rare, it is often mysterious and numinous, cloaked with a sacred aura. Having such an aura, writing could serve monumental functions, memorializing and making permanent royal decrees, official laws, or acts of emperors (such as the *Res Gestae* of Augustus), lending authority to ruling institutions and power-holders. By contrast with most writing in modern print culture, not all writing in the

---

10. Horsley, *Galilee*; and *Archaeology, History,* present preliminary analyses and dis-cussion of available evidence for the different regional history of Galilee and its implica-tions in ways that challenge standard older assumptions, approaches, and concepts. Subsequent archaeological and textual treatments of Galilee, however, have shown little interest in questioning old assumptions and approaches and often repeat the standard older generalizations rooted in the synthetic construct of Judaism and in uncritical use of sources.

11. Niditch, *Oral World.*

ancient world was (intended to be) read or consulted, as discussed in chaps. 1–2 above.

Thus in the Judean temple-state, some texts were written on scrolls as symbols of authority, and not so much as texts to be read. These scrolls were sacred objects, symbolic of and representing God and God's word which was all the more authoritative for having been set in writing. Deposited in the temple, they held an aura for the priests and people and lent their authority and sacred aura to the temple and priesthood. We can gain a sense of this from the scene in Nehemiah 8, the portrayal of the prototypical Judean scribe and priest, Ezra, presenting the scroll of the torah of Moses to the Judeans assembled before the temple. "Ezra opened the scroll in the sight of all the people, for he was standing above all the people (on a raised platform); and when he opened it, all the people stood up. Then Ezra blessed Yahweh, the great God, and all the people answered, "Amen, Amen," lifting up their hands. Then they bowed their heads and worshiped Yahweh with their faces to the ground." In this idealized scene, the people assembled first bowed before the sacred object and then heard the torah of Moses proclaimed aloud. Since the people probably did not understand the archaic literary language of Hebrew, however, real communication would have come in a second step of oral translation/interpretation.

### Scribal Oral Cultivation of Texts (and Oral Tradition)

As scholars of rabbinic learning and books of the Pentateuch have pointed out, the term *qr'*, often previously (mis-) translated with "read," really meant "recite" or "proclaim"—including when what was orally proclaimed was also written. "He [Moses] took the book of the covenant and he proclaimed (*qr'*) it in the ears of the people" (Exod 24:7; cf. Deut 31:11).[12] Similarly, when Scripture was being referenced, God or Moses was understood as *speaking*, as in the well-known "formula quotations" in the Gospel of Matthew. As has been recognized for some time, the rabbis taught their students Torah, Mishnah, and rabbinic debates by repeated oral recitation. In this same tradition of learning, as is finally being recognized in recent studies, second-temple Judean scribes, the literate elite, learned texts that were also written on scrolls by repeated *recitation*.[13] The texts thus became "written on the tablet of the heart," that is, in their memory. The text was then accessed

---

12. Boyarin, "Placing Reading," 13.

13. Jafee, *Torah in the Mouth*; Carr, *Tablet of the Heart*; Horsley, *Scribes, Visionaries*, chap. 5.

through memory, not by consulting a written copy.[14] A telling illustration of his point is the procedure for a meeting of ten "recorded" in the Community Rule handbook from Qumran in a passage that is often somewhat mistranslated. At their nightly gatherings they "recite the writing (*sefer*) and search the ruling (*mišpat*) and bless in common" (1QS 6:6–8).[15] Assuming that "the writing" refers to a written text of torah and "the ruling" to the community's own ordinances, the Qumranites were regularly calling up from memory and ritually reciting passages both of scripture and their own legal rulings that were also inscribed on scrolls possessed by the community. But this was not unique to Qumran. It was standard practice of the very scribes who copied texts on scrolls to learn the text by repeated recitation so that they could call up passages from memory as appropriate to various situations, whether in personal devotion or debates with one another or councils of state. In certain circumstances their recitation was a command performance before an audience of officials, with the gravity of a ceremonial ritual.[16]

### *Hebrew Scriptural Books: Different Versions, Still Developing*

The discovery of scores of scrolls of books of scripture among the DSS made possible a quantum leap in our knowledge of the history of the development of those texts. The standard older view was of an "official Hebrew text of the Jewish community which had reached a point of stabilization in the first century AD."[17] As discussed in chap. 1, Eugene Ulrich's careful research on the manuscripts of books of the Pentateuch and Prophets found at Qumran has concluded, on the contrary, that there is no evidence up through the end of second-temple times that there was either a fixed list of books or a fixed text either of individual books or of the collection of books.[18] The implications of his close analysis of manuscripts of books that were later included in the Hebrew Bible focus on two closely related points. First, evidence from Qumran demonstrates that there were multiple textual traditions, indeed multiple versions of books that were later included in the Hebrew Bible.[19] This suggests that there no "normative Judaism," and indicates that there

---

14. Jaffee, "Oral-Cultural Context," 53.

15. The standard translations of "read the Book" and "study the Law" are potentially misleading, insofar as those terms have distinctive connotations in modern typographic culture, particularly in academic circles.

16. Jaffe, *Torah in the Mouth*, 16.

17. Childs, *Introduction to the Old Testament as Scripture*, 100.

18. Ulrich, *Dead Sea Scrolls*, 59.

19. Ibid., 9–11, 14.

was also no standard text of scripture that was authoritative in the temple-state and Judean scribal circles. Second, the different versions of books later included in the Hebrew Bible were still developing. In a continuation of the process of composition from earlier in the second-temple period, scribes were still inserting new material and making other changes in scriptural books.[20]

About the book of Isaiah in particular (which has special relevance to the speech in Q/Luke 7:18–35), Ulrich says that the textual history is complex. On the one hand the scrolls of Isaiah from Qumran do not provide evidence of different versions of the book. But its text was unstable, still undergoing development in late second-temple times, as Talmon explained four decades ago.[21] The other Isaiah scrolls discovered at Qumran make it clear that the *Great Isaiah Scroll* (1QIsaᵃ) that "displayed multifaceted disagreement with the Masoretic *textus receptus*," hence initially thought to be distinctive to the Qumran community, was representative of the state of development of the text shared across Judean (scribal) groups.[22]

*Alternative Texts of Torah and Israelite Tradition in Contemporary Judean Texts*

Side by side with the variant versions of books that were later included in the Hebrew Bible and the LXX, both at Qumran and elsewhere, were alternative versions of torah and alternative versions of Israelite historical tradition, as discussed in chaps. 2 and 3. Books such as *Jubilees*, the *Biblical Antiquities* of Pseudo-Philo, and Josephus' *Antiquities* became categorized as "rewritten Bible." As I argued in chap. 3, however, these books were not a rewriting of the written texts that were later included in the Hebrew Bible, but alternative versions of Israelite history and torah that drew on a wider Judean cultural tradition.[23] The Temple Scroll is an alternative text of torah, not a "rewriting" of sections of the written books of Exodus, Leviticus, and/or Deuteronomy. One obvious implication is that we can no longer think in terms of (Mosaic) torah as being identical simply with the five books of Moses, the Pentateuch. Rather, different and probably rival versions of torah and Israelite historical traditions shared authority among the scribal and priestly groups of late second-temple Judea.

---

20. Ulrich, *Dead Sea Scrolls*, 11–12, 23–24, 75, 77.

21. Talmon, "DSIa as a Witness"; Ulrich, *Dead Sea Scrolls*, 61–62.

22. Ulrich, *Dead Sea Scrolls*, 8.

23. Further discussion in Horsley, *Scribes, Visionaries*.

*The Diversity of Scribal Groups and Authoritative Texts and Traditions*

Corresponding to the diversity of authoritative texts of torah and historical tradition were the diverse circles and parties among the scribal retainers who cultivated Israelite cultural traditions. The concept of "sects" was applied to the various movements and small church bodies that arose during the Reformation in Europe as alternatives to the officials sanctioned state "churches." This concept, however, simply does not fit the various Judean scribal circles that emerged at times in late second-temple Judea. Rather, in a sustained series of political-religious crises, several different circles or factions emerged among the scribal retainers who served in the temple-state. Some remained loyal to the incumbent high priestly regimes. Others became dissidents in varying degrees, at times actively opposing the dominant high priestly regime or simply withdrawing into the wilderness.[24]

In the escalating political-religious crisis of the Hellenizing reform starting in 175 BCE and the emperor Antiochus Epiphanes' invasion of Jerusalem to enforce it, the activities and/or the texts of at least three different scribal factions are evident. The *hasidim* appear to have joined the Maccabean Revolt, then made a special truce with the new usurping high priest Alcimus and his Seleucid imperial backers (2:42; 7:12–13). The *maskilim* who produced the historical visions-and-interprerations in Daniel 7, 8, 10–12 resisted the reform, its high priestly sponsors, and the imperial invasion, to the point of being martyred. A parallel circle of dissident scribes who looked to the primordial hero Enoch as their inspiration sharply condemned the wealthy and power rulers and found revelation in historical visions-and-interpretations (the Animal Vision, *1 Enoch* 85–90, the Ten-Week Vision, *1 Enoch* 93:1–10; 91:11–17, and the Epistle of Enoch, *1 Enoch* 94–105). If the large number of manuscripts of these visionary texts found at Qumran is any indication, these texts quickly achieved an authority that rivaled that of some of the books that were later included in the Hebrew Bible, and of course the book of Daniel was included.

Under the Hasmonean high priests, who were seeking less restraint from Judean tradition and greater lee-way to expand their rule over Idumea as well as Samaria and Galilee, emerged the well-known rivalry between the Pharisees and the Sadducees for influence on the regime. The more establishment Sadducees recognized as authoritative only the laws of Moses that were written on scrolls. The Pharisees, on the other hand, promulgated and cultivated additional "traditions of the elders" that held a certain authority parallel to and/or rivaling that of the laws of Moses that had been written

---

24. On the following see the more extensive analysis and discussion in Horsley, *Sribes, Visionaries.*

on scrolls. Less recognized is that this conflict involved pendulum swings in the high priestly administration of Judea, as successive Hasmonean rulers included or rescinded or re-instated the Pharisaic "traditions of the elders" as part of official state law "(*Ant.* 13.293–98, 408–10). Qumran texts now provide evidence for yet another scribal-priestly faction that had not only its own *mišpatim* that were apparently counterparts to the Pharisaic "traditions of the elders" and parallel in authority to the *sepher* of torah, but also their own *pešarim* of prophetic texts. Contrary to what was previously claimed, there is no evidence in the Qumran texts or for the Pharisees that either the justice-rulings at Qumran or the Pharisees' "traditions of the ancestors" were derived from interpretation of particular scriptural passages. Thus, not only were different version of Israelite tradition that we know from written texts competing for authority, but other versions in oral texts and/or in written texts that are no longer extant were operative in various groups in Judea.

### Composition in Memory and Oral Performance

Recent research suggests that not only did the ancient literate elite cultivate their texts that were also written by oral recitation, but they also composed new texts in their minds, drawing on the considerable store of material in their memory. The modern experience and concepts of an "author" "writing" a text (i.e., composing it in writing) that is then read in writing (by hand or in print) by readers is quite inapplicable to the ancient world. The composition and the writing down were separate processes. Texts, including those quickly inscribed on parchment or papyrus, were composed in oral performance, in many cases in an on-going cumulative process of composition from memory.

Classicists, for example, have explored how authors such as Pliny composed in their minds from materials in memory and then performed their texts and/or dictated them to scribes who wrote them down—perhaps for subsequent oral performance.[25] Something like that must be the way Paul composed the arguments of his letters before dictating them to a scribe. Particularly significant for the present exploration is that the process of composition from memory and the act of writing the text down were different, just as "the recited text" that depended on the text-in-memory was not necessarily the same as "the written text" on a scroll.

The process of composition was more prolonged and cumulative for many Judean texts, including proto-scriptural texts. Many Judean texts were evidently performed/composed and written down as divine [ly-inspired]

---

25. Small, *Wax Tablets of the Mind.*

writing by a process of agglomeration or accretion. We have for some time realized that most of the prophetic books such as Amos or Isaiah or Jeremiah, were at some point anthologies of fragments of oracles held in memory after their original oral performance (as, for example, in the story of Jeremiah dictating his oracles from memory to Baruch in Jeremiah 36). Those anthologies were then supplemented and expanded by additions at various points. From the Qumran Isaiah scrolls it is now evident that verses and wording of verses continued to develop. As Ulrich has explained, this process of composition of proto-scriptural books by addition and interpretation continued right on through late second-temple times. We are learning about the close relationship between continuing performance and the continuing development of manuscripts of texts in medieval Europe in studies that are suggestive for the oral cultivation and recitation of texts such as the proto-scriptural books.[26] It seems clear that the memory and oral performance of texts and related cultural memories played an important role in the continuing development or co-composition of the (proto-)scriptural books and related texts. Texts or components of larger texts, however, would not have suddenly vanished from peoples' memory once they were written down. They would continue to have been cultivated orally, since orality was the overwhelmingly dominant means of communication, and they would have been revived in memory by periodic performance or recitation, as can be recognized in the window onto Qumran practice cited from 1QS above.

∽

The results of research in these several interrelated areas clearly undermine some of the key assumptions of biblical studies, many of them rooted in the modern print culture in which the academic enterprise of scriptural study has been deeply embedded. The results of this research invite us to abandon what may have been standard assumptions and concepts that can now be seen as anachronistic and problematic. The mutual reinforcement of these interconnected areas of recent research thus make possible a new perspective on and approach to Gospel texts in general and to the Q speeches in particular.

---

26. Clanchy, *From Memory to Written Record*; Stock, *Implications of Literacy*.

## Performative Speech in
## the Q Speeches-in-Performance

Some of the recent research sketched above enables us to recognize differ-ent kinds of writing and their political-economic-cultural functions and to recognize and explore the effects that texts in oral performance had on the hearers. Embedded in the assumptions of modern print-culture, bib-lical studies has tended to look for the meaning of words, lines, phrases, and statements in what were assumed to be the stable sacred text (the word of God). In the cultural and social realities of the ancient world, however, where writing in its various forms was embedded in the dominant oral communication and texts, whether only oral or written as well as oral, were orally recited usually to a group of people, we are seeking rather the *work* that texts-in-oral-performance accomplished among the hearers.

As we move from consideration of the scribally composed, revered, and orally-learned and -recited texts such texts of torah and (Ben Sira's) speeches of instructional wisdom (in chaps. 2–4) to the speeches of Jesus in Q (in chaps. 6–9), the effects of the respective performances shifts with both composer-performer and audience. "Ezra's" ceremonial public performance of the numinous book of the torah of Moses, a sacred monumental-consti-tutional writing that bolstered the authority of temple and high priesthood, had the effect of solemnizing the people's loyalty to the temple-state. It did not matter that they could not [cognitively] understand the archaic Hebrew language of the text-in-performance, that only added to the mystery already surrounding the sacred scroll before which they bowed in awe. The regular nightly communal recitation of "the writing" (of torah) etc. in the commu-nity gatherings at Qumran effected personal and collective internalization of covenantal teaching and community regulations, hence personal and communal commitment and discipline in the community. The sustained curriculum of speeches of instructional wisdom performed to their proté-gés by learned scribes such as Ben Sira resulted in the conservative obedient character-formation necessary for scribes-sages engaged in the professional service of the temple-state.

Numinous scrolls on which the torah of God/Moses stood mysteri-ously "written" and the periodic ceremonial performance of sacred texts, however, along with the performance in the temple of daily and special annual festival sacrifices and offerings, could not overcome the inherent structural conflict between the ruling priestly aristocracy and the subordi-nated villagers. It was hardly in the villagers' interest, for example, to render up a certain percentage of their annual crops, from which they hoped to eke out a subsistence living, in tithes, offerings, taxes, tribute, and interest on debts. As discussed in chap. 4, they had their own version of Israelite tradition, including Mosaic covenantal torah, that included prohibition of interest on loans and requirements of the cancellation of debts and release of debt-slaves every seventh year. They told and retold stories of Elijah and other prophets who condemned kings and their officers for exploiting the people in violation of the covenantal commandments. Although Judean scribal texts are hardly direct sources Israelite popular tradition, reports of popular protests and popular movements in Josephus' histories provide evidence of at least some of the popular memories and Mosaic covenant commandments that were cultivated among the Judean, Samaritan, and Galilean villagers. It is common in other traditional agrarian societies for popular tradition to be cultivated, told and retold, in the course of family and village community life. One obvious venue for such cultivation would have been the regular meetings of village assemblies (*synagoge* in Greek, *knesset* in Hebrew/Aramaic), as attested in the Gospels and especially in later rabbinic sources.

When we hear the speeches of Jesus in Q in performance, the Israelite popular tradition suddenly comes alive.[27] Jesus and his first followers from whose interactive communication the Q speeches must have developed were born, socialized, and embedded in the Israelite village culture of Galilee. As the speeches were performed repeatedly in communities of a Jesus movement, the speeches on matters of concern to the people (in performance) had certain effects among the people hearing them. As we learn to appreciate these speeches-in-performance by attending to how they resonate with the hearers in their social and historical context by referencing Israelite popular tradition, we can also begin to discern the different kinds of speech that are involved.

Although the speeches in Q are short and focused on particular concerns, as are those in Sirach, they are very different kinds of speech from instructional wisdom.[28] The speech discerned behind Luke 11:2-4, 9-13, and the parallel in Matthew 6:7-13 + 7:7-11 is instruction on prayer. But in performance the speech begins in the register of prayer addressed to God: "Father, . . ." (11:2-4). The speech in Q/Luke 6:20-49 is speech of covenant renewal. Performed in a village community, it is what has been called "performative speech," that is, in speech that "makes it so," that is, effects what is spoken, as when a judge pronounces in court "Innocent!" or "Guilty as charged." In performance in a community deeply familiar with the Mo-

---

27. Fuller discussion of Israelite popular tradition in the Q speeches in Horsley with Draper, *Whoever Hears You Hears Me*, chap. 5.

28. Cf. the argument in Kloppenborg, *Formation of Q*. See further in chap. 8 below.

saic covenant that the speech references in formal components as well as allusions to traditional covenantal commandments and admonitions, the speech *enacts* a renewal of the Covenant in that community. The speech in Q/Luke 10.2–16 in performance is also performative speech. In declaring "Behold, I send you out . . . ," "Jesus" sends them out. The community, of course, already knows that envoys have already been commissioned. In subsequent performance of this speech "Jesus" commissions them again and/or sends out additional workers. The instruction to the envoys, moreover, includes both performance of healings and additional performative speech ("the kingdom of God has come near to you!") as well as the performance of a curse in performative speech ("the dust of your town . . . we wipe off against you!").

In comparison with the scriptural books produced presumably by Jerusalem scribal circles in support of the temple and its priestly aristocracy, the most striking aspect of the Q speeches may be their sharp stance against the ruling house in Jerusalem and especially the scribes and Pharisees. Indeed the speeches/speakers ("Jesus" and his followers) represent their own identity as "children," as opposed to sages and learned (10:21–24). The addresees of the Q speeches are poor villagers exploited by the rulers and their retainers who understand themselves as the successors of the earlier prophets persecuted and killed by the rulers and their advisers (6:20–26; 11:49–51). The Jesus-speaker(s) and his addressees are ordinary people sharply opposed to and opposed by the scribes and Pharisees and the Jerusalem rulers (see further chap. 8).

Consideration of the Q speeches in performance, however, helps us realize just how sharp this opposition is. The comments about Herod Antipas' luxurious palace and clothing in Q 7:24–28 are merely caustic and sarcastic, although they would have resonated with the people who had eagerly heard John the Baptist's prophesying against Antipas. In three other speeches or speech-fragments, however, the mode of speech goes far beyond mere criticism to performative speech in which the "Jesus" speaker performatively pronounces God's condemnation of the Jerusalem rulers and/or their scribal retainers. In form these speeches are prophetic, sub-forms of prophecies of God's judgment that, by anticipation, they announce as if it has already happened. The speech(-fragment) in Q/Luke 13:28–29 is a prophetic oracle of the future banquet of the renewed Israel in the kingdom of God, addressed (ostensibly) to those who claim the illustrious patriarchs Abraham, Isaac, and Jacob as their special ancestors, guaranteeing their inheritance of the kingdom—that is the Jerusalem aristocracy (cf. John's speech in 3:7–9). "Jesus'" prophetic vision, however, sees them cast out in punishment. The speech(-fragment) in Q 13:34–35 is a prophetic lament in which the prophet (Jesus), having become privy to God's judgment of the ruling house of Jerusalem for having killed the (previous) prophets, mourns over its impending desolation.[29]

Most shocking, perhaps, once we recognize the form of speech, is the series of woes pronounced on the scribes and Pharisees in 11:39–52. These are not disputes about "the Law" and they are not primarily about purity laws. With rhetorical flourishes that mock the scribes and Pharisees for their obsession with purity and tithing, the statements in this speech focus on the oppressive effects of the scribal political-economic-religious regulations and practices on the people. This speech takes the form of a series of prophetic woes, in a long Israelite tradition of such woes, that both indict the scribes and Pharisees for the exploitation of the people and then pronounce sentence/punishment against them. Heard in performance, the Q speeches are not just opposed to, but pronounce condemnation of the Jerusalem rulers and their scribal and Pharisaic retainers, the very literate professionals who cultivate the scripture and other expressions of the official or elite Israelite tradition.[30]

## Israelite Popular Tradition in Q Speeches Compared with Scribal Tradition

The life of ordinary people such as those addressed in the Q speeches would have been embedded in oral communication. If even the literate scribes composed and cultivated texts orally, even more would non-literate ordinary people have developed their stories and speeches in the processes of oral communication. And if in their composition of texts the literate elite could draw on a cultural repertoire in their memory, so could ordinary people. Only the cultural repertoire of the popular tradition, while overlapping in various ways, would have been different in various ways from the scribal tradition. As noted from the research summarized above, although villagers probably knew of the existence of the sacred books of scripture laid up in the temple, it is doubtful that villagers had direct contact with them. And although they may have heard that certain prophecies and psalms and laws were "written" on one or another sacred scroll, it seems unlikely that they could have gained much knowledge of the content of the scriptural texts that were laid up in the temple and were periodically recopied by scribes in Jerusalem. Rather they would have had their own Israelite popular tradition that articulated their own interests, cultivated orally over the generations

29. See further Horsley with Draper, *Whoever Hears You Hears Me,* 279–85.

30. See further ibid., 285–91.

in Judean and Galilean village communities. Where the contents of the popular tradition overlapped the contents of the scribal texts, moreover, the villagers had their own versions.

While only one Q speech and the temptation dialogue refer to scripture ("it is written"), the speeches of Q make repeated references and allusions to Israelite tradition. These references to Israelite tradition, moreover, include far more than famous figures such as Abraham and Solomon. They also include prophetic and covenantal forms, covenantal teachings that clearly draw on the Israelite covenantal lore, and many motifs and images that must have belonged to the Israelite cultural repertory in one connection or another. We recognize all of these because they also appear in the Hebrew Bible, other Judean literature, Jewish literature in Greek, and/or in non-literary sources. For Judeans and Galileans (and presumably Samarians) these were all part of their culture cultivated orally and, with the exception of scribal circles and presumably some priests, did not entail possession or consultation of written scrolls. It has long been standard practice in New Testament studies to look in particular verses or names or terms in a given Gospel for references to or echoes of particular verses or names or terms in "Old Testament" or "intertestamental" texts. As a result of the lines of recent research surveyed above, this practice can now be seen as rooted in the assumptions of print culture and superficially inappropriate to ancient society, attending to the mere written-textual surface layer of Judean and Galilean culture. Breaking with this old print-cultural habit attending merely to *written* "intertextuality," I will purposely focus on references in Q speeches to broader Israelite cultural patterns and/or symbols of broader historical patterns and/or power-relations. Four cases can illustrate how references to and uses of the Israelite popular tradition in Q speeches overlap but differ significantly from scripture or other scribal tradition.[31]

First, once we are aware of the fundamental divide between the Galilean and Judean villagers and their Herodian and high priestly rulers in Jerusalem, references to the figure of Abraham at two significant points in Q speeches jump out as an example of Israelite tradition contested between the ruling/scribal elite and the popular movement catalyzed by John and Jesus. Abraham became a key symbol in Jerusalem political-culture under Hasmonean and Herodian rule. Produced apparently somewhat after the Hasmoneans had established Jerusalem rule over the Idumeans (Edomites), the book of *Jubilees* emphasized Abraham's special love for and blessing of his "son" Jacob = Israel and expanded on Genesis 27 with an account of

---

31. Again see the fuller survey and analysis of Israelite tradition in Q in Horsley with Draper, *Whoever Hears You Hears Me*, chap. 5.

Jacob's sons' subjugation of Esau's sons = Edomites (*Jub* 19:16–29; 22:10–30; 23:1–3; 38).[32] Herod then enshrined the patriarchs in grand style with the construction of major monuments in both Mamre and Hebron, the traditional burial site of the patriarchs and matriarchs (Gen 23:19; 25:9; 49:31; 50:13).[33] The scribal *Psalms of Solomon* (9:9–10) insisted that God had "chosen the descendants of Abraham above all the nations." This focus on Abraham in ruling circles of Jerusalem forms the backdrop against which we should hear Abraham *rejected* as a symbol of guaranteed lineage in Q 3:7–9 and Q 13:28–29. John's challenge to "bear fruits of (Mosaic covenantal) repentance" and not to rely on one's illustrious lineage, as in the slogan "we have Abraham as our father," is a blunt rejection of pretentious wealthy families' presumption on this point. Similarly, the prophecy in Q 13:28–29, focused on the image of the gathering and restoration of Israel in a glorious banquet, is evidently directed against the elite who presumed, on the basis of their lineage and position, that they were sure to be included.

Second, in the concluding short speech in Q 22:28–30 Jesus sets up the Twelve as representative figures engaged in the renewal of (establishing justice for, delivering) Israel, symbolized in its twelve tribes.[34] In order to appreciate this declaration it is necessary to cut through the standard Christian supercessionism and (mis-) translation of *krinein* (*spt* in Hebrew) as "judging" Israel. In the Hebrew Bible and LXX God does not "judge" but "delivers" or "does justice for" the poor, oppressed, widow, orphan, etc. (e.g., Pss 9; 35; 58; 82; 94) or even the whole people (Isa 42:1, parallel with "salvation" in Isa 49:6). This is certainly how Matthew understood Q 22:28–30, in the use of *palingenesis*, i.e., "restoration" of Israel (in the same sense that Josephus uses the term, *Ant.* 11:66, 107). The restoration of the twelve tribes was one of the principal images of the future renewal of Israel. This was partly rooted in the memory of the renewal and resistance movement led by Elijah (see esp. 1 Kings 18). The "servant of Yahweh" in Isa 40–55 is called "to raise up the tribes of Jacob" (49:6). Ben Sira appeals to God to gather the tribes and give them their inheritance, and has restoring the tribes of Jacob as one of the functions of the returning Elijah (Sir 36:13; 48:10).

These references in scribally composed texts are good examples of how the image, originally operative in the popular tradition of the northern tribes, became installed into the Jerusalemite "great tradition." The scheme is also adjusted to hierarchical Jerusalemite tradition in Qumran texts, with twelve chief priests (1QM 2:2–3) as well as twelve chiefs of twelve

---

32. Mendels, *Land of Israel*, chap. 6; Doran, "New Dating of Jubilees."

33. Richardson, *Herod*, 60–61, 184.

34. Fuller analysis and discussion in Horsley, *Jesus and the Spiral*, 199–208.

tribes leading Israel along with the presumably higher-ranking "prince" and priestly leaders (1QM 5:1–3). As fits a scribal-priestly community, the twelve laymen heading the people at Qumran were conceived in sapiential as well as covenantal terms (1QS 8:1–3). *Psalm of Solomon* 17 presents another scribal-sapiential and Jerusalem-centered picture of the restoration of Israel in its twelve tribes. The most significant differences between the *Ps Sol* 17 vision and that in the Q/Luke 22:28–30 is the psalm's focus on an anointed imperial king (in the tradition of imperial kingship in Jerusalem) as God's agent and the emphasis on his restoration of a purged Jerusalem. By contrast in the Q speech the prophet Jesus designates a collective leadership representative of the symbolic twelve tribes that are to be "effecting justice" for the renewed people of Israel. And in other Q speeches, Jesus in a popular prophetic role presents a prophetic lament over the anticipated desolation of the Jerusalem ruling house and declares God's judgment on the ruling city for its exploitation of the people and killing of the earlier prophets (Q/Luke 13:34–35; 11:49–51).

Third, as noted above, in recent decades Q has been understood as informed, perhaps even organized, in terms of Deuteronomistic theology, as focused on the theme of persecution of the prophets. Yet the Q speeches display significant differences from Deuteronomistic theology. For example, the penitential prayers prefatory to covenant renewal, the most convincing examples of Deuteronomistic tradition, present fascinating differences from Q's speeches concerning prophets, which appear to stand in the popular tradition. In Nehemiah 9 and Baruch 1–3, the restored Jerusalem elite confess their ancestors' breaking of the Mosaic covenant and rejection of the prophets in their petition to God to restore them in power—apparently still confident in the validity of God's unconditional promise to Abraham. Similarly, evidently under late second-temple Herodian or high priestly rulers, in a corresponding penitential endeavor, monuments were constructed to prophets who had criticized and condemned earlier rulers. The *Lives of the Prophets*, which may be of later date yet contains earlier traditions, indicates the existence of monumental tombs or other memorials in six cases and implies memorials in another three.[35] Thus honored with monuments, and inscribed on sacred scrolls as well, the prophets were enshrined in the Jerusalem "great tradition" by the descendants of those they had castigated. But that is precisely what Q 11:47–48 condemns, from a popular viewpoint. Moreover, the Deuteronomistic scheme looks back on both the disobedience and God's punishment as having occurred in the past to the ancestors. The speeches in Q 11:39–52 and 13:34–35, however, declare judgment

---

35. Schwemer, *Fruehjuedische Prophetenlegenden*, 1.55–87.

against the present Jerusalem rulers and their representatives that is imminent, for present as well as past violence and injustice, in conjunction with the renewal of Israel over against the rulers that is underway in Jesus' proclamation and practice. These speeches, moreover, have the form of prophetic oracles, performative speech that effects what it declares.

Fourth, not only does the speech in Q/Luke 6:20–49 include numerous allusions to Mosaic covenantal teachings that we recognize from acquaintance with Exodus, Leviticus, and Deuteronomy, but the speech proceeds according to the traditional structuring components of the Mosaic Covenant (as discerned in Exodus 20; Joshua 24).[36] This first, longest, and foundational speech of Q's "Jesus" is thus deeply rooted in and expresses what may have been the most formative pattern in Israelite tradition. We recognize it as the structuring pattern in much of the legal material, the torah, in the books of the Pentateuch and the presupposition of many prophetic oracles. The covenant structure had three interrelated steps. After the declaration of God's deliverance (originally the exodus from bondage), came God's commandments for the conduct of societal life (including exclusive loyalty to God as Israel's King), followed by sanctioning mechanisms including the pronouncement of blessings and curses (for keeping or not keeping the commandments). In the texts of scribal tradition (e.g., in "Deuteronomistic theology"), the relationship between commandments and sanctions shifted. In what may well have been a well-intentioned way to motivate obedience to covenantal torah (laws), scribal texts pointed to people's poverty and other distress as evidence that they were cursed for disobedience of the covenantal laws. This can be seen throughout the book of Deuteronomy.

In Jesus' covenant renewal speech in Q/Luke 6:20–49, by contrast, the first step is to transform the blessings and curses, that had been used, in effect, to intensify people's self-blame, into the new declaration of deliverance. In performative speech, "Jesus" declares to the people, "Blessed are you who are poor, . . . hungry . . . ," giving them a "new lease on life" so that they can respond positively to the following covenantal demands for mutual assistance and cooperation in the social-economic life of their village communities.[37]

---

36. Analysis and discussion in Horsley with Draper, *Whoever Hears You Hears Me*, chap. 9; Horsley, *Covenant Economics*, chap. 6.

37. Fuller analysis and discussion in Horsley with Draper, *Whoever Hears You Hears Me*, chap. 9.

## Q Speeches and (Ostensible Quotation from) Scripture

Given the sharp condemnation of the Jerusalem rulers and their scribal retainers in some Q speeches, it is not surprising that the other Q speeches have virtually no quotation from the texts that had become scriptures of the temple-state. What is often considered to be a "quotation formula," "it is written" (*gegraptai*) appears only in the speech in Q/Luke 7:18–35 (at 7:27), which is invariably considered integral to Q, and (three times) in Jesus' replies to the devil's temptations in Luke 4:1–13//Matt 4:1–11, which is usually considered a late addition to Q. In the latter, a narrative or dialogue, which may not belong with the speeches of Q, "Jesus" may be appealing to the authority of the scripture. Three times he cites a brief proverb or commandment and/or a line of reassurance that resembles statements that we know in the book of Deuteronomy or the Psalms, saying "it is written." These citations are all very short formulaic statements (a proverbs or a commandment a reassurance) that would have been well known and frequently recited in the prevailing oral culture. Given the general lack of literacy and the unavailability of scrolls, it seems highly unlikely that some hypothetical "author" of this dialogue was working from a written text of Deuteronomy. "It is written" (*gegraptai*) is an appeal to the authority that these well-known proverbs or commandment have because they stand "written" in scripture. But the performer(s) of the dialogue may well not have known in what book. Given that the books of the Pentateuch were current in more than one version and that their texts were still developing, and given that these brief proverbs or commandment were well known and frequently cited, it would be extremely difficult to demonstrate that they were quotations from a written scroll.

The only apparent reference to scripture in one of the Q speeches, *gegraptai*, comes in the middle of the speech about Jesus as fulfilling longings for the prophetic "coming one" and John as the greatest prophet of Israel who has "prepared the way" (Q 7:18–35, at 7:27). What is recited, however, does not match precisely either of the two passages that have similar wording that we know from our written texts of Exodus 23:20 and Malachi 3:1 in the MT and LXX. As with the proverb and commandments recited in the temptation dialogue, the cited couplet/prophecy would have been widely familiar in Israelite cultural tradition. As indicated in the principal written texts that Q 7:27 resembles, the longing for a messenger who would renew Israel according to the Mosaic covenantal heritage was central to the culture. It appeared both at the popular level of village communities (presumably much of the material the Covenant code in Exodus 21–23 was originally from earlier Israelite popular tradition (Israelite "common law"), and at the level of scribal-priestly circles (or a scribal-prophetic circle) attempting to reform the temple-state according to covenantal principles (Malachi 3; cf. the scribal-priestly group at Qumran community as a renewed exodus/covenantal community). Given the way the prophecy in Malachi 3:1 picks up on the prophecy in Exod 23:20, it would not be surprising if a prophecy with very similar wording assumed to be "written" in the scripture had become widely current in the culture at both the popular and the scribal level.

We are thus coming about the issue in a historically inappropriate way if we ask whether Q/Luke 7:27 was quoting a written text of Exod 23:20 and/ or Mal 3:1. It seems highly unlikely that the composers/performers of the speech possessed and consulted a scroll of some version of Exodus and a scroll of a version of the Twelve. The implication of the recent research summarized above is that this Q speech was rooted in and was working from popular oral tradition. Given the central importance in Israelite tradition, at both the elite and popular levels, of the exodus-covenant and the prophetic figures of Moses, Elijah, and Moses- and/or Elijah-like "messengers," popular movements would surely have know that "the scripture" contained prophecies of a "messenger" of new exodus. Given their lack of literacy, lack of access to scrolls, and the still developing versions of the scriptural books, however, it is not surprising that the Q composers/performers' recitation of such a prophecy would not match the wording of the scriptural text as we know it from later stabilized textual tradition. The speech in Q 7:18–35 recited a prophecy (7:27) that was believed to stand "written" on scrolls. It did this to claim the authority of what stands "written" in the word of God for John's role in preparing the way for Jesus' coming.

The likelihood of this reconstruction of how Q is related to the authoritative written text is confirmed by the way scripture is recited in the Gospel of Mark. Mark's story even refers to specific books in reciting a prophecy: "As it is written in the prophet Isaiah" (Mark 1:2–3). But of course the recited prophecy is a combination of what we know from Malachi 3:1 and Isaiah 40:3. Almost certainly such prophecies were well known among Israelites, and not just in scribal circles such as Qumran (whose texts also referenced Isa 40:3 prominently, but by adapting paraphrase, not explicit quotation). It is not surprising if well-known lines and phrases were remembered and used according to the issue they addressed. Like the speech in Q 7:18–35, the opening of Mark's story recites a prophecy about the "messenger" from general knowledge of Israelite tradition, only the composers-performers believe that the prophecy they are citing stands "written" in Isaiah.[38]

---

38. On the ways that Mark's story depends on Israelite popular tradition in

It has also often been claimed that the speech in Q/Luke 7:18–35 is quoting Isaiah at 7:22, although the quotation formula "it is written" is missing. Such claims then move into a quandary about what passage is being "quoted". is it Isaiah 61:1 and/or 35:5–6—or possibly (also) 29:18–19 and/or 42:6–7. The results of the various lines of research sketched above, however, enable us to explore the workings of Israelite tradition without being limited to chapters-and-verses in printed texts.

Except possibly for Isa 29:18–19, these passages in Isaiah are parallel in their common focus on the restoration apparently of the Jerusalem elite[39] and, to a considerable degree, on the overlapping lists of the same or similar images used to express that restoration. Interestingly, many, perhaps most of the images in the lists are of the poor, hungry, and disabled rather than of elite who had been enjoying a more comfortable life in exile:

Isaiah 29:18–21 (an oracle of deliverance) announces that "the deaf shall hear the words of a scroll, . . . the eyes of the blind shall see . . . The meek . . . and neediest shall exult (in Yahweh)," and tyrants and those who pervert justice shall cease.

Isaiah 35:1–10 (a prophecy of deliverance that belongs with the extensive poetic drama of Isa 40–55 that is focused on the Judean elite's new exodus and return into Zion) along with imagery of the desert blooming along the "Holy Way" for God's people, has utopian restorative imagery of "the eyes of the blind shall be opened, the ears of the deaf unstopped; the lame shall leap like a deer, and the tongue of the speechless sing for joy."

Isaiah 42:1–9 (one of the "servant of Yahweh" songs in the extensive poetic drama of the new exodus and way back to Zion for the exiled Judean elite in Isa 40–55) portrays God, having placed his spirit upon Israel, as having given Israel as a covenant to the people, a light to the nations, to open the eyes that are blind, to bring out the prisoners from the dungeon."

Isaiah 61:1–11 (a general prophecy of the Jerusalem elite's return to Zion and elevation to virtual imperial prominence) portrays a prophetic figure anointed by Yahweh "to bring good news to the oppressed, to bind up the brokenhearted, to proclaim liberty to the captives, and release to the prisoners; to proclaim the year of Yahweh's favor, and the day of vengeance of our God; to comfort all who mourn, etc.

The same and parallel imagery can be found in some of the Psalms, such as 146:7–9: Yahweh the God of Jacob . . . "executes justice for the oppressed; gives food to the hungry. . . . sets the prisoners free, opens the eyes

---

referencing the authority of scripture with the formula "it is written," see further Horsley, *Hearing the Whole Story*, 59–61; and chaps. 10 and 12 below.

39. See Gottwald, "Social Class."

of the blind. Lifts up those who are bowed down, . . . watches over strangers; upholds the orphan and the widow.

The repetition of many of the same images of the restoration of the elite or of the people generally that God or God's anointed prophetic agent or a prophetically personified people will accomplish suggests *a repertory of standard images*, cultural idioms that could be drawn upon to express the restoration and renewal for which the people in general yearned, images derived from the experience of people who had been conquered and then suffered in the aftermath of the devastation. The prophecies of deliverance in Isaiah 35 and 61 and the servant psalm in Isaiah 42 all focus on a release from captivity, a new exodus and way through the wilderness, and/or restoration of the (exiled) elite in Zion/Jerusalem. Isaiah 61 focuses more on the aspect of release of the captives, while Isaiah 35 uses the imagery of healing of the blind, deaf, lame, and dumb, parallel to imagery of water breaking forth in the desert to emphasize the miraculous character of the new exodus and wilderness. Some of these same images are used in Ps 146:7–9 along with a somewhat different repertory of images of God being particularly attentive to needs of the poor, the orphan, and the widow.

That stock images of God's special concern to care for the poor and to liberate and restore the people persisted in the cultural memory of scribal groups is evident, for example, in a fragment from Qumran (4Q 521).

For the Lord will seek out the pious,

and call the righteous by name,

and his spirit will hover over the poor,

and he will renew the faithful by his might. (5–6)

For he will glorify the pious on the throne of his eternal kingdom,

releasing captives, giving sight to the blind,

and raising up those who are bowed down. (7–8)

. . . the glorious things that have not taken place the Lord will do as he said:

for he will heal the wounded, give life to the dead and preach good news to the poor

and he will satisfy the weak ones and lead those who have been cast out and enrich the hungry . . . and all of them . . . (11–12)

All of the images in line 8 are reminiscent of some of those in Ps 146:7–8 and those of releasing captives in line 8 and of preaching the good news to the poor in line 12 are reminiscent of some of those in Isa 61:1–2. Yet in this text presumably composed by a scribe who had access to written scrolls (as well as those written on the tablet of his heart) nothing suggests that the phrases in the text are being quoted from Ps 146 or Isa 61. Texts from Qumran that were not later included in the Hebrew Bible are full of language familiar to us from Hebrew biblical texts, including phrases and idioms. But that does not mean that particular passages from texts that were later included in the Hebrew Bible are being quoted or even alluded to. It simply means that the Qumran scribes who produced those texts were thoroughly familiar with the same Israelite cultural tradition from which the scriptural texts were produced. With regard to the particular images in 4Q 521, it is evidently drawing its several images of God's concern for the poor and readiness to liberate them from a store of such images in the cultural tradition of Israelites/Judeans who were longing for alleviation of their circumstances living under the continuing impact of conquest and ongoing imperial rule. Ps 146 and Isaiah 61 and Isaiah 35 and 42 are all somewhat earlier examples of scribal(-prophetic) compositions drawing on the same common repertory of images, the richness of which we can observe in noticing how the imagery in those texts overlaps here and there, yet does not constitute a set list.

Some DSS scholars have pointed out that Qumran texts such as 1QS and 4QMMT have a relationship with the text of scriptures different from that of the *pešarim* on prophetic texts. The former (1QS and 4QMMT) use terms and phrases familiar from and similar to those in the books of Moses, yet they are not quotations of or references to particular texts. The *pešarim* on prophetic texts, on the other hand, do cite a sequence of text-fragments followed by interpretations, which usually make connection with the conflictual events that the Qumran community is undergoing or will experience in the future.

The text in 11Q13 (Melchizedek) begins as a *pesher* of the year of Jubilee and God's release (which we know of in Lev 25:13 and Deut 15:2, respectively), which leads through a series of phrases cited from "the Psalms of David" (and the corresponding *pešarim*) to a longer citation about the messenger who proclaims peace (in Isa 52:7) and its "interpretation." The reference to "captives" toward the beginning leads editors of the text to fill the adjacent lacuna with the phrase about liberating captives in Isa 61:1. And the reference to "comfort" in the *pesher* on the messenger toward the end leads editors to fill the adjacent lacuna with a phrase about "comforting those who mourn" in Isa 61:2–3. It seems clear throughout this text that the scribal composers, who were evidently thoroughly imbued with scriptural texts, were reciting longer or shorter phrases, many from the Psalms, from the rich storehouse of their memory, each successive phrase serving as the *pesher* of the previous citation. What appear in translations of the text as citation of a phrase from Isa 61:1 and another from Isa 61:2–3 are supplied by editors-translators. This text of the *pesher* on the Jubilee release at first seems to offer hope to those who are economically captive, but by the end the interpretation of the comfort brought by the messenger focuses rather on understanding "all the ages of time." 11Q13, while reciting phrases from Scripture, is not drawing on the same standard traditional set of images of liberation and renewal that appear in texts such as Isa 35, 42, 61, Ps 146, and 4Q 521.

That the images of renewal in those texts are mostly of poor, disabled, and struggling people, and not the comfortable, suggests that scribes working in the "great tradition" were comforting and offering hope to the Judean elite being restored to their positions of power and privilege in Jerusalem after imperial conquest. These texts may well be cases of scribal composers borrowing images and materials from the Israelite popular tradition. The exodus and way through the wilderness that forms the dominant theme of Isaiah 40–55 is a parade example.

Coming back around to the speech in Q/Luke 7:18–35, finally, it has been claimed, as noted, that at 7:22 the speech is quoting Isa 61:1 or Isa 35:5–6. But Q 7:22 is probably not even an allusion to either of those text-fragments or any others in Isaiah. Of the six images in Q 7:22, only the "preaching good news to the poor" is found among the many images in Isa 61:1–3. To put that differently, Q 7:22 has only one of the many images in Isaiah 61:1–3. Isa 35:5–6 is closer with regard to images, having three parallels among the six images in Q 7:22. The particular wording and order, however, are not that close. "The blind recovering their sight" is paralleled in Isaiah 42:6–7 and 29:18–19 and Ps 146:7–8 as well as Isa 35:5–6, but not in Isa 61:1–3.

At 7:22 the speech in Q 7:18–35 is rather drawing upon the repertory of stock images of restoration of Israel that was cultivated at the popular level as well as in scribal circles. The various wonders that Jesus asks John's disciples to see and hear in Q 7:22 certainly refer to Jesus' healing and preaching activities. In the context of the speech as a whole and in connection with John's prophecy of the coming one in the first speech in the Q sequence, however, the focus is not on the particular healings of Jesus but on the fulfillment of long-standing yearnings for the renewal or restoration of the people of Israel. In contrast with the focus on a new exodus for the exiled elite in Isa 35, moreover, the focus in Q 7:18–35 is on the restoration of Israel among the suffering peasantry, as with the prophetic mission of Elijah (who raised the dead, which is notably missing in Isa 35 and 61). The same contrast is evident with Isa 61, which also focuses on the restoration of the elite in Zion, on which other Q speeches pronounce divine judgment (Q 11:39–52; 13:34–35).

In sum, it is difficult to find any particular relationship between Q 7:22 and any text-fragment of Isaiah. The parallel images often noted were simply drawn from a common Israelite cultural repertory and deployed in parallel yet different ways that expressed the interests of the Galilean and other peasants, on the one hand, and those of the Judean elite looking for restoration of their previous position of wealth and power on the other. One does get the sense that the set of images in Q 7:22 indeed make reference to prophetic expectations or yearnings, since it comes in connection with a "coming one" who is making things happen. But such longings for renewal had surely been cultivated in the popular tradition, having played a role in earlier prophetic movements, such as those led by Ahijah of Shiloh and Elijah and Elisha, well before the prophecies in Isaiah 35, 40–66. Indeed, elite texts such as Isaiah 35, 40–55 had appropriated their central images of exodus and the way through the wilderness from popular tradition and adapted them for an upscale audience.[40]

If we now consider the whole speech in Q/Luke 7:18–35 in performance, we can perhaps discern how the references to some of the particulars of Israelite tradition function in the rhetoric, the work they do for/on the hearers. This is one of the Q speeches that leads us to believe that these speeches were related to one another, perhaps even a sequence. It presuppose and picks up on the speech of John the Baptist in Q/Luke 3:7–9, 16–17 prophesying the one who comes after him who would baptize in both Spirit and fire, that is, renewal and judgment. In the first step of the speech, in Q/Luke 7:19, 22–23, John's disciples poses the question of whether Jesus is that "coming one." As a highly affirmative answer Jesus tells them to tell John what they have seen and heard in what Jesus has been doing in his mission, offering a list of actions based on the Israelite tradition of the people's longings for deliverance and renewal. With this referencing of Israelite tradition, Jesus' reply to John's question resonating with these deep-seated longings of the people in pronouncing that his actions constitute their fulfillment.

In the second step of the speech (7:24–29), "Jesus" draws the caustic contrast between John the Baptist, who was hardly a shaky reed out in the Jordan River, and "king" Herod Antipas, whom John had condemned—and paid with the loss of his head—all allusions dependent on the people knowing full well about the new cities and palace that Antipas had built in Sepphoris and Tiberias and John's fiery prophetic preaching. This sets up the declaration that John was "more than a prophet," elaborated in two

---

40. Gottwald, "Social Class."

remarkable statements. John was none other than the long-prophesied and -expected "messenger preparing the way" (for God or Jesus, who would bring) deliverance of the people, (as) a new exodus. Stating that this prophecy "is written" (up there in Jerusalem on one of the sacred scrolls) lends it all the greater authority. And that sets in turn sets up the even more remarkable next statement that makes a double declaration about how John's prophetic role as the messenger has prepared the way for the kingdom of God that Jesus is pronouncing and manifesting, which will be astoundingly "great." John the messenger is the greatest figure in history to this point, but the kingdom of God that is now happening in Jesus' mission is even greater.

Q scholars sometimes reconstruct the sequence of statements at this point in the parallel material in Matthew and Luke without Matt 11:12–13, since the corresponding saying in Luke, who usually represents the more "original" order of Q has it separately at Luke 16:16. Given the defensive tone of Q/Luke 7:31–35, however, some link is required with 7:19,22–23,24–28. Luke's mentioning "the Pharisees and lawyers" as those who reject the purpose of God (7:29–30) would make good sense both in the context of other Q speeches and in the historical context.[41] It would also indicate who might be referred to in *genea taute* in 7:31, which is usually translated "this generation" but can mean more generally "this type/kind" of people. But the link in Matthew's text, 11:12–13, has the advantage of being in sequence as the link between 11:2–11 (= Luke 7:19,22–23,24–28) and 11:16–19 (= Luke 7:31–35). Contrary to what has often been supposed, "the prophets and the law" in Matt 11:13 is probably not a reference to the scriptures. "The law and the prophets" is clearly a reference to texts that are known to be written in Acts 13:15, but the phrase does not have that sense in Luke 16:16. In either sequence, the phrase is probably a reference to the Israelite tradition in general, which at both scribal and popular levels was cultivated orally and recited orally. The (seemingly redundant) verb "prophesied" in Matt 11:13 indicates how it was understood if this statement was part of this speech: as voiced prophecy. In any case, the statement in Matt 11:12 paralleled by a somewhat different version in Luke 16:16 makes the point that the kingdom of God proclaimed and enacted by Jesus is suffering violence. And judging from the rest of the Synoptic Gospel tradition as well as Johannine tradition, the attacks or repression would have been coming from the rulers and/or their scribal retainers.

The final step of the speech mocks those who have attacked the kingdom of God as children who do not "get" what is being performed, joyful

41. It is pertinent to note that in Mark 2:13–17, it is the Pharisees who accuse Jesus of "eating with toll-collectors and sinners," the same charge leveled by "this kind (of people)" as in Q/Luke 7:31–35.

dance music or a funeral dirge, and respond accordingly. As in the climactic step in the speech, 7:24–28, John and "the son of man" (Jesus) stand virtually in tandem, or rather sequence, as the prophets of deliverance and the kingdom. And the final statement declares that, despite the attacks on John and Jesus, (the) wisdom (of God) is (has been) vindicated by her works/children! The climax of the performed speech comes in 7:27–28. 7:31–35 follows as a reassurance about the attacks on John and Jesus (and the hearers of the performance; cf. Q/Luke 12:2–12, discussed in chap. 7).

## Similar Uses of Prophetic Tradition by Q Speeches and Dissident Scribes

As suggested in chap. 5, however, scribes also drew upon Israelite tradition in composing texts that were hardly supportive of the priestly aristocracy. Most late second-temple texts that modern scholars classify as "apocalyptic" oppose incumbent rulers of the temple-state as well as the dominant empire. The Epistle of Enoch (*1 Enoch* 94–105) offers an example of how dissident scribes drew on Israelite prophetic tradition in a way similar to how Jesus' speech in Q 11:39–52 used it. In and through these two texts we can discern how both dissident scribes and a popular prophetic figure and his followers drew creatively upon the Israelite prophetic heritage that had been cultivated in both scribal circles and in village communities.

Ben Sira's summary of the curriculum of scribal training included all of the major segments of the Israelite-Judean cultural repertoire, prophecies and the torah of the Most High, as well as various kinds of wisdom (Sirach 38:34—39:3). Insofar as the learned scribes were virtually the only people in Judea trained in literacy, they would have been the ones who produced defined texts of the prophets and torah, as well as collections of wisdom.[42] In producing collections of the oracles of prophets such as Amos, Micah, Isaiah, and Jeremiah, however, they included many fragments of oracles that pronounced God's judgment on kings and their officers for their oppression of the people, in violation of commandments of the Mosaic covenant.

Among these oracles were series of several woes that bring indictments against rulers and their officers followed by declarations of punishment, as well as individual woes of indictment followed by statements of judgment. Such series of woes plus sentence appear in Amos 6:1–3, 4–6 + 7; Isaiah 5:18–19, 20, 21, 22–23 + 24; and Habakkuk 2:9–11, 12, 15 + 16–17, [and

---

42. See the fuller analysis and discussion in Horsley, *Scribes, Visionaries*, chaps. 3–4, 6–7.

another woe] 19. The woes are full of mockery and sarcasm, for example about the false wisdom of the elite, as in the following lines from Isaiah 5.

Woe to you who join house to house, who add field to field,

Until there is room for no one but you,

And you are left to live alone in the midst of the land! (Isa 5:8)

. . . Therefore my people go into exile without knowledge . . . (5:11)

Woe to you who are wise in your own eyes, . . .

And shrewd in your own sight! (21)

Therefore . . . for they have rejected the instruction of Yahweh of hosts. (24)

As evident in Isa 5:8, 24, and most of these woes, they focus their indictment on how the rulers and their officers exploit and abuse the people, in violation of Mosaic covenantal principles. These woes also include many particular terms and motifs typical of prophecies, such as the keeping of the torah as true wisdom and knowledge as the keeping of the Mosaic covenant and its commandments.

It is clear that in the books of the Pentateuch scribes framed and adapted what looks like early popular Israelite tradition so that it served to support the monarchy and/or temple-state. The prophetic woes and other early prophetic oracles, however, pronounce God's condemnation of the rulers. The scribal collectors and "editors" of the prophetic books did frame earlier prophetic oracles with exhortations to reform and promises of restoration of the glory of Zion/Jerusalem. It is nevertheless striking that in the books of the prophets that scribes (whose professional role was to serve as retainers in the temple-state) continued to develop, the scribal tradition included prophetic oracles that condemned rulers and their officers. The scribal tradition thus included prophetic oracles with which the ruling aristocracy of the temple-state would hardly have been comfortable.

The previously standard assumption that Israelite-Judean prophecy and prophets ceased after Malachi (that is until John the Baptist and Jesus appeared) still persists here and there biblical studies. But this is an unwarranted assumption rooted in reliance only on the books later included in the canon of the Hebrew Bible ("Old Testament"). Prophets whose oracles were collected into books that were later included in the Hebrew Bible may have ceased. But prophets whose names we do not know continued to operate in early second-temple times, judging from the sharp polemic against such in Zech 13:2–6. We have virtually no sources for the next few centuries. But when sources resume, particularly with Josephus' histories, we know of both oracular prophets, such as Jesus son of Hananiah, who delivered Jeremiah-like oracles of doom in the form of a prophetic lament, and prophetic leaders of movements, in the tradition of Moses, Joshua, and Elijah (discussed in chap. 5). Not just stories of Moses and Elijah, but knowledge of prophetic forms, rhetoric, and oracles as well continued to be cultivated in popular circles, occasionally voiced by prophets. The Israelite prophetic tradition thus continued both in the scribal tradition and the popular tradition.

At least some of the learned scribes serving in the temple-state were thus thoroughly familiar with prophetic forms and prophetic charges when the "reforming" faction in the priestly aristocracy became enamored of the dominant Hellenistic imperial political culture. The conflict came to a head when the dominant reforming faction in the aristocracy transformed the temple-state into a Hellenistic *polis*, a move clearly threatening to the scribal retainers.[43] At some point in the prolonged crisis in Jerusalem, a circle of learned scribes who identified with the primordial hero Enoch, on whom they projected their own role as wise scribes, produced the Epistle of Enoch (*1 Enoch* 94–105). In contrast with the other sections of *1 Enoch*, however, the Epistle is not an "apocalyptic" text. It rather takes the form of a sequence of several series of woes against the wealthy and powerful rulers (and their scribes), with multiple indictments followed by a pronouncement of sentence. These are strikingly similar in both form and substance, as well as mocking rhetoric, to the series of woes in the books of Amos, Isaiah, and Habakkuk, clearly rooted in the continuing cultivation of such prophetic woes. They are also clearly in *performative speech*. Whether or not the written form from which the text that we have is descended was secondary to their composition-in-performance, these woes must have been performed. It is evident from close analysis of the woes that the circle of "Enoch" scribes pronounced these woes against the wealthy and powerful rulers of the temple-state, indicting them for their oppression of the people, and declaring (in effect, calling down) God's punishment against them.[44] It is at least conceivable that they performed these woes in public in Jerusalem, although presumably not directly "in the face" of the dominant high priestly faction. Even if performed only within the "Enoch" circle of dissident scribes, however, the woes would have had the effect of powerfully reinforcing this scribal circle's bold opposition to the dominant aristocrats. As we know from the end of their Animal Vision (*1 Enoch* 85–90), these dissident scribes at some point mounted active opposition to the high priestly

43. On the following, see the fuller discussion in Horsley, *Scribes, Visionaries*, esp. chaps. 2 and 8; and "Social Relations and Social Conflict.

44. Laid out originally in Horsley, "Social Relations and Social Conflict."

rulers and their imperial backers as one of at least two scribal circles of resistance that preceded and prepared the way for the wider Maccabean Revolt.[45]

Once we are familiar with the series of woes in Amos, Isaiah, Habakkuk, and the Epistle of Enoch, it is clear that the speech in Q 11:37–52 is yet another series of prophetic woes, climaxing in a declaration of judgment.[46] "Jesus'" woes resemble those of the prophets and the "Enoch" scribes in their form, substance, and even their mocking rhetoric. Q interpreters fail to see this partly because they usually focus on individual sayings and do not investigate the traditional form of prophetic woes. They are also still influenced by the previously standard view that Jesus is here in conflict with the Pharisees, the predecessors of the rabbis and the key figures who defined "formative Judaism," over the Law, or more particularly, their obsession with ritual and purity laws. That, of course, mistakes the mocking rhetoric of the woes for the substance/point of the indictments.

Contrary to the way in which they have traditionally been read according to the older scheme of "Jesus vs. Judaism/the Pharisees," the woes against the scribes and Pharisees in Q 11:39–52 are not disputes about "the Jewish Law" or Jewish purity codes. Only at points does the rhetoric mock the scribes and Pharisees for their obsession with purity, particularly in the indictment that they themselves are like the very unmarked graves that they see as a dangerous source of contamination (11:44; cf. 11:39–41). In the performance of the speech, of course, these flourishes of mockery "set up" the scribes and Pharisees for the indictments at the core of the woes, which pertain to the effects of their retainer role on the people, to communities of which the speech addresses.

The main thrust of this series of woes is indicated best perhaps in 11:42, 46 and 47–48. Pressing rigorous tithing upon the peasants and "loading the people with heavy burdens" refer to the role of the Pharisees and scribes/lawyers in the economic burden that the temple-state placed on villagers. "Touching the burdens with one of your fingers" is ironic: given their role as scribal retainers of the temple-state, they could if they would alleviate the people's economic burden with a few strokes of their scribal pen. But of course theirs is only a pretense to wisdom, and they actually take away the key to knowledge and lock the people out of the kingdom of God insofar the effects of their role is extortion and evil, instead of covenantal justice (11:52 in both Luke's and Matthew's variation; and 11:39, 42). As the series of woes moves toward their climax in the declaration of judgment, the

---

45. See further Horsley, *Scribes, Visionaries,* chaps. 8–9.

46. Fuller analysis and discussion in Horsley with Draper, *Whoever Hears You Hears Me,* 285–91.

scribes' and Pharisees' activities in their retainer role are linked directly with the Jerusalem rulers whom they represent. And the imminent punishment pronounced in 11:49–51 comes upon both rulers and retainers. Throughout the speech in Q/Luke 11:39–52 the woes are performative speech. The "Jesus" performer is pronouncing God's indictment and judgment on the scribes and Pharisees and the Jerusalem rulers, probably to communities of villagers.

## Conclusion

Recent research in several related areas has shown that the relation between the earliest definable text in the Synoptic Gospel tradition and the Israelite tradition in which it was rooted can no longer be discussed in simple terms of quotation of and allusions to particular verses and phrases in the Hebrew Bible.

Israelite tradition was much more diverse in texts and oral tradition and diffuse in authority than the books that were later included in the Hebrew Bible, which at least through second-temple times existed in differing versions that were still being developed. Alternative texts of torah and historical tradition and "apocalyptic" texts relativized, rivaled, or supplemented the authority of the proto-biblical books, as did the rulings and regulations of the Pharisees and Qumranites, not included in "the laws of Moses," that they derived from the tradition of the ancestors and new revelation, respectively.

Since literacy was limited mainly to the scribal retainers who served the temple-state in a society dependent on and dominated by oral communication, it seems very unlikely that ordinary people, such as those involved in the Jesus movement that composed-performed and heard the Q speeches, had any direct contact with or knowledge of scriptural books or other texts in the scribal tradition. On the other hand, they would surely have been aware that there were written texts with aura and authority laid up in the temple, and would probably have known, through informal indirect oral communication, some of what stood written on those sacred scrolls, particularly prophecies or covenantal teachings that also expressed their interests.

While they did not have direct knowledge of the elite scribal (or official) tradition, however, ordinary Judeans and Galileans (and Samaritans) had their own Israelite popular tradition that expressed their concerns and interests. The popular tradition overlapped with or paralleled the scribal tradition in many respects, but it also contested and conflicted with the scribal expressions of elite interests. The speeches in Q, particularly when we hear them as speech and often as performative speech, are not only deeply rooted in Israelite popular tradition, but draw upon it in creative ways to express the concerns of Galilean and other villagers involved in the movement of renewal and resistance catalyzed by John and especially Jesus of Nazareth. The effect of the repeated performance of the Q speeches would have been to further strengthen the commitment and solidarity of the communities of the Jesus movement who produced and heard them in their renewal of those covenantal village communities and thus their motivation and ability to resist the continuing political-economic pressures by the rulers and their retainers.

# 7

# HEARING Q/LUKE 12:2–12 AS ORAL PERFORMANCE

THE EARLIEST GOSPEL TEXTS AS WELL AS MOST OF THE "SYNOP-
tic Gospel tradition" are "oral-derived" communications. Modern interpreters of Gospel texts, however, deeply immersed in the assumptions of print
culture, have focused their analysis almost exclusively on written texts as established by modern text critics. We are thus unprepared to appreciate oral
communication and oral performance. Fortunately other academic fields
with somewhat similar materials and issues have gained new perspectives
and explored new approaches that we may be able to adapt for appreciation
of Gospel materials. A few pioneers such as Werner Kelber have been calling Gospel studies to move beyond anachronistic assumptions and models
based on modern typographic culture, and to learn from historical and
theoretical studies of the relation of orality and writing.[1] Kelber explained
that Q materials present themselves as the oral performance of Jesus' words
and explained how their survival depended on their social relevancy.
Meanwhile scholars in other fields, such as anthropology, folklore, and the
study of medieval European and classical Greek literature, were carrying
out increasingly sophisticated analyses of oral performances and of written
texts that derived from originating oral performances.

Conversant with innovative work in many fields, John Miles Foley has
brought together insights from oral-formulaic theory and other studies of
oral-derived classical and medieval literature, on the one side, and sociolin-
guistics, ethnopoetics, and the ethnography of performance, on the other,
into highly suggestive theorizing of "immanent art" and oral performance.[2]

---

1. Kelber, *The Oral and the Written Gospel*, esp. chaps. 1–2; "Jesus and Tradition."

2. Foley, *Immanent Art*; *Singer of Tales in Performance*; and *How to Read an Oral*

I have attempted to adapt this interplay and combination of historical investigation, ethnography, experimentation, comparative reflection, and theory
for exploration of the speeches of Jesus that are standardly referred to as
"Q" (short for *Quelle*, "source").[3] Insofar as Matthew and Luke reproduced
speech material of Jesus in parallel form with many marks of oral performance, we have access to what Foley calls an "oral-derived text" or a "voice
from the past." These Jesus-speeches that were evidently recited repeatedly
in communities of Jesus' followers thus offer an unusual opportunity to appreciate how they may have "worked" in oral performance.

## Approaching Jesus' Speeches in "Q" as Oral Performance

The treatment of Jesus' teachings as individual sayings is one of the results
of reading the Bible in print. Speech becomes abstracted from a context of
communication, reified as text-fragments, and treated as separate artifacts,
each of which supposedly has a meaning in itself. What has been called
"composition criticism" of Jesus' speech material paralleled in Matthew and
Luke, however, has recognized that it is organized in "clusters" of sayings (a
concept rooted in the assumptions of typographical culture).[4] Upon closer
examination, particularly with sensitivity to the oral communication environment in antiquity, those "clusters" turn out to be short speeches on
various subjects of concern to communities of Jesus' followers.[5] It is thus inappropriate to focus on what individual sayings in themselves might mean.
Perhaps it might be appropriate for us to speculate about the meaning that
individual meditators found in the separate logia of the *Gospel of Thomas*
as objects of contemplation, given the hermeneutical principle in its first
logion. Individual sayings, however, were not basic units of communication. To find units of communication we must focus rather on the speeches
still discernible in the parallel materials in Matthew and Luke. Then we can
inquire into how communication happened in the oral performance of the
speeches communicated to communities of listeners.

    In considering any act of communication, it is necessary to consider
the interaction between speaker and hearers as they live out of their cultural
tradition in a particular context.[6] Insofar as the speeches of Jesus parallel in

---

*Poem.*

3. Horsley with Draper, *Whoever Hears You Hears Me.*

4. Kloppenborg, *Formation of Q*; see further, Kirk, *Composition.*

5. Horsley with Draper, *Whoever Hears You Hears Me*, esp. 83–93.

6. Halliday, *Language as Social Semiotic.*

Matthew and Luke are what Foley would call a "voice from the past." to hear this historical oral communication appropriately we must attempt to "hear" them in their own historical cultural and social context. Drawing on Foley's theoretical reflections, I would like to focus analysis on four interrelated aspects. To hear Jesus' speeches in oral performance, we must determine the contours of the "*text*" (or *message*), attend to the performance *context* in which the speaker addresses the hearers, sense the *register* of the speech appropriate to that context, and cultivate knowledge of the cultural *tradition* out of which the speech resonates with the hearers.[7]

*Text*

The first step is to figure out what the shape and content of the "*text*" or message communicated was. I place "text" in quote marks to remind us that, despite its connotations of something in print for us, in antiquity texts were "inscribed" on the heart (memory) even of the literate (e.g., scribes, Pharisees, rabbis) as much or more than on scrolls.[8] Scrolls, of course, were not only expensive but cumbersome to use. Hence especially authoritative texts that existed in writing (e.g., laid up in the temple) were recited from memory.[9] For an "orally-derived" text for which we are dependent on two written versions, we have little more than two variant "librettos" before us, and both of those in a printed version based on a synthetic modern construct from ancient manuscripts.[10] (This is, in effect, what the International Q Project has produced, working on the print-cultural assumptions standard in biblical studies.)[11] It is particularly important to resist the previous habit of treating Q as a collection of separate sayings and to *listen* for/to what may be (complete/genuine) units of communication, the particular speeches detectable by comparison of the two versions we have before us. Individual sayings or verses were not intelligible units of communication, but merely fragments thereof. In an analogy from musical performances, we want to consider not just a few bars or measures in the score, but whole arias in the larger context of the complete libretto of a cantata, all the while using our imagination to hear what it might sound like in performance. The intelligible units of communication would presumably be particular

---

7. Foley, *Singer of Tales in Performance*; Horsley with Draper, *Whoever Hears You Hears*, esp. 160–74.

8. Jaffee, *Torah in the Mouth*; Carr, *Writing on the Tablet of the Heart*.

9. Jaffee, "Figuring Early Rabbinic Literary Culture."

10. Parker, *Living Text of the Gospels*.

11. Robinson, Hoffmann, and Kloppenborg, eds., *Critical Edition of Q*.

speeches focused on particular issues.[12] It would also help to hear those as components of the complete sequence of speeches that constituted Q.

## Context

Particular messages are addressed to people in particular contexts. A candidate for office delivers a campaign speech to a political rally; a lover speaks terms of endearment to a partner in an intimate embrace. Messages and their meaning depend on their context. We have all experienced the words we speak having been "taken out of context." Thus in order to understand a message or communication properly it is necessary to hear it in the appropriate *context*. Context determines the expectation and the appropriate hearing of the message. It is standard, indeed intentional practice in established study of the Gospels and Jesus to separate individual sayings from their literary context in order to establish their meaning in themselves virtually "out of context." The ("out of context") context is then supplied by the modern scholar-interpreter, often unawares. The group of Jesus-sayings that includes "love your enemies" and "turn the other cheek" in Matthew's Sermon on the Mount (Matt 5:45–48; cf. Luke 6:27–35) were taken by modern pacifists such as myself, for example, in the context of international relations. We imagined Jesus to have been addressing a corresponding context in antiquity, Roman conquest and occupation of Judea and Galilee. Over twenty-five years ago I suggested that, closely examined, that set of sayings indicated their own context as quarrels among villagers, which in turn resulted from the disintegrative effects of Roman domination.[13] As illustrated by that example, context is often, perhaps usually, complex: local *and* translocal; the immediate context of delivering and hearing a message *and* the more general circumstances of the lives of speaker and hearers. Often to tune into a message we adjust to particular contexts within a general context of communication. In the general context of a Christian church service, for example, we shift from one particular context to another, e.g., from prayer to scripture reading to sermon to offering.

Appreciation of Jesus' speeches as communication by a speaker to a collective audience thus requires the interpreter to combine critical attention to the context (simultaneously) with critical attention to the text. Rudolf Bultmann and Martin Dibelius, the principal founders of form-criticism,

---

12. Kirk, *Composition*; Horsley with Draper, *Whoever Hears You Hears Me*, 83–93, 166–68.

13. Horsley, "Ethics and Exegesis"; and *Jesus and the Spiral*, 255–73. For a reassertion of the traditional pacifist reading, see Wink, "Neither Passivity nor Violence."

both insisted that form could not be considered apart from social function—which many in the next generation of form-critics promptly ignored
in their focus on form abstracted from social context. Their scholarly heirs
among recent interpreters of "the Sayings Gospel" assumed that they could
establish the meaning of sayings first, separate from consideration of the
context (including cultural tradition), and then deduce the social context
from what they had established as the meaning of the sayings. Texts-in-performance, however, like any messages in communication, are always already
in a relational context. Just as the performance context of the liturgy of the
mass is presumably a congregation gathered for worship, so the performance context of Jesus' speeches was presumably a community gathering of
participants in a Jesus movement.[14] And the wider context was the Roman
conquest and domination of the eastern Mediterranean, the installation of
client rulers, and the effects on the people.

The context of Jesus' speeches in recitation, however, is more complicated than that of epic poems such as the Iliad or Beowulf, key "texts"
on which the theory of verbal art has been developed. The performance
context of the Iliad or Beowulf was standardized over many generations
of repeated performances. The context of the Jesus speeches was gatherings of a community in a nascent social movement apparently among the
peasantry in Galilee and beyond. If we are to attempt to hear Q speeches in
their performance context, therefore, the historical context must be considered with as much precision as possible. Modern essentialist constructs
such as "Judaism" and "apocalypticism" and other anachronistic concepts
block rather than facilitate access to historical context.[15] Recent researches,
however, have made accessible the multiple political-economic-religious
conflicts that characterized Roman Palestine at the time of the early Jesus
movements.[16]

### Register

In order not to be "taken out of context" the message/text must then fit the
context, that is, must be in the appropriate *register*. One would not deliver
a funeral dirge at a wedding. A candidate attempting to deliver a campaign
speech at a baseball game or soccer match would be told to "shut up" in no

14. Horsley with Draper, *Whoever Hears You Hears Me*, 168–70.

15. Further discussion in Horsley, *Revolt of the Scribes*; Horsley and Tiller, *After Apocalyptic*.

16. My own contributions specifically on Galilee include *Galilee*; and *Archaeology, History*. See also Horsley, *Sociology and the Jesus Movement*; and Hanson and Oakman, *Palestine in the Time of Jesus*.

uncertain terms. The appropriate register depends on three factors: the subject matter being communicated, who is participating in the communication, and the mode of communication. The language of love would thus be the appropriate register for an intimate embrace. A certain set of language, including body language and paralinguistic gestures, is often "dedicated" to a certain context of communication. A particular register of speech is often activated by certain cues, sounds or phrases that set up expectations in the listeners, signaling the communication context and the kind of discourse about to be heard. Those situated in the right context and clued into the register for a regularly repeated performance already know what is being communicated. "Dearly beloved, we are gathered together . . ." "The Lord be with you. . .." In one of his speeches, Jesus complains of "this generation's" failure to appreciate the register and context of his and John's prophetic message of the renewal of Israel:

> We played the flute for you, and you did not dance;
> We wailed, and you did not weep. (Q/Luke 7:32)

The speaker often also assumes a role appropriate to the register of communication. Funerals are usually conducted by priests or ministers. Campaign speeches at political rallies are delivered by candidates for office. In the training of ancient scribes a teacher delivered short instructional speeches to his "children" in his "house of instruction" (Sirach 2:1; 3:1; 4:1; 6:18; etc.). Yeshua ben Hananiah is an example of an oracular prophetic role at the popular level ("a crude peasant," says Josephus, *War* 6.300–309). During the decade leading up to the great revolt against the Romans and client priestly rulers in Jerusalem, he repeatedly pronounced a lament over the imminent fate of the ruling city Jerusalem, a message in a prophetic register heard by crowds and overheard by an anxious aristocracy.

### *Tradition and Metonymic Referencing*

We may now be ready to appreciate how a performed text "works." When the speaker performs the message to the audience in the register appropriate to the context, its resonates with them by referencing the cultural *tradition* that they share with the performer. In every one of the communication contexts and registers offered as illustrations above, there is a cultural tradition out of which the hearers resonate with the message, whether at funerals, political rallies, even in intimate embraces. The cultural tradition, however, is far more important for communication through oral performance of texts in a traditional society where oral communication is predominant than in a highly literate modern society. For biblical scholars still striving to cut through the assumptions of print culture in which we are so deeply embedded it may be difficult, yet is crucially important, to recognize this.

Recent literary analysis of biblical narrative, while important in helping biblical scholars previously focused on text-fragments to appreciate more complete units of communication, such as the complete story of Mark's Gospel, may have perpetuated the assumptions of print culture. Such literary criticism has taken its cues mainly from literary analysis of modern novels. A modern novelist's communication with a silent reader, however, differs dramatically from an ancient performance of the Iliad or Beowulf or the Gospel of Mark.[17] A modern novelist *confers* meaning on her fresh new literary creation by individually manipulating inherited or idiosyncratic materials in a new direction or from a new perspective for a private, silent reader. The traditional oral performer, on the other hand, thoroughly grounded in standard strategies long familiar to his or her collective audience, summons conventional connotations of conventional structures evoking a meaning that is *inherent*.

A performance of Jesus' speeches or of the Gospel of Mark, therefore, would have depended much more heavily on extra-textual factors as meaning was evoked metonymically from the tradition with which the listeners were familiar. In contrast to the originality of conferred meaning in modern literary texts, traditional oral performance could not depart from, because it depended upon, traditional references of symbols, phrases, and formulas. Each performance caused what was immanent to come to life in the present; it recreated the networks of inherent meaning. The what and how of communication in a performance of a text such as a speech of Jesus or a Gospel depended on a whole range of cultural memory in which the social identity and self-image of a people or community was embedded. To emphasize just how important cultural tradition would have been in the communication that presumably happened through Gospel materials such Jesus speeches and the story of Mark, Werner Kelber has compared it to a biosphere in which a people's whole life is encompassed and nurtured.[18]

As interpreters who stand at a considerable distance from the original historical context of a text such as Q we are also unusually dependent on the cultural tradition in our attempts to hear the message appropriately. In contrast with the first followers of Jesus, however, we are not embedded in the Israelite tradition simply by virtue of our upbringing. It is thus particularly

17. Foley, *Immanent Art*; Foley, *Singer of Tales*; Horsley with Draper, *Whoever Hears You Hears Me*, 170–74; and Horsley, *Hearing the Whole Story*, chap. 3.

18. Kelber, "Jesus and Tradition," esp. 152–59.

important for us to become as thoroughly acquainted as possible with the tradition out of which the performer spoke and the hearers resonated.

It seems fairly clear that the Q speeches are rooted in Israelite tradition. Yet we can no longer imagine that we can gain knowledge of this tradition simply by reading the books of the Hebrew Bible and other Judean literature. Recent research into the cultural life of ancient Judean and Galilean society, however, is indicating that Israelite cultural tradition at the time of Jesus was not simple and unitary. Contrary to the common assumption in biblical studies, no standardized version of "the Law and the Prophets" existed, probably until well after the Roman destruction of the temple.[19] As mentioned above, moreover, scrolls would have been extremely costly and unwieldy; the limited number that existed belonged in the temple and in scribal circles.[20] In any case, few Galileans would have been literate. Much less, as Aramaic speakers, would they have been able to read a scroll in Hebrew. And Galileans had come under the rule of the Jerusalem high priestly regime and "the laws of the Judeans" only about a century before the birth of Jesus, and even then it is unclear how they would have become acquainted with texts produced by the Judeans. The Pharisees, the intellectual "retainers" of the Jerusalem temple-state that had no jurisdiction over Galilee anyhow during the lifetime of Jesus, certainly had no basis in the synagogues of Galilee, which in the first century were not (yet) "Jewish" religious buildings (archaeologists have not yet found such), but Galilean village assemblies which met to discuss community affairs as well as to hold prayers.[21]

The Israelite tradition based in Galilee in which Jesus speeches were rooted, therefore, was almost certainly what anthropologists would call the Israelite "little tradition."[22] Assuming that Galileans were descendants of ancient Israelites and/or of Israelite heritage, they cultivated popular Israelite tradition orally in their village communities. Galilean Israelite popular tradition probably came into some interaction with the Jerusalem-based "great" tradition during the first century BCE. Yet the still developing books that were later included in the Hebrew Bible at best provide only a dim reflection of the Galilean popular tradition, not a direct source. A modern scholar can only extrapolate from it, fully aware that it has been shaped and

19. Ulrich, *The Dead Sea Scrolls*.

20. Hezser, *Jewish Literacy*.

21. Horsley, *Galilee*, chaps. 6, 10; and *Archaeology, History*, chap. 6.

22. Scott, "Protest and Profanation"; and Horsley, "Jesus, Paul and the 'Arts of Resistance.'"

edited by Jerusalem scribal circles working for and articulating the perspective and interests of the ruling Jerusalem priestly aristocracy.[23]

## Hearing Q 12:2–12 as Oral Performance

To imagine the *hearing* of a speech in oral performance, it may be helpful to read them aloud, following this transliteration and translation, arranged in lines and stanzas.[24] Chapter-and-verse numbers that divert attention from the poetic patterns and flow of the speech have been replaced by a line-by-line outline of the flow of the speech. As print-oriented listeners we are in the awkward and ironic position of needing to rely on a printed text as an aid in imagining how a text-in-performance may have sounded. The focal "text" is printed here in transliteration so that even those who cannot read the Greek script can take two related steps: (1) note with the eyes, from the visual appearance of words, word-endings, and verbal forms (in parallel poetic lines!), that the text is full of repeated sounds; and (2) read the text aloud (multiple times, perhaps with the help of someone who does know how the Greek text would have sounded) in order to appreciate the repetition of sounds and the statement and restatement in parallel "lines" of the text.

23. On Israelite popular tradition, see further Horsley with Draper, *Whoever Hears You Hears Me*, chap. 5.

24. See the explanation of this "blocking" of Jesus speeches into verse for easier appreciation of its oral performance in Horsley with Draper, *Whoever Hears You Hears Me*, chaps. 7–8; the discernment of patterns in the speeches owes much to the ethnographer of performance, Dell Hymes. I have made some changes in the text and its translation from the previously published version in *Whoever Hears You Hears Me*, 271. Nearly all of the Q speeches appear "blocked" for oral performance in Horsley, *Jesus in Context*, 229–45.

**Q 12:2–12 in measured verse of performance**
**(following Matthew rather than IQP at end)**

| | | | |
|---|---|---|---|
| A. 1. Ouden kekalummenon estin | ho ouk | apokalyphthesetai | |
| Kai | krupton | ho ou | gnosthesetai |
| 2. Ho lego hymin | en te skotia | eipate | en to photi, |
| Kai ho eis to ous | akouete | keruxate | epi ton domaton. |
| B. 1. Kai me phobeisthe | apo ton apoktennonton | to soma, | |
| Ten de psychen | me dynamenon | apokteinai. | |
| 2. Phobeisthe de | [mallon] | ton dynamenon | |
| Kai psyche kai soma | apolesai | en te geene. | |
| C. 1. Ouchi [duo] | strouthia a | ssariou | poleitai; |
| Kai hen ex auron | ou peseitai | epi ten gen | aneu tou [patros hymon]. |
| 2. Hymon [de] kai | ai triches tes kephales | pasai erithmentai, | |
| Me phobeisthe | pollon strouthion | diapherete. | |
| D. 1. Pas hos [an] | homologese[e] | en emoi | emprosthen ton anthropon, |
| Ka[i ho huios tou anthropou] | homologese[ei] | en auto | emprosthen ton aggelon, |
| 2. Hos d'an | arnesetai | me | emprosthen ton anthropon, |
| | arne[thesetai] | | emprosthen ton aggelon. |
| E. 1. Kai hos ean | eipe logon | eis ton huion tou anthropou | aphethesetai auto, |
| 2. Hos d'an | [eip]e | eis to hagion pneuma | ouk aphethesetai auto. |
| F. 1. Hotan de paradosin | humas, | me merimnesate | pos e ti lalesate. |
| 2. Dothesetai gar | humin | en ekeine te hora | ti lalesate. |

## Translation of Q 12:2–12 blocked in measured verse of performance

| | | | | |
|---|---|---|---|---|
| A. 1. | Nothing is covered | which will not | be revealed | |
| | And (is) hidden | which will not | be made known. | |
| 2. | What I tell you | in the dark | speak | in the light, |
| | and what you hear | in your ear | proclaim | on the housetops. |
| B. 1. | And do not fear | those who kill | the body, | |
| | but the soul | are not able | to kill. | |
| 2. | Fear | rather | the one able | |
| | both soul and body | to destroy | in Gehenna. | |
| C. 1. | Are not two | sparrows | sold for | an assarios? |
| | and one of them | will not fall | to earth | without God. |
| 2. | Even the hairs | of your head | all have been numbered. | |
| | Do not fear, | you are worth more | than many sparrows. | |
| D. 1. | Every one | who confesses | me | before people |
| | Also the son of man | will confess | him/her | before the angels of C |
| 2. | But whoever | denies | me | before people |
| | | will be denied | | before the angels of C |
| E. 1. | And whoever | speaks a word | against the son of man | will be forgiven; |
| 2. | but whoever | blasphemes | against the holy spirit | will not be forgiven. |
| F. 1. | {When} you | are delivered up | do not be anxious about | what you will say; |
| 2. | for {it will be given | to you} | in that hour | what you will say. |

As noted above, a key marker of oral-derived texts is the repetition of words, sounds, and verbal forms as well as the parallelism of lines and sets of lines. The speech in Q 12:2–12 is one of the most striking examples in the sequence of speeches in Q. These repetitions occur abundantly in the structure of the speech as a whole and particularly within verses and stanzas. Not only the theme of speaking, but the repetition of verbs (*eipate/eipe*) and verb forms/sounds (*-thesetai*) in the concluding lines of the opening stanza provide an *inclusio* unifying the whole speech and bringing it to a conclusion. In the first stanza the repetition of the same ending and verbal form in the first two lines is followed by the repetition of verb form (*-ate/-ete/-ate*) and repetition of *–o-*, *-ou-* and *–k-* sounds in the second two lines. In the second stanza, the repetition of the verb/verb form *phobeisthe* is compounded by the repetition of the verb *apokteinai* in the first two lines and the repetition of *dynamenon* in lines two and three, and the repetition of the *–ai* verb ending, which also repeats from the previous stanza. The second verse also plays on the terms *soma* and *psyche* from the first verse. Besides repeating but reversing the imperative *phobeisthe* of the previous stanza, the third stanza repeats the verb form –*eitai* and the closely similar –*entai*, repeats many –*ei/e* sounds, and the term *strouthia/on*. Here alternating and/or successive lines are almost completely comprised of repeated words and phrases. Most strikingly of all, the fourth stanza is almost completely comprised of repeated words and phrases in alternating and/or successive lines. The concluding stanzas repeat the opening pronouns and ending verb forms and have the same sound/form in the last line, along with many long –*a*- sounds.

Many of what the performance critic, Richard Bauman and the ethnographer of performance, Dell Hymes suggest as the keys to oral performance are thus immediately evident in Q 12:2–12.[25] The stanzas flow in parallel lines throughout the speech. Figurative language abounds ("in the ears," "from the house(top)s," "the hairs of your head"), and special formulae appear ("the son of man . . . before the angels").

## Text

Again, the first step is to determine the message that is being communicated. As noted above, the standard approach to Q and other Gospel materials takes Gospel materials as discrete (written) textual artifacts to be examined, as if in a museum case. Like most interpreters, Christopher Tuckett treats each saying as a separate abstract entity as if it had meaning in itself.[26] Not even 12:4–7 can be seen as belonging together. The saying in 12:6–7 is "a call to put all one's trust and confidence in the God who is here presented as a caring, trustworthy person who banishes 'fear.'" The saying in 12:4–5, however, says that "one *should* fear. . . . 'Fear' here is thus something which *is* appropriate in relation to God" (316). Even though he senses a connection between 12:4–5 and 12:8–9, Tuckett's reasoning about the striking differences he finds in 12:4–5 and 6–7 as separate sayings leads him away from any concrete situation of persecution.

The determinative principle in Kloppenborg's analysis of the composition of Q is to classify all sayings into the categories of "sapiential" and "apocalyptic" (including mainly "prophetic" and "judgmental"). On the assumption that the ancient scribal composers of Q worked on the basis of these broad general classifications, this requires that the "apocalyptic" saying

---

25. See Bauman, *Verbal Art as Performance*; Hymes, "*In Vain I Tried to Tell You*," 79–141.

26. Tuckett, *Q and Early Christianity*, 315–18.

in 12:8–9 must have been a secondary insertion into the "sapiential" cluster of 12:2, 3, 4–7, 11–12, and must have been addressed to a different audience, i.e., outsiders.[27] Kloppenborg's approach still proceeds by focusing on individual sayings. The treatment of so-called "apocalyptic" sayings such as 12:8–9 as "secondary" insertions, which must be understood in relation to the rest of the "secondary" redactional stratum, effectively blocks appreciation of how 12:2–12 (or at least 12:2–9) comprised a coherent discourse.[28]

If we attempt to view, or rather to hear Q 12:2–12 without those assumptions, however, there are a number of indications that Q 12:2–9 (-12) was a coherent unit of communication. Both Matthew (10:26–32) and Luke (12:2–9) have this material in a continuous block. Moreover, Matthew uses the saying in Luke 12:11–12 = Matt 10:19 earlier in the same expanded mission discourse where he uses 10:26–32 = Luke 12:2–9. Only Q 12:10 evokes serious doubts about how it fits with the rest of the discourse and the rest of Q.[29] The repetition in the concluding lines, 12:11–12, of the theme of speaking and the same verbs and verb forms as appear in the opening lines, 12:2–3, provide an inclusio that unifies the whole speech.

Taking a few cues from socio-linguistic analysis can help us discern a number of aspects of the language patterns within the stanzas and the connections and cohesion of the stanzas in the overall speech.[30] The lines of A.2 give a more specific sense to those of A.1. In B, the second verse completes the thought begun in the first, "do not fear," with the contrast, "fear rather," and the combination of body and soul, which had been contrasted in the first. C.1. provides a comparison for the main point in C.2. "Do not fear" in C.2. also counters the anxiety and threat announced by B.1–2 with a reassurance of God's care. D.1 and D.2 present parallel positive and negative sides of the ultimate sanction of divine judgment. F.2 completes and explains the admonition of F.1, continues the reassurance of C.2 and D.1, and comes back around to the theme of speaking. Particularly striking in this speech is that every stanza consists of a fairly simple direct binary contrast in which one side succeeds or overcomes the other. In A revelation succeeds to hiddenness. In B God is far more of a threat than a repressive ruler. In the double contrast of C, people are far more important than sparrows and the previous threat of God's judgment in B is overpowered by God's care

27. Kloppenborg, *Formation of* Q, 208–216.

28. Kirk, *Composition*, 203–215, provides a masterful summary and criticism of previous analyses of Q/Luke 12:2–12 in terms of separate sayings, showing rather how this discourse can be read as a coherent whole.

29. See Kloppenborg's discussion, *Formation of* Q, 211–14.

30. Gee, *Social Linguistics and Literacies*, 106–14.

for people. In D the divine judgment succeeds and overrules the human political situation.

"Do not fear those who kill the body" in B.1 immediately following "proclaim. . ." in A.2 indicates in no uncertain terms that the proclamation may bring down repressive violence. But B.2 puts that in perspective: God is far more fearsome. Stanza B thus provides the political context for the admonition in stanza A. Stanza C further emphasizes the danger, while assuring those exhorted to proclaim of God's providential care. The parallel lines of sanction in D.1 and 2 combine the themes of stanzas A and B: confess and (whatever the repressive violence) be confessed at the divine judgment, deny (under threat of death) and be judged by divine court (the one who can destroy both body and soul). This in fact completes the line of thought of the speech, which could, and perhaps did once, end with stanza D. Stanza F, the current closing, comes back to the theme of "speak," but now to the situation of the speaker on trial, narrowed from the wide proclamation at the beginning of the speech.[31]

## Context

The *context* (Foley's "performance arena") in which this message was delivered was, in the general sense, meetings of communities of a movement that adhered to Jesus as its prophet-founder. More particularly, the audience-context was a movement that was experiencing periodic repression by the rulers, apparently because it was challenging or disrupting the social-political order. It is difficult to miss how the contents of the exhortations in the speech point to the context that they address. "Those who kill the body" in B.1 must be the rulers with power to execute, to whom members of the movement might well be "delivered up" and before whom they might have to speak in F.1–2. In D.1–2 is portrayed the heavenly court scene of "the angels of God" that corresponds to the rulers' earthy court before whom Jesus' followers might be hauled to face condemnation.

The context in which Q 12:2–12 was performed cannot be determined and considered apart from Q as a larger sequence of speeches (e.g., what was being proclaimed) and the historical political and cultural context in which Q belongs (e.g., "those who kill the body," and "before the angels

---

31. Kirk, *Composition*, 206–13, while still using some of some of the standard theologically-rooted modern constructs that I believe block appreciation of Jesus' speeches (e.g., "last days," "end-time," "cosmic"), provides a literary analysis that demonstrates the coherent rhetoric of this speech. His analysis explains clearly that sanctioning sayings such as Q 12:8–9 belong in such admonitory speeches, and offer no basis for separating one layer from another and one "theology' from another.

of God"). A number of Q speeches, other passages in the synoptic Gospel tradition, and other references in the books of Acts, Revelation, and Paul's letters offer multiple indications that the movements of Jesus-followers came under suspicion and experienced acts of repression by the authorities. Jesus and his followers formed a movement that proclaimed and practiced, in healings/exorcisms and communal social solidarity, the kingdom of God (evident throughout the sequence of Q speeches and the Gospel of Mark).[32] The message and practice of the kingdom meant disruption and conflict (12:49–56). Q included prophetic speeches in which Jesus pronounced God's condemnation of the rulers and woes against their representatives (13:34–35; 11:39–52). Jesus was the climax of a long line of prophets who had been killed by the Jerusalem rulers and their representatives (11:39–52; 13:34–35). His envoys had been sent out as "sheep in the midst of wolves" (10:2–16). His followers saw themselves as implicated in the same sustained political conflict, which required commitment, discipline, and solidarity (6:23; 14:26–27). This is the context in which the speech of 12:2–12 was delivered.

*Register*

The speech of 12:2–12, moreover, is in a *register* appropriate to this context. At first it might appear that there is a tension between what is indicated in 12:2–3 and 12:11–12. In 12:2–3 the emphasis seems to be on proclamation (of the kingdom), with the rest as sanction and reassurance, while a trial before rulers is the scene envisioned in 12:11–12, and is suggested in 12:8–9 as well. The tension is merely a perceived one, however, since it was clearly the proclamation and practice of the kingdom that was resulting in repression by the authorities. The one led to the other. And that is just what this speech addresses. That a register of speech appropriate to and addressed to situations of repression and persecution had developed is indicated in Judean literature prior to and contemporary with the Q movement and in other literature from parallel Jesus movements. Persecution and martyrdom during the Maccabean struggle against the oppressive emperor Antiochus Epiphanes became a focus of continuing reflection on faithful adherence to Israelite covenant and people even under violent tyranny (2 Macc 7; 4 Maccabees, see esp 13:14–15). Admonition to faithful adherence to the people and/or the group and reassurance that the righteous would be defended and/or rewarded at the divine court of judgment before all the angels

---

32. Elaborated in Horsley with Draper, *Whoever Hears You Hears Me*; and Horsley, *Hearing the Whole Story*.

apparently became standard in some scribal circles (in 1 *Enoch* 94–104; e.g., 97:5–6; 99:3; 100:4–5; 104:1; cf. esp Q 12:8–9).

Gospel and other literatures of movements of Jesus-believers (e.g., 1 Thess 1:2–9; 5:1–11; Phil 1:27–29; 2;1–18; 1 Peter 4:12–19; Rev 3:3–6, 8–13) exhibit a good deal of material belonging to this general register or exhortation to commitment and solidarity under repression (only some of which show influence from apocalyptic traditions). Sometimes the focus is specifically on the trial situation, as in Mark 8:34–38; 13:9–11 and parallels. Sometimes the possibility of martyrdom is used in an exhortation about how serious the commitment is in the face of a struggle that will be severe (Q 14:26–27. Many of the images in the speech of Q 12:2–12 also appear in the parallel discourse in Mark 8:34–38 (see esp. the theme of losing one's life and the sanctioning judgment in the heavenly court involving the son of man and the angels), i.e., presumably from a parallel Jesus-movement. In Mark 8:34–38 the focus is more clearly on the severity and risks of the struggle in following on the way of Jesus. The Q speech has a wider focus on general exhortation to bold proclamation of the kingdom with emphasis on reassurance of God's care and guidance if and when the faithful become subject to repressive action.[33]

*Tradition*

Many images and phrases in the speech in Q 12:2–12 would have resonated metonymically among the hearers out of the cultural tradition in which they were rooted. This is clearly the most difficult aspect of the performance of texts like this because we modern hearers/interpreters live at such a distance from the original hearers—not just chronologically, but also in terms of social location, language, and basic cultural assumptions, etc. as well. Moreover, we have only indirect access to the Israelite "little tradition" that Q speeches reference by extrapolation from the later canonized version of the Jerusalemite "great tradition."

The referencing of the broader Israelite tradition is far less pervasive and rich in Q 12:2–12 than it is in the covenantal speech in Q 6:20–49. As touched upon already in discussion of the register of the speech in 12:2–12, however, we can detect a good deal of resonance with both the broader Israelite tradition and the Jesus tradition that grows out of it. Those references resonate all the more once we are aware of the conflictual historical context of the performance.

---

33. See further the more extensive comparison of these speeches in chap. 8.

That nothing "is hidden that will not be made known" is indeed vague and general in the extreme, if taken in the abstract, as it is by many Q interpreters. But such statements have no meaning in the abstract. Like any statements, this one depends on context, in cultural tradition as well as in historical social (performance) context. In the context of the Jesus movements and the developing Jesus-tradition, the reference of the statement, while general, is not vague at all, especially when made more specific in the next lines, "what I tell you in the dark, speak in the light." Clearly in the rest of the Q speeches, Jesus was understood to have been proclaiming the kingdom of God. And the kingdom was indeed something that could not be hidden or kept secret. It was a whole new stage in history, a dramatic reversal of the fortunes of the hearers, a qualitative leap in the quality of life for the recipients (e.g., Q 7:18–35; 6:20–26; 11:2–4; 11:14–26; 12:22–31). It is evident from other Q speeches (such as those just cited), moreover, that Jesus' proclamation and manifestation of the kingdom of God was understood as the fulfillment of long-standing Israelite expectations and longings. Once we recognize that Judeans and Galileans were largely non-literate and that the oral cultivation of cultural tradition was dominant, it would be quite unwarranted to imagine that the term "be revealed" (*apokalyphthesetai*) alluded to portrayals of revelation in apocalyptic literature. Ordinary people, and the prophets who arose from among them, received revelations that were orally communicated and never written. It would be unwarranted to imagine that popular leaders and movements thought in the same forms as scribal circles who produced apocalyptic literature, even though there may well have been some interaction and shared images and terms.

To gain some perspective on the images of body and soul in the next stanza of the speech we might reflect on how these statements would be quite unintelligible in most Greek philosophical schools. But they would certainly resonate in a tradition basic to which was the sense that personal human life consisted not of the soul or spirit separate from the body, but was an embodied life. Moreover, basic to Israelite tradition was the distinction between a human ruler and the divine ruler. God was the ultimate and proper ruler of Israelites and both demanded just relations in social-economic-political relations and promised/threatened to enforce those demands by punishing or destroying unjust rulers. That invited people to challenge and oppose oppressive rule and rulers and to respond to divine initiatives, which might in turn be sanctioned by the sense of God as ultimate ruler and judge. Gehenna/Ge-hinnom, originally a valley outside of Jerusalem, had long since become an image of the fiery judgment to which the divine judge would confine the unrighteous for punishment/destruction.

The image of a trial before "the angels of God," with "the son of man" acting as advocate, is clearly a specifically Israelite portrayal of the divine judgment. New Testament scholars who work on the assumptions of print culture standardly posit a "heavenly" or "future son of man" that derives from the written text of Daniel 7:13. Not only is the image here not the same as that in Daniel 7:13, but it is unwarranted to imagine that there was a standardized image that derived from that written text. Since oral communication and cultivation of Israelite tradition was dominant in ancient Judea and Galilee, we should imagine things working the other way around. It has been suggested long since that the visionary behind Daniel 7 was drawing upon an existing cultural image or at least an idiom, "the son of man," which appears as a dream-image referring to "the people of the saints of the Most High." But that image would not have disappeared from the culture and was still available for other uses, one of which became an advocate figure at the divine court in session with all the angels. The special twist/skill here is in linking the confession of Jesus ("me") with the reciprocal confession by "the son of man" in the divine court.

## How Communication Happened in Performance of Q 12:2–12

Standard interpretations of Q attempt to find the meaning of individual sayings in themselves as abstract entities. To gain a sense of a Q speech such as 12:2–12 in oral performance, however, requires us to appreciate how communication happens in such performance. The communication that happened in performance of this speech involved a complex network of conflictual historical and political relations. In a sequence of stanzas of two sets of two lines each Q 12:2–12 sets up a sequence of overlapping binary contrasts whose impact is compounded with each new stanza: the proclaimed vs. the secret, in the context of a repressive situation that their proclamation is apparently challenging; the human vs. the divine ruler/judge with power to punish/enforce subordination and obedience; the caring God vs. the bodily-destructive ruler. The sequence of poetic stanzas in Q 12:2–12 communicates by referring, with sharp evaluation rooted in deep emotion, to those interrelated sets of relationships and contrasts which it sets up. For the modern interpreter to ponder whether the main point is bold proclamation in general despite potential repression or bold confession before a court after repression is underway sets up a false dichotomy that oversimplifies the situation and the communication. The situation and set of political relations that the sequence of binary conflicts points to and holds together is far more complex. In Q 12:2–12 "Jesus" admonishes members and communities of a Jesus movement to proclaim boldly the kingdom of God. Despite the possibility that the rulers whose position their proclamation threatens will apprehend, judge, and kill them, they can be confident that the ultimate judge who is now empowering their movement of renewal will further inspire and defend them. "Jesus" in Q 12:2–12 speaks out of and to the ethos and agenda of a movement caught up in the excitement over the kingdom of God now being realized among them, their yearnings for sufficiency and justice being fulfilled, yet realistically recognizing that surveillance and repression will continue, perhaps even intensify.

# 8

# THE SPEECHES OF YESHUA BEN SIRA—
# AND THE SPEECHES OF YESHUA BAR
# MARYA

THERE APPEAR TO BE SEVERAL INTERRELATED REASONS WHY interpreters of "the Sayings Source" ("Q," short for the German *Quelle* = source) sought and found the key to interpretation in a supposedly formative stratum that they claimed was sapiential instruction. Given the deeply ingrained habit of reading the Gospels verse by verse and the assumption that Jesus' teachings took the form of individual sayings, the source of Jesus' teachings parallel in Matthew and Luke (but not in Mark) was assumed to be a collection of sayings. The recently discovered *Gospel of Thomas* seemed to confirm this, and its lack or softening of prophetic/judgmental (or "apocalyptic") sayings led interpreters to favor the parables, proverbs, and other seemingly "sapiential" sayings in Q. James M Robinson delineated a genre of *Logoi Sophon*, "Sayings of the Wise," and suggested that this was the catalyst for the collection-in-writing of Jesus' sayings, (with the supposed effect of stabilizing their wording).[1] Since many of the sayings included in Q were not susceptible of (re-)classification as "sapiential," however, the logical final step was taken by Helmut Koester and John Kloppenborg in the hypothesis of a secondary "apocalyptic" layer superimposed on the formative "sapiential" collection.[2] Ironically, what goes almost unnoticed is that in his "composition criticism" Kloppenborg also argued that Q, even in its formative sapiential layer, was a series of "clusters" or discourses, and not just a collection of sayings.

---

1. Robinson, "*LOGOI SOPHON*."
2. Koester, "Apocryphal and Canonical Gospels"; Kloppenborg, *Formation of Q.*

This hypothesis of a written collection of sapiential sayings as the formative layer of Q, thus presumably the earliest and most reliable source for the teaching of Jesus, reinforced critical liberals' arguments that the "sapiential" sayings were the earliest and most "authentic" teachings of Jesus. Dismissing "apocalyptic" and judgmental sayings as the later products of "early Christians," liberal interpreters looked to wisdom sayings not only as the model for Jesus' teaching but also as the longer cultural tradition in which his teaching can be understood. This became the basis for the claim by leading members of the Jesus Seminar that Jesus was "a sage."[3]

Another (and closely related) factor in the focus on instructional wisdom as the key to the teaching of Jesus, however, given the print-cultural assumptions of modern biblical studies, was that scholars could not imagine "the Sayings Source" as a stable text, hence reliable source for the sayings of Jesus, without it having been written, that is, composed in writing. This was more implicit, although also explicit, in the definition of the genre *Logoi Sophon*. But it came sharply to the fore when John Kloppenborg attempted to comprehend, on print-cultural assumptions, that the formative sapiential layer was a written document (composed in writing) despite the agrarian ethos attested by the content of the supposedly sapiential sayings. Accordingly he also hypothesized that there existed in the small towns and villages of Galilee and surrounding areas some low-status scribes who nevertheless had sufficient education that they could compose in clusters of sapiential sayings (in some of which they must have been trained).[4]

This recent, distinctively American interpretation of "Q," and the corresponding distinctively American interpretation of Jesus as a "sage," consists of one hypothesis stacked on top of another, all resting on assumptions that are being challenged by recent research in various areas. It is all a "house of cards" now collapsing because it lacks a solid basis in evidence. Some of the recent research in these areas that undermine this set of hypotheses and assumptions about Q have been summarized in the essays above: that oral communication was dominant in ancient societies, with literacy being limited to an educated elite; that written texts had various functions, were inaccessible, and directly known only to an educated elite; that even the literate elite learned texts by repeated oral recitation and recited texts orally from memory; that even the literate elite composed in their minds, drawing

---

3. Crossan, *Historical Jesus,* quickly became by far the most influential presentation.

4. Kloppenborg, "Social History of the Q People," 82–89; repeated in *Excavating Q;* followed by his student Arnal, *Village Scribes.* Cf. the explanation of the lack of evidence for such "village scribes" in Horsley, "Introduction" to *Oral Performance, Popular Tradition,* esp. 8–15.

heavily on material in memory; that ordinary people had their own popular version of cultural tradition, while aware of the existence of written texts.

Now it might seem that this research would provide support for the hypothesis of a formative sapiential layer of Q, only on the new basis of oral cultivation and composition of speeches by scribes/sages. Yet this is not the case, as is evident from a comparison of the speeches of Yeshua bar Marya in Q with the speeches of Yeshua ben Sira collected in Sirach, the source of Judean instructional wisdom closest in time to Q and other Gospel texts. A comparison of the two indicates rather the dramatic differences between them, despite the common oral communication and some similarities in the form of their speeches.

It may not be obvious to some why I am referring to these figures as Yeshua ben Sira and Yeshua bar Marya instead of using the usual ben Sira and Jesus. The latter, of course, is the English form derived from the Greek *Iesous*, which translated the Semitic *Yeshua*. The latter was a very common name at the time. From the Judean historian we know of at least two other famous Yeshuas in mid-first century CE, one a leading high priests who attempted to keep the lid on the popular revolt of 66–70, and the other a villager-turned-bandit-chieftan in the escalating political-turmoil of the mid-first century. We could indicate the sharp social (and regional) divide between the earlier learned scribe who served the Oniad high priesthood in Jerusalem and the Galilean villager by referring to them as Ben Sira of Jerusalem and Jesus of Nazareth. But Yeshua ben Sira and Yeshua bar Marya do this more poignantly and add significant overtones of the social differences. The Hebrew form *ben* (son of) and his father's (or grandfather's) name, *Sira*, represent also that he evidently taught in Hebrew, an archaic ceremonial and literary language cultivated mainly by scribes and priests, and symbolize the extreme importance in the respectable circles of learned scribes and prominent priestly families of prominent figures being identified as sons of their fathers. By contrast, the popular prophet from the Galilean village of Nazareth was known as the son of his mother, Mary, or *Marya* in Aramaic, the language spoken, in various dialects, by ordinary people, with Joseph (*Yosef*) being supplied in legends that provided him with a father in the dominant patriarchal society.[5]

---

5. See especially the original critical analysis in Schaberg, *Illegitimacy of Jesus*.

## An Alternative Approach to the Yeshuas' Speeches as "Oral-Derived" Texts

The teachings both of Yeshua bar Marya (in Q) and of Yeshua ben Sira (in Sirach) were not isolated sayings or aphorisms that were addressed to everyone in general and no one in particular. They were rather speeches that involved interactive interpersonal communication. Once we recognize this, it is important to probe not for the meaning of isolated sayings in themselves (which is standard in biblical studies) but for what happens in the performance of the speeches (*text*) in *context* in the *register* appropriate to the context as they resonate with hearers by referencing shared cultural *tradition*. This approach, derived from the theory of oral performance of John Miles Foley, is sketched in connection with the speeches of Yeshua ben Sira and Yeshua bar Marya, respectively, in chaps. 4 and 7 above.

In moving into the comparison between their speeches, however, it is necessary to clarify further what is meant by *tradition*, since it has been understood so narrowly in interpretation of the teaching of Yeshua bar Marya. Because of its central importance for understanding the Christian Gospels and the historical Jesus, the synoptic Gospel tradition, or more widely, the tradition of Jesus' teachings, has been intensively analyzed as "oral" tradition. In this connection "tradition" has meant primarily two things: the contents of Jesus' teaching and the "handing down" or "handing on" of those teachings. For various reasons the tradition as content was simply assumed to take the fragmentary form of tiny units, the simplest forms of individual verses, sayings, or parables. Tradition as the handing on was understood in the reductionist form of mere transmission of those fragments of content from one to another to another person until someone combined them in literary, i.e., written form.

Both of these senses of tradition are problematic. Tradition as tiny fragments, as individual sayings, makes them into artifacts abstracted from life in which no human communication was involved. After all, no one can *communicate* in aphorisms. The growing appreciation of the Gospel of Mark and other Gospels as fuller narratives and recent more sophisticated appreciation of "Q" as a series of speeches may well lead to wider recognition that the fundamental units of communication in Jesus' teaching were not individual sayings, but speeches on various issues and perhaps sequences of wonder-stories and parables. Tradition as mere transmission also ignores real-life communication. As Werner Kelber pointed out thirty years ago in *The Oral and the Written Gospel*, the teachings of Jesus were remembered because they resonated with people in the contexts of their lives.[6] Both of these recognitions point in the same direction: the teaching of Jesus took forms of *communication* larger and more complex than individual sayings, and continued to be cultivated as *communication* about issues of concern in concrete contexts of social-political life.

These recognitions can be reinforced by a reminder about what we are borrowing and adapting from other fields in the exploration of oral tradition and oral performance. In the first flush of excitement over the rediscovery of the oral features, for example, of the Gospel of Mark in performance, biblical scholars focused their attention on the possible marks of orality. As Foley has reminded us, however, in the concept of "oral traditional" in texts as developed by Milman Parry, the *traditional* was just as important as (and inseparable from) the *oral*. Through certain cues, formulae, and highly familiar terms, performed texts resonate with hearers by referencing the cultural tradition in which people are rooted.

In order to appreciate this better in the speeches of Yeshua bar Marya we will consider not just a speech in Q but parallel speeches in the Gospel of Mark. It is commonly recognized that Q and Mark present parallel speeches in which Jesus sends disciples as his envoys to expand his mission (Q/Luke 10:2–16; Mark 6:6–13) and parallel speeches in which Jesus responds to the charge that he is possessed by Beelzebul (Q/Luke 11:14–20; Mark 3:22–28). But they also both have less strikingly parallel speeches on covenant renewal (Q/Luke 6:20–49; Mark 10:2–45) and on bold confession in circumstances of persecution or trial (Q/Luke 12:2–12; Mark 8:34–38; 13:9–13), as well. Because the speeches on bold confession express Yeshua bar Marya's stance toward the rulers that corresponds to Yeshua ben Sira's stance toward the rulers, we will focus on them below. Insofar as seeking wisdom is the central concern of learned scribes such as Yeshua ben Sira, we begin with his many speeches on this central topic.

## The Orally Performed Speeches of Yeshua ben Sira

The recent American hypotheses about Q assume that it was a written text and look to earlier examples of the presumed genre of *logoi sophon* as its precursors and evidence for sapiential instruction as written compositions. Of course later manuscripts of Matthew and Luke attest that, at some point in the transmission of the speeches in Q, the series of speeches became the basis of two different but very similar traditions of those speeches (in the respective Gospels) that were eventually inscribed on codices. And the

---

6. Kelber, *The Oral and the Written Gospel*, chap. 1.

anthology of Ben Sira's wisdom produced by his "grandson" (Sirach 1) was inscribed on scrolls and/or codices in both Hebrew and Greek versions.

When we look at the representation of the instructional wisdom of Yeshua ben Sira in the book of Sirach, however, writing and reading are nowhere to be found (as discussed in chap. 4). As a professional scribe/sage, of course, Ben Sira would have been thoroughly literate. But he never quotes anything from a book and, most important, he presents his own teaching as oral and his students' learning as aural—repeatedly.

> For wisdom becomes known through speech,
>
> > and education through the words of the tongue. (4:24)
>
> Do not slight the discourse of the sages, . . .
>
> Because from them you will learn discipline
>
> > and how to serve princes. (8:8–9; see further 6:23; 16:24–25)

Ben Sira teaches in his "house of instruction" by "opening his mouth," not by having his students open some cumbersome scroll (51:23–25). Senior scribes such as Ben Sira also had a more public role as a speaker in assemblies of the temple-state aristocracy (37:16–26). But of course it could not have been otherwise in a historical context where not only was the general social ethos dominated by oral communication (5:10–11, 13—6:1; 6:5; 14:1; 22:22, 27; 23:7–12; 27:11–15; 33:4; 37:16), but where communication in the court or assembly of the ruling aristocracy was oral as well (11:7–9; 15:5; 21:15–17).[7]

Yeshua Ben Sira, the professional scribe who served the rulers, moreover, stood in a long tradition of learned scribes for whom wisdom was communicated by speech (Prov 12:18; 15:2; 16:21, 23) and learning happened not through reading and writing, but through oral communication, mainly repeated recitation (Prov 15:31; 12:15; 18:15; 23:12). The only use of the verb *katab* ("to write") is metaphorical or symbolic, that their students should write their instruction on the tablet of their heart (Prov 3:3; 7:3). As discussed in earlier chapters, recent studies of scribal culture in Mesopotamia, Egypt, and (by implication) Judah have demonstrated that the teaching and learning of a wide range of cultural curricula was done by oral recitation and repetition.[8] Martin Jaffee has explained how the (literate) priests and scribes at Qumran, like the later rabbis, recited texts that had become inscribed in their memories rather than consult written scrolls and

---

7. See further chap. 4 above and Horsley, *Scribes, Visionaries*, chap. 5.

8. Carr, *Writing on the Tablet of the Heart,* has summarized the results of studies by specialists on Mesopotamian, Egyptian, and other scribal cultures and drawn out their implications for scribal practice in Judah/Judea; focus on Ben Sira in Horsley, *Scribes, Visionaries*, esp. chaps. 3–7.

continued to cultivate them orally.[9] What we have in the book of Sirach is a collection of the instructional speeches, hymns to wisdom, and other kinds of wisdom that had been orally performed by Yeshua ben Sira (see chap. 4).

Not only that, but the speeches of ben Sira were not mere clusters of individual sayings, such as proverbs and aphorisms. Directly contrary to standard treatment in biblical studies in which the "literary" genre of instructional wisdom is defined narrowly as the *mashal*, or proverb, aphorism, maxim, saying,[10] virtually all of the instructional wisdom presented in the book of Sirach takes the form of short speeches focused on particular topics (as discussed in chap. 4). In contrast to those sections of the book of Proverbs (chapters 10–22, 25–29) that consist of one proverb after another (i.e., mere lists that do not involve interpersonal communication), Ben Sira's teaching resembles that in Proverbs 1–9; 22:17—24:34; and 31:10–31, which also takes the form of speeches on various topics. In the *text* of particular speeches, an argument is easily discernible. The teaching employs certain rhetorical devices to make a case to the student hearers. The particular structure of the argument may be different in nearly every speech. But they have certain common typical features that can be readily detected and thus enable us to appreciate how their respective arguments proceed.[11]

Most basic may be an admonition followed by a motive clause. The admonition and/or the motive clause may be multiplied, and a similar, parallel admonition may form an inclusio at the end of the speech. Often a proverb or maxim functions as an admonition or a sanctioning motive clause. Reinforcing the basic point made in the admonition(s) may be illustrative examples and maxims or proverbs. And a proverb or other saying can provide a sanctioning promise of reward or threat of punishment, often at the end of the speech. This shifting back and forth from admonitions to proverbs and illustrative examples also involves a shifting from second person or imperative address to third person (which thus should not be taken as shifts to new units of communication). Similar patterns of speeches can be found in a wide range of instructional literature from the ancient Near East, particularly in Egyptian texts.[12]

---

9. Jaffee, *Torah in the Mouth*.

10. Skehan and DiLella, *Wisdom of Ben Sira*, 21–27; cf. McKane, *Proverbs*, 3 (that the fundamental form-critical unit of the instruction is the imperative or admonition); Crenshaw, *Old Testament Wisdom*, 17–19 (similarly focuses on "proverbial sentences," having the older material in Proverbs 10–22 primarily in mind.

11. Kirk, *Composition*, chaps. 2–3. See further the fuller discussion based on Kirk's work in chap. 4 above.

12. Kirk, *Composition*, 93–104, 130–151.

Insofar as these speeches of instructional wisdom all seem to be offered to students about their relationships with wives, families, rulers, or poor peasants, and their functions in service of the temple-state, the (social and textual) *context* is the relatively confined one of the training of fledgling scribes. Recent studies of scribal training in Judah/Judea, like that in ancient Egypt and Mesopotamia, has shown that instruction was given by senior scribes/sages to small groups of their "chidren/sons" (students) in their "house of instruction."[13]

The collection of Ben Sira's instructional speeches in Sirach includes two or more speeches on many different topics, such as seeking wisdom or relations between husband and wife, parents and children, rich and poor, or the sages and the rulers they served. The multiple speeches by Ben Sira on a given topic, moreover, display many of the same images, motifs, and phrases and even similar lines (as discussed in chap. 4). In cases where Proverbs has speeches on the same topics as Sirach, those speeches also display many of the same images and motifs and even variant versions of the same proverbs, maxims, or admonitions. And the collection of proverbs in other sections of Proverbs include many on the same topics as the speeches in Sirach. It is thus clear that there was a particular traditional set of language for each topic of instruction, i.e., a *register* dedicated to each topic from which the well-trained scribe such as Ben Sira drew in composing and performing instructional speeches. In the speeches of Ben Sira, the speech *register* has, in effect, become or taken the place of what in other speeches would have been the cultural tradition that the performed speeches referenced. Speeches of instructional wisdom, performed in the confined circle of a "house of instruction," were embedded in and drew upon a standard set of self-referential language registers.

In order to make a comparison between the speeches of Yeshua ben Sira and those of Yeshua bar Marya, we will focus on the former's speeches on what is the most central concern for sages such as ben Sira, the seeking of wisdom, and on the speeches that articulate his stance toward the rulers of the society.

### Seeking Wisdom

The book of Sirach includes several speeches on seeking and finding wisdom. These speeches articulate what was apparently the very center of Ben Sira's teaching. Each of these speeches has distinctive features. Yet they all draw on the same motifs, images, and phrases and combine them in similar

---

13. Carr, *Writing on the Tablet of the Heart.*

ways. This suggests that there was a standard traditional "discourse" or "register" dedicated to the topic of seeking and finding wisdom. In attempting to appreciate how Yeshua ben Sira could *compose-in-performance* several somewhat different speeches by drawing on this dedicated set of motifs, images, phrases, and proverbs with which he was thoroughly familiar in his memory, I included in chap. 4 above a synopsis of this register as used in the speeches in Sir 4:11–19; 6:18–37; 14:20—15:10; and parallels in Proverbs (see again the synopsis on page 90 above). Here we can further appreciate ben Sira's composition-in-performance of the speech in Sirach 14:20—15:10 by noting the traditional dedicated language of "seeking wisdom" as evident in the other speeches on the same topic in Sirach and Proverbs (in the right-hand column). Note also the close, indeed intimate relationship between the sage and a personified Wisdom.

**The text of Sirach 14:20—15:10 With Key Motifs and Images in Other Speeches**

| | |
|---|---|
| 20) Happy is the person who meditates on wisdom | (Happy those who find wisdom |
| and reasons intelligently, | Prov 3:13) |
| 21) who reflects in his heart on her ways | (Her ways. . .paths of peace, Pr 3:17) |
| and ponders her secrets, | (Happy. . .who keep my ways, 8:32) |
| 22) pursuing her like a hunter | |
| and lying in wait on her paths; | |
| 23) who peers through her windows | (Happy the one watching my gates, |
| and listens at her doors; | waiting beside my doors. Prov 8:34) |
| | (gazing in at the windows, Cant 9:2) |
| 24) who camps near her house | (Wisdom has built her house Pr 9:1) |
| and fastens his tent peg to her walls; | (Wisdom's house: Prov 7:6f ; |
| 25) who pitches his tent near her, | 24:3; tent. . . Job 8:22; 22:23; 29:4) |
| and so occupies an excellent lodging place; | |
| 26) who places his children under her shelter, | (Wisdom as a tree, Sir 24:13–17) |
| and lodges under her boughs; | |
| 27) who is sheltered by her from the heat, | |
| and dwells in the midst of her glory. | |
| | |
| 15:1) Whoever fears the Lord will do this, | (main theme in Sirach, e.g. 1:10–31) |
| and whoever holds to the law will obtain wisdom. | (main theme in Sirach) |
| 2) She will come to meet him like a mother, | (mother, Prov 7:1ff; wife, Prov 5:18; |
| and like a young bride she will welcome him. | bride, Cant 4:9,12; 5:1–2) |

(3) She will feed him with the bread of learning,     (wisdom's bread and wine, Prov 9:5)

and give him the water of wisdom to drink.

(4) He will lean on her and not fall,

and he will rely on her and not be put to shame.

(5) She will exalt him above his neighbors,     (exalted: Sir 4:13; 6:31; 1:30)

and will open his mouth in the midst of the     (Sir 1:30; 38:33, etc.)
assembly.

(6) He will find gladness and a crown of rejoicing,     (crown: Sir 6:31; name: 39:9–11)

and will inherit an everlasting name.

(7) The foolish will not obtain her,     (contrast with fools: 6:20;

and sinners will not see her.     (contrast with sinners:

(8) She is far from arrogance,

and liars will never think of her.

(9) Praise is unseemly on the lips of a sinner,

for it has not been sent from the Lord.

(10) For in wisdom must praise be uttered,

and the Lord will make it prosper.

### Scribes' Relations with the Rulers

In a political-economic structure in which learned scribes served the rulers in various connections, it is not surprising that their relations with their wealthy and powerful patrons ("the great/rulers" etc.) was an important topic of instruction. Along with many passing comments on this subject (e.g., 4:7, 27; 7:4–7; 8:1–2; 9:13; 20:27–31), Sirach has speeches both on the general topic of association with the great and on the more particular sub-topic of behavior at banquets (dining and drinking) hosted by the wealthy and powerful (13:1–13; 31:12—32:13). In both cases it is evident that these speeches are rooted in deep traditions of instructional speech whose language registers were devoted to these particular subjects.

Older proverbs collected in Proverbs exemplify the collective wisdom derived from generations of scribes' experience at royal courts about the fine line they tread in relations with their patrons.

A servant who deals wisely has the king's favor. (Prov 14:35)

Those who are gracious in speech will have the king as a friend. (22:11)

The dread anger of a king is like the growling of a lion;

anyone who provokes him to anger forfeits life itself. (20:2 = 19:12)

Learned scribes also shaped such wisdom into brief instructional speeches.

My child, fear the Lord and the king,

and do not disobey either of them;

for disaster comes from them suddenly,

and who knows the ruin that both can bring? (Prov 24:21–22)

Do not put yourself forward in the king's presence

or stand in the place of the great;

for it is better to be told, "Come up here,"

than to be put lower in the presence of a noble. (Prov 25:6–7)

Sirach 13:1–13 is a more elaborate speech in this same speech-register of scribal relations with rulers, combining proverbs, admonitions, analogies/similes, and (proverbial) illustrations.[14] The formulations in Sir 13:8–10 are addressed to the same situation and its perils as indicated in Prov 25:6–7, and give virtually the same advice.

When a ruler invites you, be reserved,
And he will invite you all the more insistently.
Do not be forward, or you may be rebuffed;
Do not stand aloof, or you will be forgotten. (Sir 13:9–10)

And the concluding admonition (picking up the illustrations of Sir 13:3–4, 7) repeats the same ominous concern as Prov 20:2 (cf. Sir 9:13).

Be on your guard and very careful,
for you are walking about with your own downfall. (13:13)

Sirach includes a far more elaborate speech of ben Sira on the topic of behavior at banquets sponsored by patrons among the aristocracy, in 31:12—32:13. Wise scribes had known for some time the problems of over-indulgence in wine.

Wine is a mocker, strong drink a brawler,
and whoever is led astray by it is not wise. (Prov 20:1; cf. 21:17)

Well before the time of Ben Sira, speeches warning against drinking had become standard in instructional wisdom ("Hear my child, and be wise, do not be among the winebibbers and gluttons" Prov 23:19–22). Longer

---

14. On who the wealthy/powerful/rulers are: to the *nadib* of 13:9, cf. Job 21:28; 34:18; Prov 8:16, etc. An earlier Egyptian form of instruction on the same topic is in Phibis x 12—xi 23, as discussed by Sanders, *Ben Sira and Demotic Wisdom*, 92–93.

speeches combining rhetorical questions, proverbs, and illustrations were built around admonitions such as "look not upon the wine when it is red. . . and goes down smoothly" (Prov 23:29–35). And the scribal retainers of kings knew from generations of experience that "it is not for kings to drink wine . . . lest they forget what they had decreed" (Prov 31:4–5). Their concern for their own positions, however, focused on how to conduct themselves at banquets. Proverbs includes a short speech warning about the potential risks involved in "sitting down to eat with a ruler" (23:1–3). And such speeches by earlier Judean scribes had deeper roots in instructional speech of Egypt, where banqueting with rulers was a standard topic, as evident in several extant collections.[15]

Ben Sira' speech stands directly in this tradition of instructional discourse on the topic of banqueting. The first long section (speech), Sir 31:12–24 is an elaboration, mainly in admonitions, of earlier speeches such as Prov 23:1–3, warning hungry sages against appearing greedy at the table of the great. Of course, Ben Sira does add the practical suggestion that, should one overeat, one should "get up to vomit" (31:21). Besides the standard traditional Judean and ancient Near Eastern proverbial wisdom on the importance of moderation in wine-drinking (31:25–31), Ben Sira addresses the possibility of a scribe being made "master of the feast"—which requires all the more moderation along with a diplomatic humility (32:1–2). The ensuing advice first to the more senior sages and then to the more junior indicates a situation in which guests talk during the music, not afterwards, in contrast to the Greek custom (cf. Plato's *Symposium* 176E) of dismissing the flute-girl before the discourse begins in earnest, and again draws on the traditional idiom of Judean scribal instruction on moderation in speech (32:3–12)—and concludes with a nod to God, as the source of such blessings (32:13).[16]

By noting the resemblances between his different speeches on these two issues, we can begin to appreciate how the Judean sage Yeshua ben Sira composed instructional speeches in performance. As a learned scribe who had himself undergone intensive scribal training, he would have been thoroughly familiar with the various registers and patterns of speech dedicated to the standard topics of scribal instruction. The purpose and life-long preoccupation of the wise scribe was to seek wisdom by learning "the wisdom of all the ancients, [including] . . .sayings, . . . parables, . . . and proverbs," along with the torah of the Most High (understood as identical

---

15. E.g., the Instruction of Ptah-hotep, the Instruction of Kagemi, and the Instruction of Amenemope, as discussed by Sanders, *Ben Sira and Demonic Wisdom*, 67.

16. Collins, *Jewish Wisdom*, 32–33.

with wisdom) (38:34—39:3). On the basis of these traditional sets of dedicated language that he had internalized, he could formulate speeches, as appropriate to the instructional context, on a wide range of standard topics. To his students as well as himself, each of those speeches would have been readily memorable (although not in the sense of verbatim memorization). And from the storehouse of such wisdom in his memory, Ben Sira could again and again compose speeches on topics such as the seeking of wisdom and scribes'/sages' delicate relations with their patrons among the ruling aristocracy.

## The Orally Performed Speeches of Yeshua bar Marya

It is finally being recognized, at least by key scholars in North America, that Q was no mere collection of individual sayings but a series of Jesus' speeches on various issues of concern to (a) Jesus movement(s).[17] Similarly, along with the recognition that the Gospel of Mark was a sustained story of interlocking episodes, it is being recognized that some of those episodes are Jesus' speeches on some of the same or similar issues. Thus, as noted above, Q and Mark have parallel speeches of Jesus on several matters, such as his commission of disciples for mission, his response to the charge of being possessed by Beelzebul, covenant renewal, and bold confession under persecution and repression. It could be said that in some cases we have access in the Synoptic Gospels to three, four, or five different versions of speeches on some issues, such as the commission for mission: one in Mark, a second discernible through Luke's and Matthew's parallel speech material, i.e., presumably from Q, and then a third in Mathew's conflation of the first two and Luke's adaptation of both Mark's version and Q's version. To simplify presentation here, however, we will focus on what are believed to be the earliest versions of Jesus' speeches to which we have access, those in Q and Mark.

It has long been recognized that Jesus' teaching was cultivated and continued in oral tradition, that is, in (continuing compostion in) oral performance. New—with the recent research showing the dominance of oral communication among ordinary people in particular and showing that texts such as Jesus' speeches and even whole Gospel stories continue to be performed orally after they were also written down—is that not individual sayings but Jesus' speeches were repeatedly orally (composed-and-) performed. This was the process by which the series of speeches in Q was

---

17. Argued in Horsley with Draper, *Whoever Hears You Hears Me*, chap. 4.

formed, and the process continued (probably) in the continuing use of Q speeches and in the creative re-composition on the basis of Q speeches in the Gospels of Matthew and Luke.

The teaching of Yeshua bar Marya thus resembles that of Yeshua ben Sira insofar as they both took the form of speeches on various issues and were both orally performed. Beyond that, however, the differences between them begin to appear and mount up under critical analysis.

In clarifying what is the *text* of their respective speeches, for starters, the anthology in Sirach presents what appear to be discrete short speeches on given topics. This may be partially true for the speeches in the Q series, as well. Yet the series of speeches in Q has a certain sequence that suggests that it was a coherent set of speeches cultivated by at least one Jesus movement, and as a whole set of speeches had a certain theme (the kingdom of God) and agenda (renewal of the people in opposition to their rulers). In Mark the speeches of Yeshua bar Marya are components of a longer, complex story—whose theme and agenda (the coming of the kingdom in the renewal of Israel, vs. the rulers) were virtually the same as in the sequence of speeches in Q. The speeches must thus be heard in the context of the overall text of the sequence of speeches in Q or the overall narrative in Mark. Especially noticeable in Mark, the speeches are narratively contextualized in the overall story, while their arguments as particular speeches on key issues are still evident.

More dramatic and decisive differences come to the fore when we inquire into the *context*. As with the speeches of Yeshua ben Sira, the general and particular contexts and their relationship must be considered. Whereas the general context of speeches of instructional wisdom was the confined one of training of fledgling scribes for their service of the temple-state, including the formation of cautious and conservative personal character necessary for their role, the general context of the speeches of Yeshua bar Marya was gatherings of communities of the newly emergent popular movement of renewal and resistance that was spreading beyond the frontiers of Galilee into nearby areas. Judging from the issues addressed in Yeshua's speeches, the people in the movement were struggling with the effects of economic exploitation, such as hunger and debts, various illnesses and spirit possession, and periodic political repression. Accordingly, in both the Gospel of Mark and the series of speeches in Q, particular speeches address the particular issues, hence particular life-contexts of debts and subsistence living, healing and exorcism, and political repression. These were the serious, recurrent particular aspects of the people's life-context.

The *register* appropriate to the context and the cultural *tradition* that the performed speeches referenced were quite different matters for the speeches of Yeshua bar Marya than for those of instructional wisdom, or for those of performance of a traditional epic such as *The Iliad* or *Beowulf*. As noted above, the *registers* of speech devoted to particular topics in the training of fledgling scribes/sages had become or in effect replaced the (broader) cultural tradition. The tradition referenced in performance of a traditional epic that had been performed for generations or centuries had long become standardized and deeply familiar among the audience of the performance. The cultural tradition of the Jesus movements was new, just developing in the very performance of the speeches of Yeshua bar Marya, and the registers of speech appropriate to key issues still crystallizing. Yet the mission of Yeshua bar Marya and the nascent movement were deeply rooted in popular Israelite tradition, often claiming to be the renewal and fulfillment of various facets of Israelite tradition. The speeches of covenant renewal (Q/ Luke 6:20–49; Mark 10:2–45), for example, are filled with references to the components, motifs, and particular rulings of the Mosaic covenant.[18]

### *Seeking Wisdom*

The most striking difference between the speeches of Yeshua bar Marya and those of Yeshua ben Sira is the absence of the central concern of instructional wisdom, seeking wisdom, in both the Q speeches and the Gospel of Mark. There appears to be no interest in or typical features of instructional wisdom in Mark. And several episodes of the Gospel portray sharp conflict between the scribal and Pharisaic successors of scribes/sages such as Ben Sira and the people among whom Jesus works. Mark represents Yeshua bar Marya as sharply condemning the scribes and Pharisees for imposing their "traditions of the elders" on the people and for "devouring widows' houses," that is, economically exploiting the people.

Striking in its irony is that the supposedly formative sapiential speeches of Q are not particularly sapiential and certainly give no hint that seeking wisdom is important. Indeed some of the leading scholars who formulated and perpetuated the hypothesis that the formative layer of Q speeches are "sapiential" and stand in the tradition of instructional wisdom have admitted how problematic their arguments are.[19] Pressed on their case, they admitted that of the five supposedly "sapiential" speeches in Q, the bulk

18. First sketched in *Jesus and the Spiral*, chap. 8; with broader perspective in *Covenant Economics*, chaps. 6–7.

19. Mack, *Myth of Innocence*, following Kloppenborg, *Formation of Q*, where claims about the sapiential character of the speeches of the supposedly formative stratum are accompanied by caveats that their kind of wisdom is somewhat different from that of the learned scribes.

of material in two of them (Q 10:2–16 on mission and Q 11:2–4, 9–13 on prayer) was not typically sapiential at all. They acknowledged further that the material in the formative stratum as a whole is not sapiential "with respect to traditional forms of conventional wisdom," but appears "sapiential" only by comparison with the "apocalyptic" secondary layer.[20] But in that regard, Kloppenborg admitted that the "apocalyptic" character of the supposed secondary stratum could not be stressed.[21] At one point, a supposedly "sapiential" speech appears downright hostile to sages (Q/Luke 10:21).

| I praise you | Father, | Lord of heaven | and earth |
| That you hid | these things | from the wise | and learned |
| and revealed | them | to children. | |

In addressing hearers who are hungry, in debt, and deeply anxious about where the next meal is coming from, Jesus teaches them (in the supposedly sapiential speeches) to pray for the coming of the kingdom of God and to "seek first the kingdom of God" (11:2–4; 12:22–31). In one Q speech, as in some dialogues in Mark, Jesus sharply condemns the scribes and Pharisees, the successors of Ben Sira in cultivation of instructional wisdom, for their role in exploiting the people and charges them with collaboration in the repression of the prophets who cried out for justice (11:39–52). That Q speech, like the Gospel of Mark, represents the scribes and Pharisees as working in the service of the temple-state, in close collaboration with the high priestly rulers—that is, serving in the professional role for which Yeshua ben Sira represents training in instructional wisdom as their preparation, at the center of which was seeking wisdom.

### Relations with the Rulers

Among the speeches that occur largely verbatim in Matthew and Luke is the one focused on bold confession when brought before a court in Luke 12:2–9//Matt 10:26–33. The speech appears to have run through Luke 12:10 and 11–12 as well, although Matthew has the parallels at 12:32 and 10:19, respectively. The text of this speech, discussed in chap. 7 above, is arranged so that one can appreciate how it might sound in performance on pp 165–66, where readers can voice it aloud (again).

Although not usually discussed among the parallel speeches shared by Mark and Q, Mark has two short speeches that are somewhat parallel at

20. Mack, "Kingdom that Didn't Come." 613.
21. Kloppenborg, "Formation of Q Revisited," 208.

8:34–38 and 13:9–13 (26)—printed here in translation with indications of parallel motifs or lines in the Q speech.

## Mark 8:34–38

34 If any want to become my follower,

   Let them deny themselves and take up their cross and follow me.  (cf. Q 12:4–5)

35 For those who want to save their life will lose it,

   and those who lose their life for my sake, and for the sake of the gospel, will save it.

36 For what will it profit them to gain the whole world, and forfeit their life?

37 Indeed, what can they give in return for their life?          (cf. Q 12:4–5)

38 Those who are ashamed of me & of my words in this adulterous and sinful generation,

38 of them the son of man will also be ashamed when he comes in the glory of his Father

       with the holy angels.                          (cf. Q 12:8–9)


## Mark 13:9–13 (–26–27)

9   As for yourselves, beware;

    for they will hand you over to councils;                   (cf. Q 12:11)

    and you will be beaten in assemblies (*synagogai*);

    and you will stand before governors and kings because of me,

    as a testimony to them.

10  And the gospel must first be proclaimed to all peoples.      (cf. Q 12:2–3)

11  When they bring you to trial and hand you over,

    do not worry beforehand about what you are to say;

    but say whatever is given you at that time,

    for it is not you who speak, but the Holy Spirit.           (cf. Q 12:11–12)

12  Brother will betray brother to death,

    and father his child,

    and children will rise against parents and have them put to death;  (cf. Q 12:51–53)

    and you will be hated by all because of my name.

13  But the one who endures to the end will be saved.           (cf. Q 12:7,8–9)

    (26–27 the son of man comes, sends the angels, gathers his elect)   (cf. Q 12:8–9)

*Yeshua ben Marya's Speeches on Persistence under*
*Repression/Steadfastness in Trial*

Contrary to previous interpretations that assume that the sayings in these speeches were "originally" separate, stand in tension, and were only secondarily combined by literary editing and redaction,[22] these three speeches on steadfastness under trial are all coherent *texts*. Most striking in contrast with recent American Q interpreters' division between the "sapiential" sayings in Q/Luke 12:2–7 and the "apocalyptic" (judgment) sayings in Q/Luke 12:8–9 into separate strata is that the parallel speech in Mark 8:34–38 has the same combination of seemingly "sapiential" sayings followed by sanctioning judgmental sayings about heavenly judgment (involving the "son of man").

In addition to the rich repetition of sounds, verbal forms, words, and phrases, several connecting features in the Q/Luke 12:2–12 speech made it readily memorable and performable. The repetition in the concluding lines, 12:11–12, of the theme of speaking and the same verbs and verb forms as appear in the opening lines, 12:2–3, provide an inclusio that unifies the whole speech. We can discern a number of other connections and cohesion among the stanzas in the overall speech. The provision of what to say in 12:12 completes the admonition not to be anxious in 12:2, continues the reassurance in 12:7 that your hairs a numbered and in 12:8 that the confessor will be confessed, and comes back around to the theme of speaking with which the speech started in 12:2–3.

Particularly striking in this speech is that every stanza consists of a fairly simple direct binary contrast in which one side succeeds or overcomes the other. For example in 12:4–5, God is far more of a threat than a repressive ruler, and in 12:8–9 the divine judgment succeeds and overrules the human political situation. The lines in 12:4–5 (and 12:11) indicate the political context for the admonition to proclaim in 12:2–3. The admonition not to fear in 12:6–7 further emphasizes the danger, while assuring those exhorted to proclaim fearlessly of God's providential care. The parallel lines sanctioning judgment in 12:8–9 combine the themes of bold proclamation and confession in 12:2–3 and 4–5: confess and (whatever the repressive violence) be confessed at the divine judgment, deny (under threat of death) and be judged by divine court (the one who can destroy both body and soul). The lines in 12:11–12 come back around to the theme of "speak," but now narrowed to the situation of the speaker on trial from its original wider public proclamation at the beginning of the speech.

22. Sketched briefly in chap. 7.

The two parallel speeches in Mark have both been adapted to their respective contexts in the Markan narrative. Mark 8:34–38 addresses the disciples' misunderstanding of what is entailed in following Jesus' way. Mark 13:9–13 is part of the final speech in Mark about what to expect in the impending crisis and glorious fulfillment of the near future. The close parallels of themes, even lines, and sequence with the speech in Q/Luke 12:2–12, however, suggests that the continuing composition-in-performance of Mark's story was working with a standard speech on persistence under repression. After the link to the narrative context in 8:34, the lines on saving and losing one's life in 8:35–37 followed by the judgment scene in 8:38 stand strikingly parallel to the substance and sequence of Q/Luke 12:4–5 and 12:8–9. Similarly in 13:9–13, the statement of the trial setting in 13:9 and 11 parallel that in Q 12:11–12, and the theme of proclaiming the gospel in 13:10 parallels that in Q 12:2–3, while the sanctioning judgment headed by the son of man figure occurs later in the longer speech, at 13:26–27.

The *context* of these speeches in particular was that of periodic repression by the rulers, apparently because the Jesus movements were challenging or disrupting the social-political order. A number of other Q speeches, other passages in the synoptic Gospel tradition, along with references in the books of Acts, Revelation, and Paul's letters offer multiple indications that the movements of Jesus-believers and communities of Christ-believers came under suspicion and experienced acts of repression by the authorities. The message and practice of the kingdom meant disruption and conflict (Q 12:49–56). Q included prophetic speeches in which Jesus pronounced God's condemnation of the rulers and woes against their representatives (13:34–35; 11:39–52). Jesus was the climax of a long line of prophets who had been killed by the Jerusalem rulers and their representatives (11:39–52; 13:34–35). His envoys had been sent out as "sheep in the midst of wolves" (10:2–16). His followers saw themselves as implicated in the same sustained political conflict, which required commitment, discipline, and solidarity (6:23; 14:26–27). The dominant plot in Mark portrays Yeshua bar Marya sharply opposed to and opposed by the Jerusalem, Herodian, and Roman rulers.

The speeches in Q12:2–12, Mark 8:34–38 and 13:9–13, moreover, are all couched in a *register* of language dedicated to this context and concern. The very existence of these parallel speeches on the same issue enables us to discern the register of dedicated language on which they all drew. In the standard older focus on individual sayings no connection, in fact even tension, was seen between the proclamation (of the gospel, of the kingdom, Q 12:2–3; Mark 13:10) and trials before rulers (Q 12:11–12; Mark 13:9, 11).

But as noted just context above, the one led to the other. The proclamation and practice of the kingdom had evoked repression by the authorities.

Indeed in Judean/Israelite *tradition* long before the emergence of Jesus movements a register of speech addressed to situations of repression and persecution had developed. Such dedicated language can be found in Judean literature prior to and contemporary with Q and Mark. Persecution and martyrdom during the Maccabean struggle against Antiochus Epiphanes became a focus of continuing reflection on faithful adherence to Israelite covenant and people even under violent tyranny (2 Macc 7; 4 Maccabees, see esp 13:14–15). Admonition to faithful adherence to the people and/or the group and reassurance that the righteous would be defended and/or rewarded at the divine court of judgment before all the angels apparently became standard in some scribal circles (in *1 Enoch* 94–104; e.g., 97:5–6; 99:3; 100:4–5; 104:1; cf. esp Q 12:8–9).

Other texts from movements of Jesus-believers (e.g., 1 Thess 1:2–9; 5:1–11; Phil 1:27–29; 2;1–18; 1 Peter 4:12–19; Rev 3:3–6, 8–13) also attest this register of exhortation to commitment and solidarity under repression. In many of these texts the focus is specifically on the trial situation, as in Q 12:2–12 and Mark 13:9–11. Sometimes the possibility of martyrdom is used in an exhortation about how serious the commitment is in the face of a struggle that will be severe (Q 14:26–27). While most of the images in the speech of Q 12:2–12 also appear in the parallel discourse in Mark 8:34–38 (see esp. the theme of losing one's life and the sanctioning judgment in the heavenly court involving the son of man and the angels), the focus in Mark 8:34–38 is on the severity and risks of the struggle in following on the way of Jesus. The Q speech has a wider focus on general exhortation to bold proclamation of the kingdom with emphasis on reassurance of God's care and guidance if and when the faithful become subject to repressive action.

The speeches in Q 12:2–12 and Mark 8:34–38 and 13:9–12, finally, resonated with the hearers by metonymically referencing the cultural *tradition* in which they were rooted. The language register itself would have quickly become "traditional" in Jesus movements, and as noted above, it was even more deeply rooted in older Israelite tradition of persistence in the traditional way of life, even to the point of martyrdom. The referencing of Israelite tradition is far less pervasive and rich in Q 12:2–12 and Mark 8:34–38 and 13:9–13 than it is, for example, in the covenantal speeches in Q 6:20–49 and Mark 10. Nevertheless we can detect several key references to the broader Jesus tradition and/or to the broader Israelite tradition.

That nothing ". . . is hidden that will not be made known" is indeed vague and general in the extreme, if taken in the abstract, as it is by many Q interpreters. But such statements have no meaning in the abstract. Like any statements, this one depends on cultural tradition as well as on historical social context. In the context of the Jesus movements and the developing Jesus-tradition, the reference is not vague at all, especially when made more specific in the next lines, "what I tell you in the dark, speak in the light." In his teaching in general Jesus was understood to have been proclaiming the kingdom of God. And the kingdom was indeed something that could not be hidden or kept secret. It was a whole new stage in history, a dramatic reversal of the fortunes of the hearers, a qualitative leap in the quality of life for the recipients (e.g., Q 7:18–35; 6:20–26; 11:2–4; 11:14–26; 12:22–31). It is evident from other Q speeches (such as those just cited), moreover, that Yeshua bar Marya's proclamation and manifestation of the kingdom of God was understood as the fulfillment of long-standing Israelite expectations and longings.

The images of body and soul in Q 12:4–5 would be quite unintelligible in most Greek philosophical schools. But they would certainly resonate in a tradition basic to which was the sense that personal human life consisted not of the soul or spirit separate from the body, but was the embodied life. Moreover, basic to Israelite tradition was the distinction between a human ruler and the divine ruler. God was the ultimate and proper ruler of Israelites and both demanded just relations in social-economic-political relations and promised/threatened to enforce those demands by punishing or destroying unjust rulers. That invited people to challenge and oppose oppressive rule and rulers and to respond to divine initiatives, which might in turn be sanctioned by the sense of God as ultimate ruler and judge. Gehenna/Ge-hinnom, originally a valley outside of Jerusalem, had long since become an image of the fiery judgment to which the divine judge would confine the unrighteous for punishment. The son of man had long been deployed in scenes of divine judgment, as a symbol of the people whom God was delivering or restoring in the divine judgment.

## Conclusion

Much of the recent North American analysis of the sayings of Jesus in Q (the "source" of Jesus' teachings closely parallel in Matthew and Luke) by classification (e.g., as "sapiential) and on the basis of print-cultural assumptions has been flat and formalistic. This analysis focused flatly on the form of sayings and clusters or collections of sayings, without attending to their substance, the issues and social-political relations they address. Interpreters who wanted to ascertain the social location of the "authors" who "wrote" the collection of Jesus sayings they had already deemed as "sapiential," still projecting modern print-cultural assumptions into antiquity, posited "village scribes" as a sufficiently "educated" social stratum in contact with the agrarian ethos presupposed by Q materials. Again they did this without noticing the respective substance of the speeches of Yeshua bar Marya compared with sapiential instruction.

The several lines of recent research sketched in chap. 1 (and applied to various texts and issues in the subsequent chapters) make possible a more complex and probing analysis of the teaching of Yeshua bar Marya by comparison and contrast with the results of a parallel analysis of sapiential instruction such as the speeches of Yeshua ben Sira. The instructional speeches of Ben Sira collected in Sirach indicate that they were delivered orally as part of the training of fledgling scribes. We can learn from other fields how we might analyze such "oral-derived" texts as texts-in-performance, attending to the *context* of the instruction and the *register* of speech it draws upon that is rooted in the (scribal) cultural *tradition* that it references.

Ben Sira's instructional speeches focus on the fundamental concerns of learned scribes in their own role in service of the state and in their often delicate relations with their wealthy patrons in the ruling aristocracy. This confirms and is confirmed by the findings of recent research into scribal practice in the Judean temple-state and the imperial courts of the ancient Near East. Ben Sira's instructional speeches are centrally concerned with finding wisdom, which was essential for his and other scribes' role as advisers to the ruling aristocracy. In addition to speeches on distinctively scribal concerns such as eloquent speech and personal discipline, Sirach includes speeches that caution about staying on the good side of the rulers whom they served and on whom they were evidently dependent.

A corresponding analysis of the speeches of Yeshua bar Marya in Q suggests that there is nothing in these speeches or the rest of the Gospel tradition to lead us to suspect that those who continued to perform and shape these speeches had undergone training as scribes/sages, much less that Jesus himself was a sage. The Q speeches present Yeshua bar Marya speaking in the role of a prophet (and killed by the rulers as a prophet). The typical concerns of the sage, including the central concern of seeking wisdom, are nowhere to be found in the Q speeches. Indeed, in what is perhaps the most "sapiential"-sounding speech, Q 10:21–22, Yeshua bar Marya contrasts the ordinary people he addresses with "the wise and the learned," and in one speech pronounces a string of woes against the scribes and Pharisees for aiding in the exploitation of the people (11:39–52; dismissed as a secondary judgmental speech by many American Q- and Jesus- interpreters). With regard to relations with the rulers, the speeches of Yeshua bar Marya present a sharp contrast with those of Yeshua Ben Sira. In their role of service to the temple-state, learned scribes such as Ben Sira were anxious to "stay on the good side" of their patrons. Yeshua bar Marya's speeches, by contrast, address people who are already (likely to be) arrested and on trial by the rulers. Indeed the Q speech exhorting Jesus' followers to stand steadfast in resistance to their repression is paralleled by two similar speeches included in the Gospel story of Mark.

Comparative analysis of the speeches of Yeshua ben Sira and Yeshua bar Marya as orally-performed speeches thus leads to the recognition that, far from Jesus having been a sage in the tradition of earlier Judean learned scribes, he was understood and presented by his followers in the role of a prophet of a movement that was being persecuted by the very rules whom (most of) the learned scribes advised and represented.

# 9

# THE LANGUAGE(S) OF THE KINGDOM

## From Aramaic to Greek and Galilee to Syria

IN RECENT YEARS IS IT BECOMING CLEARER THAT JESUS AND his followers in Galilee almost certainly spoke Aramaic. Yet the principal texts of the Gospel tradition are in Greek, and were evidently composed-and-performed in Greek. So how can the Jesus movements that cultivated those Gospel materials so quickly have begun communicating in Greek? And how can scholars be so confident in focusing on Jesus' sayings, which were in Aramaic, when the only sources we have are in Greek? Gospel scholars have avoided asking such questions, probably because we did not have even minimal clues about how we might go about answering them.

Recent developments in research, however, may well have prepared the way for us to ask these and related questions. Additional ancient texts in Aramaic have become available, greatly expanding our knowledge of Aramaic. Socio-linguists have called attention to social-political influences on languages and their usage. The language situations in Syria and Galilee are becoming a bit clearer. And specialists have become more sophisticated in linguistic analysis. There is also an increasing recognition that the principal division in society of Roman Syria/Palestine was not between "Jews" and "Gentiles," but between rulers and ruled. That division included diversity of cultural levels compounded by regional diversity, which can be partially comprehended with the distinction commonly made among anthropologists between the "great tradition" cultivated by ruling and scribal circles and the "popular tradition" cultivated in village communities in Judea, Samaria, and Galilee. This means, among other things, that Galilean peasants almost certainly did not share the priestly and Pharisaic concerns about "Jewish" purity codes and separation from "Gentiles." More recently it has been "discovered" that communication, certainly among ordinary people, was oral; and it has been recognized that even if they had also taken written form, "texts" were generally recited orally before groups of people.

In this paper, I want to make some initial forays into the move that Jesus movements made from Aramaic into Greek as they moved from Galilee into areas of Syria. Given that the earliest Gospel texts are in Greek and not the language Jesus and his first followers spoke, can we learn anything from investigations into the possible relationship between the oral-derived Gospel texts in Greek to which we have access and their possible but ill-defined Aramaic linguistic and cultural substratum? The investigation will proceed in four steps: the historical political power-relations that determined the general language situation; the use of languages in Syria and Galilee; the largely oral communication environment in which texts were (repeatedly) composed in oral performance (perhaps including the limited use of written texts); and finally an exploratory probe for Aramaic influence in one of the speeches in Q (7:18–28/35).

## Politics

The fundamental divide in late second-temple Palestine was between the wealthy and powerful Herodian and priestly aristocracies, on the one hand, and the vast majority of people living in hundreds of villages around the country, on the other. As in any traditional agrarian society, the ruling elite maintained their power and privilege by expropriating resources from the peasantry in the form of taxes, tithes, and offerings. The Pharisees and other scribal groups, including the predecessors of the Qumranites before they withdrew to the wilderness, belonged on the elite side of this divide.[1] One need only read Ben Sira's comments about various roles in society (Sirach 38:24—39:11) to understand that the learned scribes' role was service in the temple-state. They may well have attempted to mitigate some of the worst exploitation of the peasants by their aristocratic patrons, but they were apparently economically dependent on the priestly aristocracy. Gospel materials, like Josephus' accounts, give much evidence of scribal collaboration with the ruling elite and popular resentment of scribal functions. The Judean and Galilean peasants and even the ordinary people in Jerusalem mounted repeated protests, movements of resistance, and even widespread revolts against their rulers in early Roman times. According to the ac-

---

1. Horsley, *Galilee*, 149–52; *Hearing the Whole Story*, 151–156.

counts in Josephus, most of those protests and movements and revolts were informed by and patterned after Israelite traditions and prophecies, such as stories of Moses and Joshua leading the exodus/entry into the land.

Compounding the differences between rulers and ruled, scribal circles and peasants, were the differences in historical experience between Galilee and Judea and the built-in historical structural conflict between the people of Galilee and Jerusalem rulers and their representatives.[2] The people of Galilee were presumably descendants of the most northerly tribes of Israel who were left on the land after the Assyrians deported the ruling class in Samaria. After having been independent of Jerusalem rule for many centuries, Galilee was taken over by the Hasmonean high priesthood a hundred years before Jesus was born. Galileans were then subjected to "the laws of the Judeans" and ruled by Jerusalem for a hundred years before being placed under the separate jurisdiction of Herod Antipas during the lifetime of Jesus and thereafter remaining independent of Jerusalem jurisdiction except for the brief reign of Agrippa I (41–44). Since these regional differences have not often been recognized, the implications have not been much explored.[3]

A similar division between rulers and ruled also dominated the various areas of Syria to the north. Phrases in the Gospel of Mark are indicative of this fundamental political-economic structure: "the region of (ruled by) Tyre/the Decapolis," or "the villages of (subject to) Caesarea Philippi" (Mark 7:31; 8:27). As in Galilee, there had been periodic historical changes at the top, one set of rulers replacing another (e.g., Seleucids by Romans), while the basic structure remained the same (imperial and client rulers extracting revenues from peasantry).

What had the greatest impact on the languages used in all areas was the succession of imperial rulers. The Persians had used Aramaic as the administrative language and *lingua franca* of the western areas of their empire. Alexander and his Ptolemaic and Seleucid successors imposed Greek as the language of administration in the cities that controlled the various districts of their empires. When the Romans conquered the eastern Mediterranean areas they retained Greek as the official administrative language. The Roman imposition of client rulers such as the Herodians in Palestine, besides adding additional layers of economic demands on the peasant producers (tribute and/or taxes on top of tithes and offerings), had obvious implications for intensifying the use and influence of Greek among subject peoples.

---

2. See further Horsley, *Galilee,* chaps. 1–3, 6.

3. See, e.g., Freyne, "Behind the Names;" Horsley, *Galilee.*

## Languages

*Expanding the Approach to Languages in New Testament Studies*

Biblical scholars focused on second-temple Judean languages and literatures and on Gospel literature have previously proceeded on a rather flat plane of language represented in writing, such as scrolls and inscriptions, as if that gave us the whole picture. Many New Testament interpreters have been working on the general assumption that all key issues can be reduced to a conflict between an essentialist "Judaism" articulated in Biblical Hebrew and an essentialist "Hellenism" carried in Greek. This is complicated only by the half-hearted recognition that "the Jews" in Palestine probably spoke Aramaic. Many scholars have also tended to assume that any extant example of writing provides evidence for the common usage of a language. Burial inscriptions or graffiti, for example, were taken as evidence of what language was used not only in the site where they were found (e.g., Beth Shearim in late antiquity) but in the whole area and over an extended period of time. Archaeologists who unearthed inscriptions in Galilee suggested that, simply on the surface of things, they indicated the language spoken by the people.[4] That is, if the majority of inscriptions found along the shore of the Sea of Galilee were in Greek, therefore the language spoken in lower Galilee was predominantly Greek.

The relationship between evidence such as inscriptions, language usage, and society is far more complex, however, than much previous scholarship has discerned. Inscriptions are not reliable indicators of general language usage. Far more importantly, language usage is closely linked with culture and cultural tradition. And language and cultural differences often correspond to the political-economic divisions. Just because Greek may have been used by the literate elite in Herodian administrations in Jerusalem or Sepphoris and Tiberias does not mean that it was spoken in the hundreds of village communities of Judea and Galilee. Furthermore, in an imperial situation in which the conquerors' language has encroached on and become prominent among subject peoples, the latter can sometimes use "the master's tools" in opposition to the dominant culture and politics. No doubt some accommodation to the dominant culture was entailed when villagers began speaking Greek (in addition to Aramaic), but they could

---

4. See the critical survey of studies on language in Judea and Galilee in Horsley, *Archaeology, History,* chap. 7, disagreeing with assumptions, procedures, and conclusions, e.g., in Meyers and Strange, *Archaeology,* 62–91.

now articulate their interests and discontents in the same language spoken by those who dominated them.

## Languages in Syria

Linguists and classical historians who have learned from social and historical linguistics are far ahead of us biblical scholars in dealing with such issues of language, culture, and power-relations. So it makes sense to start with recent studies of bi-(or multi-)lingualism and diglossia in the broader area of Syria, of which Galilee and Judea were the southwestern-most corner, and then come back to Galilee with a more complicated set of interrelated factors in mind.[5]

When we find linguistic diversity (e.g., a mixed-language text) we are likely to find ethnic and class diversity. Thus the languages and their relationship cannot be assessed purely in linguistic terms. "Non-linguistic issues, such as political, social, cultural, and religious factors, must not be forgotten."[6] To take political and social differences into account linguists now distinguish between the H(igh) and L(ow) codes coexisting in various societies, where H is supposedly used for formal functions and the L for informal. But in some areas of antiquity, such as East Syria (Edessa, Palmyra) that dichotomy is too simple; both Greek and Aramaic function as High, and Aramaic and other languages as Low.[7]

In north Syria generally, judging mainly from inscriptional evidence, Greek was the High language and Aramaic the Low. Greek in the Near East was to a large extent the language of the conquests by Alexander the Great. Economic, military, and political power was in the hands of Greek speakers settled in cities founded to control the conquered territories.[8] Greek replaced Aramaic in the political sphere. Josephus was well aware of the Greeks' reliance on "gunboat linguistics" to shore up their belief in the imaginary racial unity of their new territories: "They appropriated even the glories of the past, and prettified the nations with names they [i.e., the Greeks] could understand and imposed on them forms of government as though they were their own descendants" (*Ant.* 1.121). Quite apart from soldiers, veterans, and government officials, it seems clear that significant numbers of people in northern Syria, even outside the cities, had productive control of Greek,

---

5. The following depends heavily on Adams and Swain, "Introduction"; and Taylor, "Bilingualism and Diglossa."

6. Adams and Swain, "Inroduction, 3; Taylor, "Bilingualism and Diglossa," 299–300.

7. Taylor, "Bilingualism and Diglossa."

8. Adams and Swain, "Introduction," 12; Taylor, "Bilingualism and Diglossa."

although their accent and standards of literacy may have appalled scholars of the Athenian academics (as it has more recent scholars).[9]

The ubiquity of Greek inscriptions in North Syria, however, is mainly a consequence of local diglossia that accorded Greek the status of an H variety and should not be interpreted as a reflection of the totality of the regional language system. The dominant use of Greek in inscriptions is not proof that it was widely understood. The suspicion that it was not is encouraged by an analysis of the inscriptional materials further south in the Hauran. There also all the inscriptions from this period are preserved in Greek and Latin and on the surface the region seems thoroughly Hellenized. Yet as one inscription (*IGR* iii, 1191) indicates, it was necessary for a translator to travel with the procurator so that he could communicate with the people.[10] Also, we are becoming more aware from critical analysis of the function of official inscribed monuments and statues that ordinary people themselves would have understood as instruments of domination (regardless of whether they could have read the inscriptions and understood themcognitively!). Such propaganda devices may have had the effect of intimidating the indigenous people and alienating them from the rulers' language.

With their political and cultural dominance the Greeks suppressed indigenous cultural memory—and identity—and substituted their own culture in their own language, although in degrees that surely varied by location. The dominance of Greek over the local Aramaics of north-west Syria and the Lebanon makes it reasonable to assume a sort of cultural amnesia in these zones.[11] The cultural power of Greek and its public-political guarantee by Rome made it the sole high language in use. But many elite users of Greek apparently continued to speak and to produce literature in a local language, particularly in Palestine and Egypt.[12] And in Syria in general, various dialects of Aramaic were spoken, including somewhat different dialects in Galilee, Samaria, and Judea. A well known Talmud passage (*bT Erubin* 53b ) indicates the rivalry of dialects and potential for confusion, mocking the Galilean pronunciation of guttural and vowel sounds: "Now, as for that Galilean who said: 'Who has '*amar*? Who has '*amar*?' They said to him: "You stupid Galilean! (do you mean) an ass [*hamar*] to ride on? Or wine [*hamar*] to drink? Wool ['*amar*] for clothing? Or a sheepskin ['*imar*] for a covering?"[13] The general language situation among villages and towns

---

9. Taylor, "Bilinguialism and Diglossa," 314.

10. Alexander, " ," 307; Jones, *Geek City*, 290.

11. Millar, *Roman Near East*.

12. Adams and Swain, "Introduction," 13.

13. Taylor, "Bilingualism and Diglossa," 303.

in Syria thus appears to have been mixed, with Greek having been spoken in many villages, various dialects of Aramaic (or Syriac) in others, and both (versions of koine) Greek and Aramaic (dialects) in others, with some of the people being effectively bilingual.

For our purposes here, however, a significant variation on the general pattern is that by late antiquity Greek seems to have been particularly associated with Christianity and Aramaic with pagan religious practices.[14] The Christian movement "spread through northern Syria at rates that differed from massif to massif and from village to village"[15] and *prima facie* it does not seem unreasonable to suppose that language skills and usage will have similarly varied from one small community to the next.[16] Greek is clearly the language of the earliest Christian liturgies in the region, for there are numerous inscriptions above the doorways of private houses as well as churches, which contain citations from these liturgies. Greek inscriptions were often placed above doorways in Syria to proclaim the conversion of the household to Christianity, and there are many more which seem to have had an apotropaic function.[17] This suggests that in the early period of Christian expansion Greek was explicitly identified as the language of Christian faith and worship.[18]

The continuing vitality of indigenous culture, in Aramaic and then in Greek, is behind its spectacular metamorphosis in the Christian period. One of the main impacts of Christianity was to weaken the link between Greek language and Greek culture. Many Christian authors writing in Greek trumpet their new-found freedom in this regard.[19] We can think of a Matthew or a Paul as early examples. As recent research has indicated, Paul surely knew and used standard Greek rhetorical forms, although probably not from any formal schooling and in ways opposed to the dominant use of rhetoric.[20] But Paul reveals precious little by way of Greek cultural content beyond his rhetorical modes and some of his discourse that can also be noted among some philosophers, but had apparently become commonplace by the first century CE. It is difficult to find much Greek cultural content at

---

14. Adams and Swain, "Introduction," 9.

15. Trombley, *Hellenic Religion*, 247–315, esp. 311.

16. Taylor, "Bilingualism and Diglossa," 306.

17. Trombley, *Hellenic Religion*, chap. 10.

18. Taylor, "Bilingualism and Diglossa," 315.

19. Adams & Swain, "Introduction," 14.

20. See my attempt to place Paul's use of rhetorical forms in the broader context of the Roman empire, in Horsley, "Rhetoric and Empire," 72–102.

all in Matthew's Gospel. In Paul and especially in Matthew Judean/Israelite cultural memory and thought forms are dominant.

## Languages in Judea and Galilee

Earlier attempts to construct an Aramaic stratum behind Gospel materials in Greek proved unconvincing for some obvious reasons. Knowledge of Aramaic was limited. Christian New Testament scholars were trained more fully in Greek than in Semitic languages and had a distinct cultural bias toward the supposed universalism of Hellenistic culture into which "early Christianity" moved from the supposedly more parochial and particularistic Palestinian "Jewish" culture from which it originated. Archaeologists, who tend to focus on urban areas in which they can find monumental structures that satisfy funding sources, along with liberal Jesus-scholars, went through a phase in the late twentieth century where they projected an almost cosmopolitan culture in Galilee.[21] They simply assumed that the cities built by Herod Antipas meant Hellenistic culture, and they argued from the evidence for use of Greek throughout Palestine, including Greek inscriptions in Galilee, as evidence that Greek was widely spoken in Galilee, conceivably even by Jesus and his followers.[22]

The language situation in Galilee, as well as Judea, however, has been clarified by more critical assessment of available evidence.[23] It is unwarranted, for example, to base conclusions about language in first-century Galilee in general from predominantly Greek burial inscriptions at Beth Shearim. These inscriptions are late and in a site with heavy Hellenistic cultural influence, beginning at least when it was an administrative town in the royal lands of the Great Plain (not in Galilee itself). Nor can we generalize from the combination of Greek and Aramaic and Hebrew used in documents from Murabba'at and Nahal Hever in the Judean wilderness or from the similar combination in the correspondence of Bar Kokhba in the revolt of 132–35. Both are socially more "upscale" than most Galilean villagers. It seems likely that some villagers in Lower Galilee around the cities, where

21. For example, Meyers, "Cultural Setting of Galilee," 687–98; Crossan, *Historical Jesus*, 18–19.

22. For a recent argument for the Greek as more commonly used among the people, such that Jesus could converse in Greek, see Porter, "Jesus and the Use of Greek."

23. The earlier survey by Fitzmyer, "Languages of Palestine," was in many ways more critical than some subsequent treatments of evidence. See also the discussion of languages in Chancey, *Myth of Gentile Galilee*; *Greco-Roman Culture*. The following paragraph draws on the critical analysis of studies of languages in Palestine in Horsley, *Galilee*, 247–50; see references there.

the administrative language was Greek, knew a little pidgin Greek. But in Upper Galilee very few inscriptions were found in Greek, and in Lower Galilee Aramaic was most frequently represented in inscriptions. Surprising is the appearance of evidence for Hebrew, which apparently was never completely supplanted by Aramaic. But Aramaic appears to have been the dominant spoken language. That the rabbis found they had to allow "any language" in the recitation of common oaths, prayers, and benedictions suggest that Aramaic must have been the only language of many (*m. Sota* 7:1; cf. *t. Git.* 7(9).11). Embedded in rabbinic literature in Hebrew, moreover, are traditional Aramaic proverbs introduced by phrases such as "this is what the people used to say" (e.g., *b. Ta'an.* 23a; *b. B. Qam.* 92b; *Gen. Rab.* 86:7).[24]

Maurice Casey's recent surveys of languages in Judea and Galilee confirm the picture critically constructed by Fitzmyer in 1970.[25] Latin was the language of imperial power, e.g., used for formal inscriptions by the Roman governors such as Pontius Pilate in Caesarea, the Roman capital of the province of Judea. Greek was still the language of the dominant imperial culture, a carry-over from Hellenistic imperial control of Palestine in the previous three centuries. This is evident from official inscriptions, inscriptions on jars of goods produced for Herod the Great, and the use of Greek in international trade, largely in luxury goods for the elite. The many tomb inscriptions must be critically assessed for their social (political-economic) location. That Josephus wrote his *Jewish War* originally in Aramaic and needed a good deal of help to put it into intelligible Greek is a good indication that even the political-economic and cultural elite of Jerusalem was by no means comfortable and fluent in Greek—although they surely could carry on adequate diplomatic negotiations in high places, such as the imperial court in Rome and the Roman governors' audiences in Caesarea and Jerusalem.

Hebrew continued as the language of the Israelite/Judean cultural heritage in the temple and in scribal circles. Scrolls that might be called "scriptural" were written in Hebrew, and scribes had learned and could recite texts in Hebrew, even write as well as compose texts in archaizing Hebrew, as in the last chapters (8–12) of the book of Daniel and many of the DSS composed by and for the Qumran community itself. Hebrew underwent a revival in proto-rabbinic circles. The Mishnah, an extensive compilation of learned rulings and teachings, is entirely in Hebrew, indicating that its cultivation in nascent rabbinic circles was also in Hebrew.

24. See further Horsley, *Galilee*, 249 and 344n26.
25. Casey, *Aramaic Sources of Mark*; Casey, *Aramaic Approach to Q*.

Aramaic, however, was the spoken language at every level of Judean society and among the people of Galilee as well. Ordinary people apparently could not understand Hebrew, so as early as the time of Ezra, at formal performances of Judean texts of torah in Hebrew, they were "interpreted" (translated) in Aramaic (Nehemiah 8). The DSS included some scrolls written in Aramaic, such as Targumic texts and instructions for observance of Yom Kippur.

Casey also derives evidence from what is called "interference" by one language into the spoken and written use of another to argue that speakers of Aramaic at the time of Jesus were not bilingual in Greek. On the other hand, Greek was certainly in use in the Herodian administrations in Jerusalem and Sepphoris and Tiberius, in the Greek-speaking cities such as Caesarea and Scythopolis (Beth Shean), and in inscriptions here and there. If we put credence in the legend that Joseph and Jesus were "builders" it seems likely that they would have used a sort of pidgin Greek for communication in Sepphoris, in the rebuilding of which they may have found work. Similarly, insofar as fishing was done by teams of four or five men operating boats leased by a fishing enterprise controlled by Herod Antipas, then Jesus' followers such as Cephas, Andrew, Jacobus, and John may also have known some simple Greek to communicate with the brokers and officers of Antipas regime. But it seems fairly certain now that (a dialect of) Aramaic, and not Greek, was the language of communication in Galilean and Judean village communities, the language spoken by Jesus and his first followers, hence the language in which Jesus' teachings and Jesus stories were first formulated and remembered and resonated with communities of people. And, with the study of Aramaic documents among the DSS and other developments, there may now be a "critical mass" of knowledge of Aramaic to warrant careful probing of the Greek text of Gospel materials for evidence of an Aramaic substratum.[26]

## Oral Communication and Writing

As a product of the print culture of the modern western world, biblical studies has understandably projected the assumptions of print culture onto the ancient world in which the "Scriptures" it interprets originated. It has been assumed that the ancient "Jews," as "the people of the book" were literate, regularly "read" the books of the Hebrew Bible that were supposedly readily available, and that the "writers/authors" of the "early Christian" communities

26. Fitzmyer, "Languages of Palestine"; Casey, *Aramaic Sources of Mark*; Casey, *Aramaic Approach to Q.*

also "wrote" books (composed them in writing). Recent research, however, has demonstrated that virtually none of the aspects of that standard picture are warranted.[27]

### Oral Communication and Limited Literacy

Research in the last several decades is demonstrating again and again that literacy was very limited in the ancient Roman world, including in Judea and Galilee. Even in the cities of the Roman empire only about fifteen percent of the people were literate, mainly the elite and those who served them in various ways.[28] In the face of the continuing presumption that somehow ancient Judeans were an exception to this picture, the extensive recent survey by Catherine Hezser documents beyond the possibility of continuing denial that in late second-temple and early rabbinic times literacy was limited mainly to scribal circles, and limited in use to documents used by the wealthy and powerful.[29] The Babatha letters, for example, represent only a pretentious upper layer of society, and not typical practice for society in general. Writing material was as scarce as literacy. Scrolls such as those found at Qumran were not only expensive, but cumbersome, both to handle and to read. Consequently scrolls of texts would have been kept mainly in the temple and perhaps among scribal circles such as the Qumran community. Given the limited literacy, it is clear that an oral communication environment prevailed in Judean and Galilean society. Furthermore, it is not clear that ancient "biblical" Hebrew, the language in which the books later included in the Hebrew Bible were written, was still spoken or understood by anyone outside of scribal circles.

The problems this poses for our study of late second-temple Judean and Galilean society, diaspora Jewish communities, and the texts that they used and/or produced can be illustrated most dramatically by focusing on what we have assumed were its "scriptures." How would scripture, i.e., written scrolls of the principal versions of the books of Moses and the books of the Prophets such as Isaiah, have functioned in a predominantly oral communications environment? We have hardly begun to explore this whole new reality that has been hiding from biblical scholarship working on the assumptions of print-culture. Close study of the scrolls of the Pentateuchal

27. The recognition of the oral communication environment in antiquity and of the complex relationship between orality and literacy with regard to ancient Jewish and Christian texts was innovatively pioneered by Werner Kelber. See esp. Kelber, *The Oral and the Written Gospel*.

28. Harris, *Ancient Literacy*.

29. Hezser, *Jewish Literacy*.

and Prophetic books found among the DSS and studies of the close relation of orality and literacy are beginning to clarify some key aspects of the
situation.

### The Instability of Multiple Versions of the Nascent Hebrew Scriptures

The discovery of scores of scrolls of the books of scripture among the DSS
made possible a quantum leap in our knowledge of the history of the development of those books (including Isaiah, which is supposedly quoted
frequently in New Testament texts such as Q/Luke 7:18–35). Eugene Ulrich
draws two closely related conclusions. (1) "Evidence from Qumran demonstrates that there were multiple editions of the biblical books in antiquity—one form of which survives in each of the books of the MT collection
[Masoretic Text], while other forms may or may not have had the good for-
tune to survive in the SP [Samaritan Pentateuch], the LXX [Septuagint], at
Qumran, or elsewhere."[30] (2) The different versions of books were unstable
and still developing. "Sometimes the scribes intentionally inserted new material... they were actively handing on the tradition, but they were adding to
it, enriching it, making it relevant..."[31] As for the text of the book of Isaiah
(which is supposedly "quoted" in Q/Luke 7:18–23), Ulrich says that while
there is no evidence of different versions of the book, its text was unstable,
still undergoing development in late second-temple times.[32]

This new evidence for the unstable state of the "scriptural" books has
significant implications for how we understand the social and cultural context of Jesus, early Jesus movements, and their cultivation of both Israelite
tradition and Jesus traditions. Not only was there no "normative Judaism,"
there was also no acceptance of a single text of scripture as binding or authoritative in Judean tradition. Insofar as literacy was limited to scribes
and scrolls were cumbersome and expensive, scriptural scrolls were basically confined to the temple and scribal circles such as Qumran. Yet even in
scribal circles, the scriptural texts were multiform and still developing. Judean peasants would presumably have known of the existence of the books
of Torah and Prophets, perhaps even revered them as numenous sacred
writings laid up in the temple. Insofar as they spoke Aramaic and could
not read at all, much less read the archaic Hebrew in which the scriptural

---

30. Ulrich, *Dead Sea Scrolls*, 11, 9–11, 14, 59.

31. Ibid., 11–12, 23–24, 75, 77.

32. Ibid., 8, 61–62. If Q-interpreters were to continue to imagine that of the several
items listed in Q 7:22, two are quotes of Isa 61:1, for example, which version(s) of Isaiah
was Q following: a version like the MT or one like the LXX or one like 1QIsa[a] or one
like 1QIsa[m] or one like 4QIsa[b]?

books were written, they would not have been well-acquainted with any of the different versions of the books of the Pentateuch and prophetic books (i.e., as opposed to their own popular version of covenantal teaching and prophetic oracles).

Even less would Galilean peasants have been acquainted with the text of nascent scriptural books that were written in Hebrew, given the historical regional differences between Galilee and Judea. We have virtually no evidence that any of the various versions of proto-scriptural books or other texts that were produced in Jerusalem would have been known in the villages of Galilee. Presumably some of the contents of these Jerusalemite traditions and books would have been among "the laws of the Judeans" that the Hasmonean regime that took control of Galilee in 104 BCE required the inhabitants to observe if they wanted to remain on their lands (Josephus, *Ant.* 13.318–19; cf. 13.257–58).[33] But there is no unambiguous evidence of activity in Galilee by Pharisees or other scribal figures as the representatives of the Hasmonean high priestly regime engaged in "re-socializing" Galileans according to the "the laws of the Judeans." The Gospels are the only sources for the Pharisees and scribes which place them in Galilee prior to the Pharisaic companions of Josephus in 66 CE. There is also no good evidence of Judeans, other than Herodian officers and troops, moving north into Galilee. So we can only speculate about how Galileans such as Jesus and his followers who cultivated the Jesus traditions might have become acquainted with Judean texts and traditions.[34] Yet just because they had no direct contact with the scriptures in Hebrew and could not have read them if they had does not mean that Judean peasants or Galileans such as Jesus and his followers did not know Israelite tradition, as we shall see below.

### Oral Performance of Texts and Cultivation of Tradition

In the predominantly oral communication environment of antiquity, even when a text existed in written form, it was usually recited ("performed") orally in a group context.[35] This is easily understandable with regard to a village assembly (*synagoge*) or an assembly (*ekklesia*) of a Jesus movement in which the people were largely non-literate. What may be surprising is that scribal groups such as rabbinic circles also apparently cultivated (learned

33. Horsley, *Galilee*, 39–52.

34. Horsley, *Galilee*; Horsely, *Archaeology, History*.

35. Understanding of "oral-derived texts" and of oral performance has been significantly advanced by the work of John Miles Foley. See esp. Foley, *Singer of Tales*; Foley, *How to Hear an Oral Poem*.

and recited) their texts orally. Martin Jaffee has generalized from the oral recitation of Torah in rabbinic circles and synagogues to the relation of written texts and oral performance generally. Fully aware of how cumbersome and costly scrolls were in antiquity, as emphasized by studies of ancient literacy, he points out that "a scroll was virtually useless as a handy source of information." But that was no obstacle since the text that was inscribed on the scroll "was as much a fact of their [a scribal group's] memory as it was a physical object . . . 'reading' was the activity of declaiming a text before an audience in a social performance approaching the gravity of ceremonial ritual."[36] The text was accessed through memory, not by consulting a written copy.[37] A telling illustration of his point is the procedure for a meeting of ten "recorded" in the Community Rule handbook from Qumran:

> And the Congregation shall watch in community for a third of every night of the year, to recite the book (*sefer*) and to search the ruling (*mišpat*) and to bless in common. (1QS 6:6–8, my translation)[38]

Assuming that the *sepher* refers to a text of torah (the book of Deuteronomy?) and the *mišpat* to the community's own ordinances, the Qumranites were regularly engaging in ritual oral recitation of both scripture and their own legal rulings that were also inscribed on scrolls possessed by the community (as in 1QS itself). Thus it was standard practice even in literate scribal circles that possessed written scrolls for texts to be recited orally from memory.

That even scribal groups knew and recited their texts orally from memory should make it all the more credible that the Judean and Galilean peasantry cultivated their versions of Israelite tradition orally, in the comings and goings, the households and the community assemblies (*synagogai*) of village life. As in other agrarian societies studied by anthropologists and historians, Galilean and Judean villagers lived out of their own "little tradition" that was parallel to the "great tradition" of the scribal circles but distinctively relevant to their own life situation and political-economic-religious interests.[39] Given the political-economic division in which the rulers expropriated the produce of the peasantry and drew them into

---

36. Jaffee, *Torah in the Mouth*, 16.

37. Ibid., 53.

38. The standard translations of "*read* the Book" and "*study* the Law" are potentially misleading, insofar as those terms have distinctive connotations in modern typographic culture, particularly in academic circles.

39. Scott, "Protest and Profanation"; Horsley, *Galilee*, 148–156; Horsley, *Archaeology, History,* 171–75; Horsley, "Unearthing a People's History"; and esp. Horsley with Draper, *Whoever Hears You Hears Me*, 95–204.

hunger and debt and denied their dignity, popular Israelite tradition was cultivated in opposition to the "great tradition" that legitimated Jerusalem rule (as well as in opposition to the dominant Hellenistic culture of Roman imperial rule). Galilean and Judean peasants thus cultivated their version of Israelite tradition in their village communities as a "hidden transcript," beyond the surveillance of the rulers and their representatives, in opposition to the "official transcript" of the Jerusalem temple and scribal circles (or the Herodian court in Sepphoris or Tiberias).[40] The Israelite popular tradition (or "hidden transcript") in Galilee or Judea would have been cultivated orally in Aramaic. Even in the accounts of Josephus addressed to Hellenistic Greek readers it is clear that the popular movements led by prophets such as Theudas or by popularly acclaimed "kings" such as Judas son of Hezekiah or Simon bar Giora were informed by the memories of the deliverance led by Moses and Joshua and the resistance to the Philistines led by the young David, respectively.[41] And it is the Galilean Israelite popular tradition that informs the earliest Jesus movements as they represent Jesus as a prophet like Moses and/or Elijah.[42]

## Discerning an Aramaic Substratum
## in Q/Luke 7:18–35

On the basis of the socio-linguistic situation and the indication of oral cultivation of Israelite popular tradition sketched above, I would like to probe a particular text in Greek, Q/Luke 7:18–35, for evidence of an Aramaic substratum. Casey has made a strong case for there now being a "critical mass" of evidence for Aramaic in first-century CE Judea and Galilee that can provide a "backdrop" against which we can project hypothetical Aramaic terms and phrases that might lie behind passages in Mark and Q. His approach is basically what used to be called "literary critical," working with a rich knowledge of words and phrases that were likely current in the first century CE in both Greek and Aramaic. I am suggesting that his approach can be undergirded and given a firmer social and cultural foundation from recent recognition of the socio-linguistic situation in Galilee and Syria, the lack of stability in texts of Israelite tradition, and the oral-literary forms in which

---

40. Scott, *Domination and Resistance*; Horsley, "Jesus, Paul—and the Arts of Resistance."

41. Horsley, "Popular Messianic Movements"; Horsley, "Popular Prophets."

42. Horsley with Draper, *Whoever Hears You Hears Me*; Horsley, *Hearing the Whole Story*.

developing Jesus materials, like Israelite cultural traditions, were regularly recited in popular communities.

## Q as an Oral-Derived Text

From the outset of its being identified as the speech material not in Mark but paralleled in Matthew and Luke Q has been understood in New Testament studies as a written document—according to the assumptions of print culture standard in the field.[43] Those assumptions undergird the International Q Project's reconstruction of the "(original) text" of the document behind the parallel speeches in Matthew and Luke, now published with elaborate justification in multivolume detail.[44] Because Gospel scholarship tended to focus on individual sayings of Jesus, Q was also assumed to be a collection of sayings ("The Sayings Source"). Only recently have American scholars in particular recognized that Q was a series of "clusters" or short speeches of Jesus.[45] On the model of modern literature as written by authors that governs biblical studies, Q is still assumed to have been written by one or more writers. In fact Q, almost by definition in the field, is assumed to have been probably the earliest step in which "sayings" that had previously been transmitted by oral tradition were given written, hence stabilized, form in a writing that modern scholars can "control" in their analysis based on modern print culture (and the texts that text critics "establish" according to its assumptions and procedures).

Recent analysis of the "social location" of Q, however, discerns material addressed to an agrarian village situation in Galilee. That poses the question of how material that originated in Galilean villages and is addressed to agrarian circumstances came to be written when literacy was lacking in such a context. Facing the interrelated issues of the predominance of oral communication and popular orientation squarely, John Kloppenborg hypothesizes on the basis of the inscriptions in the Hauran that "lower level administrators" and "village scribes" existed in the towns of Galilee. He argues that such low-level scribes had sufficient education to make them capable of composition in writing in the genre of instruction, on which he sees Q having been modeled.[46]

43. See especially the critique of the print-cultural assumptions and procedures in study of Gospel materials in Kelber, "Jesus in Tradition."

44. Robinson et al., *Critical Edition of Q*.

45. Kloppenborg, *Formation of Q*; Robinson, "Introduction"; Horsley with Draper, *Whoever Hears You Hears Me*.

46. Kloppenborg, "Literary Convention," 85–86; similarly Arnal, *Jesus and the Village Scribes*, 151–52.

The literary and inscriptional evidence adduced, however, does not support this hypothesis. The Greek terms used for village leaders in the Hauran inscriptions may parallel those of Greek city officials, but their duties parallel those of village assemblies in rabbinic and other Jewish literature.[47] As noted above, that the imperial finance officer had to use an interpreter suggests that such village leaders were not scribes with a degree of education in Greek in a "sophisticated rural administrative system."[48] In her thorough search through the evidence, Hezser finds a general lack of scribes in towns and villages, and concludes that they were rare in rural areas until the third century.[49] Evidence for *komogrammateis* in Egyptian papyri, ironically, suggests that they were virtually illiterate, able to inscribe only their own name on records—by copying a model. These "village scribes" were local government appointees responsible for keeping records of tax-collection, with little or no education that would have enabled them to compose more than a simple formulaic letter to a district superior.[50] It is hardly by accident that the only occurrence of the term *komogrammateis* in Judean literature comes in a caustic threat by two of Herod's younger sons that makes a sarcastic reference to the Hellenistic-Roman education (*War* 1.479; *Ant.* 16.203).

The implication of the research summarized above, however, is that we can no longer think of Q in terms of authorial written composition in modern typographic culture. Whether or not texts such as the series of speeches in Q or Mark's story of Jesus existed in writing, they were almost certainly performed orally from memory in communities of Jesus movements, just as "the book" and "the ruling" were recited from memory in the Qumran community. If we were to imagine Q's speeches as "instructional," as Kloppenborg suggests (albeit at a popular level, in contrast to all known instructional texts from the ancient Near East and Ben Sira), then it is worth noting that in his own self-representation, Ben Sira's instruction is all oral–aural, spoken and heard. If we compare the material in the book of Sirach with that in the book of Proverbs, it is evident that Ben Sira belongs in a long tradition of continuing development of instruction by repeated performance. If the concept of "composition" is apt, then it was composition in repeated performance.

47. Horsley, *Galilee*, 227–233.

48. Kloppenborg, "Literary Convention," 85–86; Macadam, "Epigraphy and Village Life," 106–8.

49. Hezser, *Jewish Literacy*, 118–26; for the Roman empire generally, see Wolff, "Literacy," 877.

50. Youtie, *"Agrammatos"*; Horsley with Draper, *Whoever Hears You Hears Me*, 126, and references there.

There is no reason other than the habits of modern biblical studies to imagine that "in the beginning were individual sayings" that later were combined (in writing) by the "author" of Q. Communication does not happen in isolated sayings, but in larger messages. Judging from the parallels to some of the Q speeches, such as the mission discourse and Beelzebul discourse, it is far more likely that such short speeches constituted such units of communication. And, as illustrated by the variant versions in Matthew and Luke, those speeches were continually adapted and developed in regular performance. In the bilingual situation that apparently existed in many Syrian villages where a Jesus movement may have spread there is then no reason to imagine that "composition" happened for the first time in Greek. Rather, it seems appropriate to the situation sketched above to hypothesize that communication in speeches that were further developed in performance was happening in Aramaic in Galilee before continuing in Greek in Syrian villages.

### Aramaic Features Discernible in the Greek text of Q 7:18–35

As an illustrative example I focus attention on Q/Luke 7:18–35 because it not only references Israelite tradition but even appears to recite it. In fact, interpreters have usually assumed that at two points it actually quotes from the Hebrew Bible. This passage therefore, on the alternative reconstruction of the cultural situation above, not only offers a likely possibility of a recitation of Israelite tradition in Aramaic behind the Greek text as we have it, but also a potential illustration of how recitation in Aramaic from Israelite popular tradition is a better explanation than quotation of a written Hebrew text. To start with, the passage should be heard as if in oral performance in order to appreciate the repetition of sounds in the parallel lines of the poetic text on pp 25–26.

NB: See the transliteration of the speech in Q/Luke 7:18–28 toward the end of chap. 1, printed in blocked verse illustrative of oral recitation.

The pattern of parallel lines consisting of three or four principal terms strongly resembles those found in Hebrew and Aramaic poetry and prophecies. Hebrew and Aramaic poetic lines are built up in parallel statements with much repetition of sounds and words.[51] Needless to say, in the following lines (printed just below), where presumably behind the repeated Greek words were repeated Aramaic words, we can hear the repetition of words

---

51. I stay with the standard term "lines" that is presumably rooted in assumptions of typographic culture, but now as a metaphoric indicator for the parallel statements of oral performance.

and sounds in the sets of parallel lines (of course since Aramaic has no case endings the repetition of sounds would not necessarily have included the ending of words). Moreover, as often in the rhetoric of Hebrew and Aramaic poetry, the first lines set up the subsequent lines. Here two parallel questions in the first four lines set up the sharp contrast of the last two. In the latter, moreover, the last line escalates the thought over the penultimate line.

| | | | |
|---|---|---|---|
| *Ti exelthate* | *eis ten eremon* | *theasasthai?* | |
| *Kalamon* | *hupo anemou* | *saleuomenon ?* | |
| *Alla* | *ti exelthate* | *idein ?* | |
| *Anthropon* | *en malakois* | *emphiesmenon?* | |
| *Alla* | *ti exelthate* | *idein ?* | *Propheten ?* |
| *Nai lego* | *hymin,* | *kai perissoteron* | *prophetou !* |

This is all the more striking when we consider some of the differences between Greek and Aramaic that could account for the Greek not conforming any more closely to an Aramaic or Hebrew poetic line. Aramaic has no definite article, few adjectives, and a different verbal system (e.g., seldom using a verb "is/are"). As in Hebrew, possessives are indicated in attached suffixes, so few personal pronouns appear. Performance or writing in idiomatic Greek would require using separate words for such elements, as the following lines illustrate.

| | | |
|---|---|---|
| *Apostello* | *ton* aggelon *mou* | pro prosopou *sou* |
| hos kataskeuasei | *ten* hodon *sou* | emprosthen *sou.* |

| | | | | |
|---|---|---|---|---|
| | *Ouk egegertai* | *en genneous* | *gynaikon* | *meizon Ioannou* |
| *ho de mikroteros* | *en te basileia* | *tou thou* | *meizon autou estin.* | |

One reason that this passage provides a telling example of a likely Aramaic background is that two sets of lines make clear reference to Israelite cultural tradition, the one being ostensibly a quotation. Indeed, it is usually claimed that both pairs of lines are direct quotations of "Scripture" (the "Hebrew Bible," "Old Testament"). Given recent research into the status of the Hebrew text—i.e., multiform and still developing—it now seems out of the question to argue that they were quotations of written scrolls, either of a scroll in Hebrew or of a written copy of the Septuagint (see chaps. 1, 5, 6). The lines supposedly quoted (*gegraptai*)

| | | |
|---|---|---|
| *Idou!* | | |
| *Apostello* | *ton aggelon mou* | *pro prosopou sou* |
| *hos kataskeuasei* | *ten hodon sou* | *emprosthen sou.* |

do not correspond closely with either the LXX or the MT of Mal 3:1, nor do they correspond closely with either the LXX or the MT of Ex 23:20. From what we are learning about literacy in Hebrew or Aramaic or Greek as being confined to the scribal elite and the rarity of scrolls, it seems highly unlikely that either the composer(s)/performer(s) of this and other speeches in Q or those who may have cultivated such speeches behind the Greek version would have possessed written copies of Exodus or Malachi and been reading them.

Encouraged by the increasing evidence that literacy was extremely limited in popular circles, among which Q speeches seem to have been produced, I am becoming bolder in pressing my hypothesis of popular Israelite tradition in Galilee as the source of this "quotation." Popular circles knew of the existence of written versions of Exodus and of the Prophets, and from interaction with representatives of the "great tradition" they knew the basic content, the gist, of stories, covenantal legal materials, and prophecies that were of significance to them. The contents of Exod 23:20 were from the exodus narrative about Israel coming into its land. Malachi 3:1 was about the messenger of the covenant. Both would have had significance in the popular cultural memory, even though they would not have been identified "by chapter and verse," as it were, or even by their source/book (Exodus or Malachi). And because they are about similar themes and/or figures, they would likely have been associated or confused with each other. It is well known from the scribal/rabbinic level that references to sacred tradition were often grouped by significant theme or motif. E.g., *Exodus Rabbah* 33 (93d), which scholars have misleadingly abridged as a parallel to just this Q/Matt passage, has a whole collage of references (to what we know in our "established" texts), starting with Exod 23:20 and ending with Mal 3:1, but including Gen 24:7, 48:16; Exod 3:2, 4:9; and Judg 6:11–14. People who were actively cultivating the popular tradition, particularly to interpret the significance of John and Jesus, would have known that some such promise stood "written" in the official written texts of Israelite great tradition.

It has been standard to claim that in reply to John's disciples' question, Q's Jesus is quoting Isaiah.

| | | | | |
|---|---|---|---|---|
| *Tuphloi* | *anablepousin* | *kai* | *choloi* | *peripatousin* |
| *leproi* | *katharizontai* | *kai* | *kophoi* | *akouousin* |
| *kai nekroi* | *egeirontai* | *kai* | *ptochoi* | *euaggelizontai.* |

The only trouble is that it is impossible to identify which "text" is "quoted"—whether Isa 61:1 or 35:5–6 or 42:6–7 or yet another (again as noted in chap. 6). Each of these mentions one or more of the kinds of malaise that are healed, but none of them mentions more than two or three. Something is wrong with this picture. Again looking to the popular Israelite tradition gives us what is almost an obvious alternative to "quotation of scripture" in an oral communication environment (with no chirographs available in popular circles). The similarity of all those passages in Isaiah suggests that in earlier Israelite tradition there was a standard set of images used to express the longings of the people for deliverance, particularly of deliverance for the lowly who suffered such maladies as a result of their political-economic circumstances. This traditional set of images was a cultural source from which earlier "prophets" in the "Isaiah" succession drew in composing the lines in 35:5–6; 42:6–7; 61:1. That "Isaiah," perhaps the best known prophet in late second-temple times, and the one most alluded to, used these images made them all the more significant, perhaps particularly in popular circles. The composers of Q speeches, especially at the level of an earlier Aramaic version, was drawing on a common cultural repertoire of images, probably unaware of or not needing to "quote" Isaiah to establish "scriptural" authority for the standard and long-standing popular longings that had at long last been fulfilled by Jesus.

We can also identify certain words and phrases that are not usual in Greek but that reflect an Aramaic background. One of these is *egegertai*, "has arisen," which, even without the previous reference to John as a prophet, references a long Israelite tradition of prophets arising at a time of crisis to lead the people or to prophesy against oppressive rulers. Also the expression *en gennetois gunaikon* ("among those born of women") is not natural in Greek, but is found both in later "biblical" Hebrew and in later Aramaic.[52]

There may also be touches of "local color" from Aramaic-speaking Galilee in this speech. The "reed shaken by the wind," while it would also fit wetlands elsewhere, would surely match the experience of anyone who had visited the banks of the Jordan River, either as it entered or exited the Sea of Galilee. "A man in soft raiment" and "royal palaces" also fits Galilee, where Herod Antipas (known as a "king" locally, even though technically he had the title of "tetrarch") had built a palace overlooking his second capital city in Tiberias, although there were other petty Roman client "kings" in Syria.

There may also be cases of grammatical "interference" in this speech. Since Aramaic is a Semitic language and Greek is Indo-European, there are many differences, such as that Aramaic has no case endings, no definite article, no comparative or superlative, few adjectives, and a radically different

---

52. It would probably be fruitful also to investigate "(not) eating and drinking" and "a drunkard and glutton" for their possible Aramaic origins.

verbal system (as noted above). Precisely at these points interference can be detected.[53]

To make this investigation more complete—for which there is no space here—we would have to come back around the other direction, asking how a speech such as Q 7:18–35 would resonate with non-Israelites in Syrian villages, whether they were mainly Greek-speaking or bi-lingual in Greek and Aramaic. And a key factor in this connection would be the imperial situation in which Greek had become the dominant language and indigenous cultures suppressed, compounding the usual economic exploitation of villagers. In such circumstances so parallel to those of peoples of Israelite heritage in Galilee where the speeches of Jesus included in Q had originated, Greek- or Aramaic- speaking Syrian villagers might readily have responded when they heard them performed.

---

53. For examples of "interference," see Casey, *Aramaic Sources of Mark*, 308.

# 10

# ORAL PERFORMANCE AND THE GOSPEL OF MARK

It was not necessary that the Gospel performer know how to read. The performer could learn the Gospel from hearing oral performances . . . It is quite possible, and indeed even likely, that many Gospel performers were themselves illiterate . . . It was certainly possible for an oral performer to develop a narrative with this level of structural complexity . . . In Mark the number of interconnections between parts of the narrative are quite extraordinary.
—WHITNEY SHINER (2003)

WERNER KELBER'S *THE ORAL AND THE WRITTEN GOSPEL* WAS A major breakthrough in biblical studies in general as well as in Gospels studies in particular. The book challenged some of the most fundamental assumptions and constructs in the field. It undermined the assumptions and concepts of subdisciplines such as text criticism, form criticism, literary criticism, and standard phrase-by-phrase exegesis. On the other hand, *The Oral and the Written Gospel* (OWG) has stimulated extensive exploration of oral features in Mark's Gospel. I would like to explore the implications of Kelber's breakthrough work for understanding the composition and oral performance of the Gospel, taking into account subsequent research both within and outside the field of biblical studies.

# Liberating Biblical Studies from Its Captivity to Print Culture

Kelber engaged in biblical interpretation with a far broader interdisciplinary and historical perspective than most scholars. Perhaps his principal concern in *OWG* was the dominant orientation toward print culture in the field of biblical studies.[1] New Testament studies was conducting its business largely in "the Gutenberg galaxy." So pervasive were the assumptions and procedures of print culture that the form critics, despite having taken many cues from folklore studies, never explored genuinely oral communication. While boldly declaring its "historical-critical" awareness of the difference between ancient and modern, the original text and modern cultural assumptions, form criticism had developed little critical reflection on how distinctive, historically, were its own assumptions and procedures.

Kelber discerned and boldly presented the implications for New Testament studies of the pioneering investigations of Milman Parry and Albert Lord on Homeric epics, of Eric Havelock on Plato's attack on poetry, of Walter Ong's groundbreaking theorization of the distinctive media of orality and literacy, and of Ruth Finnegan's reflections on the relation between oral poetry and writing. Kelber stated a strong thesis in order "to break theoretical ground and to challenge the chirographic–typographic hegemony that rules biblical scholarship and many of the human sciences."[2] Accordingly, it seems at many points in *OWG* that what Kelber has in mind in the concept "textuality" is the print mentality of biblical scholarship and its typical concerns with original forms, copies, and textual accuracy,[3] all of which are modern concerns that were evidently of no interest even to the ancient scribes who handled the "biblical" manuscripts.

Over against form critics and other New Testament scholars, who had been conceptualizing oral tradition on the assumptions of print culture, Kelber presented ways of understanding oral communication based on recent studies in a range of cognate fields, including classics, folklore, and anthropology. This, along with the challenge to the print orientation of biblical studies generally, may have been the most influential and significant contribution of *OWG*. Biblical scholars, however, have steadfastly resisted the challenge. And only a small but now expanding number have joined Kelber in further exploration of the relation between orality and writing, of oral tradition, and of oral performance.

1. Kelber, "Introduction," xv, xxii.

2. Ibid., xxii.

3. Kelber, *The Oral and the Written Gospel*, 44, 94, 105.

Only a handful of colleagues, moreover, have picked up on one of the most significant aspects of oral tradition into which Kelber offered such innovative insight: that of social identification. "Survival and continuity of spoken words was thus not simply a matter of passive transmission, but rather was intimately connected with their social relevancy."[4] The orally cultivated materials in the Synoptic Gospel tradition that survived were those with which both speakers and hearers alike identified. This makes all the more important serious attention to the broader social and even political context of oral tradition incorporated into the Gospel of Mark. Bultmann and Dibelius, the two principal formulators of New Testament form criticism, considered the social functions of traditions together with their forms. But second- and third-generation form critics tended to forget about the social context and function in their refined reflection on forms.

In contrast to many scholars, Kelber clearly discerned the differences between the social location of Jesus and his followers and that of the priestly–scribal Qumran community that left the DSS. In his view, their "conspicuous differences must alert us against projecting the literary proficiency of the Qumran scribal experts upon early synoptic processes of transmission."[5] More generally, Kelber has noted explicitly how nonlinguistic features enter into communication, particularly oral discourse. The broader context in which oral communication occurs includes multiple political and economic as well as religious, cultural, and aesthetic factors. Not only does oral communication receive powerful ideological and situational support from the social context in which it is embedded, but "nonlinguistic features have priority over linguistic ones."[6]

Kelber has been unfairly accused of advocating the "Great Divide" between literacy and orality. While he presented a "strong thesis" to gain traction against the grip of print culture on the field, his treatment of Mark as a written text is subtle and nuanced. This is abundantly evident in three interrelated connections that are central to his analysis of Mark's plotted story and the cultural circumstances of its composition.

First, after it existed as a written text, Mark continued to operate in a predominantly oral communication environment. Kelber states repeatedly that Mark and other written texts were meant to be read aloud and heard by an audience.[7] Well into the second century CE and beyond, Mark's Gospel was heard in a culture that valued the spoken word over the written. The

---

4. Ibid., 24.
5. Ibid., 16–17.
6. Ibid., 75.
7. Ibid., 93–94, 217–18.

church "fathers" were reticent, even apologetic, about their own writing, lest it compromise the (oral) Gospel.[8] Kelber devoted an entire chapter of *OWG* to exploration of the oral materials of various forms that comprise most of the written Gospel. He observes that Mark's narrative was composed "by frequent recourse to orality,"[9] although without elaborating the point. Thus Mark, along with the other Gospels, has a "performative quality."[10]

Second, in dealing with the Markan passion narrative, in which he finds death closely related to writing, Kelber notes carefully the numerous allusions to and influences of the Hebrew Scriptures. These allusions and influences suggest, however, that "much of Scripture, like much literature in antiquity, was mentally accessible to an oral mode of appropriation."[11] As he had noted earlier, texts used in the composition of other texts "were often assimilated through hearing and 'interior dictation,'" a blurring of the lines often drawn between orality and writing.[12] Although he did not have an adequate theoretical model to describe this phenomenon in *OWG*, Kelber soon became conversant with the burgeoning discussion of cultural memory in European academic circles. A text's investment in tradition may not involve a physical intertextuality, but rather oral–memorial access to a shared *cultural memory*. What is more, cultural memory does not simply involve oral–memorial knowledge of written texts. Once he had conceptualized this phenomenon, Kelber could clarify that the composition of Mark involved "plugging into a copious reservoir of memories, retrieving and reshuffling what was accessible memorially."[13] In retrospect, Kelber realized that the composition of Mark was unthinkable without cultural memory, which served not primarily to preserve Jesus materials but rather to edify the community or movement and its collective identity. With the breakthrough concept of cultural memory, as with the breakthrough to recognition of the difference and relationship of orality and writing, Kelber was the pioneer in biblical studies.[14]

Third and finally in this connection, and an integral component of the concept of cultural memory but an important point in itself, Kelber calls attention to the ways that written texts functioned in oral contexts

---

8. Ibid., 93.

9. Ibid., 95.

10. Kelber, "Introduction," xxiii.

11. Kelber, *The Oral and the Written Gospel*, 197.

12. Ibid., 23.

13. Kelber, "Introduction," xxiii.

14. See the essays in Kirk and Thatcher, eds., *Memory, Tradition, and Text*; and Horsley et al., eds., *Performing the Gospel*.

prior to the rise of print culture. Written from dictation, recited orally, and heard aurally, manuscripts were embedded in the dominant oral medium of communication. Texts—of torah as well as of the *Iliad* or *Beowulf*—were dictated to scribes and recited aloud to audiences. "Most manuscripts were, therefore, meant to be heard and processed in memory."[15] Kelber's point here is elaborated in discussion by Walter Ong,[16] in studies of the operations of medieval texts such as Beowulf,[17] and more recently in studies of ancient Judean and rabbinic texts.[18]

Kelber developed all of these crucial insights and points in close dialogue with the most recent and well–received scholarship on the principal subjects on which his investigation focused, such as the sayings of Jesus (especially in Q), Jesus' parables, the Gospel of Mark, and Paul's letters. And, with the notable exception of the most fundamental assumptions and approaches he was challenging, he couched his investigation in the assumptions, approaches, and concepts of New Testament studies that were standard in the early1980's, such as form criticism, Christology, the synthetic construct of a monolithic "Judaism," and "the living/exalted Lord."[19] It is therefore most impressive, upon rereading *OWG* thirty later, to realize the remarkable extent to which many of the then–accepted scholarly generalizations and standard assumptions, approaches, and concepts are now questionable. Meanwhile Kelber's insights are steadily gaining attention and being further developed by those he inspired.

## Related Recent Research and Reflection

Investigation into the relations of orality and literacy and of oral performance since *OWG*, both by biblical scholars who have followed Kelber's initiatives and by scholars in other fields, has confirmed Kelber's discussion of the oral materials incorporated in Mark's story. It also leads to an application of Kelber's insights on pre-Markan materials to the Gospel as a whole narrative, orally performed. Such research has resulted in a far more precise understanding of society, culture, and political affairs in the Roman empire and particularly in Judea and Galilee.

---

15. Kelber, "Introduction," xxii.

16. Ong, *Orality and Literacy*.

17. Clanchy, *Memory to Written Record*; O'Keefe, *Visible Song*.

18. Jaffee, *Torah in the Mouth*; Carr, *Tablet of the Heart*; Horsley, *Scribes, Visionaries*, chaps. 5–6.

19. Kelber, *The Oral and the Written Gospel*, 93, 100, 215–16.

Kelber presented his challenges to the field in close conversation with the standard discourse and scholarship of New Testament studies where it stood thirty years ago. The fuller implications of his challenge, however, can be more appropriately explored by moving more into the ordinary language of history and the human sciences and by moving into the appreciation of oral-derived and orally-performed texts in other fields no longer so determined by the assumptions and conceptualizations of print culture. Where appropriate, we can note when particular assumptions, approaches, and concepts of New Testament studies must be abandoned or seriously qualified.

## A World of Oral Communication and Limited Uses of Writing

Research during the thirty years since the publication of OWG has confirmed and deepened our understanding of just how limited literacy and writing were in antiquity (as discussed in chap. 1). Thoroughly researched studies have shown that writing was limited basically to the social and cultural elite.[20] One sobering bit of older research had pointed out that the "village scribes" in Roman Egypt, recently claimed as a model on which to imagine lower level scribes who could have "written" (composed) the "Sayings Collection" Q,[21] were not even functionally literate. Inscriptions show, for example, that Petaus, the village clerk of Ptolemais Hormou, could sign his name only by copying a model.[22] Not only did literacy correspond to social position, but the wealthy and powerful used writing to exert their power. With most transactions conducted in face-to-face interaction, urban artisans and rural peasants alike had little use for writing.

Literacy was even more obviously limited to the political and cultural elite in Roman Palestine,[23] seriously challenging older generalizations about the ubiquity of schools and reading among the Jews (based on a misreading of key documents that refer rather to recitation of texts from memory). A key aspect of the limits of literacy was the limited accessibility of scrolls, which were both expensive and cumbersome. Scrolls of scriptural texts were laid up in the temple, as part of their aura of authority. Scribal groups also possessed scrolls of authoritative texts, but apparently did not consult them physically on a regular basis. Josephus mentions the burning of a sacred scroll by Roman soldiers in a Judean village and someone holding up a

---

20. Harris, *Ancient Literacy*; Beard, *Literacy in the Roman World*; Woolf, "Literacy."

21. Kloppenborg, "Literary Convention;" Arnal, *Village Scribes*.

22. Youtie, "*Agrammatos*."

23. Hezser, *Jewish Literacy*.

scroll of the laws of Moses in an assembly in Tarichaeae (*Life* 134). But the presence of scrolls in such villages and towns must have been rare. Ordinary people could not have read them even if they were available.

The relation of written texts to the appropriation of those texts may be as illuminating of the predominantly oral communication environment as is the limited literacy of the population. Almost all of what we think of as "literature" in ancient Greece, Rome, and Judea involved oral communication: manuscripts were recited or performed, not read silently. We are generally aware that Greek and Latin poetry was chanted or sung and that plays were performed in city theaters in elaborately staged productions. If we think about the dialogue form of ancient philosophy, we can imagine the dialogical oral debate involved. But history and other "literary" forms were also recited orally to groups by their composers. Some of these recitations may have involved a kind of reading. But given the extreme difficulty of physically deciphering ancient manuscript writing, with no breaks between words and paragraphs, "reading" from a manuscript would have require considerable previous familiarity with the text. Written copies of most texts existed, but the existence of written copies did not disrupt the continuity of oral performance. "Literature" was thus experienced orally-aurally in public performances or, for the elite, private banquets. Kelber's observation that ancient manuscripts functioned in a predominantly oral communication environment pointed to what was a major aspect of the relation of written texts and the oral–aural appropriation of texts, and his thesis has been confirmed and elaborated with every new study of particular texts in their historical contexts.

### Authoritative Texts in Writing and Their Continuing Oral Performance

Especially pertinent to understanding the origins of the Gospel of Mark, the synoptic Gospel materials from which it was composed, and the process by which it was composed, are the Hebrew scriptures of the Judean temple-state. Traditional understandings of the social role of these texts offer a prime example of how biblical studies has been captive to modern print culture. But these scriptures also offer a prime example of how such texts can be fruitfully reconceived as components of a broader cultural memory. If we have "ears to hear" as well as "eyes to see," we may now stand close to a confluence of heretofore separate strands of research that may soon join together into a new stream of critical awareness of how ancient cultural repertoires functioned. Since some of these strands of research are still in elementary stages of development, the following sketch may be somewhat tentative at points. Yet the direction of confluence seems clear enough.

Projecting modern assumptions about widespread literacy and avail-ability of books into antiquity, biblical scholars have imagined the Jews as a people of the Book, with the spin-off Christian movement quick to develop a collection of its own sacred books.[24] Even after scholars had become aware of the limited literacy in the Roman imperial context of early "Judaism" (and early "Christianity"), they still cited passages from the Flavian Judean apologist Josephus and later rabbinic documents as proof that schools were ubiquitous in Jewish communities and that children were taught to read, especially the sacred texts of torah that were presumed readily available and readily legible. In fact, these passages indicate rather that those ancient Jewish communities were largely nonliterate and that communication was largely oral. The texts mentioned in these passages, moreover—or perhaps rather the oral recitation of the texts—are supposedly almost "magical" in their effect: by *hearing* the sacred laws spoken aloud the laws become "en-graved on their [the Jews'] souls . . . and guarded in their memory" (see *Ant.* 4.210; 16.43; *c. Apion.* 2.175, 178, 204; cf. Philo, *ad Gaium* 115, 210). More-over, rabbinic fragments once taken to attest people *reading* refer instead to people *reciting* certain well known psalms and prayers from memory. And rabbinic passages once cited to prove general literacy and the prevalence of schools refer only to the tiny circles of the rabbis and their students. Recent researches thus paint a very different picture of scriptural texts and how they were cultivated by the tiny literate elite of professional intellectuals, the scribes.[25]

Further, the scriptures of the Judean temple-state were not confined to a particular set of books and their 'text' had not been standardized and stabilized—suggesting that modern scholarly references to "the Hebrew Bible," "the Torah," or "the Old Testament" with reference to the late second-temple period are largely anachronistic (as discussed in chap. 1). Not until much later were certain books included in what is called the Hebrew Bible. Detailed analysis of the manuscripts of the books of the Pentateuch and the books of the Prophets found among the DSS has found that there were multiple versions or textual traditions of these texts.[26] Many of these texts, moreover, were undergoing continuing "composition," somewhat as schol-ars had previously imagined the continuing composition of the book of Isa-

---

24. See the studies cited in Gamble, *Books and Readers*, 7–8.

25. Jaffee, *Torah in the Mouth*; Carr, *Tablet of the Heart*; Horsley, *Scribes, Visionaries*, chaps. 5–6.

26. Ulrich, *Dead Sea Scrolls*.

iah centuries earlier. Part of the explanation for the continuing development and variant versions of these already scriptural texts becomes evident when text critics compare notes with scholars who have been studying the relationship between written texts and the continuing memorization and oral recitation of those texts in scribal circles. On the basis of his illuminating probe of the oral traditions of Jesus' sayings, Kelber challenged the very concept of "original" wording, even of the original structure. Now we must come to grips with the virtual certainty that the "original text" of a "biblical" book is a chimera of the modern print-cultural imagination.

In addition to the Pentateuchal books, other books of torah were also found at Qumran. While these texts have been labeled according to the print-cultural concept of "rewritten Bible," they were rather alternative texts of (Mosaic) torah, composed by scribes immersed in torah idiom and torah tradition (as discussed in chap. 3).[27] And texts like these point to the rich reservoir of traditional materials that were available in the Judean cultural memory, which was hardly confined to cumbersome written scrolls.

### Scribal Oral Recitation/Performance of Authoritative Texts

As several Jewish scholars have pointed out, texts of torah were not *read* (a modern misunderstanding) but rather *proclaimed* or *recited*. This reality can be seen repeatedly in passages of Deuteronomy and the prophets.[28] For example,

> When all of Israel come to appear before the LORD . . . , *qr'* [recite/proclaim] this torah in the presence of all Israel, in their ears . . . in order that they hear. . . that they learn . . . and perform all of the words of this torah. (Deut 31:11)

The rabbis distinguished between "what is written" (*kethuv*) and "what is recited" (*qere', miqra*); they viewed the *sefer torah* as "a holy object, a thing to be venerated, . . . with its holy and allegedly changeless writing."[29] The tradition of *qere'* ("what is read"), including the essential vowels, accents, stresses, and pauses, along with euphemisms and the customary rhythm and inflexion (melody?) in which the text was chanted, which were not properties of the script, was different from *ketiv* ("what is written"; *b. Ber.* 62a; *Meg.* 32a). Clearly there was a long tradition of oral recitation that proceeded semi- independently of what lay written on scrolls, and when the

---

27. Horsley, *Scribes, Visionaries*, chap. 6.

28. Boyarin, "Placing Reading."

29. Green, "Writing with Scripture," 14–15.

rabbis did consult written scrolls they articulated this difference. But the difference did not appear, to them, to require an explanation, much less an adjustment in the text recited or the manuscript tradition(s). Thus even the literate cultural elite, the later rabbis and the earlier scribal circles, cultivated (i.e., learned, used, and adapted) texts by oral recitation.

Given the print-cultural orientation of biblical studies, it is not surprising that specialists on the DSS have typically constructed the scribes and priests of the Qumran community somewhat in their own image, as engaged in "studying" and "interpreting" the Torah and other texts. And, indeed, they did produce written documents of the "interpretation" (*pešarim*) of Habakkuk and other prophetic texts. But passages that might indicate study and interpretation of the Torah are difficult to find.[30] Again as explained above, a key passage used to attest such study, the instructions for the nightly gatherings of ten or more members in 1QS 6:6–8, refers rather to the oral recitation of "the writing" (*sefer*). Like the later rabbis, the scribes and priests at Qumran had texts of torah and their own regulations (*mišpatim*) "inscribed" on their memories as well as on scrolls.

Recent studies have laid out a fuller picture of scribal practice in ancient Judea against the background of traditional scribal culture in the ancient Near East more generally. These studies confirm what we have sketched so far from bits and pieces of evidence at Qumran and from rabbinic practice. Learned scribes, the literate elite who served as administrators and advisers in temple-state and the royal and imperial regimes, were also the professional cultivators of the official cultural repertoire.[31] They learned writing and reading as part of their elementary education, and were available to write down letters for delivery in oral presentation to the recipient, to make additional copies of written texts, and to read written texts as necessary. Their more comprehensive learning of the wider repertoire of legal, historical, mythic, mantic, and other texts, however, was by recitation and memorization. With most of the texts of the cultural repertoire "written on the tablets of the heart," they could recite them on the appropriate occasions and teach the next generation of scribes (often literally their sons). Written copies of texts may well have been available, although in some cases the written texts were laid up in temples or palaces or in storage somewhere (although not like modern archives, where documents are available for consultation). The fact that these texts existed in written form in such institutions gave them a certain aura and authority. But most scribal learning and

---

30. Horsley, *Scribes, Visionaries*, chap. 6.

31. Fuller discussion in Carr, *Tablet of the Heart*; Horsley, *Scribes, Visionaries*, chaps. 4–6.

knowledge was oral–memorial: texts were stored in memory, were recited orally, and were not usually read physically from manuscripts.

### Cultural Patterns Evident in Text and Performance

Much of the material in the written and orally recited texts in the ancient Judean cultural repertoire had certain discernible cultural forms or patterns. We focus on four particular examples.

Of special importance, first, was the Mosaic covenantal pattern. A well known example would be the book of Deuteronomy, which not only contains material recognizable as covenantal teaching in the tradition of the covenant principles in Exodus 20 and the covenantal laws in Exodus 21–23 but also takes the overall form of the Mosaic covenant, as evident in Exodus 20 and Joshua 24. That the Mosaic covenant pattern was very much alive and operative in late second-temple times is attested by the Community Rule of the Qumran community (1QS). Not only does the *Rule* contain what are clearly covenantal rulings and instructions, but the overall outline of the *Rule* displays the components of the covenant pattern.[32] The first section of the scroll contains instructions for conducting ceremonies of covenant renewal in which new members were inducted into the covenant community. It is thus evident that in these covenant renewal ceremonies, community members were not physically reading an unwieldy scroll, but were orally performing blessings and curses and reciting the long "historical prologue" that included the division of history under the domination of the two spirits. Further, it should be noted that the fragmentary copies of the Community Rule found in cave 4 near Qumran contain wording very different from 1QS, another illustration of the difference between "what was written" and "what was recited" (or in this case more elaborately performed). A later section of the Community Rule contains the kinds of *mišpatim* that might have been "searched" in the ritual of the nightly meetings (1QS 6:6–8). The Qumran Community Rule thus offers a signal indication of the relation between written texts and oral performance of important "cultural patterns." It illustrates clearly that the traditional pattern of the Mosaic covenant was not just written on manuscripts of certain texts, but was also actively operative in the oral performance of renewal ceremonies of communities of people.

Second, clearly related to the basic covenantal pattern evident in written texts and operative in communal oral performance, we can occasionally discern in prophetic books a form of (God's) indictments for violation of covenant principles. Particularly striking arc scrics of woes and/

---

32. Baltzer, *Covenant Formulary*; Horsley, *Covenant Economics*.

or declarations of punishment against the rulers and/or their officers who have done the injustices. These prophetic indictments and pronouncements were oral declarations, now written down in what we know as anthologies of (often fragmentary) prophetic oracles. It is important to note that the unit of communication in these books is not an individual statement or saying, but prophetic speech of many lines in an argumentative sequence or a more complex prophetic rhetorical form.

Third, the Hymn Scroll from Qumran indicates that new hymns were being composed in Hebrew, patterned after traditional hymns that we know about from the canonical book of Psalms that was evidently defined (as we know it) somewhat later. Again, while 1QHod[a] gives us a written collection of these new psalms, these and other psalms were surely being performed from memory in community life at Qumran and perhaps elsewhere as well. The "communal blessings" mentioned in the procedure for the nightly gatherings would presumably have been a similar or parallel (or overlapping) continuing oral composition-and-performance in the community.

Fourth, we can also discern the principal speech-pattern of instructional wisdom in books of wisdom (as discussed in chap. 4 above). This instructional wisdom takes the form, not of individual proverbs, but of short speeches on topics important in the training of scribes, often with two or more speeches on a given topic. These speeches were clearly delivered orally, the book of Sirach being a written collection of many such speeches of the leaned scribe Yeshua ben Sira.

The Judean cultural repertoire included many such cultural patterns that, besides being evident in many written texts, were functioning creatively in scribal circles and community life in late second-temple times, as texts were learned and recited orally, as part of the broader Judean cultural repertoire.

### Israelite Popular Tradition

As Kelber recognized, we cannot extrapolate directly from the Qumran community or any other scribal circle or text to the Jesus movements and the synoptic gospel tradition. Jesus and his followers originated and were active in the villages of Galilee, and synoptic gospel material and the earliest Gospel texts, Mark and Q, all remained at the popular level. There were no scrolls and no reading and writing in village communities. But lack of literacy does not mean ignorance of cultural tradition. As suggested by many cross-cultural studies of agrarian societies, popular Israelite cultural tradition was alive and well in village communities (discussed in chap. 5).[33] In societies where the rulers are of the same ethnic and cultural background as the peasants, the elite tradition and the popular tradition tend to be parallel, variations of one another, while articulating the different interests of the elite and peasants, respectively, as anthropologists and historians have explained.[34] Two distinctive patterns operative in Galilean as well as Judean popular tradition are evident in the emergence of popular prophetic movements patterned after the stories of Moses and Joshua and popular messianic movements patterned after the anointing of the young David to lead the people against the invading Philistines.[35] It is evident from Josephus' accounts of events in 66–67 CE that Galileans were energetic in defending Mosaic covenantal principles, interestingly against elite Judeans compromised by their assimilation to the dominant Hellenistic-Roman culture.[36] It is in the context of this evolving Israelite popular tradition in Galilee that Jesus traditions and their cultivation and development must be understood.

### Relinquishing Concepts that Now Appear to be Anachronistic

In view of the above considerations, it should be immediately evident that some key aspects of the previous construction of Jesus tradition and its development in New Testament studies must be rejected, and a more appropriate understanding put in their place.

First, the authenticity of Jesus' teaching is typically measured on the basis of how it differs from "Jewish" (Israelite) cultural materials. A variation of this principle is to find Jesus' teachings to be "countercultural" or "unconventional." All such concepts fail to recognize the differences between the elite tradition, in which most of our textual sources stand, and the popular tradition, for which of course we have very few written sources—outside of the Gospel materials themselves. The cultural memory of Jesus' actions and prophetic teaching was rooted in Israelite cultural memory. But the latter was cultivated at the popular level, parallel to but over-against the elite scribal tradition in Jerusalem. Since we have precious few sources for Galilean Israelite popular tradition, we can resort to extrapolation from the elite texts that comprise the majority of our sources. But we can do so only with

---

33. Horsley, *Galilee*, 152–55; Horsley with Draper, *Whoever Hears You Hears Me*, chap. 5.

34. See especially Scott, "Protest and Profanation."

35. Horsley, "Popular Messianic Movements;" and Horsley, "Two Types of Prophets."

36. Horsley, *Galilee*, 147–55.

critically aware historical imagination that takes the difference between elite tradition and popular tradition fully into account.

The second key aspect of Jesus scholarship that must be rejected, a fundamental building block of form criticism and subsequent approaches to Jesus materials and their development, is the assumption that "in the beginning" were the separate sayings and aphorisms of Jesus. This assumption is questionable simply on the face of things, since no one, including the great revealer Jesus, can communicate in "one-liners" or isolated sayings.

Once we recognize how Israelite cultural traditions worked and the patterns they assumed, however, as discernible in written textual sources, we can be bolder in recognizing similar forms and patterns in the synoptic gospel materials. As noted just above, the cultural memory of Jesus' teachings and actions, like those teachings and actions themselves, was rooted and embedded in Israelite popular tradition. Cultural memories do not consist of mere fragments, discrete dates and names and proverbs, but rather of patterns that inform group identity, such as the Mosaic covenant and memories of prophets such as Moses and Elijah. It should not be surprising that just these particular cultural patterns are readily discernible in both the Q speeches and in the Gospel of Mark as well as in the revolt against Rome in Galilee in 66–67 CE and in popular movements contemporary with Jesus.[37] The first and longest speech of Jesus in Q 6:20–49 focuses on covenant renewal and the series of dialogues in Mark 10:2–45 comprise a similar covenant renewal, with explicit recitation of covenant principles in two of the dialogues.[38] In Mark's story, Jesus' sea-crossings and feedings in the wilderness are reminiscent of Moses in the exodus and wilderness journey and his healings resemble those of Elijah (with whom he then appears on the mountain).

Finally, in seeking to identify the cultural patterns by which otherwise seemingly isolated fragments of cultural memory are given coherence, it is anachronistic and inappropriate to impose synthetic modern scholarly constructs such as "apocalypticism" or theological concepts such as "christology," which are not attested as operative patterns in contemporary Judean texts.[39]

---

37. Horsley, "Popular Messianic Movements;" Horsley, "Two Types of Popular Prophets;" *Galilee*, 152–55.

38. Horsley with Draper, *Whoever Hears You Hears Me*, chap. 9; Horsley, *Hearing the Whole Story*, chap. 8.

39. Horsley, *Scribes, Visionaries*, "Conclusion"; Horsley, *Revolt of the Scribes*; Horsley, *Prophet Jesus*, chap. 4; and the implications of Horsley, "Popular Messianic Movements."

*References to Israelite Tradition in Mark*

Yet another recent line of research into the relations of oral communication and writing that reinforces Kelber's insights on Mark is investigation of how the Judean scriptures are referred to in the Gospel itself. Insofar as scribes were trained in writing and reading, their recitation may well assume acquaintance with manuscripts. Communication among ordinary people, on the other hand, was almost exclusively oral; they cultivated Israelite popular tradition orally in the course of family and community life. While they were surely aware of the existence of sacred writing ("scripture") in the temple or some other distant place, which was awesome for people in a society where writing was rare, it seems doubtful that they would have had any first-hand acquaintance with the written texts (cumbersome scrolls). The allusions and references to Israelite tradition in Mark and/or in pre-Markan material may provide an illuminating illustration of a number of the points just discussed, especially the difference between the elite and the popular Israelite tradition and the oral cultivation of Israelite tradition at the popular level.

Embedded in the assumptions of print culture, standard studies of Mark's Gospel refer to its "quotation" of "the Bible" or the "Old Testament." The Gospel of Mark, however, gives no indication that written texts were involved in its references to Israelite traditions.

Some of these references to Israelite tradition are simply to cultural memories that stand behind and inform Jesus' actions or speech. Jesus' entry into Jerusalem is an allusion to the image articulated by the prophet Zechariah of a popular king coming not on a war chariot ("triumphant and victorious") but on an ass, a peasant mode of transportation (Mark 11:2–8; cf. Zech 9:9). In one controversy story, Jesus refers to David and his men eating bread taken from an altar, but the references are not consistent with the written text that has come down to us in 1 Samuel, with the names of priests, for example, being different (Mark 2:23–28; cf. Mark 2:25–26 and 1 Sam 21:1–6; 2 Sam 15:35). It seems rather than the references in the controversy story in Mark 2:23–28 were rooted in popular cultural memory. Similarly, the Markan "passion narrative" has numerous allusions to well known psalms, especially the one we know as Psalm 22. But especially in the case of commonly sung psalms and commonly recited prayers, it would be pedestrian to think that they were quotations from written texts.

Other references to Israelite tradition are to what characters in the story said, and not to written texts (Mark 10:4; 11:9–10; 12:36). Yet other references, such as "honor your father and mother," are to the most fundamental and memorable Israelite principles that would have been well known to most Galileans and Judeans (e.g., Mark 7:9–10; 10:19). Even in cases that are presented explicitly as citations of "scripture," the words evidently come from memory, not written texts. Mark 1:2–3, for example, ostensibly cites the prophet Isaiah, but begins with a recitation of lines that resemble what we know as Exod 23:20 and Mal 3:1. The prophecy in Mark 1:2–3 appears to be a (composite) recitation from popular Israelite memory of prophetic tradition, not a combination resulting from consultation of scrolls.

The lines in Mark introduced by the terms "it is written (in the prophet . . .)" or "scripture" (*gegraptai* and *graphe*, respectively) have usually been read as quotations of written texts. What "it is written" or "scripture" referred to in Mark, however, may appear quite different once we become aware of the different kinds (and functions) of writing in antiquity, as clarified by recent investigation into orality and writing (discussed in chap. 1). In ancient Athens, laws or decrees passed by the assembly were inscribed on public monuments, even though Athenians in general mistrusted writing and the courts relied on professional "remembrancers" to know what the laws were. The act of writing the laws on public monuments functioned to enhance the authority of the laws. Something similar was operative in the Judean temple-state when "the torah/laws (of Moses)" were inscribed on scrolls (books of the Pentateuch) and laid up in the temple. As noted in chap. 2, an early illustration of this can be seen in the account in Nehemiah 8, where Ezra, with great flourish, displays "the scroll of the torah/law of Moses" before the people, who acclaim and bow down to the sacred scroll, and then recites (the torah from) the scroll before the assembly. The scrolls of scripture stored in the temple were symbols of transcendent authority, numinous sacred objects of veneration that authorized the temple as the ruling political-economic-religious center of Judean society.[40]

If we now take into consideration not only the limited literacy of the general population and the availability of scrolls only to elite circles of priesta and scribes, but also the functional value of sacred scrolls laid up in the sacred precincts of the temple as symbols of authority, we must reconsider whether the formula "it is written" or "the writing" means that Mark was quoting from written texts. When we also recognize that the words supposedly quoted do not accord with what have been judged to be the best early manuscripts of the texts supposedly quoted—and that those texts often existed in variant versions, anyhow—it seems highly likely that the composers-performers of Mark were quoting from memory while also claiming that what was being quoted stood written on a sacred scroll, i.e., had authority. The same may be true of other early "Christian" texts and of many contemporary Judean texts.

40. Van der Toorn, "Iconic Book."

In the case of Mark's Gospel, a close examination of the ostensible "quotations of scripture" leads us to a previously unrecognized aspect of Jesus' apparent citations of scripture.[41] In many of the passages where Jesus refers explicitly to "what is written," he is engaged in polemic response to the official guardians and interpreters of the sacred writings. For example, when he cites Isaiah against the scribes and Pharisees (7:6) and then cites "Jeremiah" and a festival psalm against the rulers of the temple (11:17; 12:10), he is appealing, against the literate elite, to the very authority that they claim as the basis for their power and authority. We can see the same general tactic at several other points in Mark's narrative. In response to the Pharisees' leading question about divorce Jesus counters with a reference to the written Mosaic ruling that they claim as their authority (Mark 10:3–5; which we know in Deut 24:1–4). In response to the Sadducees, Jesus appeals to the written text of Moses to refute the high priestly party that stubbornly accepted only the written laws of Moses, and not other, oral traditions of (Mosaic) torah, as authoritative (Mark 12:18–27).

Only in explaining the events surrounding Jesus' confrontation with the rulers in Jerusalem that may have been difficult to understand—betrayal, arrest, crucifixion, desertion by the disciples—does Mark appeal directly to the general authority of the scripture (14:21, 27, 49). This is similar to the way that the "creed" that Paul cites in 1 Cor 15:3–5 appeals to the general authority of "scripture" to explain and authorize the death and resurrection of Jesus.

Mark's references to "it is written" and "written" are thus appealing to the *authority* of Scripture. And when the Gospel story cites lines ostensibly from a particular text, the citation is from memory, evidently at the popular level. In contrast to the standard view in Gospel research, there is no evidence that (the composers-performers of) Mark's Gospel had direct knowledge of written texts. But the Gospel story was rooted in knowledge of what prophets had pronounced and Mosaic covenantal principles and psalms in the popular Israelite cultural memory. The Galilean popular tradition may even have known what "texts" the Pharisees would cite as authorization for their interpretation and rulings (e.g., what we know from Deut 24:1–4, in Mark 10:2–9), just as some of the "traditions of the elders" were known (e.g., *qorban*, in Mark 7:1–13). Not only does Mark's story cite (the content of) scripture from memory, but the citations reveal the ambiguous popular attitude toward "what was written" and the conflict between the popular tradition and its spokespeople (Jesus) and the elite tradition (including scripture) and its representatives (scribes and Pharisees).

41. Horsley, *Hearing the Whole Story,* 59–61.

*Implications of More Precise Knowledge of the Historical Context*

Another area of significant research that has developed since the publication of *OWG* relates to the historical context in which the synoptic gospel tradition developed. Despite the limited sources available, it is remarkable how much more precise our understanding of life in Judea and Galilee has become in the past thirty years. This research, moreover, has taken into account the various dimensions of context that Kelber emphasized, including the political and economic as well as the cultural. It is no longer appropriate to use vague synthetic concepts such as "Judaism" and "the Jews," since we can now be far more precise about groups and movements, their social and regional location, and their distinctive characteristics. And we are much more aware of the dynamics of the political–economic and cultural conflicts that persisted between the Roman, Herodian, and high priestly rulers, on the one hand, and the Judean and Galilean villagers, on the other.

To mention just a few examples directly relevant to issues discussed in *OWG* and their subsequent treatment, we are now aware that it is an oversimplification and anachronism to imagine "Jewish" and "Gentile" sides of the Sea of Galilee, such that Jesus' voyages back and forth symbolically mediate between "Jews" and "Gentiles." Jesus' "sea crossings" in Mark, heard in the cultural context of Israelite tradition, would much more likely have resonated with memories of Moses and the Exodus—especially when linked with wilderness feedings (Mark 4:35–41; 6:47–52; cf. 6:30–44; 8:1–9). Now that we are more fully aware that the Pharisees served as scribal–legal "retainers" representing the Jerusalem temple-state, the controversy stories can be seen to have serious political implications.[42] Being aware now also that there is no evidence outside the Gospels that the Pharisees, based in Jerusalem, were active in Galilee during the lifetime of Jesus, the controversy stories appear to be expressions of a more general class and regional conflict between official Jerusalem cultural tradition and Galilean popular tradition.

## Features of Mark's Gospel in Oral Performance

If we now combine Kelber's insights about the oral cultivation of Jesus materials and cultural memory with the implications of recent research on historical context of Mark and broader units of communication and cultural patterns, then there appears to have been much less of a gulf between Jesus' stories and speeches and the composition and performance of the whole Gospel story. The obvious place to start this exploration is by noting how

---

42. Horsley, *Hearing the Whole Story*, chap. 7.

some of Kelber's observations about the individual oral components of the Gospel of Mark may apply also to Mark as a whole. These observations fall into three categories: the stylistic features of oral narrative; the close fit between the theme and plot of the Gospel and the historical context that it addressed; and the parabolic plot of the overall narrative, which incorporates many parabolic paradigms of oral performance.

### Some Features of Oral Narrative that Facilitate Performance

The many episodes of the Gospel are linked together by stereotypical connective devices.[43] Besides the abundant use of paratactic *kai*, not only within episodes but as a connection between episodes (see Mark 9:2; 11:20; 15:42), we find links such as pleonastic *archesthai* with infinitive verbs (see 1:45; 2:23; 6:7; 8:31), the adverb *(kai) euthys* (see 1:29; 3:6; 6:54), the iterative *(kai) palin* (see 2:1; 4:1; 7:31; 10:1, 10), and the formulaic *kai ginetai/egeneto* (see 1:9; 2:15, 23). Some of these connectives may have come from the oral stories that Mark incorporated into the overall narrative, and the overall narrative may have stimulated some of these typical oral connectives. The effect is an exciting, action packed narrative of "one thing after another."

Among the other features that contribute to Mark's oral feel, Kelber pointed to the folkloristic triads that appear prominently in the narrative.[44] The healing stories always unfold in three steps. Parables, such as that of the tenants, feature three messengers. That Peter denies Jesus three times (Mark 14:66–72), and even that Jesus asks the disciples to watch with him three times in the garden (Mark 14:32–42), might be explained as features of oral stories that Mark incorporated. In addition, however, Mark's story has recurrent appearances of "threes" that cannot be accounted for on the basis of the many oral stories that were combined in the overall Gospel. For example, Jesus predicts his arrest, execution, and rising three times (8:31; 9:31; 10:33–34), clearly the key sequence in the middle step of the narrative focused on Jesus and the disciples. Three disciples are distinguished within the twelve (Peter, James, and John) for special focus, and Jesus enters Jerusalem three times (11:11; 11:15; 11:27), again the guiding sequence in the climactic narrative step of the story.

The devices typical of oral storytelling that structure the larger narrative of the Gospel of Mark, not just its component stories, suggest that we

---

43. Most of these connective devices disappear in modern translations (English, German, etc.), which attempt to transform the Gospel narrative into good print–culture prose style.

44. Kelber, *The Oral and the Written Gospel*, 66.

may find other examples of "narrative maneuvering" similar to what Kelber finds in the shorter component episodes of Mark.[45] In the healing stories and the exorcism stories, for example, Kelber notes that the narrator has flexibility to innovate by inserting several different motifs within the overall structure. While they are not analogous in pattern (not a macrocosm of the microcosm) to the maneuvers in the healing stories, we can detect several narrative maneuvers in the broader Markan narrative. One example is the familiar Markan "sandwich" technique of juxtaposing two stories, with one framed within the other. Mark frames the scribe's charge that Jesus works in the power of Beelzebul with Jesus' family's concern that he is possessed (3:20–35), the healing of the hemorrhaging woman with the raising of the nearly dead young woman (5:21–43), Jesus' prophetic demonstration against the temple with the cursing of the fig tree (11:12–25), and Jesus' trial before the high priesthood with Peter's denial (15:52–72).

A similar but somewhat more complex oral narrative device is the concentric or chiastic structuring of several stories. Most striking, and most carefully studied, is the arrangement of the five episodes in Mark 2:1—3:6.[46] This sequence begins and ends with episodes that have both similar subjects and parallel internal structure: healing—controversy—healing. The cast of characters is even similar: Jesus, a man paralyzed or a man with a withered hand, and the scribes/Pharisees. In both, Jesus' direct address to the man sets off the controversy, and, in both, Jesus discerns the scribes'/Pharisees' unspoken objection. The reactions are diametrically opposed, but the Pharisees' and Herodians' defensive determination to destroy Jesus in the fifth episode corresponds to the people's enthusiastic response to Jesus in the first episode. The second and fourth episodes also display similarities, in subject (eating), parallel structure as controversy stories, and the cast of characters (Jesus, the disciples, and Pharisees). Both stories also conclude with parallel proverbs and parallel "I"/"son of man" sayings. The central episode in the sequence of five begins with the opposite of eating (fasting), which leads to the real issue of the whole sequence: something unusual is happening with Jesus! What is fermenting will burst through the old wineskins, just as what is happening with Jesus is breaking through the standard, old, officially promulgated social-religious forms that the scribes/Pharisees defend. Inter-related patterns, themes, internal sequences, and overall sequences such as these help both the oral performer and the hearers to remember and create relations of significance between the episodes and to communicate or as-similate the significance of the overall sequence of episodes.

---

45. Ibid., 49.
46. Dewey, *Markan Public Debate*.

Moreover, the patterning of episodes, with its combination of themes and characters, for oral performance in this sequence displays many connections with the content and themes of the Gospel as a whole. Healing (including exorcism) and eating (including the wilderness feedings and covenantal meal at Passover) are two of Jesus' principal activities throughout Mark's narrative. Both actions anticipate but also manifest the coming of the kingdom of God (= the renewal of Israel), the overall theme of the Gospel. This sequence of five episodes also exemplifies how Jesus' actions challenge the dominant order in Jerusalem, as represented here by the scribes and Pharisees, a concern that is also central to the dominant plot of the Gospel as a whole. Again, it is typical of oral narrative that particular sequences of episodes/stanzas exemplify in microcosm the overall theme or plot of the narrative/epic poem.

Yet another example of oral "narrative maneuvering," where the composer/performer inserts episodes into a structure or pattern already available in the oral tradition, can be discerned in the second major narrative step of Mark's story, following Jesus' first long speech in and about parables. For some time now, close readings of Mark have discerned two chains of stories with the same order behind the sequence of episodes in Mark 4:35–8:26. The first "chain" consists of a sea crossing, an exorcism, two healings (arranged in one of Mark's "sandwich" formations), and a wilderness feeding (4:35–41; 5:1–20; 5:21–24+35–43; 5:24–34; 6:30–44). The second has the same sequence up to the last two stories: sea crossing, exorcism, healing, wilderness feeding, healing (6:45–52; 7:24–30; 7:31–37; 8:1–10; 8:22–26). In this second chain, the second healing is placed last in order to frame the next major narrative step (8:22—10:52), with a healing of blind figures at the beginning and end (yet another feature that would aid in oral performance and hearing). Evidently, prior to or parallel to the composition/performance of the Gospel of Mark, sets of stories were told that clearly carried the message of how Jesus was enacting the renewal of Israel as a prophet like Moses and Elijah, the great founder (sea crossing and wilderness feeding) and renewer (healings) of Israel, respectively, in popular Israelite cultural memory.

The overarching Markan Gospel story incorporates these chains and elaborates and reinforces the message of the renewal of Israel by inserting additional episodes into the developing narrative. The so-called "rejection" at Nazareth (6:1–6) indicates that Jesus is far more than a mere local figure. In the mission of the Twelve (6:7–13), representative of the twelve tribes, Jesus indicates in no uncertain terms that his program of the kingdom of God is a renewal of Israel. The story of Herod Antipas' arrest and execution of the Baptist (6:16–28) prefigures and exemplifies what happens to prophets engaged in a renewal of Israel, and specifically what is about the happen to Jesus. In the controversy with the scribes and Pharisees (7:5–13), Jesus' appeal to the basic covenantal commandment of God to insist that the people's produce is needed to feed the people, over against the temple representatives' attempt, by their "traditions of the elders" (*qorban*), to extricate support for the temple—as this episode both exemplifies and anticipates the escalating conflict between Jesus and the rulers of Israel and their representatives. The theme and narrative line of the Gospel as a whole is the same as that of the component "chains" of stories that supply the framework of the Markan narrative, but now considerably elaborated by the insertion of additional stories in which Jesus is carrying out a renewal of Israel over against the rulers of Israel.

### Oral Narrative Engaged with Historical Context

As has become evident in the last few paragraphs above, Mark's overall narrative, like its oral components, directly engages a particular historical context. In contrast with some treatments of oral poetry or narrative in other fields, Kelber's discussion of "Mark's Oral Legacy" discerns that oral communication is embedded in its context. In contrast with many biblical scholars and other humanists, moreover, Kelber recognizes that the context had not only cultural and aesthetic aspects but political and economic as well. In fact, "nonlinguistic features have priority over linguistic ones"[47] Oral communication receives powerful ideological and situational support from its context.

At points in his discussion of the various forms of the oral materials incorporated into the Gospel of Mark, Kelber notes how particular stories engage the political conflict inherent in the historical conflict. The storyteller's departure from the standard narrative formula in the account of the Gerasene demoniac (Mark 5:1–20)—not only naming the demon with the code word *legion* but narrating at length the self–destruction of the "battalion" of swine in the sea—"vents anti-Roman sentiments and encourages wishful thinking with regard to the occupying troops."[48] Political or political-economic conflict is evident in other exorcism stories and in many healing stories as well. In many cases, research on the historical context of Roman Palestine (certainly the context of Markan materials and clearly the background of Mark) since the publication of *OWG*, such as investigation of the division between rulers and peasants and the regional differences between

---

47. Kelber, *The Oral and the Written Gospel*, 75.
48. Ibid., 53.

Galilee and Jerusalem/Judea, enables us to see this. Even if the mention of "the scribes (from Jerusalem)" in the Beelzebul controversy comes from the Markan narrator, the story still displays a sharp conflict between Jerusalem rulers and Galilean prophet (3.22–27). Further, as we now recognize from a term used in analogous fashion in the DSS, Jesus' "defeat" of the demon in the Capernaum assembly (*synagoge*, 1:22–28) alludes clearly to the defeat of an imperial enemy. If we attend to important textual variants in the early manuscript evidence—that Jesus is "moved to anger," not "by pity"—then the story of the healing of the "leper" at Mark 1:40–45 clearly represents Jesus in conflict with the temple system and its "scriptural" codes. Other healing stories bring Jesus directly into confrontation with the scribes and Pharisees (2:1–12; 3:1–6). In the oral tradition of stories about Jesus, the striking aspect of conflict is not simply a matter of oral storytelling, but is rooted in the conflictual political-economic structures in which both storyteller and the hearers, as well as Jesus, were embedded.[49]

If we look more closely, now with the benefit of recent research into several key aspects of the historical context of Mark, we can discern that political-economic and (inseparably) cultural conflict are also portrayed in the other forms of oral tradition that have been incorporated into Mark: the parables and the controversy and didactic stories. Given the cultural memory of the song of the vineyard and the persistent conflict between villagers and the temple high priesthood, the parable of the tenants (Mark 12:1–8) would certainly have alluded to and evoked the fundamental political–economic conflict of rulers and ruled. Recent research makes the most dramatic difference for our ability to recognize the persistent conflict between Jesus and the Jerusalem priestly rulers and their scribal/Pharisaic representatives, and even his conflict with Roman rule, portrayed in the controversy/didactic stories.[50] The sharpest conflicts are surely Jesus' condemnation of the scribes and Pharisees for attempting to expropriate local food production that was desperately needed by Galilean families for support of the temple (via the device of *qorban*, Mark 7:1–13), and Jesus' skillful dodge of the attempted entrapment question of whether tribute to Rome was "lawful" by focusing on "the things of God" (everything) versus "the things of Caesar" (nothing; 12:13–17).[51]

Again, we can go a step further, from the oral components of Mark's Gospel to the Gospel as a whole. Not only do most of the component oral stories exhibit the conflict inherent in the historical context in which, says

---

49. Ibid., 54–55.

50. Cf. ibid., 71–77.

51. Horsley, *Jesus and the Spiral of Violence*, 306–17.

Kelber, the oral communication is embedded and on which it is dependent. The broader narrative of the Gospel even more explicitly and fully displays the conflict inherent in the historical context. Almost certainly the Gospel narrative is responsible for the explicit mention of "the scribes from Jerusalem" who oppose Jesus (in the framing of the controversies, Mark 3:22; 7:1–2), and probably also for the Pharisees' and Herodians' conspiracy to destroy him (already in 3:6). The Gospel narrative must be responsible for Jesus' explanation of the parable of the sower, which includes "persecution" among the difficulties encountered by the seed/word (4:17). The overall plotting of the Gospel is responsible for the insertion of episodes into the two chains of stories (4:35–8:26) that embellish Jesus' renewal of Israel over against the rulers of Israel. And the plotting of the Gospel as an overall story is responsible for making Jesus' renewal of Israel over against the Jerusalem and Roman rulers the main conflict of the Markan narrative. Oral narrative is embedded in a particular context, and Mark's narrative is very closely interrelated with the conflicts inherent in Judea and Galilee under Roman rule in the first century BCE.

## Parables and the Parabolic Gospel

One of the highlights of *OWG* is Kelber's discussion of parables as the quintessential form of oral communication among the oral components incorporated into the Gospel of Mark. Not surprisingly, some aspects of the interpretation of the parables in the early 1980s, on which Kelber's discussion draws, were rooted in the print culture of established biblical studies. Despite his deployment of some of this language, Kelber's own discussion cuts through inappropriate concepts. Perhaps the first step in understanding parables is to recognize that they not only have *no original form*, but also have *no meaning* in themselves.[52] As a distinctive form of communication, a parable is spoken by a speaker to hearers in a particular context. Indeed, as Kelber himself points out, the very contents of Jesus' parables are "slices of life" drawn from the experiences of Galilean peasants.[53] It hardly needs pointing out that, as oral communication to hearers, the voicing of a parable would be accompanied by extra–verbal elements such as tone of voice, gestures, and other aspects of the speaking/hearing context. Parables are mnemonically shaped to facilitate speaking and hearing.[54]

---

52. Kelber, *The Oral and the Written Gospel*, 62.

53. Ibid., 59.

54. Ibid., 58.

The communication that happens in the telling of a parable is utterly dependent on both hearers and context.[55] Far from having a meaning in itself that the hearer must interpret, a parable metaphorically invites a hearer to recognize a situation and take the appropriate action, one that the story/content of the parable evokes. This also sets up a situation in which some hearers "get it" and others do not, thus creating a potential dichotomy between insiders and outsiders. For example, the parables of the growing seed and the mustard seed included in Jesus' parables speech (Mark 4:26–29, 30–32) invite hearers to recognize what the kingdom of God is like, to have confidence in its eventual fulfillment, and to join in advancing that fulfillment. More elaborate parables invite hearers into the story and ask them to identify with what is happening so that they can recognize the relationship between the story and a situation in their own life circumstances.[56]

One of Kelber's key insights in *OWG* is that Mark's Gospel as a whole is a parable. This observation makes it possible to recognize that, since parables are the quintessential form of oral communication, the Gospel as a whole must be oral communication, performed to hearers in a particular context. As Kelber notes, "for the Markan Jesus, it seems, the significance of speaking in parables goes beyond those stories technically called parables."[57] We begin to "get" this point in several connections. The parable of the tenants (Mark 12:1–12) not only fits well in its immediate narrative context, but can be heard as a story analogous to Mark's story as a whole,[58] a story that stands in continuity with—indeed, presents Jesus' mission as the fulfillment of—the (hi)story of Israel. As is often observed, Jesus' parable of the tenants of the vineyard is an "updated" version of Isaiah's "song of the vineyard" (Isaiah 5), which functioned as a prophetic indictment of the monarchic rulers of the people. Moreover, not only do the high priestly rulers of Israel in Mark's story recognize that they are implicated in the parable Jesus just told to them as the hearers standing on their own "turf" (the temple), but the hearers of Mark's Gospel story are invited to recognize that Jesus, in telling the parable, as part of Mark's overall parabolic story, has just pronounced God's condemnation on the rulers of Israel, who not only exploited the people (Israel, traditionally symbolized by the vineyard) but were about to arrest Jesus to hand him over to be killed by the Romans. Some of the details that now appear in Marks' telling of the parable may have emerged

---

55. Ibid., 62, 112.
56. Ibid., 61.
57. Ibid., 58.
58. Ibid., 112–13.

in repeated retellings, because the parable was so invitingly analogous to the history it invited hearers to recognize.

Kelber also suggests that, just as a speaker tells a parable to move people to action, so Mark's overall story aims to move people to action—in imitation of Jesus. Jesus' discussions with the disciples after his first and third announcements that he must be arrested, killed, and rise (8:27–38; 10:32–45) have implications for the hearers of the Gospel. And if modern, print-oriented readers did not "get it" before, the "open ending" of this parabolic oral narrative (Mark 16:1–8) might well stimulate some leading questions. Mark's ending is not just open, but parabolic, insofar as the hearer—prepared by earlier indications in the narrative that Jesus will be going back up to "Galilee," the setting of his mission, after his crucifixion—is invited to recognize that not only the disciples but they themselves are to meet him and, presumably, to continue the renewal of Israel. As Kelber notes, like the parables included in the Gospel, Mark's overall story of the coming of the kingdom of God points beyond itself to the kingdom of God.[59]

59. Ibid., 123–24.

## 11

# IMAGINING MARK'S STORY COMPOSED IN ORAL PERFORMANCE

The stories of prophets may be better understood as history rather than
biography . . . Mark's Gospel is less a life of Jesus than a history of the . . .
events that come to a head in him . . . A composing performer embodies in
him or herself the tradition people are waiting to hear . . . What holds Mark
together is not only oral and communal and grounded in the prophetic
role. Mark holds the broadest canvas for its news of a historical reversal of
this world's power structure.

—ANTOINETTE CLARK WIRE (2011)

IT HAS BEEN DIFFICULT IN THE EXTREME FOR INTERPRETERS
of texts in fields deeply embedded in modern western print culture to break
free of their bondage to its assumptions and concepts. This is especially difficult for biblical scholars, whose careers are dedicated to and dependent
on interpretation of Scripture, the Holy *Writ*. Those who have pioneered
the exploration of various facets of oral communication and performance
have taken their cues largely from other fields of study, often from studies
of peoples and periods of history where writing or print culture had not yet
become prominent or dominant. The pioneers of such exploration in biblical studies, as well-trained academics, have carefully defined and limited
their investigations, departing from or challenging print culture in cautious
steps one aspect at a time. This has been professionally prudent, considering
the inertia or outright resistance in a field devoted to (sacred) *written* texts.

Much of the exploration of oral performance of texts that were later
included in the New Testament has focused on the Gospel of Mark. The

major breakthrough was made by Werner Kelber in *The Oral and the Written Gospel* (1983). Having read widely in groundbreaking studies of orality and oral tradition in other fields, he discerned that the concept (of the "behavior") of oral tradition operative in studies of the Synoptic Gospel tradition was based on the adaptation of (what were assumed to be) one written text (Mark) by another (Matthew or Luke). On the basis of studies of (genuinely) oral tradition in other fields, he presented a highly illuminating alternative understanding of the cultivation in oral tradition of the sayings and parables of Jesus and the stories about Jesus. The assumptions of print-culture, however, continued to dominate interpretation of Mark's Gospel as well as biblical studies in general, as illustrated in a major critical study of the origins of Mark.

> Mark's Gospel . . . was composed at a desk in a scholar's study lined with texts . . . In Mark's study were chains of miracle stories, collections of pronouncement stories in various states of elaboration, some form of Q, memos on parables and proof texts, the scriptures, including the prophets, written materials from the Christ cult, and other literature representative of Hellenistic Judaism.[1]

Nevertheless, continuing explorations of oral-performative features in the Gospel of Mark in the 1990s generated ever more confident assertions that it would have been performed orally. The oral formulas identified by Parry and Lord in the Iliad and Odyssey had been suggestive for interpreters of Mark. Pieter Botha took the important step of looking not for the same formulas as in the *Iliad* and *Odyssey*, but for the corresponding formulas and cues distinctive to the Markan narrative.[2] In a whole series of articles, Joanna Dewey taught us to listen for oral narrative devices in the interwoven tapestry of Mark's story, and to discern features of the Gospel as an "oral/aural event."[3] The oral narrative patterns and devices in the different kinds of pre-Markan stories identified by Kelber,[4] moreover, can be discerned also in the overall Markan narrative as well (as discussed in chap. 10). On the basis of these and other explorations, those of us involved in the investigation of the oral features of the Gospel of Mark were ever more

---

1. Mack, *Myth of Innocence*, 322–23.

2. Botha, "Mark's Story as Oral-Traditional Literature," now in *Orality and Literacy*, chap. 2.

3. See especially Dewey, "Mark as Interwoven Tapestry," and "Gospel of Mark as an Oral–aural Event."

4. Kelber, *The Oral and the Written Gospel*.

confident in our exploration of the story as having been orally performed in communities of a Jesus movement.[5]

Yet our discussion of Mark in oral performance often involved an apologetic qualification. After we had recognized that in the ancient world texts continued to be performed orally even if they had been inscribed on papyrus, it did not seem important to determine how a given text was composed in order to appreciate the text-in-performance. Our explorations of the features and aspects of the Markan story in performance, "even after it may have existed in writing," seems to reflect two remaining cautions. It seemed easier to induce colleagues to appreciate the Gospel in/as oral performance if we did not confront them simultaneously with the reasons why Mark' story would have been composed in performance, which would pose an even broader challenge to the print-cultural assumptions in which the field is rooted. Given the elementary stage of our own investigations of oral performance, moreover, we could not yet ourselves confidently imagine just how Mark's story could have been composed in (continuing) performance. Even though we had become aware of many orally composed and performed epics that are much longer and more complex than Mark, we still had difficulty imagining how a text of such length and complexity could have been composed other than in writing.

Now, however, Anne Wire has stated a strong "case for Mark composed in performance."[6] In a carefully crafted, step by step presentation she has addressed the inevitable objections from a field deeply embedded in print culture, drawing judiciously on much of the telling implications of recent lines of research discussed in the chapters above. And she makes a suggestive case that the story pattern of contemporary popular prophets and their movements was formative for the composition of the Markan story. Emboldened by her initiative, I would like to try to deepen, broaden, and thus strengthen the case.

Much of the consideration of Mark as story and comparisons with other, near contemporary stories does not delve very deeply into what kind of story Mark is, much less attempt to "read" or "hear" the story in its historical context considered in its complexity. Indeed, much of the early interpretation of Mark (and the other Gospels) as story consisted of the application of types of literary criticism developed on modern prose fiction (such as "reader-response criticism"). Some of the features on which interpretation focused, such as "character-development," that are characteristic of modern

---

5. See the summary discussion of "Mark as Oral Performance," in Horsley, *Hearing the Whole Story*, chap. 2; and Dewey, "Good Story."

6. Wire, *Mark Composed in Performance*.

prose, are difficult to find in ancient stories. Even the suggestive studies of folk-lore, of various kinds of stories, and of other orally-performed texts such as epic poems have attended primarily to matters such as "literary" form, narrative patterns, (repetition of) motifs, and repeated formulas and narrative cues. The highly complex, interdisciplinary theory of John Miles Foley that I have found so stimulating, for example, in insisting on the importance of *context* and (metonymic references to cultural) *tradition*, as well as analysis of the *text*, refers mainly to the immediate context of the "performance arena" and the performance tradition of a particular form of epic or poetry (such as of the "Homeric" epics).[7]

In Foley's multidisciplinary theory, however, analysis of *text*, *context*, and *tradition* are integral steps toward the goal of appreciating not so much the *meaning* of a text as the *work* that a performed text does in the community of hearers. Unless a given performed story is little more than entertainment (which still does work of cultural maintenance), however, it seems necessary to understand the social, even the broader historical context of the text and its hearers. The story of a hero who takes bold action, for example, can inspire the followers also to take action and/or to form a movement of solidarity focused on the hero. Finding Foley's theory of oral performance highly suggestive for understanding how cultural forms and features are embedded with and interact with social-political contexts, particularly in crisis situations, I have attempted to include social-political circumstances as well as cultural features in analysis of text, context, and tradition.[8] Consideration of the *text* thus includes discernment of the kinds of texts in relation to their social location and social function. Consideration of the *context* includes the historical circumstances of the audience. And consideration of how the text (metonymically) references the *tradition* is extended to include the broader tradition from which the performer and hearers live and work, which Kelber has compared to the "biosphere" in which they live.[9]

I am now becoming convinced that consideration of these three interrelated facets of any text, broadened and deepened in further exploration of Mark, may enable us to gain a clearer sense of how the Gospel story was composed (developed) in a movement of Jesus' followers. The first step would be to have a clear sense of the basic story, the main plot (as indicated in the dominant conflict) of the Gospel story. The Gospel of Mark

7. Foley, *Immanent Art*; Foley, *Singer of Tales in Performance*; Foley, *How to Read an Oral Poem*.

8. For example, Horsley with Draper, *Whoever Hears You Hears Me*; Horsley, *Hearing the Whole Story*; Horsley, *Jesus in Context*.

9. Kelber, "Jesus and Tradition," 151–62, esp, 159.

(as we have it) presents a complex story, elaborated into a rich tapestry of interwoven themes and subplots developed in a sequence of repetitious episodes.[10] Even though the main plot is not linear, does not build through suspense to an unexpected climax, it does have a main plot. I am imagining something like the "already existing narrative tradition" or "framework" that Dewey projects behind the more elaborate Markan story as we have it.[11] But since we have access to a basic story only through the fuller Markan story, I imagine a basic story that is already fairly complex—certainly more so than a narrative framework of Jesus' ministry, death, and resurrection, which seems like later reductive creedal summaries.

The second step will be to note how some of the principal features of the basic story are given in the broader historical context of its origins and how some of the ostensible history of Jesus' mission portrayed in Mark fits in the history of the Galilean and Judean people under Roman rule, as known from other sources. To a considerable extent the characters, settings, and sequence of events of the (historical) story (the *text*) are the same as or continue into the *context* in which the story is performed.

The third step will be to recognize how the Markan story (history) of Jesus' mission and the historical movements that it parallels were rooted in and resonated with Israelite cultural tradition, particularly Israelite popular tradition (sometimes in opposition to the official Judean tradition) as carried in the people's social memory. This would have been operative in the interaction between Jesus and his followers and opponents as well as in the (Markan) Jesus movement that resulted from that interaction. In how the story is shaped by and resonates with tradition we are considering not just the developing "Jesus-tradition," but the much broader and deeper Israelite tradition in which the narrower Jesus-tradition was itself deeply rooted.

As will become increasingly evident in the following discussion, the aspects of the story-in-performance that will be analyzed in sequence, text, context, and tradition, are inseparable in the basic story as well as in its component episodes. It is impossible to summarize the basic story of the Gospel of Mark without noting the prominent references to and reminiscences of Israelite history and tradition. And the story gives explicit indications of the context in which the history it narrates (ostensibly) takes place.

In taking all of these three main steps it will be important to avoid or to cut through some of the most basic synthetic modern scholarly and/ or Christian theological constructs that obscure the Markan story and the

---

10. See again Dewey, "Mark as Interwoven Tapestry"; and Dewey, "Gospel of Mark as an Oral–aural Event."

11. Dewey, "Good Story," 496–97.

complex historical context in which it originated and the Israelite (popular) cultural tradition in which it was based and with which it resonated. Principal among these synthetic constructs are "(early) Judaism" and "(early) Christianity" and "the (Hebrew) Bible," none of which existed yet as standardly imagined in the field of "biblical" studies. Also seriously problematic as well as anachronistic are the synthetic constructs of "apocalyptic(ism)" (and "eschatological") and "the Messiah/messianic." Recent expansion and increasing precision of our knowledge of a variety of near contemporary written textual sources, political-economic-religious structures and dynamics, and historical movements and events enable us to be fairly specific in making references and in discerning particular social forms, social relations, power relations, and political conflicts.

In previous books and articles I have explored all of these three steps just outlined.[12] Drawing on those previous discussions I will attempt to bring them together in support of the case for the Markan story composed in performance. Before launching into these three steps, however, the implications of some other recent researches further open the way to consideration of how Mark's story may have been composed in (ongoing) performance.

## Recent Research That Converges toward Composition in Performance

In the decade or so since those of us working on features of oral performance in Mark became able to imagine the whole story in oral performance, largely separate lines of research in areas that are closely related have reached conclusions that can strongly reinforce the case for composition in performance.

First, contrary to the standard assumption in biblical studies, it has become evident that composition is separable from writing and education. Biblical scholars, particularly those specialists on the Gospel tradition, have worked on the assumption that oral tradition consisted merely of separate sayings, parables, or brief (controversy or "miracle") stories; and that anything more complex, such as a collection of sayings or stories involved writing by an author or "evangelist." Scholars who recognized the popular origins of Jesus' sayings or parables, for example, still sought literate people who could have composed the "collection" of (clusters of) sayings commonly called "Q." They suggested that lower level administrators and bureaucrats

---

12. All of these steps are included in Horsley, *Hearing the Whole Story*; and Horsley, *Jesus in Context*, chaps. 4, 7, and 9, but not adduced to make a case for Mark's story as composed in performance.

("village scribes") in Galilee and nearby areas possessed sufficient education to have composed in the "relatively learned and characteristically
scribal genre" of instruction previously identified as what had crystalized
the collection of sayings into "Q"[13] Closer examination, however, indicated
that the literary and inscriptional references adduced did not support the
hypothesis.[14] Inscriptions from Egypt referring to "village scribes" (*komogrammateis*), for example, indicate that, far from having sufficient education to compose in writing, they could barely inscribe their own names.[15]
As anthropologists and folklorists have explained, non-literate uneducated
peoples are capable of delivering shorter or longer speeches and of telling
complex stories, some of which draw heavily on the "little traditions" that
they cultivate orally (see chap. 5 above). And as any of us who have attended
community meetings can attest, people without much formal education can
tell sustained stories and deliver effective speeches.

While the training of professional scribes who served in ancient regimes such as the temple-state in Jerusalem were trained in reading and
writing, the scribe who composed-and-dictated a text might well be different from the scribe who inscribed the text on parchment or papyrus. It
now seems clear that the (nonliterate) apostle Paul composed-and-dictated
the complex arguments in his letters in the hearing of a scribe (with good
craft-literacy) and probably also of the envoy who would transmit the letter to the assembly to which it was addressed and "deliver" it orally, with
manuscript in hand."[16] Composition (-dictation) and education and writing
were separable and often separate.

Second, recent research of text critics, both of books of the Hebrew
Bible and of the Gospels, provides strong support to the case for composition in performance. As discussed in chap. 1, close examination of the manuscripts found at Qumran of books later included in the Hebrew Bible has
led to the conclusion that these texts existed in more than one version and
were still developing in late second-temple times.[17] Composition of these
texts was a process that continued in their cultivation by oral recitation even
in scribal circles. Recent research into ancient scribal practice, heretofore
separate from text-critical research, strongly reinforces these new findings

---

13. Kloppenborg, *Literary Convention; Excavating Q* ; Arnal, *Jesus and the Village
Scribes.*

14. Horsley, "Introduction" to *Oral Performance*, 10–15.

15. Youtie, "*Agrammatos.*"

16. Botha, "Letter Writing," 21–24.

17. Ulrich, *Dead Sea Scrolls*; most recently, Tov, *Textual Criticism.*

of text critics.[18] Judean scribes, like their ancient Near Eastern counterparts, were trained to read and write and inscribed key texts on scrolls. But they learned and cultivated those same texts by recitation, so that they were "inscribed on the tablet of the heart" (in their memory). This continuing scribal oral cultivation of authoritative texts, and the resulting multiformity of texts in oral tradition, would seem to have been closely related to the multiformity of those same texts in written form. The implications of these very recent lines of research, however, especially in combination, seriously undermine one of the most basic assumptions of biblical studies: that oral tradition is fluid and "unreliable" but that the writing down of the tradition provides permanence and reliability. It can now be recognized that the fixity of written texts is an assumption rooted in print-culture and is not applicable to ancient written texts any more than ancient performed texts.

Recent text-criticism of the Gospels is finding that the (fragmentary) texts were extremely varied into the fourth century, when some standardization begins to be evident.[19] Considerable variation is evident especially in passages that would have been particularly important in community life, such as Jesus' statements about marriage. Text critics are thus suggesting that it is impossible to "establish" an early text of a Gospel—which also reminds us that the Greek texts of the Gospels that form the basis of translations and that scholars interpret are modern constructions of text-critical scholars. That is, the text of the particular phrases, sayings, and little stories that we biblical scholars have been trained to interpret may well have been variable, "unstable."

This makes all the more important what we can learn from scholars in other fields who study lengthy performed texts: while particular lines and stanzas vary from performance to performance, the larger story tends to remain constant. Drawing on studies of orally performed epics and stories from several different cultures, Foley made this point repeatedly.[20] On the basis of his extensive acquaintance with African oral histories, Jan Vansina found that as stories were fused from several earlier accounts they quickly acquired a stable form. Thereafter in continuing performance the main plot and sequence of episodes remained fairly stable, changing only slowly.[21] The clear implication of such cross-cultural studies combined with the recent text critical work for the Gospel of Mark and other Gospels is that in per-

18. Carr, *Tablet of the Heart*; Jaffee, *Torah in the Mouth*, chap. 1; Horsley, *Scribes, Visionaries*, chaps. 5–6.

19. Parker, *Living Text*; Epp, "Multivalence"; Epp, "Oxyrhynchus"; Haines-Eitzen, *Guardians of Letters*.

20. For example, in Foley, *How to Read an Oral Poem*.

21. Vansina, *Oral Tradition*, 12–17.

formed texts the overall story may well be more stable and dependable (for our analysis and interpretation) than the particular components.

Third, we can learn from the recent studies by classics scholars on composition practices among the (highly literate) Greek and Roman elite and from traditional storytelling of lengthy and complex stories in a wide variety of (pre-print nonliterate) peoples.

Pliny left a telling account of his own compositional practice, even of highly discursive texts.

> [When I wake] If I have anything on hand I work it out in my head, choosing and correcting the wording, and the amount I achieve depends on the ease or difficulty with which my thoughts can be marshaled and kept in my head. Then I call my secretary, the shutters are opened, and I dictate what I have put into shape; he goes out, is recalled, and again dismissed. Three or four hours after I first wake I betake myself according to the weather either to the terrace or the covered arcade, work out the rest of my subject, and dictate it. (Letters 9.36).

Pliny would later perform the text he had composed in his head to a group of friends. As Jocelyn Penny Small, who cites and discusses many such passages from Greek and Roman elite figures, points out, "the English word 'dictate' and its relatives go directly back to the Latin *dicto*, which meant either our 'dictate' or—and this is significant—'compose.'"[22] The common way of composing something was through dictation—and "compose" was the more common meaning of *dicto* well into the middle ages. In another window onto how the Greek and Roman elite composed mentally in preparation for a performance, Quintilian explains that orators composed their speeches, in general structure and words, relying on the resourcefulness of memory, and "without any recourse to writing" (10.6.1).[23]

For repeated composition in performance by the nonliterate, the book of Jeremiah includes the story of how Jeremiah dictated (performed) all the prophecies that Yahweh had spoken to him for over a decade to the scribe Baruch, who wrote them on a scroll and then in turn proclaimed the prophecies to the audience in the Lord's house. After the outraged king defiantly burned the scroll, Jeremiah again recited all those prophecies while Baruch wrote them on another scroll (Jeremiah 36:2–6, 16–18, 21–26, 32). Having all of the speeches God had spoken to him in memory, Jeremiah could recite them again and again. Disciples of prophets and circles of scribes continued such abilities and practices. The spokespersons who continued to

22. Small, *Wax Tablets*, 185.

23. Ibid. 182.

perform the prophetic speeches of Jesus appear to stand in just such a tradition, as suggested at points in Q speeches themselves (Q 6:20–26; 7:18–35; 11:39–52; 13:34–35).

Even more directly pertinent to the composition of a complex story such as Mark's Gospel in memory-and-oral performance are the many, many nonliterate storytellers that ethnographers, anthropologists, and folklorists have recorded, documented, and studied, for example, among Native American or African peoples. Such storytellers hold (the templates of) often long and complex stories and "histories" in their memory, from which they can perform the story or history anew in ceremonial or other community occasions. As often as not the setting and characters and their interaction in the stories are given in the setting, circumstances, and social-political interaction of the people's or community's life-situation. It is difficult for us moderns who have relied for generations now on print culture for the storage of memory to imagine the deep capacity of the individual and collective memory in traditional (pre-print) societies. In her remarkable and now highly influential study of memory, Mary Carruthers remarks that "many things I believed could not be done, such as composing difficult works at length from memory, had to be entertained as possibilities—even as expected and much admired behavior."[24]

It is thus inappropriate for biblical scholars rooted in the assumptions of print culture to impose the limitations of their own imagination onto composition in antiquity. Texts such as the complex arguments of Paul, the Q speeches, and the Markan story themselves call for sensitivity and appreciation of how their composition, supported by memory, was embedded in oral communication, emerged from periodic oral performance, and "worked" in oral performance. Parallel to the lettered Greco-Roman elite such as Pliny, nonliterate ordinary people could also compose songs and speeches and tell complex stories. And if a particular story proved compelling and was told repeatedly, it could take on distinctive form as an oral text in continuing performance.

In accord with the way I am imagining the composition (development) of the Gospel of Mark in repeated performance as given in the historical situation and events and shaped from/by Israelite tradition, and to incorporate the agency of composers-performers who gave shape and embellishment to the story, I will speak in terms of plural composers in the following analysis. By this I do not mean composition by committee. I mean rather that we cannot judge precisely where and when in the process

---

24. Carruthers, *Book of Memory*, 260. I owe the reminder about Carruther's telling observation to Pieter Botha, *Orality and Literacy*, 112.

of the story's development the basic story had taken form and when various subplots and other features emerged. Given the ancient oral communication environment and the integral relationship between Mark's story and the community or movement from which it emerged and that it addressed, we must imagine (a series of) multiple performer-composers.

## The Basic Story in the Gospel of Mark

Earlier interpreters of the Gospels sought in other ancient stories for a genre that Mark was evidently following. Scholars who became aware that Mark's Gospel consists of a narrative in episodes have somewhat similarly been on the look-out for an ancient story-pattern that would "explain" the arrangement of episodes in their Markan sequence. An alternative way to begin would be to discern the basic story or plot of the Gospel. While it unfolds in a sequence of episodes, the basic plot of the overall story would be something simpler and different from that sequence: the main program and actions of the protagonist in interaction with the other main characters who react, in the context of the historical situation, leading to the climactic conflict.

The recognition of the Gospel of Mark as a sustained narrative in the 1970s and 1980s[25] did not lead to clarity about its plot. Prior to the discovery of Mark as a story, modern theological interpreters had taken the Gospel to be about discipleship. Following this tradition of interpretation, many of those who recognized that Mark is a narrative still read the Gospel as a primarily religious story focused on the conflict between Jesus and his disciples. After being called and commissioned to assist in Jesus' "ministry," the disciples became afraid and misunderstood the character of Jesus' messiahship. Finally as Jesus was arrested, tried, and crucified, the disciples abandoned and denied him. The new-found narrative criticism was used to embellish the modern individualistic understanding of the Gospel as a paradigmatic story of the struggle to be faithful disciples. While Mark's story does indeed portray a conflict between Jesus and the disciples, that is only one of several interrelated conflicts woven into the narrative.[26]

The key to the main plot of a story is usually its dominant conflict, and the key to the latter is the climax of the story. In Mark's story this is surely Jesus' sustained confrontation of the Jerusalem rulers in the temple,

---

25. Among the most discerning early "readings" were Kelber, *Mark's Story*; and Rhoads and Michie, *Mark as Story*; excellent critical review of "narrative criticism" in Moore, *Literary Criticism*.

26. More extensive discussion in Horsley, *Hearing the Whole Story*, esp. chaps. 1–5.

followed by his arrest by the high priests and his crucifixion as a leader of insurrection by the Roman governor. Even though the high priests do not appear earlier in the narrative set in Galilee, the earlier steps in the story also tell of the same basic conflict that later comes to a climax in Jerusalem. The scribes and Pharisees who "come down from Jerusalem" as representatives of the high priests accuse Jesus of usurping the prerogatives of the temple and priesthood, for example in declaring the forgiveness of sin. Early in the story the Pharisees and Herodians plot to destroy him, and Jesus condemns the scribes and Pharisees for working against the interest of the people.

Meanwhile, what he is doing that evokes such opposition is preaching that the kingdom of God is at hand and manifesting the direct rule of God in exorcisms of invasive spirits and healing various illnesses in the villages of Galilee and beyond, while recruiting disciples and commissioning them to extend his own program of preaching and healing to other villages. As clearly indicated in the appointment of the twelve and in his performance of acts of power such as sea-crossings, healings, and wilderness feedings, and clinched by his appearance on the mountain with Moses and Elijah, Jesus is engaged in the renewal of the people of Israel as a prophet like Moses and Elijah. Indeed, as he is heading toward Jerusalem for the climactic confrontation with the rulers, he engages in a series of dialogues that, citing the covenantal commandments, constitute a renewal of the Mosaic covenant.

It is clear that the basic story in the Gospel is about how Jesus is generating the renewal of Israel in opposition to and by the high priests and the Romans who maintained them in power. The Gospel unfolds as a sequence of episodes, "one thing after another." But all of the episodes, all of Jesus' proclamation and action, his announcement of the kingdom and his healings and exorcisms, as well as his conflicts with the Pharisees and his confrontations with the rulers, are components of the basic story of his renewal of the people over against the rulers.

## The Historical Context

The basic story of the Gospel of Mark is not only closely tied to a particular historical context, but many of the most fundamental features of the story are given in and determined by the historical context in which it is set and, evidently, originated. It was previously standard to locate the "author" who "wrote" the Gospel of Mark in Rome, explicitly or implicitly following the early tradition articulated by Papias that "Mark" was Peter's interpreter (*hermeneutes*; Eusebius, *Hist. eccl.* 3.39.1–4). But there is no reason internal to

Mark's story to locate it in Rome.[27] The "Latinisms" such as "Legion" were key features of Roman imperial rule in most places. More recently the Gospel has been located in Syria or even Galilee.[28] Indeed, the narrative has Jesus and his disciples leaving their "footprints" in villages or regions immediately north and east of Galilee. The point is that Mark's story fits what is known from extra-Gospel sources, particularly the accounts of the contemporary Judean historian Josephus, of the political-economic-religious structure and dynamics of Roman Palestine and is strikingly parallel to other popular movements in the same historical context.

As Josephus indicates repeatedly, there was a deep gulf and structural conflict between the Roman rulers and the client rulers they appointed and the vast majority of people who lived in hundreds of village communities.[29] The fundamental conflict in the Markan story is thus given in and determined by the historical situation during Jesus' lifetime as ultimately dictated by the Romans. They had imposed "Herod" Antipas as the ruler in Galilee, assisted by "Herodian" officers (in the two new cities he built), and elevated the high priestly aristocracy of the Jerusalem temple-state as rulers of Judea under the oversight of the Roman governor who came to Jerusalem at Passover time with a cohort of soldiers in anticipation of popular disruption. Since the mid-second century BCE, "scribes and Pharisees" had served the temple-state as advisers and representatives especially knowledgeable in Judean laws and traditions, the Pharisees having their own "traditions of the ancestors" that had often been included in the officially recognized laws.[30] For Jesus or any popular leader of Israelite heritage originating in Galilee, this would be the cast of characters of the rulers and their representatives with whom he would have come into conflict simply as a villager and especially as a spokesperson and leader. That that other popular prophet, John the Baptist, came into conflict with Herod Antipas, who arrested and killed him, is confirmed by Josephus, hence another example of what was given in and derived from the historical context.

The people lived in semi-independent village communities, with local "assemblies" (*synagogai*) as their form of governance.[31] Archaeological explorations confirm Josephus' report (*Life* 235) that there were roughly

---

27. Summary of arguments against Roman origins of Mark in Marcus, *Mark 1–8*, 21–37.

28. For evidence and arguments, see Black, *Apostolic Interpreter*, 77–113; Horsley, *Whole Story*, chap. 2.

29. Detailed analysis and documentation in Horsley, *Galilee*; more recent discussion in Horsley and Tiller, *After* Apocalyptic; and Horsley, *Jesus and the Politics*, chap. 2.

30. See further Horsley, *Jesus and the Politics*, chap. 6.

31. More detailed discussion in Horsley, *Galilee*, chaps. 8–10.

200 villages in Galilee, such as Nazareth, Capernaum, Chorazin, and a large village or town whose traditional name was Magdala. During the first century CE, the multiple layers of rulers made claims to a portion of the villagers' produce for the Roman tribute, taxes to Herod Antipas, and perhaps tithes and offerings to the priests and temple. Josephus reports that in his attempts to organize (control!) the Galileans in 66–67, the villagers were seriously hostile to the (newly built) governing cities of Sepphoris and Tiberias.[32] Again, that a popular prophet would work in villages, including in their assemblies, send his representatives into villages, and avoid the ruling cities is given in the historical context.

Special attention may be required for particular historical circumstances evident in the Markan story that have been obscured by the continuing influence of the synthetic constructs of standard biblical studies, in particular "Judaism" and the supposed division between "Jews" and "Gentiles." Even in recent literary or narrative criticism of the Gospel, it was common to read Jesus' crossing the Sea of Galilee as a mediation between "the Jewish" side and "the Gentile" side. But there are no such concepts, there is no such divide in the Markan story. In Mark, as in Josephus' histories and the Gospel of John and other sources, "the Judeans" is a regional reference, as are "the Galileans" and "the Samaritans." Josephus is consistent in his use of these regional terms in reference to the people of these different regions. The source of confusion in the Gospel of John, in which Jesus works in all of these regions, is that "the Judeans" most often refers to particular Judeans, the rulers, which are synonymous in the story with the high priests and the Pharisees. But the people of all of these regions were evidently of Israelite heritage, the term of common identification having been "Israel."[33]

The regional references and differences were rooted in the different regional history of the centuries prior to Roman times. Following the Assyrian and Babylonian conquests, these regions were under separate imperial regional jurisdictions, the Judeans under the Jerusalem temple-state, the Samaritans under a parallel aristocracy and temple, and the Galileans under a separate imperial division.[34] But the Hasmonean high priesthood conquered Samaria and destroyed its temple and took over Galilee only a hundred years before Jesus' birth. Yet during Jesus' lifetime, Galilee had been placed under the separate rule of Antipas, as noted above.

---

32. Horsley, "Power Vacuum."

33. See further Horsley, *Galilee*; and the summary discussion in Horsley and Thatcher, *John Jesus*, chap. 2. On the implications for Jesus, see Elliott, "Jesus the Israelite."

34. See analysis and discussion in Horsley, *Galilee*, chap. 1.

This means that in two regards the basic Markan story of Jesus' mission may have a more complicated relation to the historical situation during Jesus' mission. First, Mark (followed by both Matthew and Luke) is the principal source that represents the scribes and Pharisees as active in Galilee. The other sources, principally Josephus' accounts, have them active mainly in Jerusalem.[35] Had scribes and Pharisees been active in Galilee during the century of rule by Jerusalem? Or did the composers of the Markan story just know of their role as agents of the temple-state and extrapolate to Galilee? Second, and more easily explained in the historical context of Roman Palestine, is why a prophet who worked mainly in Galilean villages would have marched up to Jerusalem, where critical historians as well most Gospel sources have him coming into the conflict with the rulers that resulted in his execution. During the century of rule by the temple and high priesthood, Galileans had likely come to view Jerusalem as the capital of Israel—and, as will be discussed below, a major part of a prophets "job-definition" in the common Israelite tradition would have been to confront the rulers of Israel.

Given the pervasive influence of the synthetic construct of "Judaism" on the view of the temple and high priests in study of the Gospels, it is important to review attitudes in late second-temple Judean sources. Rabbinic texts have a highly positive view of the temple—after it had been destroyed by the Romans. From its very foundation and continuing into early Roman times, however, the Jerusalem temple-state was sponsored by imperial rulers and served as their local representative. The scribal texts we classify as "apocalyptic" were composed in opposition to the high priests as well as the imperial regimes that supported them.[36] While some late prophetic texts were composed in support of the temple, "apocalyptic" texts left no place for a temple and high priesthood in their vision of the restoration of Israel, the Animal Vision (in *1 Enoch* 85–90) pointedly so. Herod the Great had massively rebuilt the temple-complex into one of the wonders of the Roman imperial world and appointed families from outside Judea to the high priesthood. In the first century, the high priests who headed the temple-state were appointed by the Roman governor, were responsible for the collection of the tribute to Caesar, and generally collaborated in Roman rule. According to Josephus, they became downright predatory on the people, sending out their gangs of toughs to seize the tithes from the threshing floors (*Ant.* 20.181, 206–207, 214).[37] Shortly after the mission of

35. Horsley, *Jesus and the Politics*, chap. 6.

36. Explained in Horsley, *Scribes, Visionaries*, chaps. 8–9; and *Revolt of the Scribes*.

37. On extractions from the peasantry, see more generally Hanson and Oakman, *Palestine*, 105–11.

Jesus, a number of their own scribal retainers, evidently in despair over their collaboration, began selective assassinations of high priestly figures (*War* 2.254–56; *Ant.* 20.208–10). Basically the high priestly aristocracy lacked legitimacy in the eyes of many of the scribal retainers as well as among the people they were trying to rule.[38] In its climactic episodes in Jerusalem the Markan story again fits the historical context of Roman Palestine.

What both framed and filled the historical context of the Markan story were the widespread popular revolts roughly a generation before and a generation after Jesus mission and the many popular protests and movements in between.[39] Collective actions and movements among the people in resistance to the rulers were virtually driving history, with the rulers reacting to suppress the resistance. Jesus and his movement, as narrated in Mark, far from being unique, were paralleled by other leaders and movements. Particularly noteworthy were two types of leaders-and-movements distinctive to people of Israelite heritage, the movements led by popularly acclaimed "kings" and those led by prophets, and a widespread "strike" among villagers in Galilee in protest over Roman provocation.

This peasant "strike," like the popular movements, illustrates the ability of peasants to organize across individual village communities, contrary to generalizations often made by modern intellectuals. In a widespread and sustained collective action that threatened their own survival as well as a crop-failure that would have denied the Romans their tribute, Galilean peasants refused to seed their fields in protest over Roman troops marching through the countryside carrying the bust of Gaius (Caligula).[40] Modern scholars can only wonder at the communication across village communities that would have been necessary to sustain this agrarian "strike" in the face of threatened suppression.

The principal social form taken by the widespread revolts against Roman and Jerusalem rule in 4 BCE and again in 67–70 CE was a succession of what I have called "popular messianic movements."[41] In his histories of these revolts Josephus includes accounts of several movements in which the people acclaimed a leader as "king," who led them in attacks on Herodian or Roman storehouses to "take back" goods that had been taken there (*War* 2.56–75; *Ant.* 17.271–85). Distinctive features of each of these movements, as recounted by Josephus, shows how a particular action taken by Jesus and his followers in Mark's story (or the very origins of his leadership and move-

38. Goodman, *Ruling Class*; Horsley, *Jesus and the Politics*, chap. 2.

39. Rhoads, *Israel in Revolution*; Horsley, *Jesus and the Spiral*, chaps. 2–4.

40. Discussion and documentation in Horsley, *Jesus and the Spiral*, 110–116.

41. Horsley, "Popular Messianic Movements."

ment) can have been derived from (influenced by) events in the historical context. One of these movements, led by the son of a Galilean popular hero, the brigand-chieftan Hezekiah, who had been martyred by the arrogant young military strongman Herod, emerged in the area around the fortress at Sepphoris, near Nazareth. The ensuing Roman military suppression of the movement would have left a collective social trauma in (that area of) Galilee, fertile ground for another leader and movement a generation later. The movement led by the strapping shepherd Athronges in the hill country of Judea in 4 BCE was able to sustain its independence of Roman and high priestly rule for nearly three years. This indicates that it was possible for a movement of resistance and renewal to spread across many village communities before the rulers could effectively suppress it (and crucify the leaders). Simon bar Giora, acclaimed king in an even more widespread movement in Judea after the great revolt began in 66 CE, proclaimed liberation of captives, cancellation of debts, and people's restoration to their land (which was their family inheritance; *War* 4.507–13, 529–34). Again elements of the basic Markan story of Jesus renewal of Israel in opposition to the rulers, such as the spread of the movement across many villages and the popular desire (desperation) for cancellation of debts were given in the historical context.

Closer to the time of Jesus' mission, indeed in the immediately following decades, when the Synoptic Gospel tradition was developing, were several movements led by popular prophets.[42] Josephus provides accounts of three that were particularly prominent and memorable, one in Samaria and two in Judea (*Ant.* 18.85–87; 20.97–98, 169–71; *War* 2.261–63).

These movements have been inappropriately labeled "sign prophets" by some modern scholars working without the benefit of more probing source criticism of Josephus's accounts.[43] It is necessary not only to cut through Josephus' denigration of the popular leaders that he utterly despises, but to sort out the various figures and groups that he associates in his retrospective alarmist portrait of the intensifying turmoil that eventually erupted in widespread revolt in the summer of 66—a portrait that modern scholars for some time mistook as "the Zealots" as a sustained movement agitating for armed revolt. Only in two summary references does Josephus mention "signs" and "wonders." In parallel summary references to "deceivers and impostors" or "charlatans" prior to the great revolt he says that they or God would show their followers "signs of deliverance " or "wonders and signs in accord with God's plan" out in the wilderness (*War* 2.259; *Ant.* 20.268–69).

---

42. Analysis and references in Horsley, "Two Types of Popular Prophets."

43. Influential has been Barnett, "Jewish Sign-Prophets." Cf. Horsley, "Two Types of Popular Prophets."

Later in his account of the Roman military siege of Jerusalem he says that "numerous (false) prophets" and charlatans exhorted the desperate people who had taken refuge in the temple to await "signs of their salvation" from God, portents such as a sword-like star or a meteor over the city or omens such as a cow giving birth to a lamb, which the sacred scribes interpreted more ominously (*War* 6:285–300). Josephus' terms and clauses in these summary passages suggest omens and portents familiar from scribal lore, known in ancient Near Eastern cosmological wisdom, a sample of which is collected in the Book of Luminaries in *1 Enoch* 72–82. The further "sign" of celestial chariots and battalions hurtling through the sky is also reminiscent of scribal lore, the theophany of the heavenly hosts coming to rescue the people familiar in some "apocalyptic" texts (for example, *Testament of Moses* 10:3–7). Josephus' accounts of the three prominent prophets and their movements, however, make no references to signs (*Ant.* 18.85–87; 20.97–98; 169–71; *War* 2.261–63).

Once we sort critically through his accounts, the Samaritan prophet, the prophet Theudas, and the prophet (returned) from Egypt and their respective movements seem to follow more or less the same sequence of events, all more or less inherent in and determined by the same general historical situation in which Jesus was working. Only the particular new act of deliverance they promise their followers is distinctive to each. First, in order to have generated and led such a sizeable following, these prophets were speaking and organizing in the countryside (*chora*) across many village communities for a prolonged period of time. Second, what Josephus focuses on, these prophets took specific action in leading their followers in anticipation of a new divine act of deliverance that corresponded to a foundational action of the hoary past (a recovery of the vessels Moses had deposited on the sacred mount Gerizim; a crossing of the Jordan River in a new exodus and/or entry of the land; witnessing a Jericho-like collapse of the walls of the ruling city). Finally, in response to the opposition and threat to the established imperial order, the Roman governor took action to kill the prophets and suppress their movements.

For these prophets and their movements, as for Jesus and his movement in Mark's story, the basic conflict in Roman Palestine, the main cast of characters, and the basic sequence of events are all given in the historical context. The principal difference between them is in the particular act of deliverance they preached and anticipated. The principal difference between Jesus in Mark's story and these other popular prophets is that he was generating renewal in and of the village communities themselves, whereas the other prophets called the people out of their communities to participate in the new deliverance. To explore the similarities and differences of these prophets and their movements, however, it is necessary to shift focus to the Israelite tradition in which they were all grounded and by which the composition of their stories were informed, whether in Josephus' accounts or the Markan story (and other Gospel texts).

## Israelite Tradition, Official and Popular

There would be neither story nor history without tradition. Stories and histories are not generic. Stories and histories are rooted in and informed by particular cultural traditions as carried and shaped in social memories of particular peoples in particular larger historical contexts. Much of the recent "quest" of the historical Jesus is strikingly unhistorical. One of the basic reasons for this is that, still refining the old form-critical approach focused on individual sayings, the questers not only ignore the Gospel stories, leaving the sayings without (historical) meaning-context, but also largely ignore the Israelite tradition in which the stories, including their component sayings and episodes, and the history of Jesus-in-movement-in-story are rooted and informed.

Recent application of the social sciences to the Gospels and Jesus has been suggestive, particularly in countering the individualist construction of Jesus as unencumbered by historical social forms and social-political interaction—what both story and history are about. But it is not clear what is gained by constructing Jesus as a (generic) "charismatic" figure, even if the emphasis were to be on the relationship between leader and followers in a crisis situation, since it is the cultural tradition in which leader and followers are rooted that determines the way they interact and act in a particular historical crisis.[44] Similarly, it is not clear what is gained by applying the cross-cultural construct of "millenarian prophet" to Jesus,[45] again even with a wide-angle focus on the relations of prophet and followers.[46] It is the culture (tradition) in which both prophet and followers are rooted that determines how they respond to a crisis for their society and its culture. The "cargo cults" in Melanesia studied by anthropologists emerged in societies with little previous "contact" with powerful colonial forces. By contrast, Jesus and his movement(s) were deeply rooted in Israelite culture at the core of which was a long tradition of resistance both to imperial domina-

---

44. See, for example, the discussion by Kee, *Christian Origins*, which seems unaware of the explicitly relational restatement of the constitutive three-way relationship of leader, followers, and crisis situation by Worsley, *Trumpet Shall Sound*.

45. See Allison, *Jesus of Nazareth, Millenarian Prophet*.

46. Done over twenty years earlier by Gager, *Kingdom and Community*, more in accord with key anthropological studies.

tion and to more local centralization of power. It was surely no historical "coincidence" that Judeans and Galileans mounted persistent resistance to Roman imperial domination before finally being "pacified" by the Roman devastation in 67–70 and 132–35 CE. To understand the composition and performance of the Markan story and the history it recounts it is essential to investigate how they are informed by and draw upon Israelite tradition.

It is impossible, moreover, to peel away the story from the history in analysis of how they draw upon and are informed by Israelite tradition. The same tradition with which the Markan story resonated informed how Jesus interacted with his followers and opponents, including the "roles" that Jesus played and/or his followers and opponents projected onto his actions, the (different) ways their interactions were understood. However clear it may be that the most basic characters and events of Jesus' mission were given by the historical situation, Israelite tradition determined the events and, not all that long thereafter, the composition and performance of the Markan story about them.

In a serious complication of our consideration, again contrary to the oversimplification of the synthetic construct "Judaism," Israelite tradition was not unified or monolithic, and consisted of far more than and ran far deeper than extant Judean written texts. As discussed extensively in previous chapters, those texts were produced by, and available mainly to, the tiny literate scribal elite, and were just "the tip of the iceberg" of official or elite (largely Judean) tradition. In the historical events, the high priests and their scribal and Pharisaic representatives would have been acting out of the official tradition, which articulated their interests and helped legitimate their position. And to the extent that ordinary people knew of the existence of the official tradition, including its authoritative written texts, the latter probably influenced their actions and the stories they produced at points (as when the Gospel of Mark appeals to the authority of "what is written" in the elite tradition in arguments against the Pharisees: "have you not read. . .?"). The ordinary people with whom Jesus interacted and among whom the Markan story developed, however, were rooted in and informed by the popular Israelite tradition that they cultivated orally in their village communities (again as discussed above, particularly in chap. 5). Insofar as we have few direct sources for the popular tradition, of course, discussion of its operation involves some educated "guesswork" and extrapolation on the basis of extant sources from the cultural elite.

Another preliminary observation is crucial, largely because of how difficult it is to overcome the intellectual habits and practices of modern print culture. Determined probably by the print culture in which biblical texts appear to the eye as individual verses in chapters, scholars tend to focus on individual verses. A motif or a figure or a saying in a Gospel is understood as influenced by or an allusion to a particular verse in the Hebrew Bible or other earlier text. But culture, cultural tradition, does not work that way. Cultural tradition is shaped and works in broad "patterns" or "forms" (inadequate visual/spatial metaphors) or, often, in stories that include interaction of leaders and followers in crisis situations. In the Community Rule and the Damascus Rule found among the DSS we can discern the continuing life and operation of the broader exodus tradition and the broader pattern of the Mosaic covenant so prominent in the books later included in the Hebrew Bible.[47] These broader narratives and patterns not only are adapted in the written texts left by the Qumran community but informed and even determined the actions they took in their own (new) exodus from the temple-state and formation of a (renewed) covenantal community. In our attempt to discern how the Markan story was composed, therefore, it is appropriate to discern broader cultural patterns of tradition as well as particular allusions, which may well also be (metonymic = part stands for whole) cues to broader cultural patterns and memories.

It may now be possible to appreciate more fully how the Markan story could have been composed by exploring how the historical story of Jesus' mission was informed and shaped by Israelite tradition, how the (hi)story was given particular shape and embellishment from the tradition.[48] Comparison with other figures-and-movements will be crucial. While the basic characters and events of Mark's story (and the parallel popular prophetic movements in Josephus' accounts) are given in the historical situation of Galilee and Judea under Roman rule, their shaping by Israelite tradition is what makes them distinctive. The prophets and villagers involved were not just striking out in random anarchic acts of frustration. These movements all assumed a particular social form. These (hi)stories were shaped according to a particular pattern distinctive to (popular) Israelite tradition carried actively in contemporary social memory.[49]

These movements were all acting in the same historical crisis for their society, and they were all suppressed by the Roman and/or high priestly rulers. The main social form of all of these leaders-and-movements was a prophet-and-followers acting in anticipation of new deliverance by God patterned after historical deliverance of God under the leadership of a prophet in formative Israelite tradition. Within that distinctive general form, each prophet-and-movement was patterned after one or more of the legendary

---

47. Horsley, *Covenant Economics*, 100–103.

48. Explored initially in Horsley, *Hearing the Whole Story*, chap. 10.

49. Sources and analysis in Horsley, "Two Types of Popular Prophets."

foundational acts of deliverance in hoary Israelite tradition. The Samaritan prophet as a new Moses promised that his followers would recover the tabernacle vessels deposited by Moses on Mount Gerizim, the sacred mountain of early Israel. The prophet Theudas in the role of a new Moses (and/or Joshua) led the people to the Jordan River to experience a new exodus and/or new entry into their land (the two were often fused in Israelite tradition). The prophet (returned) from Egypt became a new Joshua gathering his followers to witness the collapse of the walls of the ruling city of Jerusalem, as the early Israelites had experienced at Jericho.

That several prophets and their movements in mid-first century took this distinctively Israelite social form indicates that this general pattern in Israelite popular tradition was very much alive among villagers. It may well have been formative in the interaction between Jesus and his immediate followers. And it would have continued as a prominent pattern in the movements of Jesus' followers in which Jesus traditions developed, continuing into the movement/communities in which and for which the Markan story was composed and performed. The Israelite tradition of prophets of deliverance and renewal of the people in resistance to their rulers, moreover, was far richer and more complex than evident in the three particular movements that Josephus recounts. Other legendary events, such as the feeding in the wilderness, were attributed to (a prophet like) Moses in Israelite tradition, "events" that we know from reading Judean texts, such as Exodus and Numbers and *Jubilees,* but which almost certainly were cultivated orally as stories in village communities. Stories of Joshua's leadership would have been similarly cultivated.

There have long been hints here and there in (written) sources that stories of Elijah (and his protégé Elisha) were very much alive in the popular tradition. Indeed, these were so important among the people that they were taken up into the official tradition and its written texts. This began in the Deuteronomistic history, where the cycle of Elijah and Elisha stories (1 Kings 17–19, 21; 2 Kings 1–9) stand out from the more courtly style of the rest of the history of the kings. This cycle of stories presents Elijah, assisted by his disciple Elisha, as the restorer of Israel, symbolized according to its "twelve" tribes (represented by the twelve stones), confronting the rulers about their oppression of the people, including prophecies against the regime and a commission by God to foment insurrection against oppressive and/or foreign rule, and healing and providing provisions for people struggling in their hardships. Later the pro-temple-state prophet Malachi and the scribal propagandist for the Oniad high priestly regime Ben Sira both include references to the future role of (a new) Elijah in renewal of the people. In its origins and in it continuing social memory, Elijah (with his protégé Elisha) was the legendary prophet of renewal of Israel in resistance to oppressive and/or foreign rulers.

Along with his legendary role as leader of the exodus, celebrated annually in the Passover festival (the *seder* of which was hardly dependent on inscribed scrolls and literacy), the founding prophet Moses was prominent in Israelite tradition as leader of the exodus but equally prominent as the mediator of the "Mosaic" covenant, its basic commandments, and other covenantal teaching (*torah*) that included principles and mechanisms by which the people were to aid one another in times of need and share resources in their village communities. Moses' mediation of the covenant also included presiding at the ceremony of covenant making on Sinai. While nonliterate ordinary Judeans, Galileans, and Samaritans did not have direct contact with cumbersome and expensive scrolls of torah, they were familiar with the Mosaic covenant, the commandments, and covenantal teaching as the basis of social-economic interaction in their communities. All of these segments, patterns, customs, and particular stories of Israelite tradition were regularly cultivated in the village communities and the popular Jesus movement(s) in which the Markan story originated. These segments, patterns, customs, themes were in the social memory of the people who composed and performed and developed the Markan story, just as they were in the social memory of those who cultivated and shaped Jesus-tradition and, before that, in the social memory of Jesus and those with whom he interacted.

Perhaps a good starting point would be the two sets of "acts of power" that come in (mostly) the same sequence in Mark (4:35 to 8:26): sea-crossing, exorcism, healing, healing, wilderness feeding. That the second set in Mark has the second healing after the wilderness feeding is attributable to the Markan framing of the ensuing (third) narrative step with healings of blind people at the beginning and end (8:22–26 and 10:46–52). It has long been suspected that these are pre-Markan "chains" of episodes of acts of power[50] arranged in a sequence that presents Jesus as a combination of new Moses (sea crossing and wilderness feeding) and new Elijah (healing people representative of Israel and beyond) engaged in a renewal of Israel. Of course the tradition of Elijah's and his protégé Elisha's multiplication of food may also have informed the wilderness feedings. In the narration of these "typical" acts of power Jesus is presented as the prophet engaged in renewal of Israel. It is impossible to judge whether such symbols of renewal of the people were integral to the acts of power "chains" or were subsequent embellishments in the composition of the larger story.

---

50. Achtemeier, "Pre-Markan Catenae."

The composer(s) of Mark's basic story, in what appears in the more embellished form that we have as the second major narrative step (4:35— 8:26), followed this double sequence rooted in and shaped by memories of Moses and Elijah, inserting other episodes or narrative bridges that represented Jesus as the new Moses and/or Elijah in other facets of their activities in Israelite tradition. The introduction to the John the Baptist episode has everyone talking about Jesus the prophet of renewal, and the episode presents (the also Elijah-like) story of John as a miniature or paradigm of Jesus' story, with Jesus as the reincarnation of John in Herod's haunted mind (Mark 6:14–29). In a parallel sequence of events, John prophesied against the ruler, who then arrested and killed him (which we know as historically-based tradition about John, thanks to Josephus' account, *Ant.* 18.116–19). In a second major addition to the two sequences of acts of power, the composers present Jesus as the new Moses insisting on observance of the covenantal commandment of Moses himself (ultimately of God) and Mosaic covenantal law in condemnation of the Pharisees, whose role in the temple-state was to cultivate the torah of Moses in "the traditions of the elders" (Mark 7:1–13).

From the very beginning of the Markan story, in numerous episodes and several interrelated ways, the composers draw upon formative Israelite tradition to portray Jesus as a prophet like Moses and Elijah engaged in a renewal of Israel. Preparing "the way of the Lord," suggesting that Jesus is about to lead a new exodus, John the Baptist appears as a prophet in the wilderness enacting renewal of the Mosaic covenant in the dramatic ritual of a baptism of repentance. The baptism with Holy Spirit empowers Jesus to carry out the new exodus and covenant renewal, that is the renewal of the people of Israel. The tradition of Elijah's forty days' testing in the wilderness in preparation for leading the renewal of Israel (and Moses' wilderness preparation for leading the exodus) is what informs Jesus' forty days' testing in the wilderness, preparation for assuming the role of the prophet of renewal. The composers of the Markan story may even be patterning Jesus' call of the first disciples after Elijah's call of Elisha and his association with the bands of prophets (1 Kings 18–19).

The tradition that Israel consisted of the symbolic twelve tribes virtually required that this symbol be prominent in the episodes of Jesus' renewal of the people. Thus the composers have Jesus commission the twelve disciples as representative of Israel undergoing renewal, reminiscent of the symbol of twelve in Israelite tradition, for example, in Elijah's construction of the altar of twelve stones. The composers feature the symbolism prominently in the second main narrative step (4:35—8:26), with the "twelve year old" woman and the woman who had been hemorrhaging "for twelve years" healed as representative of Israel, and the twelve baskets of fragments gathered up in one of the wilderness feedings. The composers give an unmistakable indication that Jesus' program is a renewal of Israel when they have Jesus go "up the mountain" and when he commissions the twelve disciples to extend his own mission of preaching and exorcism.

The composers draw further on the other principal task of Moses in Israelite tradition, his giving the covenant commandments and his presiding over the covenant making ceremony (with the basins of blood binding God and the people), in presenting Jesus' renewal of the covenant as the "constitution" (in both senses of the term) of his renewal of Israel. The covenant renewal is begun by John in the baptism. Then as the concluding episode of the first major narrative step (1:16—3:35) they have Jesus declare that those who "do the will of God" (i.e., keep the covenant commandments and laws) constitute the renewed covenantal familial community. At the conclusion of the third narrative step in the story (8:22—10:52), as Jesus completes his mission in the villages of Galilee and beyond and heads through Judea and up to Jerusalem to confront the rulers, the composers have Jesus deliver what is in effect a "charter" of renewed covenantal teaching to his followers in a series of dialogues. In the first step they draw upon the commandment prohibiting adultery and the Pharisees' relaxation of the commandment as the springboard for Jesus' new commandment that strengthens the marriage bond at the center of the family. In the third step, on egalitarian economic relations in the village community, they have Jesus recite most of the covenantal commandments explicitly, and then deliver another law- or commandment-like statement that those who are wealthy (by defrauding others) will not enter the kingdom. The core concerns of the Mosaic covenant in Israelite tradition (for the integrity of the family, the community, economic relations, and community leadership) determine the issues addressed in the composition of the dialogues.

At the Passover meal in celebration of the exodus liberation, finally, the composers draw on the key symbol of the basins of blood in the covenantal ceremony on Sinai that Moses presided over (which we know from Exodus 24), having Jesus declare in his word over the cup, "this is my blood of the covenant, which is poured out for many." The composers (perhaps following very early Jesus-tradition) thus transform the Passover meal that celebrated the exodus liberation into a covenant renewal ceremony—that will be observed regularly until its celebration anew in the fully realized direct rule of God (the term "new covenant" is in Paul, 1 Cor 11:23-26, but not Mark 14:22-25).

The Israelite tradition of a prophet leading a movement continues to inform the Markan story as Jesus confronts the high priestly and

Roman rulers in Jerusalem, although it may be less explicit and obvious than earlier in the narrative. The stories of Elijah offered a paradigm of a prophet who confronted the rulers and delivered prophecies of judgment as well as spearheaded a popular a movement of resistance and renewal. Composers-performers of the Markan story could thus continue to follow the social memory of Elijah that was prominent in the popular tradition as they moved into the climactic events in which Jesus confronted the rulers in Jerusalem. It is worth noting also criteria of the Mosaic covenant implicit in the episodes of Jesus' blockade of temple business and the parable of the tenants and more explicit in his response to the entrapment question about whether the tribute was lawful and his condemnation of the scribes for devouring widow's houses—which leads narratively directly to (God's) destruction of the temple.

Also prominent in Israelite tradition, however, was another type of prophet that had emerged after Elijah and Elisha. These prophets, no longer leading popular movements of renewal and resistance, pronounced prophecies of God's judgment against the rulers and their officers. The "classical" cases were Amos and Hosea in (northern) Israel and Micah and Isaiah in Judah, and finally Jeremiah. In stories about some of them, these prophets performed actions that symbolized or dramatized God's impending judgment. Josephus includes accounts of contemporary prophets in this other tradition, such as that other "Jesus," the son of Hananyah, who delivered oracles of judgment, but did not lead movements. Jesus of Nazareth's oracle over the Jerusalem ruling house in one of the Q speeches (13:34–35), in the traditional form of a prophetic lament known from Amos' laments, bears striking resemblance to the lament of Jesus son of Hananyah over Jerusalem thirty years later.[51] The Israelite tradition of oracular prophets was thus evidently still very much alive at the time of Jesus. It is possible that the traditions of these two types could be fused or affect one another. The *Lives of the Prophets*, which may have taken written form well after the time of Jesus but contains earlier popular (not elite) stories,[52] reimagines Ezekiel, who both had been an oracular prophet, as the leader of a movement of repentance, renewal and resistance, a virtual new Moses who leads a new exodus and preaches judgment against Jerusalem.

In the climactic confrontation in Jerusalem, the composers of the Markan story still have Jesus leading a movement, as in the previous steps of the story. His followers accompany him to Jerusalem, the demonstration against the temple is framed by a conversation with them. He teaches the disciples

---

51. Again see Horsley, "Two Types of Prophets."
52. Schwemer, *Vitae Prophetarum*, 1.65–71; cf. Satran, *Biblical Prophets*.

about the future, and the disciples are present (unfaithfully) and the women present (faithfully) when he is arrested and crucified. In portraying his blockade against the temple, his prophetic parable that condemns the high priests, and the prophecy(ies) of the destruction (and "rebuilding") of the temple, however, the composers (or Jesus) drew on the tradition of oracular prophets, particularly well-known prophecies of Jeremiah and Isaiah. And they drew on the tradition of symbolic prophetic actions.

The composers of the story, moreover, knew that prominent prophecies of Isaiah, Jeremiah, and other prophets stood "written" in the numinous, authoritative scrolls ("scriptures") laid up in the Jerusalem temple. They knew that citing these prophecies that were "written" would give all the greater authority to their story and to Jesus as the prophet of renewal. The opening quotation from what was ostensibly "written in the prophet Isaiah," but is a composite from Isaiah and Malachi in the official scribal scrolls (in the written textual tradition to which we have access) provides a good illustration of how non-literate composers-narrators could draw upon the tradition of "oracular" prophets cultivated at both the popular and the official levels.

In Jesus' confrontation with the high priests in the temple, the story composers' knowledge of prophecies informs their account of Jesus' prophetic condemnation of the rulers so that it resonates deeply with the tradition of Jeremiah and Isaiah. In the episode of Jesus' blockade (hardly a mere "cleansing") of temple business, a prophetic "demonstration" that symbolized God's judgment, the again composite quotation is identified only as "written," but not explicitly "by Jeremiah (and/or Isaiah)." However, Jeremiah's pronouncement of God's condemnation of the temple would likely have been prominent in Israelite tradition (two accounts are included in the continuously composed "book" of Jeremiah). Jesus' parable of the tenants that functions as a prophetic condemnation of the high priests in the Markan narrative built upon and applied to the rulers of Jesus' day the "song of the vineyard" oracle from Isaiah. Again from their deep knowledge of Israelite tradition the composers of the story (following early Jesus tradition?) broaden and deepen Jesus as the prophet of the renewal of the people from the wider prophetic tradition of pronouncements against oppressive rulers. Probably we do not have sufficient sources to know whether the distinctive traditions of two types of prophets had already been fused prior to the mission of Jesus. In the narrative of Jesus' confrontation with the Jerusalem rulers, however, they have drawn upon both to expand and deepen the role and effect of Jesus the prophet generating the renewal of Israel in resistance to their rulers.

In the final narrative step of the high priestly and Roman rulers taking action to apprehend and kill Jesus, the composer-narrators are still/again drawing on Israelite tradition of the prophets. It is impossible to enter into the long-standing debate about the composition of the "passion narrative," a debate heavily overlayed with Christian theological concerns.[53] It should suffice for this presentation to note that rulers' repression and killing of the prophets was an integral component of Israelite tradition. King Ahab's Canaanite wife Jezebel had sought to kill Elijah (1 Kings 19). The prophet Micah of Moresheth who had prophesied God's judgment against the Jerusalem rulers was threatened with death (Jer 26:16–19). King Jehoiakim sent his officers out to track down the prophet Uriah son of Shemaiah, who had prophesied against the regime. And Jeremiah was nearly lynched by the royal regime after his condemnation of the temple for its oppression of the people (Jer 26:10–11, 20–23). The social memory of the rulers' killing of the prophets became considerably more prominent in the Israelite popular tradition, as evident in the *Lives of the Prophets*, which portrayed most of the prophets as having been killed. Contemporary with Jesus, Antipas had arrested and killed John the Baptist for prophesying against his rule, and contemporary with the development of Jesus-tradition, the Roman governors, such as Pilate, had sent out their military to attack and kill prophets such as the Samaritan and Theudas. Arrest and killing was the tradition as well as the history of prophets.

This survey thus suggests that the basic story of the Gospel of Mark was given in history and shaped by Israelite tradition of prophets leading movements, especially Moses and Elijah, with some influence from the tradition of oracular prophets such as Isaiah and Jeremiah. The composition of the story was not a matter of following a particular type of story, but was shaped, even determined by the structure-and-dynamics of the historical situation and a particular segment of Israelite popular tradition that was particularly prominent at the time, as known from Josephus' accounts of other popular prophets who led movements of renewal and resistance.

## The Complexity in the Overall Markan Story

The Markan story as a whole, however, is more complex and embellished. Yet brief examination of some of these complications and their derivation or motivation may serve to highlight the composition of the basic story as just explored.

---

53. Recent extension of the debate into the exploration of orality, writing, and social memory in Aitken, *Jesus' Death*; and Thatcher, ed., *Jesus, the Voice,* chaps. 9 and 11.

Almost "by definition" in previously standard Christian theology the Gospels are understood to be about Jesus as the Messiah. A century ago and after, what was understood as driving the story of the Gospel of Mark was "the messianic secret"; of course Jesus is the Messiah in the Gospel, but in the little stories edited into the Gospel he frequently orders the demons he exorcises or the people he heals not to disclose his identity, which becomes evident only later.[54] After the reading and rereading of the Markan story in the last decades it is not surprising that earlier readers may have entertained the notion of a "messianic secret" in the Gospel. Read more critically as a whole story, the Gospel can be seen to downplay or even deny that Jesus was a messiah. But the matter is more complicated.[55]

Beginning around fifty years ago, critical scholars started to recognize that, contrary to standard assumption and generalization in Christian biblical interpretation, there was no standard "Jewish expectation of 'the Messiah'" in "(early) Judaism."[56] It became evident that what had been references to different divine agents had become synthesized into the composite Christian concept of "the Messiah." Then it was recognized that occurrences of the term "messiah" were remarkably rare in late second-temple Judean texts. What had been the standard Christian "prooftext" of the supposed "Jewish expectation" of a "militant Messiah" in *Psalm of Solomon* 17 turned out to be a scribal figure who would judge the imperial rulers not with the sword but with "the words of his mouth." The few references in the DSS imagined multiple messiahs, both a priestly and a royal figure, both of whom had a mainly ceremonial function. If we pause to consider who produced the extant texts, that is, scribal circles, then it should be evident from the "social location" of scribes and their high priestly patrons in the continuing (Persian-Hellenist-Roman) imperial order that there could be little role for a anointed "king of the Judeans." The notable exception, of course, was the community at Qumran that consisted mainly (we think) of dissident scribes and priests. While acting and composing mainly in the cultural pattern of exodus and Mosaic covenant, they did anticipate both an anointed priest and an anointed lay leader in the community of fulfillment (e.g., the Messianic Rule, 1 QSa 2.12–23).

While the high priestly rulers appointed by the Romans and their loyal scribal retainers had no interest in an anointed king, however, many of the local or regional revolts took the form of a movement focused on a

---

54. Classic statement by Wrede, *Messianic Secret*.

55. Discussed more extensively in Horsley, *Hearing the Whole Story*, chap. 10.

56. De Jonge, "Use of the Word 'Anointed'"; see the many essays in Charlesworth, *Messiah*; and Neusner, *Judaisms and their Messiahs*.

leader whom the people acclaimed as their "king," as recounted by Josephus. Parallel to the prophets who led popular movements patterned after Moses and Joshua, moreover, the leaders acclaimed as king by their followers were shaped ("in-formed") by the Israelite popular tradition of the young David who had been "messiahed" by the Israelites (the elders; 2 Sam 2:1–4; 5:1–4). As with the Israelite popular tradition of popular prophets leading movements, so the tradition of the young David "messiahed" by the Israelites was prominent in the people's social memory just at the time of Jesus, as known from Josephus' accounts of Judas son of Hezekiah in Galilee, Athronges in Judea, and a figure in the transJordan in 4 BCE (as discussed above).

It is evident from many texts later included in the New Testament that Jesus was understood as (the) messiah, an anointed king, by some of his followers, whether during his mission or (more likely) after. In the speeches adapted in the early chapters of the book of Acts, Jesus became the messiah upon his vindication after his crucifixion (and was expected to return as messiah). In Paul's letters "Christ" has become almost part of his name, "Jesus Christ," with his principle title being "Lord." The Gospel of John portrays Jesus primarily as (the) messiah, while also as a prophet. And in John's narrative, Jesus is not an imperial anointed king, influenced mainly from the "royal psalms" (Pss 2; 110), but the anointed king from his acclamation by his followers, in the tradition of the popular kings who led the people in resistance to the imperial rulers.[57]

Not surprisingly, therefore, one of the complications in the composition of the Markan story is whether or how Jesus was the messiah/a popular king. Historical knowledge of the popularly acclaimed kings who led (temporarily successful) revolts in 4 BCE appears to be behind the composition of how the Roman governor Pontius Pilate deals with Jesus: (even though he came from Galilee) Pilate identifies Jesus as a "king of the Judeans," orders him executed by crucifixion on that charge (of fomenting insurrection), as indicated in the inscription on the cross, and the Roman soldiers mock him as insurrectionary "king of the Judeans"—and the high priests mock him as the supposed "king of Israel." At the center of the story, at the beginning of its third main narrative step (8:22—10:52), as the disciples demonstrate their serious misunderstanding of Jesus' mission, the composers have a narrative sequence that, in effect, denies that Jesus is "the messiah," or at least that he is a popular king. In contrast to the people, who take Jesus as a prophet, Peter declares "you are 'the messiah.'" Then when Peter rebukes Jesus after he announces that he must suffer and die at the hands of the Jerusalem rulers, Jesus rebukes him right back, "get behind me Satan." Toward

---

57. See further Horsley and Thatcher, *Jesus, John*, chap. 7.

the end of this narrative step as well, in the last covenant renewal dialogue, the composers have Jesus sharply reject James' and John's misunderstanding that Jesus will gain (royal/imperial) political power. Then toward the end of Jesus confrontation with the rulers in the temple, the composers have Jesus explicitly deny that he is "the messiah the son of David" (12:35–37)—ironically on the basis of the opening line of an imperial psalm (110).

The only episode in which the composers may represent Jesus as a popular king is his entry into Jerusalem at the Passover festival (11:1–11). As with the portrayal of Jesus as a prophet like Moses and Elijah throughout the story, so here the composers draw upon popular Israelite tradition (which had at one point been drawn up into the elite tradition, at Zech 9:9). They have Jesus enter the capital city riding on an ass, a peasant mode of transportation, in fulfillment of the prophecy that the people's popular king would be triumphant vis-à-vis the rulers but be a humble popular king. In imitation of the popular acclamation of Jehu as king of (northern) Israel after Elijah's protégé Elisha had "anointed" him, moreover, the people strew their garments before him (cf. 2 Kgs 9:1–13). But in contrast with the revolution led by Jehu, this is a (prophetic) "demonstration" as part of the people's festive entry into Jerusalem for the Passover celebration of the exodus liberation. The people's cry of Hosanna (Save!), moreover, was part of the Hallel psalms (113–118) that the people sang at Passover, which began by recounting the exodus and entry into their land. By contrast with the entry in John's story, this episode in Mark's story is less "messianic." The "messianic" motifs are part of a prophetic demonstration that fits Mark's main plot of Jesus pressing the renewal of the people in opposition to the rulers.

Another of the complications of the Markan story is the "subplot" of the Jesus' commissioning of but then conflict with the disciples—so complicating that it was taken by many literary critics as the main plot. This subsidiary conflict illustrates just how complex the Markan story is, or became as it developed in repeated recomposition-in-performance. But it does not seem to have been shaped or informed by Israelite tradition, from stories such as the people's grumbling about Moses' leadership. Rather this (sub-)conflict in the story seems to reflect or respond to conflicts within the Jesus movement(s). I suggested previously that it might reflect the "Markan" movement that understood itself as continuing Jesus' mission in "Galilee" (Mark 14:28; 16:1–8, the "open ending" of the story) in tension with the disciples who had become the "pillars" of the broader movement, based in Jerusalem (the leadership and the speeches in the early chapters of Acts).[58] The conflict of Jesus and the disciples is woven into a few particular episodes

58. Horsley, *Hearing the Whole Story*, chap. 4.

of the prophet-engaged-in-renewal in the second main narrative step of the basic story (4:35—8:26). It is then developed more pointedly in narrative juxtapositions in the third main narrative step (8:22—10:52), and then becomes intense in the narrative juxtapositions of the final narrative step (the "passion narrative"). But there is no reason that such complex narrative embellishment cannot have been orally composed.

A closely related complication is the subplot of the women. As the disciples move from misunderstanding to betray, abandon, and deny Jesus, women trust, broaden, anoint, and remain in solidarity with him.[59] It is again difficult to imagine how this subplot would have been influenced from Israelite tradition—other than perhaps the archaic songs of liberation having been women's songs (Miriam, Deborah, Hannah). Feminist interpreters have pointed out tellingly that the tendency in popular movements is for women's prominence and leadership to gradually decline as deep-rooted patriarchal (or kyriarchal) patterns reassert themselves. It is therefore surprising that the "Markan" composers weave the increasing prominence and role of women in the unfolding of the story. If there are paradigms of "discipleship" in the story, it is the women. Their positive role is pointedly juxtaposed with the increasingly negative portrayal of the disciples. This is one of the reasons for thinking that, as Wire suggests, women, who were traditionally the singers of songs and the teller of tales, were (among) the composers. Again there is no reason why this theme cannot have been woven into the narrative in oral (re-)composition-performance.

## Conclusion

What I hope to have done is to undergird our ability to imagine how the Markan story of Jesus and his movement as the renewal of the people of Israel in opposition to the rulers could have been composed in performance. Yes the story is complex. But nonliterate people are fully capable of composing and performing complex stories. In the case of the Markan story, the main characters in the story and the conflict between them is given in the historical situation, as know from other sources. Both the story and its historical situation, however, are profoundly shaped by Israelite tradition in general and particulars. The fundamental conflict between rulers and people was deeply rooted in Israelite tradition. The principal prophetic (and messianic?) role(s) that Jesus adapted and in which others responded to him were very much alive in Israelite popular tradition in his historical situation, again as known from other sources. And the imagery, motifs, and

---

59. Fuller discussion in *Hearing the Whole Story*, chap. 9.

the very language of particular episodes of the story and the interactions they portray are rooted in and make rich (metonymic) references to Israelite tradition.

# ORAL PERFORMANCE IN THE EMERGENCE OF THE GOSPEL OF MARK AS SCRIPTURE

Jewish and Christian, and especially Protestant Christian, emphasis upon the sacred book and its authority have combined with scholarly interests and techniques, as well as the broader developments in the modern West. . . to fix in our minds today a rather narrow concept of scripture, a concept even more sharply culture-bound than that of "book" itself.

—WILLIAM GRAHAM (1987)

THE PROCEDURES AND CONCEPTS OF CHRISTIAN BIBLICAL studies are often teleological. The results of a historical process are assumed in study of its early stages. Until recently critical study of the books of the New Testament focused on establishing the scriptural texts and their meaning in the context of their historical origins. Ironically that was before the texts became distinctively authoritative for communities that used them and were recognized as Scripture by established ecclesial authorities. Such teleological concepts and procedures obscure what turn out to be genuine historical problems once we take a closer look.

How the Gospels, particularly the Gospel of Mark, became included in the Scriptures of established Christianity offer a striking example. On the earlier Christian theological assumption that Christianity as the religion of the Gospel made a dramatic break with Judaism as the religion of the Law, one of the principal questions was how the Christian church came to include the Jewish Scriptures in its Bible. We now see much more clearly the continuity of what became Christianity with Israel. The Gospels, especially

Matthew and Mark, portray Jesus as engaged in a renewal of Israel. The Gospel of Matthew is now generally seen as addressed to communities of Israel, not "Gentiles."[1] And while Mark was formerly taken as addressed to a "Gentile" community in Rome, it appears rather to be addressed to communities in Syria that understood themselves as the renewal of Israel.[2]

The inclusion of the Gospels in the Christian Bible is far more problematic than the inclusion of the Jewish Scripture (in Greek). The ecclesial authorities who defined the New Testament canon in the fourth and fifth centuries were men of high culture. The Gospels, however, especially the Gospel of Mark, did not meet the standards of high culture in the Hellenistic and Roman cultural world. When they were set into writing, the use of the papyrus codex "declared the Gospels to be neither sacred nor high literature, but something both different and impermanent."[3] Once they became known to the Greco-Roman cultural elite, opponents of the Christians such as Celsus (late second century) mocked the Gospels for their lack of literary distinction and their composers as ignorant people who lacked "even a primary education" (*Contra Celsum* 1.62). Fifty years later, the "church father" Origen proudly admitted that the apostles possessed "no power of speaking or of giving an ordered narrative by the standards of Greek dialectical or rhetorical arts" (*Contra Celsum* 1.62). Luke had asserted, somewhat presumptuously perhaps, that his predecessors as "evangelists" and he had, in the standard Hellenistic-Roman ideology of historiography, set down an "orderly account" of events in the Gospels. Origen, who knew better, had to agree with Celsus that the evangelists were, as the Jerusalem "rulers, elders, and scribes" in the second volume of Luke's "orderly account" said about Peter and John, "illiterate and ignorant" (*agrammatoi kai idiotai*, Acts 4:13).

Nor would the Gospels, again especially Mark, have measured up as Scripture on the model of previous Judean scriptural texts. The Gospels stand in strong continuity with Israelite-Judean cultural tradition, indeed they portray Jesus and his followers as its fulfillment. Yet they do not resemble any of the kinds of texts included in the Hebrew Bible or other Judean scribal compositions, whether books of torah (Deuteronomy, etc.), books of history (Judges; 1–2 Kings, etc.), collections of prophecies (Isaiah, Amos, etc.), collections of instructional wisdom (Proverbs 1–9; Sirach), or apocalypses (Daniel). Rather the Gospels tell the story of a popular leader they compare to Moses and Elijah who focused on the concerns of villagers

---

1. Saldarini, *Matthew's Christian Jewish Community*.
2. Horsley, *Hearing the Whole Story*.
3. Parker, *Living Text*, 197.

in opposition to the political and cultural elite and who was gruesomely executed by the Roman governor.

Consideration of the *oral* cultivation of scripture (writings that [have] become authoritative and sacred) may be one of the keys to addressing the question of how the Gospels, particularly the Gospel of Mark, became included in the Bible by the ecclesial authorities of established Christianity in the fourth and fifth centuries. Only contemporary with or after the Gospels' official recognition as part of Scripture do we find Christian intellectuals producing commentaries that are more than spiritualizing allegories or moralistic homilies on Gospel passages. Research in a number of interrelated (but often separate) areas is coalescing to suggest that the Gospel of Mark developed in a largely oral communication environment and was performed orally in communities of ordinary people in ever widening areas of the Roman empire, such that it became de facto authoritative and revered in Christian communities. In both the situation of the Gospel's origins and the circumstances of its regular recitation, written texts were known and respected as authoritative. Recent researches, however, suggest that it was through repeated oral performance that Mark's Gospel gained wide authority among the people as the basis on which it was later included in the Bible by the Church authorities.

Evidence for both the written and oral functioning of the Gospel of Mark is fragmentary and often indirect. Yet there may be sufficient evidence to consider the following aspects of the emergence of the Gospel of Mark as scriptural.

- The Gospel's relation to Scripture in comparison with scribal cultivation of Scripture.

- The predominantly oral communication environment (and oral-memorial cultivation of Israelite cultural tradition) in which the Gospel originated among ordinary people.

- The oral cultivation of the Gospel in the second and third centuries prior to its official inclusion in the Christian Bible.

- The features of the Gospel that made it memorable and performable.

- The Gospel's resonance with hearers in historical context.

An appropriate preface to these steps is to note the loosening grip of print culture in biblical studies.

## Loosening the Hold of Print-Culture on the Concept of Scripture

The concept of Scripture assumed in standard Jewish and Christian biblical studies is problematic as well as narrow because it is so deeply embedded in the assumptions of modern print-culture. Only recently have a small number of biblical scholars begun to "catch on" to pioneering discussion of the oral cultivation of the Qur'an and the Bible and of oral tradition and performance of New Testament texts.[4] If we can move behind the print-culture on which our eyes are usually fixed, what is meant by scripture becomes more diverse. In the middle ages, Christian Scripture cannot be confined to what was inscribed on codices or scrolls in Hebrew, Greek, and/or Latin translation. Scripture, broken down into short, easily memorable units, was commonly learned and recited orally by priests and monks. If we are to deal with such oral aspects of scripture then our concept must obviously include texts in oral performance. And we must take into account different forms of written scripture (a necessary redundancy) and different forms of oral appropriation. Perhaps the "most common denominator" will be the contents of the text, whether in oral-memorial or written (or visual) form. Moreover, there has often been a close relationship between the oral and the written cultivation of scriptural texts. Recent work in related fields has revealed the remarkable interrelation between orality and scribal practice with regard to other authoritative texts in medieval Europe.[5] Oral cultivation has often affected the continuing development of written texts as scribes with memorial knowledge of the text made new written copies.

Conceptually, once we back away from the modern print-cultural definition of scripture, it is more satisfactory and more historically accurate to say that the text of scripture functioned as much (or more) in scribal memory and oral recitation as in (but not independent of) writing on scrolls. Correspondingly the term "text" then would refer to the contents that are learned and recited as well as written on scrolls (as in older usage; see OED; and compare the Latin *textus* , which was what was woven, texture, and even context, and the Greek verb *rhapto*, "to stitch," behind the compound *rhaphsodeo*, "to recite"). When we want to use "text" to refer more specifically to either a text in memory and recitation or a written text, we could "mark" it as "written text" or "oral text" for clarity. Graham called for this move in the use of the term "text" twenty years ago, referencing Walter

---

4. Prime examples are Graham, *Beyond the Written Word*; and Kelber, *The Oral and the Written Gospel*.

5. Carruthers, *Book of Memory*; Clanchy, *Memory to Written Record*; Doane, "Ethnography of Scribal Writing."

Ong's observation about the relentless domination of textuality understood according to print-culture in the scholarly mind.[6]

At least the contents of Christian scripture, particularly the Gospels, moreover, far from being limited to the literate elite, have functioned in significant ways among ordinary people. The functioning of scripture among ordinary people is difficult to get a handle on. What would scripture have been for medieval peasants who could not read Latin and perhaps rarely heard texts read or recited even in Latin? Scripture as written on codices was something very holy and mysterious possessed by the Church hierarchy in cathedrals and monasteries. At least some medieval peasants, however, were not ignorant of the contents of scripture as stories, symbols, and significant figures. They heard about these in homilies, perhaps on particular saints' days, and saw them in murals and statues that decorated even tiny rural chapels. Early print editions of the *Biblia pauperum* contain replicas of murals on chapel walls that display scenes from the Gospels flanked by the analogous scenes from the "Old Testament"—a popular version of what Auerbach wrote about in his essay on *Figura*. When the contents of the Gospels in particular were suddenly made accessible in oral performance to non-literate peasants in the late middle ages they "came alive," for example among the Lollards in England, the followers of Jan Hus in Bohemia, and the peasants in SW Germany in 1524–25.[7] For non-literate ordinary people it may be difficult to distinguish between scripture and cultural memory. What we are after is relationships of people and scripture, looking at the different functions of scripture in various circumstances.

## Mark's Relation to Judean Scriptures in Comparison with Scribal Cultivation

The standard view of the Gospel of Mark in New Testament studies rooted in the assumptions of print-culture is that it was "written" by an "author" on the basis of written sources. On the standard assumptions of general literacy, particularly in Jewish society, and of the availability of books of the Hebrew Bible ("the Law and the Prophets," "Old Testament"), Mark was supposed to have "quoted" from books such as Isaiah, Jeremiah, and the Psalms. A combination of the results of the recent researches discussed in earlier chapters suggest a very different picture that takes the relationship of oral communication and written texts into account. In that different picture,

---

6. Graham, *Beyond the Written Word*.

7. Aston, *Lollards and Reformers*; Deanesly, *Lollard Bible*; Blickle, *Communal Reformation to Revolution*; Scribner, *Sake of Simple Folk*.

moreover, the Gospel of Mark seems to stand at some distance from the scribal culture in which written Judean texts were cultivated.

First, insofar as writing was limited to the cultural elite in second-temple Judea, the cultivation of written texts was concentrated in circles of scribes who had taken on this role and responsibility in the service of the Jerusalem temple-state.[8] Beyond scribal circles communication was almost completely oral.

Second, in largely non-literate societies in which writing had a numinous authority and power, certain texts inscribed on monuments or parchment were not intended for reading or consultation or interpretation. References to "writings/scrolls" of (Mosaic) torah/law in books later included in the Hebrew Bible (2 Kings 22–23; Nehemiah 8) indicate that they were written (and laid up in the temple) as what might be called "constitutional" texts that authorized the Judean temple-state.[9]

Third, as a result of the discovery of the DSS, it is now evident that the authority of the books that were later included in the Hebrew Bible held what might be called relative authority in Judean society. Not only were the texts of the Pentateuchal books still developing,[10] but shared authority with both alternative texts of torah, such as *Jubilees*, and the ordinances promulgated by the Pharisees that were included as part of official state law under some high priests (Josephus, *Antiquities* 13.296–298, 408–409).

Most important are the implications of the recent recognition that scribes themselves were engaged in oral cultivation of texts as well as in inscribing them on scrolls.[11] If even the literate scribal custodians of the written texts of the elite tradition were cultivating texts by oral recitation, then it seems certain that non-literate ordinary people who would have had little or no direct contact with scrolls were engaged in oral cultivation of Israelite tradition at the popular level.

All of these results of recent research conspire to undermine the previously standard construction of the late second-temple Judean scriptures as readily accessible and widely known to a largely literate society by reading. Instead the books later recognized as biblical, along with other authoritative

---

8. Harris, *Ancient Literacy*; Hezser, *Jewish Literacy*; Carr, *Tablet of the Heart*; Horsley, *Scribes, Visionaries*, chaps. 4–6.

9. Niditch, *Oral World and Written Word*; Horsley, *Scribes, Visionaries*, chap. 6; and chaps. 1 and 2 above.

10. Ulrich, *Dead Sea Scrolls*; Horsley, *Scribes, Visionaries*, chap. 6; and chaps. 2 and 3 above.

11. Jaffee, *Torah in the Mouth*; Carr, *Tablet of the Heart*; Horsley, *Scribes, Visionaries*, chap. 5.

written texts, were known mainly in circles of scribes who both learned them by recitation and copied them on scrolls.

The Gospel of Mark, however, does not fit this emerging picture of oral–written scribal knowledge and cultivation of Judean scriptures. The feature of the Gospel that provides the obvious "test case" is provided by Mark's references to what are presented as passages of scripture. In the previously standard construction of biblical studies, it has been assumed that Mark and the other "evangelists" were "quoting" from written texts of scripture. When we reexamine these references in the Gospel apart from the assumptions of print culture, however, it is difficult to find clear indications that written texts were involved. Indeed it seems clear that Mark's knowledge of the content of scripture is not derived from scribal or scribal-like cultivation of scripture that involved written texts in close relation to oral recitation.

The Gospel of Mark introduced "quotes" and some of its other references with the formula "(as) it is written" (*gegraptai*; 1:2; 7:6; etc.). We can conclude from this formula at least that the Gospel derives from a society in which the existence of authoritative written texts was widely known and that their existence in writing gave them a special authority. A study of the frequent use of the formula in the *Didache* ("The Teaching of the Twelve Apostles") concluded that it is an appeal to the scripture as authority, while the "quotation" appears to have been from memory.[12] That a prophecy or a law was "written" on a scroll, especially if it were a revered prophecy of great antiquity, gave it an added aura of authority, for ordinary people as much as for the literate elite. Virtually all of the instances where the Gospel of Mark uses the formula are references to a prophecy now being fulfilled. Thus in the Gospel of Mark, parallel to the *Didache*, references to what stands "written" is an appeal to authority (as noted in chap. 10). In some cases "it is written" is just a general appeal to authority, with no particular "quotation" given (9:12–13; 14:21).

In the few cases in Mark where particular words or phrases are quoted, they do not appear to have involved consultation of a written text. In two cases the "quotes" appear to us as composites from two different "biblical" texts. Mark 1:2–3, ostensibly quoting "the prophet Isaiah," begins with lines similar to what we read in our written texts of Malachi 3:1 and Isaiah 40:3. The anonymous "quotation" in Mark 11:17 includes lines similar to what we know in our written texts of Isaiah (56:7) and Jeremiah (7:11). We recognize that the anonymous "quotation" in Mark 7:6–7 derives from Isaiah, although the citation is not very close to our written texts of Isa 29:13

---

12. Henderson, "Didache and Orality."

(similarly what appears as Isa 6:9–10 in Mark 4:12). And in Mark 14:27 the short line supposedly quoted from Zech 13:7 looks like a proverb that may have been well-known, even from before the composition of the book of Zechariah. The best explanation for all of these cases, particularly the ones that appear to us as composite "quotations" and the proverb, would seem to be that Mark's composers' knowledge of this material is oral-memorial, and not from (examination of) written texts. But it is oral-memorial knowledge that does not appear close to what we would expect of professional scribes whose knowledge would presumably have been closer to one or another of the written textual traditions.

The other supposed quotations of scripture in Mark are of three sorts. (a) In two episodes of the Gospel, Jesus recites "the commandments (of God)" as commonly known oral tradition. The citations are directed, respectively, against the scribes and Pharisees from Jerusalem who have voided God's word and the man who has by implication violated the commandments in accruing great wealth (7:9–13; 10:17–22). Jesus' followers' spontaneous singing of a well-known psalm and Jesus' reference to the ecstatic David's declaration in the words of another well-known psalm are similarly derived from oral tradition (11:9–10; 12:36). (b) At three different points Mark's Jesus challenges the Pharisees, high priests and scribes, and Sadducees, respectively, with the phrase "have you never/not read," claiming that their written text supports his action or position against theirs (Mark 2:25; 12:10; 12:26). In all three cases the historical incident or statement by God or a psalm would almost certainly have been common knowledge in oral tradition. Especially in the incident about David and the bread from the altar (2:25), "Jesus'" version is strikingly different from what the Pharisees would have "read" in any of the variant written versions. (c) In the only places where Mark refers to Moses as having "written," it was for the Pharisees or the Sadducees (10:3–5; 12:19), and by implication not for ordinary people (who would not have been able to read what was written).

Mark's relation to Judean scriptures can thus be summarized in three key points. First, the Gospel and its audience knew of the existence of written texts, indeed viewed the written texts as authoritative, finding their fulfillment in Jesus' mission. Second, Mark appealed to scriptures as supporting its (Jesus') position against that of the scribes and Pharisees, who should have known them well because they could read. Third, the Gospel's citations of lines ostensibly "written" in scripture show significant discrepancies with written versions of the texts, greater than would be expected from scribal (-like) cultivation (some contact with the written text). It is thus much easier to explain Mark's (composers') knowledge of the contents of the scriptures as derived from (Galilean) popular tradition (that has come to include some knowledge of the official scribal tradition based in Jerusalem) than as coming from a scribal like cultivation of oral–written texts, which would presumably have resulted in closer acquaintance with one or more of the written versions of lines cited.[13]

A key and important difference between Qumran texts such as the Damascus Document and the Gospel of Mark, which both stand in and continue Israelite tradition, is that the former are in the *language registers* of previous scribal texts (some of which were later included in the Bible) while the Gospel narrates new events with references and allusions to figures and events known from Israelite tradition, but not in the language register of scribal texts of torah. The situation is different with regard to prophetic forms, which were popular forms that were taken up secondarily into the scribal collections of prophetic oracles. But prophetic activity, including the delivery of oracles, continued in the popular tradition, as exemplified in John the Baptist and Jesus ben Hananiah as well as Jesus of Nazareth.[14]

## Importance of Oral Communication in the Origin/ Development of the Gospel

This comparison of references to Israelite tradition in Mark's Gospel with Judean scribal oral–written cultivation of scriptures points to two further, related features of the Gospel: its origins in and orientation to ordinary people and the corollary, the origins and development of the Gospel in an oral communication environment.

As suggested by its references to tradition, Mark is not a scribal text, but focused on a popular prophet leading a movement of ordinary people. The people involved in the story and evidently its earliest audience as well were evidently located in the villages of Galilee and surrounding territories in Syria (villages of Tyre, Caesarea Philippi, the Decapolis), not in Jerusalem, from which scribal representatives "came down" in opposition. There is even a notable language difference, as Peter is recognized apparently by his "up-country" dialect (presumably of Aramaic; Mark 14:70). After Jesus' confrontation with the high priests and his Roman execution in Jerusalem, the audience is directed back to rural Galilee (Mark 14:28; 16:7). This open ending points to where the story continued among its early audience. The Gospel story originated among and was oriented to ordinary people, indeed in opposition to the rulers and their representatives.

13. Hearon, "Mapping Written and Spoken Word," 383, makes the further point that what Mark refers to as "it is written" is encountered as spoken word.

14. Horsley, "'Like One of the Prophets of Old.'"

This story of a leader-and-movement that was addressed to other ordinary people was (thus) also heavily dependent on oral communication,
as indicated in the research (discussed above) that finds literacy limited
mainly to scribal circles in Judea and the elite in the wider Roman empire.
Under the standard view rooted in assumptions of widespread literacy, it
was not possible to explain the composition of Mark and the other Gospels
without assuming the "authors'" knowledge of the Hebrew Bible (the written "Law and the Prophets"), presumed to be *the* medium in which Israelite
tradition was known. As reviewed in the first few chapters above, however,
recent researches have shown that it is extremely unlikely that written copies of scriptural books (mostly in Hebrew) were generally available and that
ordinary people (who spoke Aramaic) could not have read them anyhow.

Yet ordinary people were by no means ignorant of Israelite tradition
or dependent on the scribes and Pharisees to mediate it. As all of those
distinctively Israelite popular prophetic and messianic movements in late
second-temple times recounted by the Judean historian Josephus attest, a
popular Israelite tradition was not only alive but formative among the ordinary people (*Ant.* 17.271–285; 18.85–87; 20.97–98, 169–171; *War* 2.55–65,
259–263).[15] Although it is difficult to document, given that ordinary people
generally left no written texts, parallel to the elite or official Judean tradition produced and cultivated in scribal circles, including the written texts
(scriptures), villagers had for generations been orally cultivating their own
popular Israelite tradition.[16]

The Gospel of Mark portrays Jesus as a new Moses and Elijah in multiple sea crossings, feedings in the wilderness, healings, appointing twelve
disciples who carry on his mission, and addressing people in new (Mosaic)
covenantal teaching. None of these episodes need to be understood as dependent on knowledge of "biblical texts." They are rooted in and resonate
with the popular tradition long cultivated orally among the people. As the
developing Gospel was performed in communities of the expanding movement, it resonated with the hearers by referencing the popular tradition.

## Oral Communication, Oral Performance, and Oral–written Texts in the Context in Which Mark was Cultivated

Contrary to the standard operating assumption of New Testament studies
rooted in print culture, oral communication and oral recitation of texts,

15. Horsley, "Two Types of Popular Prophets"; "Popular Messianic Movements."
16. Scott, "Protest and Profanation."

not the reading and writing of texts, prevailed in the early centuries during which the Gospel of Mark gained authority among communities of Christians. This can be seen in communications in the Hellenistic-Roman world in general, in the communities of Christ in particular, and in evidence for the oral recitation of texts such as Mark that were eventually included in the New Testament. The Gospel of Mark thus continued to be performed orally in communities of ordinary people even after written copies were made and became more widely distributed through repeated copying.

Below the level of the literate elite, the vast majority of people had little or no need for writing, as noted above for Galilee and Judea. Communication generally was oral and cultivation of cultural traditions was oral. To appreciate that cultivation of texts was oral among ordinary people in the Roman empire generally it may help to recognize that the cultivation of texts was oral among the literate elite as well. Just as texts were learned and cultivated by oral recitation by scribes in Judea, so in Hellenistic and Roman literate circles texts that were written were processed orally, with written texts playing ancillary, monumental, and authorizing roles. Public recitation was the principal means of "publishing" a composition. "Reading" a cumbersome chirograph required prior knowledge of the text inscribed on it. Students of virtually any subject learned by recitation and memorization. Those who composed texts did not "write" them as "authors" do in print culture, but may have dictated them to a secretary or scribe.[17]

One of the foundational assumptions of modern New Testament studies is that "early Christianity" was a literate culture. It is indeed impressive that Christian communities possessed written copies of some of their revered texts already in the second century. Yet the few early Christian references to oral and/or written communication indicate that the communities of Christ and their nascent intellectual leadership did not just prefer orality, but were even reticent about or suspicious of writing.[18] In the early second century Papias, bishop of Hierapolis declared:

> I inquired about *the words* of the ancients, what Andrew or Peter or Philip or Thomas or James of John or Matthew or any other of the Lord's disciples *said*, and what Ariston and the elder John, the Lord's disciples, were *saying*. For I did not suppose that things from books would benefit me so much as *things from a living and abiding voice*. (Eusebius, *H. E.* 3.39.3–4)

---

17. Graham, *Beyond the Written Word*, chap. 3; Small, *Wax Tablets of the Mind*.

18. Achtemeier, "*Omnes verbum somnat*"; L. Alexander, "Living Voice"; Botha, "Greco-Roman Literacy"; Shiner, *Proclaiming the Gospel*.

Papias' statement indicates both the oral mode of communication and the high valuation placed on the direct oral continuity of communication from the Lord through the previous two generations of disciples. The erudite early theologian Clement of Alexandria apologized for committing the teaching of the church to writing. He was clear that written notes are weak and lifeless compared with oral discourses. The former served only instrumental purposes such as aiding the memory or preventing the loss of important teaching. And some teachings could be communicated only orally. It was dangerous to write them down, for they might fall into the hands of those who would misunderstand what he was trying to communicate.[19]

The *Shepherd of Hermas* presents a fascinating illustration of the function of "books" among the Christ-believers who were non-literate or semi-literate. In the "visions" section of this second-century text produced by a prophet in Rome, Hermas receives a visit from a heavenly revealer.

> She said to me, "Can you take this message to God's elect ones?" I said to her, "Lady, I cannot remember so much; but give me the little book to copy." "Take it," she said, "and give it back to me." I took it and went away to a certain place in the country, and *copied everything, letter by letter, for I could not distinguish the syllables* (*metegrapsamen panta pros gramma ouch heuriskon gar tas syllabas*) So when I had finished the letters of the little book, it was suddenly taken out of my hand; but I did not see by whom (*Shep. vis.* 2.1.3–4).

This scene stands in the revelatory tradition known from earlier Enoch texts, the book of Daniel, and the book of Revelation, a tradition that includes heavenly books shown to visionaries, thus lending their visions the highest authority of divine writing.[20] Hermas' vision reflects knowledge of how new copies of written copies of texts were made, and then returned to the one from whom they were borrowed.[21] Later the "ancient lady" had "additional words" for Hermas to "make known to all the elect." Hermas is to send two books, respectively, to Clement and Grapte, who would exhort the widows and orphans. Meanwhile Hermas was to "read it [the book] with the elders in charge of the assembly" (*Vis.* 2.4.2–3). But Hermas does not know how to read the book, as he has already indicated in the way he describes his copying ("letter by letter, since I could not distinguish the syllables"). He cannot make out the syllables so that he knows how the text sounds, that is, how to reoralize the letters in a recitation so that it can be communicated.

---

19. Shiner, *Proclaiming the Gospel*, 18; Haines-Eitzen, *Guardians of Letters*, 105.

20. Niditch, *Oral World Written Word*; Horsley, *Scribes, Visionaries*, chaps. 5, 6.

21. Haines-Eitzen, *Guardians of Letters*, chap. 1.

In immediate "literary" context as well as in the general cultural context, it seems clear that Hermas' "reading," like Grapte's exhortation, was oral in a group of elders. At least some of the "authors" of the revered "writings" of the apostolic and sub-apostolic "fathers" were not literate. The point is that cultivation (learning and appropriation) of texts was by oral recitation or performance.

This further communication of his revelation by the non- or semi-literate Hermas and Papias' highest valuation of "the living voice" also illustrate the third point about how oral communication predominated in the context in which Mark would have been performed. Most valuable to the subsequent generations of Christ-believers was the direct chain of oral recitation of the "words of the Lord." Written books were of secondary, ancillary value. From his close investigation of performance of texts in the Hellenistic-Roman world, Whitney Shiner concluded that a "reader" of the Gospels did not need to know how to read from a codex. "The performer could learn the Gospel from hearing oral performances or by hearing" others recite it.[22] Justin Martyr reports that at Sunday assemblies "the memoirs of the apostles or the writings of the prophets are read for as long as time permits."[23] Hippolytus says that "Scripture was read at the beginning of services by a succession of readers until all had gathered . . . This practice lasted at least to the time of Augustine." He comments that many people had learned to recite (large portions of) the Gospels themselves from hearing them recited in services.[24]

As in both Judean culture and Hellenistic-Roman culture generally, early Christians committed texts to memory in order then to recite or perform them orally. Such performers probably included some who were semi-literate. Already in the second century, and certainly in the third and fourth century at least some Christians possessed craft literacy, were copyists, secretaries, "calligraphers." His wealthy patron provided Origen with copyists and (women) calligraphers. That example, of course, also indicates that even craft literacy was not that common. As we know from the fourth-century report (*Panarion* 67.1.1–4; 67.7.9) of Hieracas in Leontopolis in Egypt, while he was a copyist, he memorized the Old and New Testaments in order to recite and comment on the texts. Or, to come at this from another angle, the striking lack of evidence "regarding copyists involved in reproducing [written] Christian texts prior to the fourth century is itself instructive."[25]

22. Shiner, *Proclaiming the Gospel*, 26.

23. Ibid., 45.

24. Ibid., 45, 107.

25. Haines-Eitzen, *Guardians of Letters*, 38–39.

The plea from a community in upper Egypt to "make and send me copies of books" indicates that they were not already readily available. Written copies of texts were revered, hence in demand. But texts were usually cultivated orally.

Detailed recent investigations by text critics are now confirming that oral recitation was probably the predominant form of appropriation and further cultivation of revered authoritative texts such as the Gospels in Christian communities. Parker and others are recognizing that manuscripts from the second and third centuries are extremely varied.[26] The majority of what are still called "textual variants" of Christian books originated in the first two centuries, in the relatively free transmission process.[27] There is more disagreement/variation among (fragmentary) manuscripts of a given Gospel than there is between the Gospels. There is a growing awareness that manuscripts cannot be neatly grouped into distinctive traditions or versions. The evidence is too varied, even chaotic. Text critics have characterized the fluid state of the texts as "uncontrolled," "unstable," "wild," "free," suggesting unlimited flexibility and even randomness.[28] They suggest this evidence may indicate that oral cultivation of the texts influenced and was reflected in the copying of the texts, a suggestion that invites further exploration. It appears that through the second and third centuries Mark, like the other Gospels, continued to be performed orally from memory. Not until the Church suddenly became eagerly responsive to the imperial state, with the initiative coming from Constantine himself, did bishops such as Eusebius order "fifty copies of the divine scriptures. . . for the instruction of the church, to be written on well-prepared parchment by copyists most skillful in the art of accurate and beautiful writing."[29]

## The Gospel of Mark as Memorable and Performable

To have been continuously performed, resonated with the people, such that it became widely used, the Gospel of Mark must have been memorable and performable in significant ways. Exploration of Mark as oral performance has barely begun among Gospel scholars. Yet there are some suggestive probes the results and implications of which can be summarized here.

---

26. Parker, *Living Text*.

27. Ibid.; Haines-Eitzen, *Guardians of Letters*, 76.

28. Haines-Eitzen, *Guardians of Letters*, 106–7.

29. As cited in Gamble, *Books and Readers*, 79, n. 132.

*Drawing on and Adapting Israelite Tradition and Larger Cultural Patterns*

Much of the literary analysis that was borrowed by Gospel interpreters in the 1970s and 1980s was developed to deal with modern prose fiction. The assumption was that students were reading novels (or a Gospel) for the first time and not familiar with the story. In the assemblies of Christ where Gospels were performed in the late first and second-third centuries, however, both performer and the community of listeners were already familiar with the story. I want to focus briefly on two key implications of the already familiar story, partly to counter the persistence in New Testament studies of the belief that the Gospels made a decisive break with "Judaism" and the residual habit of focusing mainly on text-fragments such as individual sayings or episodes.

Precisely because the Gospel was an oft-told story both the performers and the audiences were familiar not only with the Gospel story, but also with the Israelite tradition(s) in reference to which it resonated. Israelite cultural tradition travelled in and with the Gospel story. Hearers were thus on familiar cultural ground as Mark's story, for example, began with Jesus receiving a call and undergoing a test in the wilderness, as had Moses and Elijah, the founding prophet of Israel and the prophet of renewal, respectively. They would almost have expected Jesus then to call protégés, as Elijah had called Elisha to help expand his renewal of Israel, and of course there should be twelve disciples in a program of renewal of Israel (Mark 1:16–20; 3:13–19; 6:7–13). Like Moses, Jesus led sea-crossings and presided over feedings in the wilderness for a people without sufficient food, and like Elijah he performed healings (Mark 5–8). Again in the recapitulation of Moses, he not only knew and recited the covenant commandments, but gave renewed covenantal teaching for revitalized community life (Mark 10:2–45).

Israelite tradition also offered roles other than that of the prophet like Moses or Elijah that Jesus could have been adapting, such as that of the young David who, acclaimed "messiah" by his followers, led them against foreign conquerors, an issue that several episodes in Mark's Gospel struggle with. Israelite prophets such as Elijah and Jeremiah, moreover, had boldly opposed the oppressive rulers of the people and had been persecuted and hunted down. In more recent Judean tradition, those who had been martyred in resisting the foreign emperor's attempt to control or interfere with the traditional Mosaic covenantal way of life had been vindicated by God. In any number of ways that we who are not as familiar with Israelite tradition do not even "get," the episodes of the Gospel story, and even the sequence of the episodes of the Gospel story were already familiar from the cultural memory of Jesus' followers, at the center of which was Israelite tradition. Those who performed and heard the Gospel in Greek-speaking villages a few generations later and who were now using those same scriptures as their own would have been aware of how the story of Jesus resonated with stories and prophecies that had become part of their cultural memory.[30]

The other key implication is implicit in the first. While biblical scholars have standardly focused on tiny text-fragments (isolated sayings or verses) and drawn connections between one verse and another, both narratives and prophetic oracles in the scriptures are rooted in, express, and adapt larger cultural patterns. As noted above, the popular prophetic and messianic movements in Judea and Galilee at the time of Jesus were informed by the cultural patterns carried in Israelite traditions of Moses-Joshua and the young David. Both of those same broader cultural patterns can be discerned to be operative in Mark's story, which portrays Jesus as a new Moses and struggles with whether and how Jesus was a messiah like David. To take the other most evident example, the broad pattern of Mosaic covenant that was clearly operative in the texts produced by the Qumran community (the Community Rule and the Damascus Rule) can be discerned in and behind the series of dialogues in Mark 10:2–45 as well as in Matthew's "sermon on the mount."[31] The point here is that the Israelite cultural memory out of which the Gospel of Mark developed included such broad cultural patterns and their adaptation in Mark's Gospel make it memorable and performable—and thus contributed to its taking root in communities of early Christians.

### Oral Narrative Features and Devices

One of the many important contributions of Werner Kelber was to enable us to appreciate most of the Jesus-stories that were the components of the Gospel of Mark as oral performances.[32] Many of the key features of oral narrative in the component "stories" of Mark are found also in the overall narrative, as discussed in chap. 10. Oral narrative features such as formulaic connective devices (such as "and," "immediately," "and again," which are usually omitted in English translations) also link together the many episodes throughout the Gospel. The effect is an action-packed story of "one

---

30. On cultural/social memory, see Kelber, "The Case of the Gospels"; and Kirk and Thatcher, eds., *Memory, Tradition, and Text.*

31. Horsley, *Hearing the Whole Story,* chap. 8.

32. Kelber, *The Oral and the Written Gospel,* chap. 2, esp. 64–70. See also Botha, "Mark's Story"; and Dewey," Mark as Oral–aural Event."

thing after another." Another narrative features is a plethora of "folkloristic" triads.[33] Not only do healing stories and parables unfold in three steps, but the overall narrative features triads. Jesus predicts his arrest, execution, and rising three times, he enters Jerusalem three times, he asks the disciples to watch with him three times, and Peter denies Jesus three times.

The Gospel also includes various devices of "narrative maneuvering," such as the well-known Markan "sandwich" technique of juxtaposing two stories, one framing the other. Jesus' family's concern that he is possessed frames the scribes' charge that Jesus works in the power of Beelzebul (3:20–35), the healing of the twelve-year-old dead young woman frames the healing of the woman who had been hemorrhaging for twelve years (5:21–43), Jesus' cursing of the fig tree frames his prophetic demonstration against the temple (11:12–25), and Peter's denial frames Jesus' trial before the high priesthood (15:52–72). In this device of oral storytelling the focal episode and the framing episode reinforce and interpret each other.

A more subtle oral narrative device is the concentric arrangement of the five episodes (of healing—eating—celebrating—eating—healing) in Mark 2:1—3:6.[34] But these five episodes have many connections with the themes of the story as a whole. Healing, exorcism, and eating (wilderness feedings and covenantal meal at passover) Jesus' principal activities throughout the Gospel narrative. As in the chiasm of five episodes, so in the fuller narrative of healing, exorcism, and meals, Jesus' actions pose challenges to the dominant order centered in Jerusalem as represented by the scribes and Pharisees.

Another example of the oral "narrative maneuvering" that would aid in oral performance and hearing are the two series of five acts of power in the second major narrative step of the story—an oral pattern that may have preceded the development of the story as a whole.[35] Readers of Mark have long discerned in Mark 4:35—8:26 two "chains" of stories that have the same sequence of a sea-crossing, an exorcism, two healings, and a wilderness feeding (except that the last two episodes in the second chain are reversed into order to frame the next major narrative step; thus 4:35–41; 5:1–20; 5:21–24+35–43; 5:24–34; 6:30–44 and then 6:45–52; 7:24–30; 7:31–37; 8:1–10; 8:22–26).

By themselves, without insertion of other episodes, those sets of stories clearly represent Jesus as enacting the renewal of Israel as a prophet like Moses and Elijah, the great founder (sea-crossing and wilderness feeding)

33. Kelber, *The Oral and the Written Gospel*, 66.

34. Dewey, *Markan Public Debate*.

35. Laid out in Achtemeier, "Pre-Markan Catenae."

and renewer (healings) of Israel, respectively, in the popular Israelite cultural memory. By inserting additional episodes into these chains the Markan narrative expands their message of the renewal of Israel. For example, in the mission of the twelve, representative of the twelve tribes, Mark's Jesus further confirms that his program of the kingdom of God is a renewal of Israel. And the story of Herod Antipas's arrest and execution of the Baptist illustrates what happens to prophets engaged in a renewal of Israel and, more specifically, prefigures what is about to happen to Jesus. The material that expands the "chains" and the many links between episodes in the second narrative step of the Gospel and those later in the story enable the listeners to hear that the message of the Gospel as a whole is the same as that of the structuring "chains," Jesus' renewal of Israel over against the rulers of Israel.

### *The Overall Narrative Structure of the Gospel of Mark*

On the basis of these implication of Kelber's earlier work and others' insights, we can discern the narrative structure and structuring elements that must have made the Gospel of Mark a most memorable and performable text in the first several generations of its use. I will delineate the overall structure and then comment on how the "infrastructure" would help make the Gospel easily memorable. (I am aware of the irony of continuing to use visual-spatial metaphors such as "structure" and chapter-and-verse numbers to "locate" sections of a text.)

### Narrative Steps in the Gospel of Mark

**Opening**: John's announcement, Jesus' baptism and testing in wilderness (1:1–13)

**Theme**: Jesus (as prophet) proclaims that the Kingdom of God is at hand (1:14–15)

**First step**: Jesus launches renewal of Israel in Galilee (1:16—3:35)

Speech: Jesus' teaches the mystery of the kingdom in parables (4:1–34)

**Second step**: Jesus like Moses/Elijah continues renewal of Israel (4:35—8:21/26)

**Third step**: Jesus debates his role and renews covenant (8:22/27—10:52)

**Fourth step**: Jesus proclaims divine judgment of temple, high priests (11:1—13:1-2)

Speech: Jesus speaks about future, exhorting solidarity and not being misled (13:3–37)

**Fifth step**: Jesus' last supper, arrested, trial; crucifixion by the Romans (14–15)

**Open ending**: direction back to "Galilee" for continuation of movement (16:1–8)

Except for the two pauses for the speeches, the overall narrative consists of one episode after another linked with "ands" and frequent references to "immediately." As noted above, all of the narrative steps include devices that provided some intermediate patterning. In the first step (after the obligatory first move, for a prophet like Elijah, of calling protégés to assist him), Jesus enters the assembly (*synagoge*) in the village of Capernaum (1:21) and then returns "home" to Capernaum (2:1), again enters the assembly (3:1) and again goes "home" (3:19), at fairly evenly timed intervals in the narrative. As noted just above, the next narrative step (4:35—8:21/26) is organized around two series of five episodes in the same sequence that recapitulate the prophetic acts of Moses and Elijah (sea crossing, exorcism, healings, wilderness feeding), except that the last two in the second series are reversed to provide an episode of healing a blind person as an opening to frame the next narrative step. The third step in the narrative is structured by the three announcements of Jesus' arrest, crucifixion and rising that serve as foils to the dialogue episodes in this section. This step closes with another healing of a blind man that corresponding to the transitional episode from the previous narrative step, a framing that sets off the increasing blindness of the disciples to what Jesus is doing and its implication. In the fourth narrative step Jesus enters Jerusalem three times, first in a seemingly "messianic" demonstration, then in a demonstration that announces God's condemnation of the temple, and then for a sustained confrontation with the ruling high priests and their representatives. The climactic narrative step features two "sandwich" or framing devices: first the high priests' resolve to arrest and kill Jesus and Judas' betrayal frame the last supper and Jesus' prayer in Gethsemane then Peter's denial frames Jesus' trial.

In addition to the "infrastructure" of the narrative steps, there are numerous links between and across the narrative steps, including repetitions of themes that drive home the message. Between the second and third and the third and fourth narrative steps, and between the fourth narrative step and the second speech are episodes that make them overlap. These episodes belong to the previous step, but also begin the next step or speech (the healing of the first blind person, the healing of the second blind person, and the prophecy of the destruction of the temple). In the first narrative step, after an exorcism and several healings and disputes with the scribes or Pharisees, the latter conspire with the Herodians against Jesus, announcing clearly what is coming in the climax of the story. In the second next narrative step, introduced by Herod Antipas' question about who Jesus is, comes the episode in which Herod beheads John, again prefiguring the climax of the story in the arrest and execution of Jesus. In the third narrative step, the same question about Jesus' identity and Peter's adamant answer "the messiah" introduces Jesus' first announcement that he will be executed, prompting Peter's protest and Jesus' sharp rebuke "get behind me Satan."

Additional links are evident between the first and second narrative steps and the second and third steps. After calling the first four disciples and then naming the full twelve, suggesting a renewal of Israel, in the first step, Jesus then heals two women, one hemorrhaging for twelve years and the other twelve years old, suggesting a renewal of Israel, and then commissions the twelve to expand his program of preaching and healing among the villages of Israel, in the second step. After Jesus does Moses-like and Elijah-like actions in the second narrative step, he then appears on the mountain with Moses and Elijah in the third narrative step. In links and repetitions such as these the overall narrative is tied together and the performer (and audience) has cues and other devices that make the sequence of "one thing after another" come up in memory and flow out in plotted sequence.

In its various narrative devices of connectives and maneuvering, its adaptation of familiar cultural patterns, and the many connectives of its narrative structure, the Gospel of Mark was memorable and performable in the oral communication context of early Christian communities. Further exploration of Mark's narrative in oral performance should open up additional memorable and performable aspects of the Gospel.

## Mark's Resonance with Hearers in Context

As a performed text, the Gospel of Mark would have resonated with its hearers in particular historical (performance) contexts. In his discussion of "Mark's Oral Legacy," Kelber also reminds us that oral communication is embedded in its context, which has not only cultural and aesthetic aspects but political and economic as well. In fact, "nonlinguistic features have priority over linguistic ones."[36] Oral communication receives powerful ideological and situational support from its context as it resonates with the hearers. For Mark's Gospel we are attempting to understand not only its origins but its continuing performance in early Christian communi-

---

36. Kelber, *The Oral and the Written Gospel*, 75.

ties in Syria, Egypt, Asia Minor, etc. Whitney Shiner makes the important observation that in oral performance the narrative happens simultaneously in two worlds, the imagined world of the narrative and the concrete social world of the performance context. In contrast with a silent modern reader who perceives dialogue as taking place within the story world of a text, the ancient hearers of Mark would have heard dialogue within their own situation as well. There was thus "a partial collapse between the narrative dialogue and the audience."[37]

To appreciate the performance context of communities of Christ among peoples subject to the Roman empire and how the narrative may have resonated with them, modern western scholars need to cut through at least two layers of blockage to our discernment. One is the heavy layer of Christian supersessionism and anti-Judaism according to which the Gospels have been read. As noted above, in Mark and Matthew no split has yet taken place between "Christianity" and "Judaism." Both Gospels are stories of the fulfillment of Israel which has now expanded to include other, non-Israelite peoples (and there indeed are the seeds of subsequent supersessionism). The division evident in the texts is between the rulers and the ruled, not between "Jews" and "Christians." There is no question that some "Christian" texts (Luke-Acts) were playing up the Roman destruction of Jerusalem as God's punishment for the Judean rulers' collaboration in the killing of Jesus. But that is not true of Mark, which could well have originated prior to the great revolt of 66–70.[38]

The other obstruction to our understanding is our own different social location and historical situation. However, once we are sensitive to why people were poor, partly or largely because they owed rents or taxes to wealthy and powerful local magnates, we begin to sense how both particular episodes and the overall story in Mark would resonate with the people who comprised the overwhelming majority of the populace. Mark repeatedly represents Jesus as criticizing the powerful and their representatives for their demands on and exploitation of the poor. He accuses them of "devouring" widow's houses and of urging villagers to "dedicate" to the temple the economic resources they need locally to "honor their father and mother" (Mark 12:38–40; 7:9–13). Mark has Jesus insisting on cooperative non-exploitative economic life in their communities, in keeping with the covenantal commandments (versus the negative example of wealthy fellow seeking "eternal life"). "It is easier for a camel to go through the eye of a needle than for someone who is rich to enter the kingdom of God" (10:25).

37. Shiner, *Proclaiming the Gospel*, 171.

38. See the discussion in Horsley, *Hearing the Whole Story*, 131–33.

The parable of the tenants in Mark's Gospels (Mark 12:1–9) offers an illustrative episode that, working creatively from Israelite cultural tradition, would have resonated with virtually any community in antiquity. Many of the rural hearers may have become tenants of their creditors as a result of spiraling debts; and many of the urban hearers or their parents may well have migrated into the city because they or their ancestors had lost their land to absentee landlords. The parable builds on the "song of the vineyard" which Isaiah had used to indict the wealthy for their exploitation of the peasants and seizure of their land. Jesus' parable dramatizes the sharp conflict between the wealthy absentee landlords, often also the rulers, and their tenants, who had been forced off their land that the landlords now controlled. Poor listeners would have been sympathetic with the tenants. But "Jesus" turns the parable against the wealthy rulers, with the implication that the vineyard/land will be given to others, i.e., those whom the wealthy landlord has exploited.[39] The parable of the tenants as applied is a virtual microcosm of the macrocosm of the whole Gospel story, which portrays Jesus carrying out a renewal of the people over against the rulers of the people. Mark's narrative which focuses on the renewal of the people of Israel was recognizably representative of the similar conflict in other areas of the Roman empire where it was performed.

In sum, the Gospel of Mark was not a good candidate to become scripture according to the prevailing models and standards either of Judean scribal circles or of Greco-Roman intellectual circles. As a story about a popular prophetic leader of a renewal movement among ordinary people in Galilee it was evidently regularly performed orally among other communities of ordinary people in an ever widening radius. Having become revered and authoritative for the broad base of the Christian movement during the second and third centuries, Mark was among the popular texts defended by the nascent Christian literate intellectuals to their cultural detractors. With strong resonance among the people this ordinary people's story and the other Gospels were also eventually acknowledged by the emergent hierarchy of the established Church as integral to the canon of the New Testament that was added to the Jewish scriptures in Greek as Christian Scripture. But what led to its inclusion in the canon was its repeated oral performance as an

---

39. There is no indication in Mark that the "others" are "Christians" who are replacing "the Jews." It is clear that they are the ordinary people addressed throughout the story.

increasingly authoritative, scriptural text in the second and third centuries before standardized written copies were widely available.

# EPILOGUE

The steadily increasing recognition that many texts that became scriptural, that is, Holy *Writ*, had been orally performed in an oral communications environment has profound implication for the field of biblical studies and the appropriation of those texts. These implications will surely be wider-reaching than we can discern at this elementary stage of exploration. But some of them, including ways that may bring new life to biblical interpretation, are becoming clear at least in their general outlines.

First, exploration of oral communication, oral cultivation of texts and tradition, and oral performance of texts can help interpreters escape the prison of print culture that constrains the spirit, the imagination, and the creativity that foster supportive community and social action. Exegesis on the basis of the print-cultural assumptions and concepts of standard biblical studies often results in the reduction of texts to mere lines extracted from librettos left over from live performances. The focus on and analysis of individual proverbs of sages and sayings of Jesus fragments what was once genuine communication into precious but lifeless artifacts to be contemplated by isolated individual readers. Exploring texts in oral performance, on the other hand, opens the way toward discernment of what the parameters of messages (texts) of genuine communication may have been (instructional speeches, prophecies, sustained Gospel narratives, speeches of Jesus), of who their particular audiences may have been (scribes-in-training, kings and their officers, Jesus-movements), and of the particular context of performance in which the message communicated would have come alive.

Second, exploration of how texts were performed and resonated with people in historical community context by referencing the cultural tradition in which they were rooted makes necessary serious investigation of both the historical context and the cultural tradition of the performed text. It leads interpreters into deeper appreciation of how the text fit in and resonated with the historical context and cultural tradition. In this way exploration of texts in performance along the lines of theory such as that of Foley makes possible the historical understanding of texts (the previously stated agenda of biblical studies) that was blocked by the field's print-cultural assumptions and procedures.

Third, exploration of texts in oral performance has a goal or purpose very different from that in standard biblical studies. Like other humanities fields, biblical studies rooted in bourgeois (and print) culture seeks to find the *meaning* of the text, whether the meaning of a text-fragment in itself or the meaning of a passage in its supposed literary and/or historical context. Exploration of orally performed texts look rather for the *work* done by (or the effect of) a text performed in a community in its context as it references the people's cultural tradition. To illustrate from texts discussed in the chapters above, many of the maxims or other proverbs in the book of Sirach, when taken as isolated sayings (like those listed one after another in Proverbs 10:1—22:16), are virtually opaque as to their meaning-in-themselves. Proverbs "communicate" or "mean" something only when used in particular contexts, and that meaning is contextual. If we discern and explore the instructional wisdom in Sirach as speeches to scribes-in-training on subjects such as seeking wisdom, one's demeanor and deferential behavior vis-à-vis one's high priestly patrons, and one's role as a fledgling "son" (student/ protégé) of an influential "father" (teacher, sage), then we can begin to appreciate how submission to such "discipline" would shape the conservative personality necessary for those who served in the staff of the high priestly heads of the temple-state. Exploration of the Q speeches or the Gospel of Mark in oral performance can help us appreciate how repeated performance of the speeches or story in community meetings could have evoked continuing loyalty to the prophet who had generated their movement, the solidarity of the community, and their commitment to continuing resistance to the rulers that their prophet-leader had pursued to the point of becoming a martyr. In the case of written texts not intended to be read and consulted, such as the monumental/constitutional texts of torah laid up in the temple, it is also more appropriate to look for the work they did (the effect they had) in the community that acclaimed them as holy objects (and heard their contents formally proclaimed). Torah-scrolls, as numinous sacred objects on which constitutional texts stood written, lent their sacred authority to the temple and its priestly heads.

Fuller awareness of the *work* done or the *effect* of particular texts-in-performance may well affect how we choose to use them in our own political-religious context. Perpetuation or restoration of the sacred aura of authoritative monumental texts as objects of veneration and deference would be instrumental in enhancing or bolstering the authority of ecclesial or political institutions and authority figures today. Regular recitation or even reading of instructional wisdom designed to instill a conservative

obedient personal demeanor in scribes-in-training might well have a similar effect in religious education and "spiritual discipline" in our own circumstances. Hearing or simply reading a Gospel whole in a group context, on
the other hand, with its dramatic portrayal of political conflict, personal and
community renewal, and resistance to the authorities, could well stimulate
questioning of authoritative political arrangements and cooperation and
collective action in today's world.

Fourth, one of the more serious implications of the recognition that
many "biblical" texts were, in their original compositional context, orally-
performed is for how these texts can be understood and used as historical sources. The investigation and (re-)construction of history (including
"biblical" history) as it developed in modern print-culture was based on
the analysis of "archival" sources such as government and company records,
letters, journals, and treatises, whether in print or hand-written. "Biblical"
and closely related texts have been treated in more or less the same way
as historical sources. "Biblical" historians, like other historians, have developed sophisticated critical analysis of their sources. But recognition that in
their context of origin, texts such as the instructional speeches of Ben Sira
or prophetic pronouncements or a Gospel story or the speeches in Q were
orally performed will presumably change the way that historians understand the relationship between the textual sources and the historical context
for which they provide evidence. Texts explored in performance contexts
open windows onto the dynamics of social-political relationships that were
much less accessible when texts were understood as archival, even as they
lessen confidence with which historians believed they could project "what
happened" (e.g., what Jesus said or did) with some precision, on the basis of
information or "data" derived from those texts.

For the instructional speeches in Sirach, for example, historical sociological analysis makes clear that they do not provide evidence for second-
temple Judean society (much less "Judaism") generally, but mainly for the
social-political relations of learned scribes with the heads of the temple-
state above them, their own families, and the ordinary people below them.
Exploration of these speeches as oral instruction of scribes-in-training
opens onto a deeper dimension of history to which we previously did not
imagine that we might have access: the formation of scribal character and
the political (-emotional) ambivalence of the scribal role in the dynamics
of historical crises under imperial rule. This access, moreover, may enable
historians to discern more readily the mediating role not only of the scribes
but of the texts they produced and cultivated in the dynamics of the power
relations between their ruler-patrons who headed the temple-state (under

imperial oversight) and the people they controlled politically-religiously and exploited economically.

The implications for how Gospel texts are understood as related to "the historical Jesus" are particularly poignant, indeed potentially "game-changing." Recent work of text critics is confirming what was suggested by exploration of the Gospels as orally performed, that a stable text of sayings or parables or mini-stories in the Gospels cannot be established. The "data" that Jesus-scholars have produced on the basis of print-cultural assumptions turn out to be modern scholarly constructs in somewhat the same way that the "established" text of the Gospels is a modern (print-cultural) scholarly construct. To the print-cultural scholarly orientation the recognition that our principal sources for Jesus are the Gospel texts-in-performance might appear to make historical investigation and historical knowledge virtually impossible. But that would be only on the standard print-cultural assumptions of biblical studies compounded by the distinctively modern individualistic belief that a historical person, and the revealer Jesus in particular, can be known apart from the societal forms in which s/he was embedded and her/his social interaction in political-economic-religious context. That an individual person and what s/he 'actually' said and did could be isolated was a chimera of the modern western individualistic imagination. It could be argued that what has led to the recent revival of interest in the historical Jesus has been the greater awareness and more precise knowledge of the historical situation in which he lived and worked. What has hardly begun is to view and explore Jesus relationally as well as contextually engaged in societal forms and interaction as portrayed by the Gospel stories and speeches. Recognition that our principal sources for Jesus were texts-in-performance only forces us to move toward a more fully relational and contextual approach.

Since the Gospels were produced by and performed in communities of Jesus movements that responded to Jesus' mission, however, we not only cannot extract Jesus as an individual from his interaction with others in historical context, but we cannot extract Jesus-in-interaction from the movements that produced and performed the Gospels. This, of course, is the way history works anyhow, as a historically significant figure emerges from interrelationship and interaction with people in complex circumstances and in the movements or events thus catalyzed. In attempting to appreciate how the Gospel stories of Jesus' mission resonated with the communities/movements in which they were performed (respectively) we can discern how he was understood as interacting with his followers and his opponents in historical context in some of the key movements resulting from his mission. We can then make judicious, informed comparisons of those portrayals to ascertain what may have been the main agenda of Jesus' mission in historical context.

Fifth, exploration of how texts were performed and resonated with people in historical community context can help bring new life to the field of biblical studies and to the ways in which biblical texts are appropriated in church and society. Probing the meaning of terms and phrases will remain important. Awareness that what we have access to are transcripts of texts-in-performance, however, pulls us into appreciation of texts as communication in contexts of the people's lives.

In this awareness the texts themselves demand appreciation as dynamic communication, and not hardened verbal artifacts. The texts, whether letters, Gospels, speeches, or prophecies, transcend and resist attempts to pin down their "meaning" in themselves or reduction them to some theological propositions. Insofar as most texts were (and continue as) texts-in-performance-in-contexts numerous "extra-textual" factors enter into the communication involved. How the texts do their work, the effects they have depend on the context of audience and their cultural tradition, even on tone of voice and gestures. Episodes of healing or of the sharp disputes between Jesus and the Pharisees, for example, do their work as integral components (in the context) of the overall Gospel stories of Jesus' renewal of Israel in opposition to the rulers. In the Gospels Jesus' teaching does not take the form of abstract one-line "sound bites." Rather he delivers short speeches on crucial real-life issues of people, such as social-economic relations in local communities, anxiety about subsistence living, and relations with repressive authorities. Fuller awareness of texts-in-performance allows the texts (seemingly "in themselves) to come alive. The "sayings of Jesus" provide a vivid example. Working on the assumptions of print-culture, and focusing not only on separate individual sayings but also on the Greek text without much consideration of the Israelite tradition in which Jesus was working, the scholars of the International Q Project reconstructed the original or early wording of the sayings of Jesus parallel in Matthew and Luke. It was not until we attempted to appreciate the teaching of Jesus in oral performance, after recognizing that the sayings formed speeches, that it could be recognized that the speeches have the poetic form of parallel lines that have considerable similarity to and resonance with poetic speeches and prophecies in (Semitic-language) Israelite tradition. And of course poetic speech is far more communicative and memorable than declarations in prose. New translations of the teaching of Jesus in Matthew and Luke can now reflect the discernment made possible by exploration of texts-in-performance.

Sixth, the exploration of "biblical" texts in performance in historical contexts can help inform the performance of biblical texts today, one of the most stimulating ways in which biblical studies is experiencing new life. The latter was already underway well before the recent expansion of exploration of "biblical" texts in performance in their situations of origin. Contemporary performance of biblical texts is what led its practitioners to formulate biblical "performance criticism," as discussed in the Introduction. It is important that contemporary performance practice remain geared to contemporary audiences and situations, and not become an attempt to resurrect some supposedly original performance. Exploration of texts-in-performance in their context of origin, however, can inform contemporary performance in various ways. For example, fuller awareness of the historical context of a text-in-performance and the cultural tradition in which it resonated with the hearers can provide a check on allowing contemporary performance to become so domesticated for today's context that the text is no longer allowed its own integrity that may stand over against today's hearers. And exploration of likely historical performance-context and the work done by the text in that context may result in further insights into how contemporary performers can make the text come alive again in addressing a new and different context.

It is probably too early to tell whether the recognition that many biblical texts were "originally" performed in the historical oral communications context will produce a new "paradigm" that will replace the print-cultural assumptions and concepts in which mainline biblical studies developed. The field has become so diverse and splintered that many of the new initiatives and "criticisms" will likely continue along their own innovative paths. But the closely related but largely independent recent lines of new research discussed in the chapters above pose serious challenges to the standard print-cultural assumption of biblical studies and open toward exciting new possibilities for the rejuvenation of the field.

# BIBLIOGRAPHY

Achtemeier, Paul J. "Toward the Isolation of Pre-Markan Catenae." *JBL* 89 (1970) 265–91. Reprinted in Achtemeier, *Jesus and the Miracle Tradition*, 55–86. Eugene, OR: Cascade Books, 2008.

———. "*Omnes verbum somnat:* The New Testament and the Oral Environment of Late Western Antiquity." *JBL* 109 (1990) 3–27.

Adams, J. N. et al., editors. *Bilingualism in Ancient Society: Language Contact and the Written Text.* Oxford: Oxford University Press, 2002.

Adams, J. N., and Simon Swain. "Introduction." In *Bilingualism in Ancient Society: Language Contact and the Written Text,* edited by J. N. Adams et al., 1–20. Oxford: Oxford University Press, 2002.

Aitken, Ellen B. *Jesus' Death in Early Christian Memory: The Poetics of the Passion.* Studien zur Umwelt des Neuen Testaments 53. Göttingen: Vandenhoeck & Ruprecht, 2004.

Alexander, Elizabeth Shanks. "The Fixing of Oral Mishnah and the Displacement of Meaning." *Oral Tradition* 14 (1999) 100–139.

———. *Transmitting Mishnah: The Shaping Influence of Oral Tradition.* Cambridge: Cambridge University Press, 2006.

Alexander, Loveday C. A. "The Living Voice: Skepticism Towards the Written Word in Early Christianity and in Greco-Roman Texts." In *The Bible in Three Dimensions: Essays in Celebration of Forty Years of Biblical Studies in the University of Sheffield,* edited by David J. A. Clines et al., 221–47. JSOTSup 87. Sheffield: Sheffield Academic, 1990.

Alexander, Philip S. "Retelling the Old Testament." In *It is Written: Scripture Citing Scripture: Essays in Honour of Barnabas Lindars, SSF,* edited by D. A. Carson and H. G. M. Williamson, 99–121. Cambridge: Cambridge University Press, 1988.

Allison, Dale G. *Jesus of Nazareth: Millenarian Prophet.* Minneapolis: Fortress, 1998.

Arnal, William E. *Jesus and the Village Scribes: Galilean Conflicts and the Setting of Q.* Minneapolis: Fortress, 2001.

Aston, Margaret. *Lollards and Reformers: Images and Literacy in Late Medieval Religion.* London: Continuum, 1984.

Baines, John. "Literacy and Ancient Egyptian Society." *Man* 18 (1983) 572–99.

———. "Literacy, Social Organization, and the Archaeological Record." In *State and Society: The Emergence and Development of Social Hierarchy and Political Centralization,* edited by J. Gledhill et al., 192–214. One World Archaeology 4. London: Unwin Hyman, 1984.

Baines, John, and C. J. Eyre. "Four Notes on Literacy." *Göttingen Miszellen* 16 (1983) 65–74.

Baltzer, Klaus. *The Covenant Formulary: In Old Testament, Jewish, and Early Christian Writings*. Translated by David E. Green. Philadelphia: Fortress, 1971.

Bar-Ilan, Meir. "Illiteracy in the Land of Israel in the First Centuries C.E." In *Essays in the Social Scientific Study of Judaism and Jewish Society*, edited by Simcha Fishbane and Stuart Schoenfeld, 2:46–61. Hoboken, NJ: Ktav, 1992.

Barkay, Gabriel. "The Iron Age II–III." In *The Archaeology of Ancient Israel*, edited by Amnon Ben Tor. New Haven: Yale University Press, for the Open University of Israel, 1992.

Barnett, P. W. "The Jewish Sign-Prophets: Their Intentions and Origins." *New Testament Studies* 27 (1980–81) 679–97.

Bauman, Richard. *Verbal Art as Performance*. Prospect Heights, IL: Waveland, 1977.

Baumgarten, Albert I. "The Pharisaic *Paradosis*." *HTR* 80 (1987) 63–77.

Beard, Mary, editor. *Literacy in the Roman World*. Ann Arbor: Journal of Roman Archaeology, 1991.

Bernstein, Moshe J. "'Rewritten Bible': A Generic Category which Has Outlived Its Usefulness?" *Textus* 22 (2005) 169–96.

Berquist, Jon. *Judaism in Persia's Shadow: A Social and Historical Approach*. 1995. Reprinted, Eugene, OR: Wipf & Stock, 2005.

Bial, Henry. *The Performance Studies Reader*. London: Routledge, 2004.

Black, C. Clifton. *Mark: Images of an Apostolic Interpreter*. Columbia: University of South Carolina Press, 1994.

Blenkinsopp, Joseph. "The Mission of Udjahorresnet and Those of Ezra and Nehemiah." *JBL* 106 (1987) 409–21.

———. *Sage, Priest, Prophet: Religious and Intellectual Leadership in Ancient Israel*. LAI. Louisville: Westminster John Knox, 1995.

———. "Temple and Society in Achaemenid Judah." In *Second Temple Studies 1: Persian Period*, edited by P. R. Davies, 22–53. JSOTSup 117. Sheffield: Sheffield Academic Press, 1991.

———. "Was the Pentateuch the Civic and Religious Constitution of the Jewish Ethnos in the Persian Period." In *Persia and Torah*, edited by James W. Watts, 41–62. SBLSymS 17. Atlanta: Society of Biblical Literature, 2001.

Blickle, Peter. *From the Communal Reformation to the Revolution of the Common Man*. Studies in Medieval and Reformation Thought 65. Leiden: Brill, 1998.

Botha, Pieter J. J. "Greco-Roman Literacy as Setting for New Testament Writings." *Neotestamentica* 26 (1992) 206–27. Reprinted in Botha, *Orality and Literacy in Early Christianity*, 39–61. BPCS 5. Eugene, OR: Cascade Books, 2012.

———. "Letter Writing and Oral Communication in Antiquity: Suggested Implications for Interpretation of Paul's Letter to the Galatians." *Scriptura* 42 (1992) 17–34. Reprinted in Botha, *Orality and Literacy in Early Christianity*, 193–211. BPCS 5. Eugene, OR: Cascade Books, 2012.

———. "Mark's Story as Oral Traditional Literature: Rethinking the Transmission of Some Traditions about Jesus." *Hervormde Teologiese Studies* 47 (1991) 304–31. Reprinted in Botha, *Orality and Literacy in Early Christianity*, 163–90. BPCS 5. Eugene, OR: Cascade Books, 2012.

———. *Orality and Literacy in Early Christianity*. BPCS 5. Eugene, OR: Cascade Books, 2012.

Bowman, Alan K., and Greg Woolf, editors. *Literacy and Power in the Ancient World*. Cambridge: Cambridge University Press, 1994.

Boyarin, Daniel. "Placing Reading: Ancient Israel and Medieval Europe." In *The Ethnography of Reading*, edited by Jonathan Boyarin, 10–37. Berkeley: University of California Press, 1993.

Brooke, George J. "Between Authority and Canon: The Significance of Reworking the Bible for Understanding the Canonical Process." Online: http://orion.mscc.huji.ac.il/symposiums/7th/BrookeFullPaper.htm/.

———. "Rewritten Bible." In *Encyclopedia of the Dead Sea Scrolls*, 2:778. Oxford: Oxford University Press, 2000.

Carr, David M. *Writing on the Tablet of the Heart: Origins of Scripture and Literature*. New York: Oxford University Press, 2005.

Carruthers, Mary J. *The Book of Memory: A Study of Memory in Medieval Culture*. Cambridge Studies in Medieval Literature 10. Cambridge: Cambridge University Press, 1990.

Carter, Charles E. *The Emergence of Yehud in the Persian Period: A Social and Demographic Study*. JSOTSup 274. Sheffield: Sheffield Academic Press, 1999.

Casey, Maurice. *An Aramaic Approach to Q*. Cambridge: Cambridge University Press.

———. *The Aramaic Sources of Mark's Gospel*. SNTSMS 102. Cambridge: Cambridge University Press, 1998.

Chancey, Mark A. *The Myth of a Gentile Galilee*. SNTSMS 118. Cambridge: Cambridge University Press, 2002.

———. *Greco-Roman Culture and the Galilee of Jesus*. SNTSMS 134. Cambridge: Cambridge University Press, 2005.

Charlesworth, James H., editor. *The Messiah: Developments in Earliest Judaism and Christianity*. Minneapolis: Fortress, 1992.

Childs, Brevard S. *Introduction to the Old Testament as Scripture*. Philadelphia: Fortress, 1979.

Clanchy, M. T. *From Memory to Written Record: England, 1066–1307*. Cambridge: Harvard University Press, 1979.

Coggins, Richard J. *Sirach*. Guides to Apocrypha and Pseudepigrapha. Sheffield: Sheffield Academic, 1998.

Collins, John J. *Jewish Wisdom in the Hellenistic Age*. Louisville: Westminster John Knox, 1997.

Conquergood, Dwight. "Performance Studies: Interventions and Radical Research." In *The Performance Studies Reader*, edited by Henry Bial, 311–22. London: Routledge, 2004.

Coote, Robert B., editor. *Elijah and Elisha in Socioliterary Perspecctive*. Semeia Studies. Atlanta: Scholars, 1992.

Coote, Robert B. and Mary P. Coote. *Power, Politics, and the Making of the Bible*. Minneapolis: Fortress, 1990.

Crawford, Sidnie White. "Rewritten Pentateuch." In *Encyclopedia of the Dead Sea Scrolls* 2:775–76. Oxford: Oxford University Press, 2000.

Crenshaw, James L. *Old Testament Wisdom: An Introduction*. Atlanta: John Knox 1981.

———. "The Primacy of Listening in Ben Sira's Pedagogy." In *Wisdom, You are My Sister: Studies in Honor of Roland E. Murphy*, edited by Michael L. Barre, 277–87. Catholic Biblical Quarterly Monograph Series 27. Washington, DC: Catholic Biblical Association of America, 1997.

———. *Education in Ancient Israel: Across the Deadening Silence*. Anchor Bible Reference Library. New York: Doubleday, 1998.

Cross, Frank Moore. *Canaanite Myth and Hebrew Epic*. Cambridge: Harvard University Press, 1973.

Crossan, John Dominic. *The Historical Jesus: The Life of a Mediterranean Jewish Peasant*. San Francisco: Harper, 1991.

Culloy, Robert C. "Orality and Writtenness in the Prophetic Texts." In *Writings and Speech in Israelite and Ancient Near Eastern Prophecy*, edited by Ehud Ben Zvi and Michael H. Floyd, 45–64. SBLSymS 10. Atlanta: Society of Biblical Literature, 2000.

Deanesly, Margaret. *The Lollard Bible and Other Medieval Biblical Versions*. Cambridge Studies in Medieval Life and Thought. Cambridge: Cambridge University Press, 1966.

Dewey, Joanna. "The Gospel of Mark and Oral Hermeneutic." In *Jesus, the Voice, and the Text: Beyond "The Oral and Written Gospel,"* edited by Tom Thatcher, 71–88. Waco, TX: Baylor University Press, 2008.

———. "The Gospel of Mark as an Oral–Aural Event: Implications for Interpretation." In *The New Literary Criticism and the New Testament*, edited by Elizabeth Struthers Malbon and Edgar V. McKnight, 248–57. Journal for the Study of the New Testament Supplements 109. Sheffield: Sheffield Academic, 1994.

———. "Mark as Interwoven Tapestry: Forecasts and Echoes for a Listening Audience." *CBQ* 52 (1991) 221–36.

———. *Markan Public Debate*. Society of Biblical Literature Dissertation Series 48. Chico, CA: Scholars, 1979.

———. "Oral Methods of Structuring Narrative in Mark." *Interpretation* 53 (1989) 332–44.

———. "The Survival of Mark's Gospel: A Really Good Story." *JBL* 123 (2004) 495–507.

———. *The Oral Ethos of the Early Church: Speaking, Writing, and the Gospel of Mark*. BPCS 8. Eugene, OR: Cascade Books, 2013.

Doane, Alger N. "The Ethnography of Scribal Writing and Anglo-Saxon Poetry: Scribe as Performer." *Oral Tradition* 9 (1994) 420–39.

Doran, Robert. "The New Dating of Jubilees: Jub 34–38; 23:14–32 in Narrative Context." *Journal for the Study of Judaism* 20 (1989) 1–11.

Dunn, James D. G. *Jesus Remembered*. Grand Rapids: Eerdmans, 2003.

Eisenstein, Elizabeth L. *The Printing Press as an Agent of Change: Communications and Culture Transformations in Early Modern Europe*. Cambridge: Cambridge University Press, 1979.

Ehrman, Bart D. *Misquoting Jesus: The Story behind Who Changed the Bible and Why*. San Francisco: HarperSanFrancisco, 2005.

———. *The Orthodox Corruption of Scripture: The Effect of Early Christological Controversies on the Text of the New Testament*. New York: Oxford University Press, 1993.

Elliott, John H. "Jesus the Israelite Was Neither a 'Jew' nor a 'Christian': On Correcting Misleading Nomenclature." *Journal for the Study of the Historical Jesus* 5/2 (2007) 119–54.

Epp, Eldon J. "The Multivalence of the Term 'Original Text' in New Testament Text Criticism." *HTR* 92 (1999) 257–63.

———. "The Oxyrhynchus New Testament Papyri: 'Not without honor except in their own hometown'?" *JBL* 123 (2004) 3–21.

Falk, Daniel K. *The Parabiblical Texts: Strategies for Extending the Scriptures in the Dead Sea Scrolls*. Companion to the Scrolls 8. London: T. & T. Clark, 2007.

Finnegan, Ruth. *Literacy and Orality: Studies in the Technology of Communication.* Oxford: Blackwell, 1988.

Fitzmyer, Joseph A., SJ. "The Languages of Palestine in the First Century A.D." *CBQ* 32 (1970) 501–31.

Foley, John Miles. *How to Read an Oral Poem.* Urbana: University of Illinois Press, 2002.

———. *Immanent Art: From Structure to Meaning in Traditional Oral Epic.* Bloomington: Indiana University Press, 1991.

———. "Plenitude and Diversity: Interactions between Orality and Writing." In *The Interface of Orality and Writing: Speaking, Seeing, Writing in the Shaping of New Genres,* edited by Annette Weissenrieder and Robert B. Coote, 103–18. WUNT 260. Tübingen, Mohr/Siebeck, 2010.

———. *The Singer of Tales in Performance.* Voices in Performance and Text. Bloomington: Indiana University Press, 1995.

Fontaine, Carole V. *Traditional Sayings in the Old Testament: A Contextual Study.* Bible and Literature Series 5. Sheffield: Almond, 1982.

Fox, Michael. "Wisdom and the Self-Presentation of Wisdom Literature." In *Reading from Left to Right: Essays on the Hebrew Bible in Honour of David J. A. Clines,* edited by J. Cheryl Exum and H. G. M. Williamson, 153–72. JSOTSup 373. Sheffield: Sheffield Academic, 2003.

Fraade, Steven D. "Interpretive Authority in the Studying Community at Qumran." *Journal of Jewish Studies* 44 (1993) 52–68.

———. "Looking for Legal Midrash at Qumran." In *Biblical Perspectives: Early Use and Interpretation of the Bible in Light of the Dead Sea Scrolls,* edited by Michael E. Stone and Esther G. Chazon, 59–79. Studies on the Texts of the Desert of Judah 28. Leiden: Brill, 1998.

Freyne, Sean. "Behind the Names: Galileans, Samaritans, *Ioudaioi.*" In *Galilee through the Centuries: Confluence of Cultures,* edited by Eric Meyers, 39–56. Duke Judaic Studies 1. Winona Lake, IN: Eisenbrauns, 1999.

———. *Galilee from Alexander the Great to Hadrian: A Study of Second Temple Judaism.* Wilmington, DE: Glazier, 1980.

———. "The Geography, Politics, and Economics of Galilee and the Quest of the Historical Jesus." In *Studying the Historical Jesus: Evaluations of the State of Current Research,* edited by Bruce Chilton and Craig Evans, 75–121. New Testament Tools and Studies 19. Leiden: Brill, 1994.

Fried, Lisbeth S. *The Priest and the Great King: Temple-Palace Relations in the Persian Empire.* BJS 10. Winona Lake, IN: Eisenbrauns, 2004.

Gager, John G. *Kingdom and Community: The Social World of Early Christianity.* Englewood Cliffs, NJ: Prentiss-Hall, 1975.

Gamble, Harry Y. *Books and Readers in the Early Church: A History of Early Christian Texts.* New Haven: Yale University Press, 1995.

Gee, James P. *Social Linguistics and Literacies: Ideologies in Discourse.* 2nd ed. London: Taylor & Francis, 1996.

Gesche, Petra D. *Schulunterricht in Babylonien im ersten Jahrtausend v. Chr.* Münster: Ugarit-Verlag, 2001.

Goodman, Martin. *The Ruling Class of Judaea: The Origins of the Jewish Revolt against Rome A.D. 66–70.* Cambridge: Cambridge University Press, 1987.

———. *State and Society in Roman Galilee, A.D. 132–212.* Totowa, NJ: Rowman & Allenheld, 1983.

———. "Texts, Scribes, and Power in Roman Judea." In *Literacy and Power in the Ancient World*, edited by Alan Bowman and Greg Woolf, 99–108. Cambridge: Cambridge University Press, 1994.

Gottwald, Norman K. *The Politics of Ancient Israel*. LAI. Louisville: Westminster John Knox, 2000.

———. "Social Class and Ideology in Isaiah 40–55." *Semeia* 59 (1992) 43–57. Reprinted in *The Bible and Liberation: Political and Social Hermeneutics*, rev. ed., edited by Norman Gottwald and Richard Horsley, 329–42. Maryknoll, NY: Orbis, 1993.

Grabbe, Lester. *Priests, Prophets, Diviners, Sages: A Socio-Historical Study of Religious Specialists in Ancient Israel*. Valley Forge, PA: Trinity, 1995.

Graham, William A. *Beyond the Written Word: Oral Aspects of Scripture in the History of Religion*. Cambridge: Cambridge University Press, 1987.

Green, William Scott. "Writing with Scripture: The Rabbinic Uses of the Hebrew Scripture." In *Writing with Scripture: The Authority and Uses of the Hebrew Bible in the Torah of Formative Judaism*, edited by Jacob Neusner, 7–23. Minneapolis: Fortress, 1989.

Haines-Eitzen, Kim. *Guardians of Letters: Literacy, Power, and the Transmission of Early Christian Literature*. Oxford: Oxford University Press, 2000.

Halliday, M. A. K. *Language as Social Semiotic: The Social Interpretation of Language and Meaning*. Baltimore: University Park Press, 1978.

Hanson, K. C. "Alphabetic Acrostics: A Form-Critical Study." Ph.D. diss., Claremont Graduate School, 1984.

———. "'How Honorable!' 'How Shameful!' A Cultural Analysis of Matthew's Makarisms and Reproaches." *Semeia* 68 (1994[96]) 81–111.

Hanson, K. C., and Douglas Oakman. *Palestine in the Time of Jesus: Social Structures and Social Conflicts*. 2nd ed. Minneapolis: Fortress, 2008.

Harrington, Daniel J. "Palestinian Adaptations of Biblical Narratives and Prophecies." In *Early Judaism and Its Modern Interpreters*, edited by Robert A. Kraft and George Nickelsburg, 239–46. Atlanta: Scholars, 1986.

———. "Two Early Jewish Approaches to Wisdom: Sirach and Qumran Sapiential Work A." In *The Wisdom Texts from Qumran and the Development of Sapiential Thought*, edited by Charlotte Hempel et al., 263–75. Leuven: Leuven University Press, 2002.

Harris, William V. *Ancient Literacy*. Cambridge: Harvard University Press, 1989.

Hearon, Holly E. "The Implications of Orality for Studies of the Biblical Text." In *Performing the Gospel: Orality, Memory, and Mark*, edited by Richard A. Horsley et al., 3–20. Minneapolis: Fortress, 2006.

———. "Mapping Written and Spoken Word in the Gospel of Mark." In *The Interface of Orality and Writing: Speaking, Seeing, Writing in the Shaping of New Genres*, edited by Annette Weisenrieder and Robert B. Coote, 379–92. WUNT 260. Tübingen: Mohr/Siebeck, 2010.

Henderson, Ian. "Didache and Orality in Synoptic Comparison." *JBL* 111 (1992) 283–306.

Hengel, Martin. *Judaism and Hellenism*. Translated by John Bowden. Philadelphia: Fortress, 1974.

Herzog, William R. *Jesus, Justice, and the Reign of God: A Ministry of Liberation*. Louisville: Westminster John Knox, 2000.

Hezser, Catherine. *Jewish Literacy in Roman Palestine*. Texte und Studien zum antiken Judentum 81. Tübingen: Mohr/Siebeck, 2001.

Horsley, Richard A. *Archaeology, History, and Society in Galilee: The Social Context of Jesus and the Rabbis*. Harrisburg, PA: Trinity, 1996.

———. *Covenant Economics: A Biblical Vision of Justice for All*. Louisville: Westminster John Knox, 2009.

———. "Empire, Temple, and Community—But No Bourgeoisie." In *Second Temple Studies 1: Persian Period*, edited by P. R. Davies, 163–74. JSOTSup 117. Sheffield: Sheffield Academic, 1991.

———. "Ethics and Exegesis": 'Love Your Enemies' and the Doctrine of Nonviolence." *Journal of the American Academy of Religion* 54 (1986) 3–31. Reprinted in *Love of Enemy and Nonretaliation in the New Testament*, edited by Willard M. Swartley, 72–101. Louisville: Westminster John Knox, 1992.

———. *Galilee: History, Politics, People*. Harrisburg, PA: Trinity, 1995.

———. *Hearing the Whole Story: The Politics of Plot in Mark's Gospel*. Louisville: Westminster John Knox, 2001.

———, editor. *Hidden Transcripts and the Arts of the Resistance*. Semeia Studies 48. Atlanta: Society of Biblical Literature, 2004.

———. "Introduction: Jesus, Paul and the "Arts of Resistance." In *Hidden Transcripts and the Arts of the Resistance*, edited by Richard A. Horsley, 1–26. Semeia Studies 48. Atlanta: Society of Biblical Literature, 2004.

———. *Jesus and the Politics of Roman Palestine*. Columbia: University of South Carolina Press, 2013.

———. *Jesus and the Spiral of Violence: Popular Jewish Resistance in Roman Palestine*. 1987. Reprinted, Minneapolis: Fortress, 1993.

———. *Jesus in Context: Power, People, and Performance*. Minneapolis: Fortress, 2008.

———. "'Like One of the Prophets of Old': Two Types of Popular Prophets at the Time of Jesus." *CBQ* 47 (1985) 435–63.

———. "The Oral Communication Environment of Q." In Richard Horsley with Jonathan Draper, *Whoever Hears You Hears Me*, 125–59. Harrisburg, PA: Trinity, 1999.

———. "Oral Performance and Mark." In *Jesus, the Voice, and the Text: Beyond "The Oral and Written Gospel,"* edited by Tom Thatcher, 45–70. Waco, TX: Baylor University Press, 2008.

———, editor. *Oral Performance, Popular Tradition, and Hidden Transcript in Q*. Semeia Studies 60. Atlanta: Society of Biblical Literature, 2006.

———. "The Origins of the Hebrew Scriptures in Imperial Relations." In *Orality, Literacy, and Colonialism*, edited by Jonathan A. Draper, 107–34. Semeia Studies 47. Atlanta: Society of Biblical Literature, 2004.

———. "Popular Messianic Movements around the Time of Jesus." *CBQ* 46 (1984) 471–95.

———. "Power Vacuum and Power Struggle in 66–67 C.E." In *The First Jewish Revolt: Archaeology, History, and Ideology*, edited by Andrea M. Berlin and Andrew Overman, 87–109. London: Routledge, 2002.

———. *The Prophet Jesus and the Renewal of Israel: Moving Beyond a Diversionary Debate*. Grand Rapids: Eerdmans, 2012.

———. "Q and Jesus: Assumptions, Approaches, and Analyses." *Semeia* 55 (1991) 175–209.

———. "Recent Studies of Oral-Derived Literature and Q." In Richard Horsley with Jonathan Draper, *Whoever Hears You Hears Me,* 160–74. Harrisburg: Trinity, 1999,

———. *Revolt of the Scribes: Resistance and Apocalyptic Origins.* Minneapolis: Fortress, 2010.

———. "Rhetoric and Empire—and 1 Corinthians." In *Paul and Politics: Ekklesia, Israel, Imperium, Interpretation,* edited by Richard Horsley, 72–102. Harrisburg, PA: Trinity, 2000.

———. "Social Relations and Social Conflict in the *Epistle of Enoch.*" In *For A Later Generation: The Transformation of Tradition in Israel, Early Judaism, and Early Christianity,* edited by Randall Argall et al., 100–115. Harrisburg, PA: Trinity, 2000.

———. *Scribes, Visionaries, and the Politics of Second Temple Judea.* Louisville: Westminster John Knox, 2007.

———. *Sociology and the Jesus Movement.* New York: Crossroad, 1988.

———. "Unearthing a People's History." In *A People's History of Christianity.* Vol. 1, *Christian Origins,* edited by Richard Horsley, 1–20. Minneapolis: Fortress, 2005.

Horsley, Richard A., with Jonathan A. Draper. *Whoever Hears You Hears Me: Prophets, Performance and Tradition in Q.* Harrisburg, PA: Trinity, 1999.

Horsley, Richard A. et al., editors. *Performing the Gospel: Orality, Memory, and Mark: Essays Dedicated to Werner Kelber.* Minneapolis: Fortress, 2006.

Horsley, Richard, and Patrick Tiller. "Ben Sira and the Sociology of the Second Temple." In *Second Temple Studies III: Studies in Politics, Class and Material Culture,* edited by Philip R. Davies and John M. Halligan, 74–107. JSOTSup 340. Sheffield: Sheffield Academic, 2002. Reprinted in Horsley and Tiller, *After Apocalypse and Wisdom: Rethinking Texts in Context.* Eugene, OR: Cascade Books, 2012.

Horsley, Richard A., and Patrick Tiller. *After Apocalyptic and Wisdom: Rethinking Texts in Context.* Eugene, OR: Cascade Books, 2012.

Horsley, Richard, and Tom Thatcher. *John, Jesus, and the Renewal of Israel.* Grand Rapids: Eerdmans, 2013.

Humbert, Paul. *Recherches sur les sources egyptiennes de la literature sapientiale d'Israel.* Neuchatel: Secretariat de l'Universite, 1929.

Hurowitz, V. A. "Spanning the Generations: Aspects of Oral and Written Transmission in the Bible and Ancient Mesopotamia." In *Freedom and Responsibility: Exploring the Challenges of Jewish Continuity,* edited by Rela Mintz Geffen and Marsha Bryan Edelman, 11–30. New York: Ktav, 1998.

Hymes, Dell. *"In Vain I Tried to Tell You": Essays in Native American Ethnopoetics.* Studies in Native American Literature 1. Philadelphia: University of Pennsylvania Press, 1981.

———. "Ways of Speaking." In *Explorations in the Ethnography of Speaking,* edited by Richard Bauman and Joel Sherzer, 433–74. 2nd ed. Studies in the Social and Cultural Foundations of Language 8. Cambridge: Cambridge University Press, 1989.

Iverson, Kelly R. "Orality and the Gospels: A Survey of Recent Research." *Currents in Biblical Research* 8 (2009) 71–106.

Jacobson, Arland D. *The First Gospel: An Introduction to Q.* 1992. Reprinted, Eugene, OR: Wipf & Stock, 2005.

Jaffee, Martin. "Figuring Early Rabbinic Literary Culture." *Semeia* 65 (1994) 67–74.

———. "The Oral-Cultural Context of the Talmud Yerushalmi: Greco-Roman Rhetorical Paideia, Discipleship, and the Concept of Oral Torah." In *The Talmud Yerushalmi and Graeco-Roman Culture 1*, edited by Peter Schäfer, 27–61. Texte und Studien zum Antiken Judentum 71. Tübingen: Mohr/Siebeck, 1998.

———. "Oral Transmission of Knowledge as a Rabinic Sacraent." In *Study and Knowledge in Jewish Thought*, edited by Howard Kreisel, 65–79. Beer Sheva: Ben Gurion University of the Negev Press, 2006.

———. *Torah in the Mouth: Writing and Oral Tradition in Palestinian Judaism 200 B.C.E.—400 C.E.* Oxford: Oxford University Press, 2001.

Johnson, Steven R. *Seeking the Imperishable Treasure: Wealth, Wisdom, and a Jesus Saying.* Eugene, OR: Cascade, 2008.

Jones, A. H. M. *The Greek City from Alexander to Justinian.* Oxford: Oxford University Press, 1940.

Jonge, Marianus de. "The Use of the Word 'Anointed' in the Time of Jesus." *Novum Testamentum* 8 (1966) 132–48.

Kee, Howard Clark. *Christian Origins in Sociological Perspective.* Philadelphia: Westminster, 1980.

Kelber, Werner. "The Case of the Gospels: Memory's Desire and the Limits of Historical Criticism." *Oral Tradition* 17 (2002) 55–86.

———. *Imprints, Voiceprints, and Footprints of Memory: Collected Essays by Werner Kelber.* SBLRBS. Atlanta: Society of Biblical Literature, 2013.

———. "Introduction." In *The Oral and Written Gospel*, xix–xxi. Voices in Performance and Text. Bloomington: Indiana University Press, 1997.

———. "Jesus and Tradition: Words in Time, Words in Space." *Semeia* 65 (1994) 139–67.

———. *Mark's Story of Jesus.* Philadelphia: Fortress, 1979.

———. *The Oral and the Written Gospel: The Hermeneutics of Speaking and Writing in the Synoptic Tradition, Mark, Paul, and Q.* Philadelphia: Fortress, 1983.

———. "The Oral-Scribal-Memorial Arts of Communication in Early Christianity." In *Jesus, the Voice, and the Text: Beyond "The Oral and Written Gospel*," edited by Tom Thatcher, 234–62. Waco, TX: Baylor University Press, 2008.

Kirk, Alan. *The Composition of the Sayings Source: Genre, Synchrony, and Wisdom Redaction in Q.* Novum Testamentum Supplements 90. Leiden: Brill, 1998.

Kirk, Alan, and Tom Thatcher, editors., *Memory, Tradition, and Text: Uses of the Past in Early Christianity.* Semeia Studies 52. Atlanta: Society of Biblical Literature, 2005.

Kloppenborg, John S. *The Formation of Q: Trajectories in Ancient Wisdom Collections.* Philadelphia: Fortress, 1987.

———. "The Formation of Q Revisited: A Response to Richard Horsley." In *Society of Biblical Literature 1989 Seminar Papers*, edited by David J. Lull, 204–15. Atlanta: Scholars, 1989.

———. "Literary Convention, Self-Evidence, and the Social History of the Q People." *Semeia* 55 (1991) 77–102.

Kloppenborg-Verbin, John S. *Excavating Q: The History and Setting of the Sayings Gospel.* Minneapolis: Fortress, 2000.

Koester, Helmut. "Apocryphal and Canonical Gospels." *HTR* 73 (1980) 105–30.

Kovacs, Brian. "Is There a Class-Ethic in Proverbs?" In *Essays in Old Testament Ethics (J. Philip Hyatt in Memoriam)*, edited by James L. Crenshaw and John T. Willis, 171–89. New York: Ktav, 1974.

Larsen, Mogens Trolle. "What They Wrote on Clay." In *Literacy and Society*, edited by Karen Schousboe and Mogens Trolle Larsen, 121–48. Copenhagen: Akademisk, 1989.

Levine, Baruch A. "The Mo'adim of the Temple Scroll." In *Archaeology and History in the Dead Sea Scrolls*, edited by Lawrence H. Schiffman, 61–64. Journal for the Study of the Pseudepigrapha Supplements 8. Sheffield: JSOT Press, 1990.

Levine, Lee I. "The Jewish Patriarch (Nasi) in Third Century Palestine." *Aufstieg und Niedergang der römischen Welt* 2.19.2 (1979) 649–88.

————. *The Rabbinic Class of Roman Palestine in Late Antiquity.* New York: Jewish Theological Seminary of America, 1989.

MacAdam, Henry Innes. "Epigraphy and Village Life in Southern Syria during the Roman and Early Byzantine Periods." *Berytus* 31 (1983) 103–15.

Machiela, Daniel A. "Once More, with Feeling: Rewritten Scripture in Ancient Judaism—A Review of Recent Developments." *Journal of Jewish Studies* 61 (2010) 308–20.

Mack, Burton L. *A Myth of Innocence: Mark and Christian Origins.* Minneapolis: Fortress, 1988.

————. "The Kingdom that Didn't Come: A Social History of the Q Tradents." In *Society of Biblical Literature 1988 Seminar Papers*, edited by David J. Lull, 608–35. Atlanta: Scholars, 1988.

Marcus, Joel. *Mark 1–8: A New Translation with Introduction and Commentary.* Anchor Bible 27. New York: Doubleday, 2000.

McKane, William. *Proverbs: A New Approach.* Old Testament Library. Philadelphia: Westminster, 1970.

Meier, John P. "Is There *Halaka* (the Noun) at Qumran?" *JBL* 122 (2003) 150–55.

Mendels, Doron. *The Land of Israel as a Political Concept in Hasmonean Literature.* Texte und Studien zum antiken Judentum 15. Tübingen: Mohr/Siebeck, 1987.

Meyers, Eric M. "The Cultural Setting of Galilee: The Case of Regionalism and Early Judaism." *Aufstieg und Niedergang der römischen Welt* 2.19.1 (1979) 687–98.

Meyers, Eric M., and James F. Strange. *Archaeology, the Rabbis, and Early Christianity.* Nashville: Abingdon, 1981.

Middendorp, Th. *Die Stellung Jesu Ben Siras zwischen Judentum und Hellenismus.* Leiden: Brill, 1973.

Millar, Fergus G. B. *The Roman Near East, 31 B.C.—A.D. 337.* Cambridge: Harvard University Press, 1993.

Millard, Allan R. "An Assessment of the Evidence for Writing in Ancient Israel." In *Biblical Archaeology Today: Proceedings of the International Congress on Biblical Archaeology, Jerusalem, April 1984*, 301–12. Jerusalem: Israel Exploration Society, 1985.

Moore, Stephen D. *Literary Criticism and the Gospels.* New Haven: Yale University Press, 1989.

Morenz, Ludwig D. *Beiträge zur Schriftlichkeitskulture im Mittleren Reich und in der 2. Zwischenzeit: Aegypten und Altes Testament.* Wiesbaden: Harrassowitz, 1996.

Mowinckel, Sigmund. *He That Cometh: The Messiah Concept in the Old Testament and Later Judaism.* 1955. Reprinted with an Introduction by John J. Collins. Grand Rapids: Eerdmans, 2005.

Murphy, Roland E. *Wisdom Literature: Job, Proverbs, Ruth, Canticles, Ecclesiastes, and Esther.* Forms of Old Testament Literature 13. Grand Rapids: Eerdmans, 1981.

Na'aman, Nadav. "The 'Discovered Book' and the Legitimation of Josiah's Reform." *JBL* 130 (2011) 47–62.

Najman, Hindy. "Interpretation as Primordial Writing: Jubilees and its Authority Conferring Strategies." *Journal for the Study of Judaism* 30 (1999) 379–410. Reprinted in *Past Renewals*, 39–72.

———. *Past Renewals: Interpretative Authority, Renewed Revelation, and the Quest for Perfection in Jewish Antiquity.* JSJSup 53. Leiden: Brill, 2010.

———. *Seconding Sinai: The Development of Mosaic Discourse in Second Temple Judaism.* JSJSup 77. Leiden: Brill, 2003.

———. "The Symbolic Significance of Writing in Ancient Judaism." In *The Idea of Biblical Interpretation: Essays in Honor of James L. Kugel*, edited by Hindy Najman and Judith Newman, 139–73. JSJSup 83. Leiden: Brill, 2004. Reprinted in *Past Renewals*, 3–38.

Neusner, Jacob. *Judaic Law from Jesus to the Mishnah.* South Florida Studies in the History of Judaism 84. Atlanta: Scholars, 1993.

Neusner, Jacob et al., editors. *Judaisms and Their Messiahs at the Turn of the Christian Era.* Cambridge: Cambridge University Press, 1987.

Nickelsburg, George W. E. *Jewish Literature between the Bible and the Mishnah: A Historical and Literary Introduction.* 2nd ed. Minneapolis: Fortress, 2005.

Niditch, Susan. *Oral World and Written Word: Ancient Israelite Literature.* LAI. Louisville: Westminster John Knox, 1996.

O'Keefe, Katherine O'Brien. *Visible Song: Transitional Literacy in Old English Verse.* Cambridge Studies in Anglo-Saxon England 4. Cambridge: Cambridge University Press, 1990.

Ong, Walter J. *Orality and Literacy: The Technologizing of the Word.* New Accents. London: Methuen, 1982.

———. *The Presence of the Word: Some Prolegomena for Cultural and Religious History.* The Terry Lectures. New Haven: Yale University Press, 1967.

Parker, D. C. *An Introduction to the New Testament Manuscripts and Their Texts.* Cambridge: Cambridge University Press, 2008.

———. *The Living Text of the Gospels.* Cambridge: Cambridge University Press, 1997.

Petersen, Anders Klostergaard. "Rewritten Bible as a Borderline Phenomenon—Genre, Textual Strategy, or Canonical Anachronism?" In *Flores Florentino: Dead Sea Scrolls and Oher Early Jewish Studies in Honour of Florentino Garcia Martinez*, edited by Anthony Hilhorst et al., 285–306. JSJSup 122. Leiden: Brill, 2007.

Porter, Stanley E. "Jesus and the Use of Greek in Galilee." In *Studying the Historical Jesus: Evaluations of the State of Current Research*, edited by Bruce Chilton and Craig Evans, 123–54. New Testament Tools and Studies 19. Leiden: Brill, 1994.

Rendsberg, Gary A. "The Galilean Background of Mishnaic Hebrew." In *The Galilee in Late Antiquity*, edited by Lee I. Levine. New York: Jewish Theological Seminary, 1992.

Rhoads, David. *Israel in Revolution 6–74 C. E.* Philadelphia: Fortress, 1976.

———. "Performance Criticism: An Emerging Methodology in Second Testament Studies, parts I and II." *Biblical Theology Bulletin* 36 (2006) 1–16, 164–84.

———. "What Is Performance Criticism?" In *The Bible in Ancient and Modern Media: Story and Performance*, edited by Holly E. Hearon and Philip Ruge-Jones, 83–100. BPCS 1. Eugene, OR: Pickwick Publications, 2008.

———. "Biblical Performance Criticism: Performance as Research." *Oral Tradition* 25/1 (2010) 157–98. Online: http://journal.oraltradition.org/files/articles/25i/11_25.1.pdf.

———. "Performance Events in Early Christianity: New Testament Writings in an Oral Context." In *The Interface of Orality and Writing: Speaking, Seeing, Writing in the Shaping of New Genres*, edited by Annette Weissenrieder and Robert Coote, 266–93. WUNT 260. Tübingen: Mohr/Siebeck, 2010.

Rhoads, David, and Doald Michie. *Mark as Story: An Introduction to the Narrative of a Gospel.* Philadelphia: Fortress, 1982.

Richardson, Peter. *Herod: King of the Jews and Friend of the Romans.* Personalities of the New Testament. Columbia: University of South Carolina Press, 1996.

Robinson, James M. "*LOGOI SOPHON*: On the Gattung of Q." In *Trajectories through Early Christianity*, by Robinson and Helmut Koester, 71–113. 1971. Reprinted, Eugene, OR: Wipf & Stock, 2006.

———. "Introduction." In *The Critical Edition of Q*, edited by James M. Robinson, Paul Hoffmann, and John S. Kloppenborg, xix–lxxi. Hermeneia Supplements. Minneapolis: Fortress, 2000.

Safrai, Shemuel. "Education and the Study of the Torah." In *The Jewish People in the First Century*, edited by Shemuel Safrai and Menahem Stern, 945–70. Philadelphia: Fortress, 1976.

Saldarini, Anthony J. "Johanan ben Zakkai's Escape from Jerusalem: Origin and Development of a Rabbinic Story." *Journal for the Study of Judaism* 16 (1975) 189–220.

Saldarini, Anthony. *Matthew's Christian-Jewish Community.* Chicago: University of Chicago Press, 1994.

Sanders, John T. *Ben Sira and Demotic Wisdom.* Society of Biblical Literature Monograph Series 28. Chico, CA: Scholars, 1983.

Satran, David. *Biblical Prophets in Byzantine Palestine: Reassessing the Lives of the Prophets.* Studia in Veteris Testamenti Pseudepigrapha 11. Leiden: Brill, 1995.

Schaberg, Jane. *The Illegitimacy of Jesus: A Feminist Theological Interpretation of the Infancy Narratives.* San Francisco: Harper & Row, 1987.

Schaper, Joachim. "The Jerusalem Temple as an Instrument of the Achaemenid Fiscal Administration." *Vetus Testamentum* 45 (1995) 528–39.

Schechner, Richard. *Performance Studies: An Introduction.* 2nd ed. New York: Routledge, 2006.

Schechner, Richard, and Willa Appel. *By Means of Performance: Intercultural Studies of Theatre and Ritual.* Cambridge: Cambridge University Press, 1990.

Schiffman, Lawrence H. *The Halakhah at Qumran.* Studies in Judaism in Late Antiquity 16. Leiden: Brill, 1975.

———. "*Miqsat Ma'aseh ha-Torah* and the *Temple Scroll*." *Revue de Qumran* 14 (1990) 435–57.

Schmid, Konrad. "The Canon and the Cult: The Emergence of Book Religion in Ancient Israel and the Gradual Sublimation of the Temple Cult." *JBL* 132 (2012) 289–305.

Schniedewind, William M. *How the Bible Became a Book: The Textualization of Ancient Israel.* Cambridge: Cambridge University Press, 2004.

Schwemer, Anna Maria. *Studies zu den frühjüdischen Prophetenlegenden Vita Prophetarum.* 2 vols. Texte und Studien zum Antiken Judentum 49, 50. Tübingen: Mohr/Siebeck, 1995.

Scott, James C. *Domination and the Arts of Resistance: Hidden Transcripts.* New Haven: Yale University Press, 1990.

———. "Protest and Profanation: Agrarian Revolt and the Little Tradition." *Theory and Society* 4 (1977) 1–38, 211–46.

Scribner, Robert W. *For the Sake of Simple Folk: Popular Propaganda for the German Reformation.* Oxford: Oxford University Press, 1994.

Shiner, Whitney. *Proclaiming the Gospel: First-Century Performances of Mark.* Harrisburg: PA: Trinity, 2003.

———. "Memory Technology and the Composition of Mark." In *Performing the Gospel: Orality, Memory, and Mark,* edited by Richard A. Horsley et al., 147–65. Minneapolis: Fortress, 2006.

Skehan, Patrick W. "The Structure of the Song of Moses in Deuteronomy (Dt 32:1–43)." *CBQ* 13 (1951) 153–63.

Skehan, Patrick W., and A. A. DiLella. *The Wisdom of Ben Sira.* Anchor Bible 39. New York: Doubleday, 1987.

Small, Jocelyn Penny. *Wax Tablets of the Mind: Cognitive Studies of Memory and Literacy in Classical Antiquity.* New York: Routledge, 1997.

Steck, Odil Hannes. *Israel und das gewaltsame Geschick der Propheten: Untersuchungen zur Überlieferung des deuteronomistischen Geschichtsbildes im Alten Testament, Spätjudentum und Urchristentum.* Wissenschaftliche Monographien zum Alten und Neuen Testament 23. Neukirchen-Vluyn: Neukirchner, 1967.

Stendahl, Krister. *The School of St. Matthew.* 2nd ed. Philadelphia: Fortress, 1968.

Street, Brian V. *The Implications of Literacy: Written Language and Models of Interpretation in the Eleventh and Twelfth Centuries.* Princeton: Princeton University Press, 1983.

———. *Literacy in Theory and Practice.* Cambridge Studies in Oral and Literate Culture 9. Cambridge: Cambridge University Press, 1984.

Talmon, Shamaryahu. "DSIa as a Witness to Ancient Exegesis of the Book of Isaiah." *Annual of the Swedish Theological Institute* 1 (1962) 62–72.

Taylor, David G. K. 2002. "Bilingualism and Diglossa in Late Antique Syria and Mesopotamia." In *Bilingualism in Ancient Society: Language Contact and the Written Text,* edited by J. N. Adams et al., 298–331. Oxford: Oxford University Press, 2002

Tedlock, Dennis. *The Spoken Word and the Work of Interpretation.* Philadelphia: University of Pennsylvania Press, 1983.

Toorn, Karel van der. "The Iconic Book: Analogies between the Babylonian Cult of Images and the Veneration of the Torah." In *The Image and the Book: Iconic Cults, Aniconism, and the Rise of Book Religion in Israel and the Ancient Near East,* edited by Karel van der Toorn, 229–48. Contributions to Biblical Exegesis and Theology 21. Leuven: Peeters, 1997.

———. *Scribal Culture and the Making of the Hebrew Bible.* Cambridge: Harvard University Press, 2007.

Tov, Emanuel. "Biblical Texts as Reworked in Some Qumran Manuscripts with Special Attention to 4QRP and 4QParaGen-Exod." In *The Community of the Renewed Covenant: The Notre Dame Symposium on the Dead Sea Scrolls,* edited by Eugene Ulrich and James VanderKam, 112–34. Christianity and Judaism in Antiquity Series 10. Notre Dame: University of Notre Dame Press, 1994.

———. *Textual Criticism of the Hebrew Bible.* 3rd ed. Minneapolis: Fortress, 2012.

Trombley, F. R. *Hellenic Religion and Christianisation, c. 370–529.* 2 vols. Religions in the Graeco-Roman World 115. Leiden: Brill, 1994.

Tuckett, Christopher M. *Q and the History of Early Christianity.* Edinburgh: T. & T. Clark, 1996.

Ulrich, Eugene. *The Dead Sea Scrolls and the Origins of the Bible.* Grand Rapids: Eerdmans, 1999.

VanderKam, James C. *The Book of Jubilees.* Guides to Apocrypha and Pseudepigrapha. Sheffield: Sheffield Academic, 2001.

Vansina, Jan. *Oral Tradition as History.* Madison: University of Wisconsin Press, 1985.

Veldhuis, Niek. *Elementary Education in Nippur: The Lists of Trees and Wooden Objects.* Groningen: Styx, 1997.

Vermes, Geza. *Scripture and Tradition in Judaism: Haggadic Studies.* Stuia Post-Biblica 4. Leiden: Brill, 1961.

Wacholder, Ben Zion. *The Dawn of Qumran: The Sectarian Torah and the Teacher of Righteousness.* Monographs of the Hebrew Union College 8. Cincinnati: Hebrew College Press, 1983.

Watts, James W., editor. *Persian and Torah.* SBLSymS 17. Atlanta: Society of Biblical Literature, 2001.

Weinberg, Joel. *The Citizen Temple Community.* JSOTSup 117. Sheffield: Sheffield Academic, 1991.

Wink, Walter. "Neither Passivity nor Violence: Jesus' Third Way (Matt. 5:38–42 par)." In *Love of Enemy and Nonretaliation in the New Testament*, edited by Willard M. Swartley, 101–25. Louisville: Westminster John Knox, 1992.

Wire, Antoinette Clark. *The Case for Mark Composed in Performance.* BPCS 3. Eugene, OR: Cascade Books, 2011.

———. *Holy Lives, Holy Deaths: A Close Hearing Early Jewish Storytellers.* Studies in Biblical Literature 1. Leiden: Brill, 2002.

Wise, Michael O. *A Critical Study of the Temple Scroll from Qumran Cave 11.* Studies in Ancient Oriental Civilization 49. Chicago: University of Chicago Press, 1990.

Wolff, Greg D. "Literacy." In *Cambridge Ancient History*, vol. 11, edited by A. Bowman et al. 875–97. 2nd ed. Cambridge: Cambridge University Press, 2000.

Worsley, Peter. *The Trumpet Shall Sound.* New York: Schocken, 1958.

Wrede, Wilhelm. *The Messianic Secret.* London: Clarke, 1901.

Wright, Benjamin G. "Eschatology without a Messiah in the Wisdom of Ben Sira." In *The Septuagint and Messianism*, edited by Michael A. Knibb, 313–23. Bibliotheca Ephemeridum theologicarum Lovaniensium 195. Leuven: Peeters, 2006.

Youtie, H. C. "*Agrammatos*: An Aspect of Greek Society in Egypt." *Harvard Studies in Classical Philology* 75 (1971) 161–76.

Zahn, Molly M. "Genre and Rewritten Scripture: A Reassessment." *JBL* 131 (2012) 271–88.

———. "Rewritten Scripture." In *The Oxford Handbook of the Dead Sea Scrolls*, edited by Timothy H. Lim and John J. Collins, 323–36. Oxford: Oxford University Press, 2010.

# SUBJECT INDEX

# INDEX OF TEXTS DISCUSSED AND OF REFERENCES TO ANCIENT TEXTS

This index lists ancient texts and text-fragments in two different connections. (1) To encourage the reading and hearing of texts as sustained narratives (sequences of episodes) and short speeches on particular issues those stories or episodes or speeches are listed as wholes, without breakdown into particular lines or verses, and are printed in **bold** type where discussed and <u>underlined</u> where printed in translation and/or transliteration. (2) In more conventional style, texts and text-fragments are listed of shorter or longer passages from ancient texts that are cited as evidence for assertions in the discussion.

www.ingramcontent.com/pod-product-compliance
Lightning Source LLC
Chambersburg PA
CBHW021847090426
42811CB00033B/2168/J